FIFTH EDITION 2009

THE STRENGTHS PERSPECTIVE IN SOCIAL WORK PRACTICE

Edited by

DENNIS SALEEBEY, PROFESSOR EMERITUS

University of Kansas

PEARSON

Boston ■ New York ■ San Francisco
Mexico City ■ Montreal ■ Toronto ■ London ■ Madrid ■ Munich ■ Paris
Hong Kong ■ Singapore ■ Tokyo ■ Cape Town ■ Sydney

Senior Acquisitions Editor: Patricia Quinlin
Editorial Assistant: Carly Czech
Senior Marketing Manager: Wendy Albert
Managing Editor: Karen Carter
Production Supervisor: Patrick Cash-Peterson
Editorial Production and Electronic Composition Services:
   Pine Tree Composition, Inc./Laserwords, Pte. Ltd.–Chennai
Manufacturing Buyer: Debbie Rossi
Cover Administrator: Kristina Mose-Libon

For related titles and support materials, visit our online catalog at www.ablongman.com.

Between the time website information is gathered and then published, it is not unusual for some sites to have closed. Also, the transcription of URLs can result in typographical errors. The publisher would appreciate notification where these errors occur so that they may be corrected in subsequent editions.

Library of Congress Cataloging-in-Publication Data
The strengths perspective in social work practice / edited by Dennis
Saleebey. — 5th ed.
    p. cm.
 ISBN-13: 978-0-205-62441-6
 ISBN-10: 0-205-62441-3
1. Social service—Psychological aspects. I. Saleebey, Dennis.
 HV41.S827 2009
 361.3'2—dc22
                              2008029303

Printed in the United States of America

10   9   8   7   6   5   4   3   2   1   12   11   10   09   08

To my family:
My mother and father, June Hoff and Ted Saleebey, the seeds of my
strength; my children, Jennifer, David, John, and Meghan, who have grown
to adulthood in ways that amaze; and Ann, my wife, whose wisdom I count
on, and whose love I depend on.

In Memoriam

Ted Saleebey
June Celestine Hoff
Bette A. Saleebey
Liane V. Davis
Howard Goldstein
John Romanyshyn

Their strengths are found yet in the lives of others.

He who has the Why to live for can bear almost any How.

—Nietzsche

We confide in our strength, without boasting of it;
We respect that of others, without fearing it.

—Thomas Jefferson (Letter to William Carmichael and William Short)

CONTENTS

CHAPTER THREE

The Opportunities and Challenges of Strengths-Based, Person-Centered Practice: Purpose, Principles, and Applications in a Climate of Systems Integration   47

Walter E. Kisthardt

PART TWO   STRENGTHS-BASED APPRECIATIONS, ASSESSMENTS, AND APPROACHES TO PRACTICE

CHAPTER FOUR

Chronic Illness and Transilience Along My Spiritual Path   72

Edward R. Canda

CHAPTER FIVE

The Strengths Approach to Practice: Beginnings   93

Dennis Saleebey

CHAPTER SIX

Key Dimensions of the Strengths Perspective in Case Management, Clinical Practice, and Community Practice   108

Ann Weick, James Kreider, and Ronna Chamberlain

CHAPTER SEVEN

The Strengths Perspective in Criminal Justice   122

Michael D. Clark

CHAPTER EIGHT

Implementation of Brief Strengths-Based Case Management: An Evidence-Based Intervention for Improving Linkage with Care   146

Richard C. Rapp and D. Timothy Lane

CHAPTER NINE

The Strengths Model with Older Adults: Critical Practice Components   161

Holly Nelson-Becker, Rosemary Chapin, and Becky Fast

CHAPTER TEN

Assessing Strengths: Identifying Acts of Resistance to Violence
and Oppression   181

Kim M. Anderson, Charles D. Cowger, and Carol A. Snively

CHAPTER ELEVEN

A Shift in Thinking: Influencing Social Workers' Beliefs About
Individual and Family Resilience in an Effort to Enhance
Well-Being and Success for All   201

Bonnie Benard and Sara L. Truebridge

PART THREE   USING THE STRENGTHS PERSPECTIVE IN CONTEXT

CHAPTER FOURTEEN

Poverty Through the Lens of Economic Human Rights   262

Mary Bricker-Jenkins, Rosemary A. Barbera, and Carrie Young

CHAPTER FIFTEEN

The Strengths Perspective: Possibilities and Problems   281

Dennis Saleebey

FOREWORD

I am pleased to have another opportunity to write a foreword for the *Strengths Perspective in Social Work Practice*. Publication of this fifth edition suggests the continued interest in and relevance of the strengths perspective to social workers and its ongoing development both in the depth of its analyses and the scope of its applications. These developments are evident in the new and revised chapters of this edition.

What has not changed is that the strengths perspective continues to provide an important alternative to the deficit and problem-oriented approaches that still dominate social institutions and professions. This alone makes its continued viability and availability to social work educators, scholars, students, and practitioners a critical resource. There is a dynamic interdependence between what we take to be real and the language available to construe these beliefs. For many social workers, this book will provide an alternative language—of promise, resilience, generativity, and transformation—that enables them to reassess and, when necessary, "talk back" to the dominant discourses of illness and pathology. As an educator, I find it heartening to hear stories of students for whom the language of strengths provides a context from which they can question policies and practices and generate new, constructive possibilities for working with people.

When reading this book, I suggest that you consider common and new meanings of "strengths." To call something a strength is not to reveal an unassailable feature of reality, but to construe or assess one concept in terms of another. For example, when I identify an individual's "optimism" as a strength, I am ascribing a value to how this perceived way of "being in the world" functions in her life. As literary theorists have pointed out, there is no necessary relation between a word and its referent. Nothing about a person or situation demands the words "optimism" and "strength"; it is one of many possible interpretations. What we call a strength (or a deficit for that matter) can be anything. This position frees us to expand our thinking about the ways in which people manage to survive and thrive in less than optimal circumstances. We need not limit our analyses to factors presumed to represent resources or resilience, but can entertain heretofore unconsidered possibilities. We can listen to others more openly in ways less fettered to theoretical screens.

Maintaining this openness helps keep the strengths perspective from becoming another "universal good" that fails to recognize human diversity and how different perspectives function in different contexts. Despite the enthusiasm engendered by the strengths perspective, we must be mindful of how ostensibly positive concepts like social justice have been used to deflect or rationalize the perpetration of harms. Similarly, it is important that the strengths perspective not be reified, converted into a "thing" with an enumerated list of defining characteristics that functions as a kind of virtue ethic or prescription for healthy living. To do so would diminish its power to transform and reproduce the reality-generating dimension of deficit discourses that strength-oriented practitioners find so problematic.

Readers can obviate these potential risks by adopting two positions. First, preserve the status of the strengths perspective as a *perspective*, a sense-making framework. Doing so helps us to remember that the strengths perspective is one of numerous perspectives that guide our awareness and interpretations. Our interest shifts from questions about whether something is *really* a strength to how the strengths perspective functions in practice. For example: How does the donning of strength-tinted lenses affect our noticing, understandings, and relationships? Does it move us in the direction of our visions of helping and world-building? Our responses to such questions, I suggest, will help us discover the functional meanings of the strengths perspective.

Second, consider strengths as a relation rather than as an individual quality or attribute. This integrates us, as social workers, into the meaning-making process that generates strengths. It invites us to examine how we relate to the people we serve and to ask how we can coordinate our interactions to help them articulate and move toward their aspirations. It encourages a "relational responsibility" (McNamee & Gergen, 1999) that reduces the alterity of our clients.

In the spirit of the strength perspective, I advise revising the so-called "KISS principle" ("keep it simple, stupid") to "keep it complicated, smarty!" Do not let the strengths perspective's apparent simplicity lull you into thinking that it provides a quick and easy fix to the complex problems of the world. To do so, makes one vulnerable to the classic good intentions–bad results scenario. So this is a cautionary as well as a hopeful tale that I hope leads to a constructive reading of this book.

I am proud that the strengths perspective originated in social work and that it has been so widely adopted within social work education. To my mind it ranks alongside social work's commitment to a contextual (i.e., person and environment) perspective as a distinguishing intellectual and value position. I want to be associated with a profession that steadfastly considers people in a positive light; that sees difficult situations as opportunities for growth; that considers people and communities who struggle with psychological and social challenges as resourceful, resilient, and even heroic; that is interested in how people thrive and endure rather than how they deteriorate and fail; and that promotes a view of humanity in which our bootstraps are interlaced and lifted by us all. This is the social work that makes a unique and positive contribution to our collective lives. It is the one you can find in the pages of this book.

Stanley Witkin
Professor of Social Work, University of Vermont

REFERENCES

McNamee, S. & Gergen, K. J. and Associates (1999). *Relational responsibility*. Thousand Oaks, CA: Sage.

PREFACE

The interest in and work on the development of a strengths-based approach to case management, practice with individuals and groups, and community development continues not only at the School of Social Welfare, University of Kansas, but around the country and even internationally. Much remains to be done, of course, with respect to inquiry and the further development of concepts and principles as well as techniques. But it is gratifying to witness, from the views of practitioners and their clients, students, and faculty how poignant the strengths perspective has been in their pedagogy and practice. It may be, too, that the strengths perspective will remain just that: a perspective, a way of thinking about and orienting yourself to your work and obligating yourself to your clients and their families and communities.

The reactions to the first four editions of the *Strengths Perspective in Social Work Practice* have, for the most part, been encouraging and edifying. There have been critiques as well, and all the authors are aware of challenges and suggestions put forward by readers. The authors who have revised chapters for this edition have taken most of those critiques into account as they have reworked their arguments and analyzed their observations. In this edition, you will find new chapters by Robert Blundo; Diane McMillen and Jack Pransky; Michael Clark; Mary Bricker-Jenkins, Rosemary Barbera, and Carrie Young; Ann Weick, Jim Kreider, and Ronna Chamberlain; Ed Canda; Richard Rapp; and Bonnie Benard and Sara Truebridge. In addition, other chapters have been significantly revised, including those by Kim Anderson, Charles Cowger, and Carol Snively; Charlie Rapp and Pat Sullivan; Wally Kisthardt; Holly Nelson-Becker, Rosemary Chapin, and Becky Fast; and me.

A special thanks to Susana Mariscal, a Ph.D. student at the University of Kansas and a long-time believer in and practitioner of the strengths approach to practice, for her wise advice and counsel regarding this edition.

We have tried to be attentive to remembering our professional commitment to social and economic justice. Spirituality is defined in this edition as a strength, and we have provided some new examples as well as some fresh ideas about practice.

We hope, of course, that this book will assist you in developing in your own professional work and pedagogy, a genuine strengths perspective. I have been privileged to travel around the country—and, to a limited extent, abroad—and consult with groups and organizations attempting to incorporate this perspective into their work or curriculum. Believe me, there are people doing some amazing things. But I also see that it is easy to think that one is using a strengths perspective when, in some ways, that isn't the case. The problem is that it requires a dedication and depth of commitment that, on the surface, does not seem warranted. Nonetheless, the authors of these chapters—who, by the way, are not of one mind about this perspective—hope that you see the enormity of the undertaking but also the joys that come from the use of a strengths approach.

PLAN OF THE BOOK

The first part of the book, "The Philosophy, Principles, and Language of the Strengths Perspective," introduces you to the basic assumptions, the values, the guiding principles, and the lexicon of the strengths perspective. In Chapter 1, Dennis Saleebey lays out some of the assumptions and principles and contrasts them with the more dominant problem-based and medical models. In Chapter 2, Robert Blundo develops the idea of the strengths perspective as a very different kind of frame and contrasts it with other frames that have dominated social work theory and practice over the past century.

In Chapter 3, Walter Kisthardt gives the reader a broad look at the application of the ideas of strengths-based practice across a number of practice venues.

In Part Two, "Strengths-Based Appreciations, Assessments, and Approaches to Practice," Ed Canda, in Chapter 4, gives a stirring and instructive account of his struggle with cystic fibrosis and how he has managed to thrive in this daily confrontation. Dennis Saleebey, in Chapter 5, lays out some of the basic elements of strengths-based practice. Chapter 6, by Ann Weick, Jim Krieder, and Ronna Chamberlain, is a terse and useful arraying of the key dimensions of the strengths approach in clinical work, case management, and community practice. Michael Clark, in Chapter 7, provides a rich and informative accounting of the use of the strengths perspective in a difficult environment—the criminal justice system—and highlights methods that would have use in many fields of practice. Richard Rapp and Timothy Lane, in Chapter 8, give us a detailed and elaborate look at the basic ideas and the evidence-based use of brief strengths-based case management in helping people with HIV and addiction problems link up with appropriate care. In Chapter 9, Holly Nelson-Becker, Rosemary Chapin, and Becky Fast describe in detail the use of a strengths model in helping older adults adjust to their challenges and also address the issue of immigration of older adults to this society and how that affects care. Kim Anderson, Charles Cowger, and Carol Snively, in Chapter 10, discuss assessing strengths in working with women who have been abused. Importantly, they identify a major source of strength—acts of resistance to the oppressor. In Chapter 11, Bonnie Benard and Sara Truebridge provide a valuable schema for influencing social workers' beliefs about resilience and strengths, and they describe educational modules for positively affecting social workers and their understanding of resilience.

Part Three of the book moves outward to discuss understanding and using the strengths approach in various social environments. Charles Rapp and William Patrick Sullivan write of the importance of helping people find those social niches that take advantage of and enhance their strengths in Chapter 12. A discussion of the "perfect niche" provides a constructive way of thinking about the environment and strengths. In Chapter 13, Jack Pransky and Diane McMillen give us new insight into the relationship between individual and environment for the purpose of capitalizing on the inherent wisdom and strengths of people, individually and collectively. In Chapter 14, Mary Bricker-Jenkins, Rosemary Barbera, and Carrie Young argue that it is not enough to promote peoples' strengths. We must attend to the socioeconomic and political environment in which people live, focusing in particular on the status of their economic human rights before we can secure true social justice. In Part Four of the book, in the last chapter, Dennis Saleebey discusses and responds to some of the critiques of the strengths perspective and articulates some similarities between the approach and other methods of practice that honor the capacities and assets of individuals, groups, and communities.

ACKNOWLEDGMENTS

The authors who have contributed to this edition of the book have my deepest appreciation and gratitude. They are all very busy practitioners and scholars, but they are also committed to the strengths perspective. This, for them, was a labor of love—as you can tell from reading their work. I have derived great benefit and insight from reading their words, and I am sure you will too. These individuals do not just preach the sermon, they do the good work as well.

I would also like to thank the contributors to the first four editions: John Poertner, John Ronnau, Eloise Rathbone-McCuan, Julian Rappaport, Gary Holmes, Michael Yellow Bird, Jennifer C. Jones, James Taylor, and Margaret Waller. Their work on and dedication to the strengths approach continues. We would like to thank the reviewers for their suggestions: Robert Blundo, University of North Carolina, Wilmington; Brenda Bryson, Barry University; Debra Gohagan, Minnesota State University, Mankato; and Cecilia L. Thomas, University of North Texas.

The editors at Pearson Allyn & Bacon, have been extraordinarily supportive and patient. They have believed in this project from the inception of the first edition to this one. In particular, thanks to Janice Wiggins, Judith Fifer, and Karen Hanson. For this edition, the guiding hands of Patricia Quinlin, Sara Holliday, and Carly Czech have been most helpful. Without their encouragement, I am not at all sure that I would have attempted another edition of this book. I would also like to acknowledge Katie Boilard at Pine Tree Composition for her guidance through production.

Finally, a word about two special people. Howard Goldstein died in 2000. He was one of the most intellectually audacious and bold scholars I have ever known. He also was a sensitive and skilled practitioner, and his concern for others always shone through. But his moral and intellectual vision for social work was unsurpassed in its clarity and reach. He had wondrous qualities of his mind and heart. We will miss him. The profession will miss him.

My wife, Ann Weick, is an exquisite partner in life and work. She is remarkable in the steadfastness of her belief in the strengths of others, her vision for this profession, and her love for those who have come to rely on her wisdom and caring.

ABOUT THE EDITOR

Dennis Saleebey, DSW, is Professor Emeritus of Social Welfare at the School of Social Welfare, University of Kansas. He was the Lucy and Henry Moses Distinguished Visiting Professor of Social Work at Hunter College in New York, for the 2002–2003 school year. One of his primary interests has been the development of a more strengths-based approach to social work practice. For the past twenty years he has been involved in a number of strengths-based community building and community outreach projects in Fort Worth, Texas; Kansas City, Missouri; and Kansas City, Kansas. Dennis is an author and editor of the previous editions of *The Strengths Perspective in Social Work Practice* (Pearson/Allyn & Bacon). His book, *Human Behavior and Social Environments: A Biopyschosocial Approach*, was published by Columbia University Press in 2001. His latest publications include: *The Strengths Perspective: Putting Possibility and Hope to Work in Practice; Comprehensive Handbook of Social Work and Social Welfare,* (Sowers, Dulmus, & White (Eds.]); *The Strengths Perspective* (S. J. Lopez, *Handbook of Positive Psychology,*); *A Paradigm Shift? The Self in Context* (Lightburn & Sessions [Eds.], *Handbook of Community-Based Clinical Practice*).

CONTRIBUTORS

Kim M. Anderson, Ph.D., is an Assistant Professor of Social Work at the University of Missouri, Columbia. She is a licensed clinical social worker. For the past 20 years, Dr. Anderson has crossed the boundaries among the many roles that interest her—practitioner, researcher, educator, and advocate—to help survivors of family violence and the practitioners who serve them. Her scholarship bridges gaps between theory and practice by offering conceptual frameworks for survivors and practitioners that allow for variation in individual expressions of trauma, trauma recovery, and resilience. In addition, she has led training on core principles of resiliency theory and on the basics of solution-focused intervention methods to provide clinicians with tools to enhance their strengths-based practice with individuals, families, organizations, and communities.

Rosemary Barbera has been a human rights activist for over 25 years. During the oppressive military regime of Augusto Pinochet in Chile, she was a community organizer working in human rights in Santiago. She was also a member of the Sebastian Acevedo Movement against Torture and a founding member of the Committee of Pastoral Agents against Impunity. Presently, she is Assistant Professor of Social Work at Monmouth University. She is active with JUNTOS in South Philadelphia, the Pennsylvania Economic Human Rights Campaign, and *Grupo de Acción Social Concierto y Cultura, Junta de Vecinos Pablo Neruda*, and the *Agrupación de Familiares de Detenidos Desaparecidos* in Chile. She has a Masters and Doctorate in Social Work from Bryn Mawr College and a Masters in Theology from La Salle University.

For over 20 years, **Bonnie Benard,** MSW, has brought the concept of resilience to the attention of national and international audiences. She is currently a Senior Program Associate in WestEd's Health & Human Development Program in Oakland, CA. She writes widely, leads professional development, and makes presentations in the field of prevention and resilience/youth development theory, policy, and practice. Her 1991 WestEd publication, *Fostering Resiliency in Kids: Protective Factors in the Family, School, and Community*, is credited with introducing resiliency theory and application to the fields of prevention and education. Her most recent publication, *Resiliency: What We Have Learned* (2004), synthesizes more than a decade of resiliency research and describes what application of the research looks like in our most successful efforts to support young people. Benard's work in resilience has also led to the development of the California Department of Education's Healthy Kids Survey's Resilience and Youth Development Module, which surveys students throughout California and elsewhere on their perceptions of support and opportunities in their schools, homes, communities, and peer groups.

Robert Blundo, Ph.D., LCSW, is a professor in the Department of Social Work at the University of North Carolina Wilmington. He has established the Strengths Collaborative, which works on bringing strengths-based practice to his region and state through trainings and consultations. He has established a weekly collaborative team meeting of child protective service workers at the county social services helping incorporate strengths and solution-focused practice into work with families and children. The Strengths Collaborative is also working with teachers and administrators in local schools to bring strengths-based/solution-focused teaching and counseling into school settings.

Mary Bricker-Jenkins is a member of the National Staff of the Poor People's Economic Human Rights Campaign (PPEHRC) and co-convener of the School of Social Work and Social Transformation of the University of the Poor, PPEHRC's educational arm. She began her career over 40 years ago as a New York City welfare worker and has practiced, taught, and published in the areas of child welfare, feminist social work, community organizing, social welfare history, and economic human rights. Now Professor Emerita at Temple University, she has returned to her home at WIT's End Farm in Tennessee, where she continues her work with PPEHRC, teaches part-time at Dalton State College and the University of Tennessee-Chattanooga, and spends as much time as possible on the Tennessee River.

Edward R. Canda, MA, MSW, Ph.D., is a Professor at the University of Kansas School of Social Welfare. He founded the Society for Spirituality and Social Work in 1990 to promote knowledge and respect for spiritual diversity among social workers. He has more than 100 publications about cultural, religious, and philosophical aspects of social work. He lectures and consults around the world and has a special interest in international collaborations. He hosts the online Spiritual Diversity and Social Work resource center (via his homepage at **www.socwel.ku.edu/canda**), which includes essays, bibliographies, Internet links, a photo gallery, and other materials on connections among spiritual diversity, social work, and health.

Ronna Chamberlain is currently the Director of the University of Kansas Partnership Center. It was established to bring the expertise and resources of the university to assist the urban core of Kansas City, Kansas, by addressing the difficult circumstances faced by residents of the community. The focus of the partnership center is to use community practice and service learning models to help communities improve the level of education, build and preserve assets, and increase citizens' voice in public decisions through civic engagement. As one of the original developers of the strengths model, she has applied that model to the community practice strategies used in the Partnership Center's activities. Previous positions include Director of the KU School of Social Welfare Office of Policy and Community Development, Director of Mental Health for Kansas, and Director of Community Support Services for Johnson County Mental Health Center in the Kansas City area.

Dr. Rosemary Chapin, Professor, University of Kansas, School of Social Welfare, has extensive policy research and program development experience in the long-term care arena. She was also one of the initial scholars who developed strengths case management principles for older adults. She currently teaches in the graduate program at KU and also directs the Office of Aging and Long Term Care in the KU School of Social Welfare. For the past 20 years, she has been involved in doing research and providing technical assistance to states to help craft more effective state long-term care policy. She has published widely in the areas of long-term care policy and practice and was a delegate to the 2005 White House

Conference on Aging. Her newest book, *Social Policy for Effective Practice: The Strengths Approach*, was published this year by McGraw Hill. All of her research reports are available through the Office of Aging and Long Term Care website: **www.oaltc.ku.edu**

Michael D. Clark, MSW, LMSW, is a consultant, a trainer, and an addictions therapist. After serving 18 years as a probation officer and judicial magistrate, he currently directs the Center for Strengths-Based Strategies located in Michigan (**www.buildmotivation.com**). Clark is a national expert within the criminal and juvenile justice fields for application of the strengths perspective and motivational interviewing with mandated (court-ordered) clients. He has provided training to the fields of mental health, education, addictions, child welfare, probation/parole, and juvenile delinquency, and has presented throughout the United States, as well as Europe, Canada, the Caribbean and the Pacific Rim. Clark's greatest strengths are his relationships with his wife, Frances, and his children, Rebecca, Brian, Steven, and Molly.

Charles D. Cowger, Ph.D., is a Professor Emeritus of the School of Social Work at the University of Missouri, Columbia. He is the former Director of the School of Social Work at the University of Missouri, Columbia. As a former member of the faculty at the University of Illinois School of Social Work, he served in various administrative capacities. Other interests of his include woodworking, canoeing, backpacking, and pottery.

Becky Fast, MSW, MPA, is Director of Constituent Services for Kansas Congressman Dennis Moore, United States House of Representatives. She is a social work practicum instructor and has been a regular adjunct professor at the University of Kansas School of Social Welfare and Washburn University in Topeka, Kansas. Over the past 10 years she has taught classes in case management, human behavior, aging, and social policy. Prior to working with Congressman Moore, she conducted research evaluation and designed specialized training programs at the School of Social Welfare for social workers and case managers. She has developed a strengths-perspective training manual for work with older adults.

Walter E. Kisthardt, MSW, Ph.D., is the Chair of the Social Work Department and BSW Program Director at Park University, Parkville, Missouri. He has provided training and consultation with a wide range of human service providers in 42 states, England, and New Zealand. Currently, he is consulting with the Kansas Department of Addiction Prevention Services to provide strengths-based, person-centered case management, and to evaluate its effectiveness in substance abuse and co-occurring disorders.

James W. Kreider, MSW, LSCSW, is an instructor at the Graduate School of Social Welfare, University of Kansas. He is also owner of Kreider Consulting, LLC, where he provides clinical services, training, consultation, and supervision. He has been in clinical practice since 1973, working with a variety of challenging populations and specializing in collaborative, competency-based approaches such as Solution-Focused Therapy, Narrative Approach, Client-Directed Outcome-Informed Therapy, and Ericksonian Hypnotherapy. He is the author or co-author of articles and chapters on Critical Incident Stress Debriefing, Solution-Focused Brief Therapy, Teaching Spirituality in the Classroom, and the Strengths Perspective.

D. Timothy Lane, MEd, LICDC, is a researcher at the Wright State University Boonshoft School of Medicine's Center for Interventions, Treatment, and Addictions Research and is the Project Director of the Reducing Barriers to Drug Abuse Treatment Services project, funded by the National Institute on Drug Abuse. He is an Ohio-licensed Independent Chemical Dependency Counselor with 30 years of experience providing and managing substance abuse prevention and treatment services.

Diane P. McMillen, Ph.D., is an Associate Professor who has been teaching in Human Services for 28 years. She started her teaching career at Ottawa University in Kansas where she developed the Human Services program and taught for eleven years. In the fall of 1990, she accepted a position at Washburn University in Topeka, where she helped develop the Baccalaureate degree in Human Services and directed the internship program. She received her Ph.D. from the University of Kansas with a research focus on social action and community mental health. She has a longstanding interest in the field of prevention. She recently returned from a sabbatical during which she researched a new method of prevention. She continues to consult with and provide training for group homes, social service agencies, and various community agencies and programs.

Holly Nelson-Becker, LCSW, Ph.D., is Associate Professor in the School of Social Welfare at the University of Kansas, Lawrence, Kansas. She is a Hartford Faculty Scholar in Geriatric Social Work (cohort 3). From 2001–2004, she was Chair of the Interest Group in Religion, Spirituality, and Aging for the Gerontological Society of America. She is PI on a Hartford/New York Academy of Medicine Practicum Partnership for Aging Education grant to increase the numbers of age-competent social workers. She serves on the Advisory Board of the John A. Hartford Doctoral Fellows Program. She has published widely in spiritual assessment and religious and spiritual coping with diverse older populations in diverse settings including hospice and the community. Her research has embraced strengths- and resilience-based perspectives. Prior to entering academia, Holly was a geriatric psychiatric counselor for Maricopa County in Phoenix, AZ.

Jack Pransky, Ph.D., is founder/director of the Northeast Health Realization Institute. He authored the books, *Somebody Should Have Told Us!* (2006); *Prevention from the Inside-Out* (2003); *Prevention: The Critical Need* (2001/1991); *Parenting from the Heart* (2000/1997); and *Modello: A Story of Hope for the Inner City and Beyond* (1998), and co-authored *Healthy Thinking/Feeling/Doing from the Inside-Out* prevention curriculum for middle school students (2000). Pransky has worked in the field of prevention in a wide variety of capacities since 1968 and now provides consultation and training throughout the United States and internationally. He specializes in prevention from the inside out. In 2001 his book *Modello* received the Martin Luther King Storyteller's Award for the book best exemplifying King's vision of "the beloved community," and in 2004, Pransky won the Vermont Prevention Pioneer's Award.

Charles A. Rapp, MSW, Ph.D., is Professor at the University of Kansas School of Social Welfare and Director of the Office of Mental Health Research and Training. He holds a Ph.D. and MSW from the University of Illinois and a B.S. from Millikin University. His professional career has been devoted to enhancing the recovery of people with psychiatric disabilities through the development of client-centered methods and programs and advocacy for client rights and social justice. He is co-developer of the Strengths Model of Case Management and the Client-Centered Performance Model of Social Administration. The second edition of his book, *The Strengths Model: Case Management with People with Psychiatric Disabilities* (with Rick Goscha), was published by Oxford Press in 2006.

Richard C. Rapp, MSW, ACSW, is an Assistant Professor at the Wright State University School of Medicine (WSUSOM) and clinical services developer and researcher with the Center for Interventions, Treatment, and Addictions Research (CITAR). He is currently Principal Investigator for the Reducing Barriers to Drug Treatment Services Project, a National Institute on Drug Abuse clinical trial testing two brief interventions—strengths-based case management and motivational interviewing—for their effectiveness in facilitating treatment linkage among adult substance abusers. Rapp also designed the brief strengths-based intervention used in a Centers for Disease Control and Prevention Clinical Trial and implementation study.

Carol A. Snively, Ph.D., is the Director of MSW and Off Campus Programs of the School of Social Work at the University of Missouri. Her most recent community practice and research projects have focused on understanding how economically disadvantaged and sexual minority teens experience their communities and participate in community betterment activities. Prior to academia, Carol practiced for 15 years as a registered/board certified art therapist and licensed clinical social worker with youth and their families in mental health and addiction treatment.

Patrick Sullivan, Ph.D., serves as Professor at the Indiana University School of Social Work. He also served as the Director of the Indiana Division of Mental Health and Addiction from 1994–1998. While earning a Ph.D. at the University of Kansas, Sullivan helped develop the strengths model of social work practice. He has extended the model in mental health and addictions treatment. With over 60 professional publications on a diverse range of topics, he received the Distinguished Hoosier award from Governor Frank O'Bannon in 1997, and earned the Sagamore of the Wabash, the highest civilian honor awarded in Indiana, from Governor Joseph Kernan in 2004.

Sara Truebridge, MEd, is a Research Associate with the Health and Human Development Program at WestEd, focusing on prevention and resilience and youth development theory, policy, and practice. Truebridge has developed and provided resilience training to social service agencies throughout California. Most recently she conducted a series of resilience trainings for the entire staff of the Family Child Services Division of the San Francisco County/City Human Services Agency. Her professional experience includes work as the Founder and President of *Sincerely, Kids Inc.*®, a child-centered consulting firm; as a credentialed teacher; and as the Legislative Analyst for education issues in the New York State Senate. Truebridge is currently pursuing a Doctorate in Educational Leadership at Mills College and is one of two international recipients of the 2005 Howard M. Soule Fellowship for Doctoral Studies, a Phi Delta Kappa Graduate Fellowship in Educational Leadership.

Ann Weick, Ph.D., joined the faculty of the University of Kansas School of Social Welfare in 1976, after completing her doctoral degree at Brandeis University. She was chair of the Doctoral Program from 1981–1988 and was appointed Dean in 1988, a position she held until her retirement in 2006. She is currently Professor and Dean Emerita. During her career she has written two books and over 35 articles and book chapters. Her work has focused on approaches that stretch the boundaries of current knowledge and practice in social work, including postmodern, feminist, holistic, and strengths-based approaches. She was recently awarded the Council on Social Work Education Lifetime Achievement Award.

Carrie Young is a member of the National Staff of the Poor People's Economic Human Rights Campaign (PPEHRC). She is a social worker and has participated in developing models of social work practice based on economic human rights. Carrie is a member of the Kensington Welfare Rights Union (KWRU) and the School of Social Work and Social Transformation of the University of the Poor, the educational arm of PPEHRC. She is an adjunct faculty member at the School of Social Administration at Temple University and is parenting two young children.

■ ■ ■ ■ ■

CHAPTER ONE

INTRODUCTION
Power in the People

DENNIS SALEEBEY

In the lore of professional social work, the idea of building on people's strengths has become axiomatic. Authors of textbooks, educators, and practitioners all regularly acknowledge the importance of this principle. Many of these calls to attend to the capacities and competencies of clients are little more than professional cant. So let us be clear: The strengths perspective is a dramatic departure from conventional social work practice. Practicing from a strengths orientation means this—*everything* you do as a social worker will be predicated, in some way, on helping to discover and embellish, explore and exploit clients' strengths and resources in the service of assisting them to achieve their goals, realize their dreams, and shed the irons of their own inhibitions and misgivings and society's domination. This is a versatile practice approach, relying heavily on the ingenuity and creativity, the courage and common sense, of both clients and their social workers. It is a collaborative process depending on clients and workers to be purposeful agents and not mere functionaries. It is an approach honoring the innate wisdom of the human spirit, the inherent capacity for transformation of even the most humbled and abused. When you adopt the strengths approach to practice, you can expect exciting changes in the character of your work and in the tenor of your relationships with your clients.

Many of us believe (or have at one time believed) that we are building on client strengths. But sometimes we fall short. Practicing from a strengths perspective requires that we shift the way that we think about, approach, and relate to our clients. Rather than focusing exclusively or dominantly on problems, your eye turns toward possibility. In the thicket of trauma, pain, and trouble you see blooms of hope and transformation. The formula is simple: Rally clients' interests, capacities, motivations, resources, and emotions in the work of reaching their hopes and dreams, help them find pathways to those goals, and the payoff may be an enhanced quality of daily life for them. Although the recipe is uncomplicated, as you will see, the work is hard. In the chapters that follow, you will encounter descriptions of the strengths approach used with a variety of populations, in a variety of circumstances. You will be exposed to schemes of assessment, methods of employment, examples of application, and discussions of issues related to moving from a concentration on problems to a fascination with strengths.

In the past few years, there has been an increasing interest in developing strengths-based approaches to practice, case management in particular, with a variety of client groups—the elderly, youth in trouble, people with addictions, people with chronic mental illness, communities, and schools (Benard, 2004; Clark, 1997; Kretzmann & McKnight, 1993; Miller & Berg, 1995; Mills, 1995; Parsons & Cox, 1994; Pransky, 1998; Rapp & Goscha, 2006). In addition, rapidly developing literature, inquiry, and practice methods in a variety of fields bear a striking similarity to the strengths perspective—developmental resilience, healing and wellness, positive psychology, solution-focused therapy, assets-based community development, and narrative and story to name a few.

THE FASCINATION WITH PROBLEMS AND PATHOLOGY

The impetus for these efforts comes from many sources, but of singular importance is a reaction to our culture's continued obsession with psychopathology, victimization, abnormality, and moral and interpersonal aberrations. A rapidly proliferating conglomerate of businesses and professions, institutions and agencies, from medicine to pharmaceuticals, from the insurance industry to the mass media, turn handsome profits by assuring us that we are in the clutch (or soon will be) of any number of emotional, physical, or behavioral maladies. Each of us, it seems, is a reservoir of vulnerabilities and weaknesses usually born of toxic experiences in early life. The *Diagnostic and Statistical Manual* of The American Psychiatric Association (APA) has become the primary handbook for the diagnosing of mental disorders. Not only is it widely used, insurance companies typically require, for reimbursement purposes, a diagnosis fashioned from the DSM lexicon. While DSMs I and II were modest documents having less than 100 pages each of description of mental disorders (causality was also a focus), and were written by a handful of psychiatrists in predominantly psychodynamic language, DSM III was a sea change in this psychiatric glossary. Fueled by a group who wanted to emulate the descriptive precision and clarity of the early psychiatrist, Emil Kraepelin (who over time wrote eleven increasingly large editions of his psychiatric diagnostic manual), DSM III had hundreds of pages of descriptions of various categories of mental illness. It also was intended to be descriptive, not analytic. Many more disorders were included between its pages. The APA has put the DSM on a timetable. The DSMs have been extremely successful enterprises for the APA. The manual itself and the accompanying manuals and teaching guides are highly lucrative. In the realm of professional books, they are runaway best sellers. DSM IV, published in 1994, was followed in 2000 by DSM IV TR (Text Revision). DSM V is due out in 2010. Each edition has new disorders added to the existing panorama of maladies. If you want to anticipate what new pathologies will appear in the next DSM, check the back of DSM IV TR under the heading Criteria Sets and Axes Provided for Further Study. Here you have a roster of diseases-in-waiting. All of this is to say that we are in a relentless march toward hemming in each aspect of the human condition, even human nature itself, as reflective of some behavioral, emotional, and/or cognitive ills.

Not only are we mesmerized by disease and disorder, many of us have been designated as casualties by the ever-growing phalanx of mental health professionals, turning mental health into a thriving and handsomely rewarding business. Prodded by a variety of gurus, swamis, ministers, and therapists, some of us are in hot pursuit of our wounded inner children and find ourselves dripping with the residue of the poisons of our family background. If you listen carefully, you can hear the echoes of evangelism in some of these current cultural fixations. And these are cultural preoccupations as well. Tune in to talk shows and situation comedies, check out movies, blogs, CDs—the whole pageant of cultural preoccupations and enthrallments—and you will experience an expedition into our wounded and angry collective and individual selves. Kenneth Gergen (1994) sees the result of this symbiosis between mental health professions and culture, as a rapidly accelerating "cycle of progressive infirmity" (p. 155).

To make these observations is not to callously disregard the real pains and struggles of individuals, families, and communities; neither is it to casually avert our glance from the realities of abuse of all kinds inflicted on children; nor is it to deny the tenacious grip and beguiling thrall of addictions. It is, however, to foreswear the ascendancy of psychopathology as society's principal civic, moral, and medical categorical imperative. It is to denounce the idea that most people who experience hurt, trauma, and neglect inevitably suffer wounds and become less than they might be. It is to return a semblance of balance to the equation of understanding and helping those who are hurting. The balance is hard to come by because the language of strength and resilience is nascent and just developing and, therefore, scant. Sybil and Steve Wolin (1997) say this about the two paradigms (risk and resiliency):

> As a result, the resiliency paradigm is no match for the risk paradigm. Talking about the human capacity to repair from harm, inner strengths, and protective factors, professionals feel that they have entered alien territory. They grope for words and fear sounding unschooled and naïve when they replace pathology terminology with the more mundane vocabulary of resourcefulness, hope, creativity, competence, and the like . . . . We believe that the struggle can be tipped in the other direction by offering a systematic, developmental vocabulary of strengths that can stand up to pathology terminology that is standard in our field. (p. 27)

Social work, like other helping professions, has not been immune to the contagion of disease- and disorder-based thinking. Social work has constructed much of its theory and practice around the supposition that clients become clients because they have deficits, problems, pathologies, and diseases; that they are, in some essential way, flawed or weak. This orientation leaps from a past in which the certitude of conception about the moral defects of the poor, the despised, and the deviant captivated us. More sophisticated terminology prevails today, but the metaphors and narratives that guide our thinking and acting, often papered over with more salutary language, are sometimes negative constructions that are fateful for the future of those we help. The diction and symbolism of weakness, failure, and deficit shape how others regard clients, how clients regard themselves, and how resources are allocated to groups of clients. In the extreme, such designations may even invoke punitive sanctions.

The lexicon of pathology gives voice to a number of assumptions and these in turn have painted pictures of clients in vivid but not very flattering tones. Some of these assumptions and their consequences are summarized below.

The person is the problem or pathology named. Diagnostic labels of all kinds tend to become "master statuses" (Becker, 1963), designations and roles that subsume all others under their mantle. A person suffering from schizophrenia *becomes* a schizophrenic, a convention so common that we hardly give it a thought. Once labeled a schizophrenic, other elements of a person's character, experiences, knowledge, aspirations, slowly recede into the background, replaced by the language of symptom and syndrome. Inevitably, conversation about the person becomes dominated by the imagery of disease, and relationships with the ailing person re-form around such representations. To the extent that these labels take hold, the individual, through a process of surrender and increasing dependence, becomes the once alien identification (Gergen, 1994; Goffman, 1961; Scheff, 1984). These are not value neutral terms, either. They serve to separate those who suffer these "ailments" from those who do not; a distinction that if not physical (as in hospitalization) is at least moral. Those who are labeled, in ways both subtle and brutish, are degraded—certainly in terms of social regard and status. However, these labels provide a measure of relief for some suffering individuals and their families—knowing, finally, what the matter is. In addition labels are certainly better than being thought of as possessed by demons. Nonetheless they do create a situation for far too many individuals of self-enfeeblement—moral, psychological, and civil (Gergen, 1994, p. 150).

The language of pessimism and doubt; the sway of professional cynicism. Accentuating the problems of clients creates a wave of pessimistic expectations of, and predictions about, the client, the client's environment, and the client's capacity to cope with that environment. Furthermore, these labels have the insidious potential, repeated over time, to alter how individuals see themselves and how others see them. In the long run, these changes seep into the individual's identity. Paulo Freire (1996) maintained for many years that the views and expectations of oppressors have an uncanny and implacable impact on the oppressed. Under the weight of these once-foreign views, the oppressed begin to subjugate their own knowledge and understanding to those of their tormentors.

The focus on what is wrong often reveals an egregious doubt about the ability of individuals to cope with life's challenges or to rehabilitate themselves. Andrew Weil (1995) laments the profound pessimism and negativity in his own profession, medicine, about the body's innate inclination to transform, regenerate, and heal itself.

> I cannot help feeling embarrassed by my profession when I hear the myriad ways in which doctors convey their pessimism to patients. I . . . am working to require instruction in medical school about the power of words and the need for physicians to use extreme care in choosing the words they speak to patients. A larger subject is the problem of making doctors more conscious of the power projected on them by patients and the possibilities for reflecting that power back in ways that influence health for better rather than worse, that stimulate rather than retard spontaneous healing. (p. 64)

The situation is so bad that Weil refers to it as medical *hexing*—dire medical predictions and inimical attributions by physicians powerful enough to create anxiety, fear, depression, and resignation in patients. This is a common consequence of the biomedical model—a model that has profoundly influenced some fields of social work practice. The biomedical model and its more widely influential kin in the human service professions, the "Technical/Rationalist" model (Schön, 1983), are despairing of natural healing and people's capacity to know what is right. Extraordinarily materialistic, these models disregard the functional wholeness and fitness of anything under their scrutiny—including human beings. Social work's continuing emphasis on problems and disorders and the profession's increasing commerce with theories that focus on deficits and pathologies tend to promote the portrayal of individuals as sites of specific problems and as medleys of singular deficiencies. Such an attitude takes the social work profession away from its avowed and historical interest in the person-in-context, the understanding of the web of institutional and interpersonal relationships in which any person is enmeshed, and the possibility for rebirth and renewal even under dire circumstances.

Distance, power inequality, control, and manipulation mark the relationship between helper and helped. The idea that we have empirically grounded or theoretically potent techniques to apply is beguiling. But in some way it may create distance between clients and helpers. Distance itself, whether the distance of class, privileged knowledge, institutionalized role, or normative position, may imply a power inequality between helper and helped. In the end, the client's view may become fugitive or irrelevant. In discussing "resistant" clients, Miller and colleagues (1997) say this:

> If a therapist . . . suggests or implies that the client's point of view is wrong, somehow invalidates, or upstages the client, "resistance" may appear. After all, even if not already demoralized, who wants to be reminded of failure, criticized, and judged, or made to feel that you have to follow orders? What we come to call resistance may sometimes reflect the client's attempt to salvage a small portion of self-respect. As such, some cases become impossible simply because the treatment allows the client no way of "saving face" or upholding dignity. (p. 12)

The connoisseur, the grandparent of thinking about helping relationships and healthy ones generally, was Carl Rogers. This is what he said about the qualities of these relationships vis-à-vis the client. "[T]he client should experience or perceive something of the therapist's congruence, acceptance, and empathy. It is not enough that these conditions exist in the therapist. They must, to some degree, have been successfully communicated to the client" (Rogers, 1961, p. 284).

The surest route to detachment and a kind of depersonalization is the building of a case—assembling a portfolio on the client created from the identity-stripping descriptions of, for example, DSM IV TR or the juvenile justice code. Furthermore, the legal and political mandates of many agencies, the elements of social control embodied in both the institution and ethos of the agency, may strike a further blow to the possibility of partnership and collaboration between client and helper.

Context-stripping: Denying the power of context. Problem-based assessments encourage individualistic rather than ecological accounts of clients. When we transform persons into cases, we often see only them and how well they fit into a category. In this way, we miss important elements of the client's life—cultural, social, political, ethnic, spiritual, and economic—and how they contribute to, sustain, and shape a person's misery or struggles or mistakes. The irony here is that, in making a case we really do not individualize. Rather, we are in the act of finding an appropriate diagnostic niche for the individual, thus making the client one among many and not truly unique. All individuals suffering from bipolar disorder hence become more like each other and less distinctive. In doing this, we selectively destroy or at least ignore contextual information that, although not salient to our assessment scheme, might well reveal the abiding distinctiveness of the individual in this particular milieu. It might also indicate important resources for help and transformation as well as problem solving.

The supposition of disease assumes a cause for the disorder and, thus, a solution. Naming the poison leads to an antidote. But in the world of human relationships and experiences, the idea of a regression line between cause, disease, and cure ignores the steamy morass of uncertainty and complexity that is the human condition. It also happens to take out of the hands of the person, family and friends, the neighborhood—the daily lifeworld of all involved—the capacity and resources for change. There are many cultural and spiritual avenues for transformation and healing. They, rightly enough, also suppose linkages between the nature of the problem (is it natural or unnatural? spiritual or mundane?) and its relief. But to bury these tools under the weight of a medico-scientific model is to inter a variety of familial and cultural media for change.

Remedies in the lifeworld usually begin with reinterpretations of the problem that come out of continuing dialogue with the situation and with clients. These renderings are mutually crafted constructs that may only be good for this client, at this time, under these conditions. Although they may have the power to transform clients' understandings, choices, and actions, these expositions are tentative and provisional. The capacity to devise such interpretations depends not on a strict relationship between problem and solution but on intuition, tacit knowing, hunches, and conceptual risk taking (Saleebey, 1989). Schön (1983) has characterized the tension between the usual conception of professional knowing and doing and this more reflective one as that between rigor and relevance. Relevance asks these questions of us: To what extent are clients consulted about matters pertinent to them? What do they want? What do they need? How do they think they can get it? How do they see their situation—problems as well as possibilities? What values do they want to maximize? How have they managed to survive thus far? These and similar questions, as answers draw near, move us a step toward a deeper appreciation of all clients' unique attributes, abilities, and competencies, and the world of their experience. They require of the social worker and the client a degree of reflection, the interest in making meaning and making sense. Iris Murdoch said that when we return home and share our day

> We are artfully shaping material into story form. So in a way as word-users we all exist in a literary atmosphere, we live and breathe literature, we are all literary artists, we are constantly employing language to make interesting forms out of experience which perhaps originally seemed dull or incoherent. (cited in Mattingly, 1991, p. 237)

Finding the words that shout the reality of the lived experience of people, and perhaps finding other words that reflect genuine possibility and hope is, in a modest and unscientific sense, finding cause for celebration—of promise.

THE STRENGTHS PERSPECTIVE: PHILOSOPHY, CONCEPTS, AND PRINCIPLES

I want to discuss two major philosophical principles as a way of staking out the claims of the strengths perspective, but in the context of the sometimes numbing and usually complex realities of daily life.

Liberation and Empowerment: Heroism and Hope

Liberation is founded on the idea of possibility: the opportunities for choice, commitment, and action whether pursued in relative tranquility or in grievous circumstance. We have fabulous powers and potentials. Some are muted, unrealized, and immanent. Others glimmer brilliantly about us. All around are people and policies, circumstances and conventions, contingencies and conceptions that may nurture and emancipate these powers or that may crush and degrade them. Somewhere within, and we may call it by different names, lies the longing for the heroic: to transcend circumstances, to develop one's own powers, to face adversity down, to stand up and be counted. All too often social institutions, oppressors, other people, some even with good intentions, tamp out this yearning or distort it so that it serves the interests and purposes of others. Nonetheless, however muted, this precious craving abides. It is incumbent on the healer, the humane leader, the shaman, the teacher, and, yes, the social worker to find ways for this penchant for the possible and unimaginable to survive and find expression in life-affirming ways. Of course, things go more smoothly if people simply play their roles, pay their taxes, and stifle their opinions. Liberation exerts tremendous pressure on the repressive inclinations of institutions and individuals. Collectively, liberation unleashes human energy and spirit, critical thinking, the questioning of authority, challenges to the conventional wisdom, and new ways of being and doing. But liberation may also be modest and unassuming. We may try out new behaviors, forge new relationships, or make a new commitment. Hope and the belief in the possible is central to liberation. Before his death, the great pedagogue of liberation, Paulo Freire, wrote in his last book, *Pedagogy of Hope* (1996), that he had previously underestimated the power of hope.

> But the attempt to do without hope, in the struggle to improve the world, as if that struggle could be reduced to calculated acts alone, or a purely scientific approach, is a frivolous illusion. To attempt to do without hope, which is based on the need for truth as an ethical quality of the struggle, is tantamount to denying that struggler as one of its mainstays . . . [H]ope, as an ontological need, demands an anchoring in practice. . . . Without a minimum of hope, we cannot so much as start the struggle. (pp. 8–9)

I would go so far as to say that the central dynamic of the strengths perspective is precisely the rousing of hope, of tapping into the visions and the promise of that individual, family, or community. Circumstances, bad luck, unfortunate decisions, the harshness of life lived on the edge of need and vulnerability, of course, may smother these. Nonetheless, it is the flicker of possibility that can ignite the fire of hope.

Assume that all humans, somewhere within, have the urge to be heroic; to transcend circumstances, to develop their powers, to overcome adversity, to stand up and be counted, to be a part of something that surpasses the petty interests of self, to shape and realize their hopes and dreams. This is a valuable urge and it is often a fragile one. Liberation and empowerment—the heart of the work that we are privileged to do—are designed to unleash the heroic—human energy, critical thinking, possibility and purpose, challenges to the conventional wisdom, moral imagination, the humanitarian impulse, the ability to survive and surmount adversity. This all may occur within the parameters of one's daily life and may be simple things like trying out new behaviors, or entertaining new ideas, escaping the drudgery of oppressive work, or abusive relationships, sensing and using a more generous fund of communal spirit, giving help to a friend, volunteering in a community, withstanding a stressful situation or dread disease with dignity and resolve, or holding the hands of those who are marginalized, isolated, or belittled.

The heroism of everyday life is all around us. People carrying on in the midst of mind-searing stress; people coming to the fore when the needs around them require someone to act and to act out of the ordinary; people whose moral imagination allows them to see, even in distant and unfamiliar places, the utter humanity of those who suffer (Glover, 2000). 9/11 is a horrific but instructive example. Fire and police personnel, rescue teams, the people who risked their lives and faced serious harm in helping to clear away the hellish debris (Langewiesche, 2003), social workers who met with survivors and witnesses to help ease the psychological and interpersonal wreckage of the trauma; people trapped in the inferno, facing certain death, who called their loved ones to tell them goodbye and to express their love: Many of these pushed the boundaries of the heroic outward and upward. Clearly, the destruction wrought on that day was a deliberate, heinous, and murderous crime. But even on the other side, given their point of view, the terrorists thought themselves to be heroic. In a letter to his wife, speaking of his certain death, one of them wrote, ". . . Know that my death is a martyrdom, my imprisonment hermitage, my exile tourism in God's land. I would like to meet you in heaven, so please help me by waking up at night to pray, fasting during the day, and staying away from temptation" (Cullison, 2004, p. 66). Obviously, we are required here to make a moral judgment about the lethal and vicious acts they committed against us, but we must also look through their eyes to understand more fully the meaning of heroism for the human condition.

Alienation and Oppression: Anxiety and Evil

The circumstances around us will not let us deny the existence of harsh and tyrannical institutions, relationships, circumstances, and regimes. Bigotry, hatred, war, slaughter, repression, and, more quietly but no less devastating, setting people aside, treating them as the despised other, and acting as though they are not fully human, are all daily reminders of the existence of evil, brutality, and despotism. But why is the capacity for evil the seeming companion to the urge to the heroic?

How often do we stand, agape, horrified at what we see or hear about or read about? Vicious acts of cruelty, violence born of intolerance and hate—how can they happen, we cry? Yet, aren't there times when we have been propelled to act or have been a party to actions that have inflicted emotional or physical pain on others, often those who are different from us? Why?

We are small, and vulnerable. The cosmos is enormous. We tremble at the insignificance and frailty of our being when cast against the magnitude of time and the vastness of space. At times, our fear and trembling is best handled by taking matters into our own hands, individually or collectively, and dealing the instrumentalities of fear and loathing onto others. Thus we subdue our own uncertainties and obscure our cosmic smallness. It may even be that some of these acts of violence or marginalizing are "immortality projects" designed to blind us to the reality of our own organismic vulnerability and eventual demise (Becker, 1973; Fromm, 1973; Rank, 1941).

But from the ashes of destruction, mayhem, and oppression may emerge the human spirit, the capacity for the heroic. So we can never dismiss the possibility of redemption, resurrection, and regeneration. However, the sweep of history, the grandeur of wholesale creation and destruction eventually find their way into the nooks and crannies of our lives. These sweeping generalities occur in the small confines of daily life as well. You see a single mother and her 10-year-old daughter. They have come to the family service agency you work for. The mother is worried. Her daughter, once sweet and compliant, a joy to be around, is becoming morose, uncommunicative, anxious, and weepy. The quality of her work at school is plummeting, and friends seem unimportant to her. Father left the family suddenly and left them in dire financial straits. It had been a marriage of youthful misjudgments, the mother allows, but, she says, in spite of the financial hardships maybe it is better that he has gone. The mother wonders if her daughter's current woes aren't related to his leaving about six months ago. You spend considerable time over the next weeks exploring the situation with the mother and daughter. Eventually, you discover that for a period of almost two years the young girl had experienced physical and sexual depredation and brutality at the hands of her father. She had vowed to herself never to tell anyone! Never to let him know how much he had hurt her. Never! And she maintained her vow until he left. Now she was falling apart, grieving, experiencing rage, and feeling the wounds of violation. But in the ashes of devastation, this young girl's spirit, against all odds, flourished. Now the mother and the social worker must make an alliance with this tiny, amazing soul.

We have seen that the preoccupation with problems and pathologies, while producing an impressive lode of technical and theoretical writing, may be less fruitful when it comes to actually helping clients grow, develop, change directions, realize their visions, or revise their personal meanings and narratives. What follows is a brief glossary of terms supporting an orientation to strengths as well as a statement of the principles of practice central to a strengths perspective. These are meant to give you a vital sense of what a frame of mind devoted to the strengths of individuals and groups requires.

THE LEXICON OF STRENGTHS

"We can act," wrote William James (1902) in reflecting upon Immanuel Kant's notions about conceptions, "as *if* there were a God; feel as *if* we were free; consider nature as *if* she were full of special designs; lay plans as *if* we were to be immortal; and we find then that these words **do** [emphasis added] make a genuine difference in our moral life" (p. 55). Language and words have power. They can elevate and inspire or demoralize and destroy. If words are a part of the nutriment that feeds one's sense of self, then we are compelled to examine our dictionary of helping to see what our words portend for clients. Any approach to practice speaks a language that, in the end, may have a pronounced effect on the way that clients think of themselves and how they act. Not only that, our professional diction has a profound effect on the way that *we* regard clients, their world, and their troubles. In the strengths approach to practice, some words are essential and direct us to an appreciation of the assets of individuals, families, and communities.

A simple device for framing and remembering the essentials of the strengths perspective can be found in Figure 1.1.

These words capture, I think, the core values of the strengths lexicon. The central dynamic of strengths discovery and articulation lies in hope and possibility; the vision of a better future or quality of life.

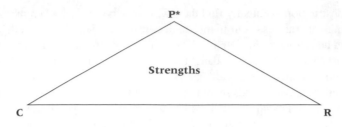

Where C stands for:

Competence, capacities, courage

And P symbolizes:

Promise, possibility, positive expectations, potential

And R signifies:

Resilience, reserves, resources, resourcefulness

FIGURE 1.1   Essentials of the Strengths Perspective
*Thanks to my daughter Meghan for suggesting this.

Plasticity (and the Placebo Effect)

It is a miracle of the brain that it "never loses the power to transform itself on the basis of experience and that the transformation can occur over short intervals. . . . your brain is different today than it was yesterday" (Restak, 2003, p. 8). It was once thought that after adolescence the brain is pretty much a structural monolith, hardly changing. But now, thanks to sophisticated imaging techniques, it is clear that the brain, in ways minute and substantial, continually undergoes change. Most of these changes take place at the synapse (the place where neurons communicate with each other) and are the result of experience and learning or simply one's current state of mind (LeDoux, 2002). These relationships are, at one site or another, in flux and are the basis of plasticity. Therefore, we have a marvelous capacity to alter, extend, and reshape behavior, feeling, and cognition. Of course, much of what happens here is beyond our conscious recognition.

The placebo effect has been long noted (even before modern medicine, although it was not called that). In contemporary usage it refers to a phenomenon in the clinical trials of various medical procedures and medications. Typically, one group is given the actual drug and another is given an inert substance (although now it is becoming more common to give a placebo that does provoke side effects so that people are less likely to guess they are being given the placebo). Neither the administrators of the drugs and placebos nor the "patients" know which is which. A drug's power is thought to be measured in the extent to which it is superior to the placebo in promoting the appropriate effects. In many clinical trials of psychoactive drugs it is not uncommon for 40 to 60 percent of the placebo group to experience the therapeutic outcome provided by the drug. And we do not really know how many of the people who get the actual drug experienced a placebo rather than a drug effect (or some combination of the two). Recently, four physicians, using the Freedom of Information Act, were able to get the results of clinical trials done over the last fifteen years from the Food and Drug Administration (FDA) for six of the most popular antidepressant drugs. Pharmaceutical companies conduct clinical trials and then send the results to the FDA. Until then no one had access to the results of these trials, so we had to take the drug company's word that its drug is effective. These researchers conducted meta-analyses of the clinical trials and found, no matter how generous or conservative their statistical analysis, that there were no clinically significant differences between the placebos and the drugs (Kirsch et al., 2003). Whatever else this means, it does, I think, bespeak the power of hope, positive expectations, and belief in the healing ministration. It seems odd that we would not have made more of the placebo effect (even if it is only a short-term one).

Empowerment

In danger of becoming hackneyed, empowerment indicates the intent to, and the processes of, assisting individuals, groups, families, and communities to discover and expend the resources and tools within and around them. Rapp and Goscha (2006) argue that " '[t]o be empowered' a person or group requires an environment that provides options and ascribes authority to the person to choose" (p. 27). It also requires, they suggest, that a person must be aware of those options, have the authority to act, and must have the resources and ability to act on them. Finally, empowerment only becomes a transformative phenomenon when it is constructed through dialogue and action.

To discover the power within people and communities, we must subvert and abjure pejorative labels; provide opportunities for connections to family, institutional, and communal resources; assail the victim mindset; foreswear paternalism; trust people's intuitions, accounts, perspectives, and energies; and believe in people's dreams. Barbara Levy Simon (1994) builds the concept of empowerment with five necessary ideas: collaborative partnerships with clients and constituents; an emphasis on the expansion of client strengths and capacities; a focus on both the individual or family and the environment; assuming that clients are active subjects and agents; and directing one's energies to the historically disenfranchised and oppressed. Pursuing the empowerment agenda requires a deep conviction about the necessity of democracy. It requires us to address the tensions and conflicts, the institutions and people that subdue and limit those we help, and compels us to help people free themselves from these restraints (Pinderhughes, 1994). Too often, helping professions (although social work has been very wary of falling into this trap) have thwarted this imperative by assuming a paternalistic posture, informing people about what is good for them and exhorting people to do the right thing. The strengths approach imposes a different attitude and commitment. The strengths of individuals and communities are renewable and expandable resources. Furthermore, the assets of individuals almost always lie embedded in a community of interest and involvement. Thus, the ideas of community and membership are central to the strengths approach.

Membership

To be without membership, writes Michael Walzer, is to be in a "condition of infinite danger" (1983, p. 32). To be without membership is to be alienated, to be at risk for marginalization and oppression. People need to be citizens, responsible and valued members of a community. To sever people from the roots of their "place" subverts, for all, civic and moral vigor. The strengths orientation proceeds from the recognition that all of those whom we serve are, like ourselves, members of a species, entitled to the dignity, respect, and responsibility that comes with such membership. But, too often, people we help have either no place to be (or to be comfortable) or no sense of belonging. The sigh of relief from those who come to be members and citizens and bask in the attendant rights and responsibilities, assurances and securities, is the first breath of empowerment. There is another meaning of membership and that is that people must often band together to make their voices heard, get their needs met, to redress inequities, and to reach their dreams. Jonathon Kozol (2000) writes eloquently about the lived experience of people, especially children, who are poor and struggle with the ignorance, hostility, lack of regard, and destructive policies of the outside world. He describes places of refuge, resurrection, and membership. St. Ann's Church and School in the South Bronx is one such place. Here, Mother Martha, the pastor, invites the membership of children and adults. The reality of segregation and separation from the mainstream is never very far from the halls of St. Ann's.

> Despite the isolation and betrayal that may be suggested by these governing realities, St. Ann's is not a place of sorrow, but at least during the hours when children fill its corridors and classrooms with their voices and their questions and their paperpads and their notebooks and their games, it is a place of irresistible vitality and energy and sometimes complicated hope, and now and then uncomplicated joy. For grown-ups in the neighborhood, it is an energizing place as well, although the burdens that they bring with them when they come here in times of crisis to seek out the priest can often seem at first overwhelming. (p. 33)

The same kind of trustful energy is poured into community-building and neighborhood development projects all over this country. In her investigation of programs that work, Lisbeth Schorr (1997) says this about successful community-building programs:

> Community building . . . is more an orientation than a technique, more a mission than a program, more an outlook than an activity. It catalyzes a process of change grounded in local life and priorities. Community building addresses the developmental needs of individuals, families, and organizations within the neighborhood. It changes the nature of the relationship between the neighborhood and the systems outside its boundaries. A community's own strengths—whether they are found in churches, block clubs, local leadership, or its problem-solving abilities—are seen as central. (pp. 361–362)

You can see that the ingredients of the strengths perspective abound in this definition of community building—empowerment, membership, and, certainly, indigenous resilience.

Resilience

A growing body of inquiry and practice makes it clear that the rule, not the exception, in human affairs is that people do rebound from serious trouble, that individuals and communities do surmount and overcome serious and troubling adversity. "In fact, for just about any population of children that research has found to be at greater risk than normal for later problems . . . —more of these make it than do not. In most studies the figure seems to average 70 to 75%" (Benard, 2004, p. 7). These percentages include children who have been abused, whose parents divorced, who faced abandonment, developmental delays, who had parents who were seriously mentally ill and so forth. As a matter of fact, you could identify any misfortune likely to afflict children and these findings would stand.

Much of this literature documents and demonstrates that particularly demanding and stressful experiences, even ongoing ones, *do not lead inevitably to vulnerability, failure to adapt, and psychopathology* (Benard, 2004; Katz, 1997; Werner & Smith, 1992; Wolin & Wolin, 1996). Resilience is not the cheerful disregard of one's difficult and traumatic life experiences; neither is it the naive discounting of life's pains. It is, rather, the ability to bear up in spite of these ordeals. Damage has been done. Emotional and physical scars bear witness to that. In spite of the wounds, however, for many the trials have been instructive and propitious. Resilience is a process—the continuing growth and articulation of capacities, knowledge, insight, and virtues derived through meeting the demands and challenges of one's world, however chastening.

Healing and Wholeness

Healing implies both wholeness and the inborn facility of the body and the mind to regenerate and resist when faced with disorder, disease, and disruption. Healing also requires a beneficent relationship between the individual and the larger social and physical environment. The natural state of affairs for human beings, evolved over eons of time and at every level of organization from cell to self-image, is the repair of one's mind and body. Just as the resilience literature assures us that individuals have naturally occurring self-righting tendencies, even though they can be compromised (Werner & Smith, 1992), it seems also the case that all human organisms have the inclination for healing. This evolutionary legacy, of course, can be compromised by trauma, by environmental toxins, by bodily disorganization, and, not the least, by some of our professional intervention philosophies and systems. But, the bottom line is this: If spontaneous healing occurs miraculously in one human being, you can expect it to occur in another and another. Such organismic ingenuity only makes common sense. Otherwise, how could we have survived as a species for hundreds of thousands of years without hospitals, HMOs, physicians, psychiatrists, pharmacists, or talk show hosts? Healing occurs when the healer or the individual makes an alliance with, or instigates the power of, the organism to restore itself (Cousins, 1989; Pelletier, 2000; Weil, 1995). Healing and self-regeneration are intrinsic life support systems, always working and, for most of us, most of the time, on call. Healing almost always is relationship bound and occurs in a context that generates and supports it. Some milieus—whether family, group, community, or social network—are more health promoting than others. Lois Holzman (2002), one of the developers of the East Side Institute for Short-Term Therapy in New York City, observes that the therapeutic work that she and her colleagues do at the Institute as essentially community-building—"a collective, creative process of people bringing into existence a new social unit and sharing collective commitment to its sustainability" (p. 2).

Dialogue and Collaboration

Humans can only come into being through a creative and emergent relationship with others. Without such transactions, there can be no discovery and testing of one's powers, no knowledge, no heightening of one's awareness and internal strengths. In dialogue, we confirm the importance of others and begin to heal the rift between self, other, and institution.

Dialogue requires empathy, identification with, and the inclusion of other people. Paulo Freire (1973) was convinced, based on his years of work with oppressed peoples, that only humble and loving dialogue can surmount the barrier of mistrust built from years of paternalism and the rampant subjugation of the knowledge and wisdom of the oppressed. "Founding itself upon love, humility, and faith, dialogue becomes a horizontal relationship of which mutual trust between the dialoguers is the logical consequence" (pp. 79–80). A caring community is a community that confirms otherness, in part by giving each person and group a ground of their own and affirming this ground through encounters that are egalitarian and dedicated to healing and empowerment.

The idea of collaboration has a more specific focus. When we work together with clients, we become their agents, their consultants, stakeholders with them in mutually crafted projects. This requires us to be open to negotiation and to appreciate the authenticity of the views and aspirations of those with whom we collaborate. Our voices may have to be quieted so that we can give voice to our clients. Comfortably ensconced in the expert role, sometimes we may have great difficulty assuming such a conjoint posture.

Suspension of Disbelief

It would be hard to exaggerate the extent of disbelief of clients' words and stories in the culture of professionalism. While social work because of its enduring values may fancy itself less culpable in this regard than other professions, a little circumspection is warranted. Like other helping professions, we have presumptions and preferences, often driven by the context in which we work, that frame the people and problems we confront. The weight of the DSM IV TR and other agency protocols, for example, may obscure the person who seeks our help. Myths and narratives about groups of clients, from, say, people who physically abuse their children to those who abuse substances, can raise a curtain of certainty before us where we should proceed with circumspection and restraint. Sometimes we act on our beliefs because we think that, encouraged by the profession and agency, they are valid representations of reality.

But, the idea that there are valid representations of reality is questionable. That is, there are many representations of the real world. Is, say, a Lakota understanding of fever any less relevant in context than a Manhattan internist's? Second, to begin work with clients in this frame of mind would seem to subvert the idea that clients often do know exactly what they are talking about and that they are experts on their own lives. And, are social workers' own interpretations less subject to faulty recall, or their own interpretive forestructures less likely to be slathered over clients' own understanding? Perhaps the suspension of belief in clients' accounts comes from the radiation of scientific thinking throughout our culture and into the professions. The ideal of the scientific investigator as objective and dispassionate observer has been transfigured into a certain incredulity about, and distancing from, clients. If the rise of the professions (and the ideology of professionalism) was part of the extension and reinforcement of the institutions of socialization and social control during the Victorian era, then a certain detachment and restraint in accepting clients and their stories made sense (Bledstein, 1978).

Professionals have checked the affirmation of clients in a number of ways:

- By imposing their own theories over the theories and accounts of clients.
- By using assessment in an interrogative style designed to ascertain certain diagnostic and largely preemptive hypotheses that, in the end, confirm suspicions about the client.

- By engaging in self-protective maneuvers (like skepticism) designed to prevent the ultimate embarrassment for a professional—being fooled by or lied to by a cunning client.

The frequent talk about manipulative and resistant clients in many social agencies may stem from the fear of being made the fool. To protect self-esteem, nonnormative lifestyles, self-interests, or benefits, clients may have a vested interest in not telling the truth. But we must consider the possibility that avoiding the truth may be a function of the manner in which the professional pursues and/or asserts the truth. The professional's knowledge, information, and perspective are privileged and carry institutional and legal weight. The client's do not.

In summary, the lexicon of strengths provides us with a vocabulary of appreciation and not aspersion about those with whom we work. In essence, the effort is to move away from defining professional work as the articulation of the power of expert knowledge toward collaboration with the power within the individual or community toward a life that is palpably better—and better on the clients' own terms.

PRINCIPLES OF THE STRENGTHS PERSPECTIVE

What exactly is a perspective? It is not a theory. Theories seek to explain some phenomena, or at least describe them analytically. It is not a model. Models are meant to represent, logically and graphically, some aspect of the world. A perspective is somewhat harder to define. At the least it is a standpoint, a way of viewing and understanding certain aspects of experience. It is a lens through which we choose to perceive and appreciate. It provides us with a slant on the world, built of words and principles. We have already reviewed some of the words. What follows now are some of the principles.

The principles that follow are the guiding assumptions and regulating understandings of the strengths perspective. They are tentative, still evolving, and subject to revision. They do, however, give a flavor of what practicing from a strengths appreciation involves.

1. *Every Individual, Group, Family, and Community Has Strengths.* For a variety of reasons—professional identities and credos, cultural preferences, or agency norms, who knows?—it is sometimes hard to take the stance that the individual, family, or community that you intend to help comes to you already possessing knowledge, wisdom, goals, and assets that, at least at the outset, you know nothing about. First *and* foremost, the strengths perspective is about discerning those resources, and respecting them and the potential they may have for reversing misfortune, countering illness, easing pain, and reaching goals. To detect strengths, however, the social work practitioner must be genuinely interested in, and respectful of, clients' stories, narratives, and accounts—the interpretive angles they take on their own experiences. These are important "theories" that can guide practice. The unearthing of clients' identities and realities does not come only from a ritual litany of troubles, embarrassments, snares, foibles, and barriers. Rather, clients come into view when you assume that they know something, have learned lessons from experience, have hopes, have interests, and can do some things masterfully. These may be obscured by the stresses of the moment, submerged under the weight of crisis, oppression, or illness but, nonetheless, they abide.

In the end, clients want to know that you actually care about them, that how they fare makes a difference to you, that you will listen to them, that you will respect them no matter what their history, and that you believe that they can build something of value with the resources within and around them. *But most of all, clients want to know that you really believe they can surmount adversity and begin the climb toward transformation and growth.*

2. ***Trauma and Abuse, Illness and Struggle May Be Injurious, but They May also Be Sources of Challenge and Opportunity.*** The Wolins (1997) point out that the "damage model" of development so prevalent in today's thinking only leads to discouragement, pessimism, and the victim mindset. It also foretells a continuing future of psychopathology and troubled relationships. Individuals exposed to a variety of abuses, especially in childhood, are thought always to be victims or to be damaged in ways that obscure or override any strengths or possibilities for rebound. In the Wolins' "challenge model," children are not seen as merely passive recipients of parental unpredictability, abuse, disappointment, or violence. Rather, children are seen as active and developing individuals who, through these trials, learn skills and develop personal attributes that stand them in good stead in adulthood. Not that they do not suffer. They do. Not that they do not bear scars. They do. But they also may acquire traits and capacities that are preservative and life affirming. There is dignity to be drawn from having prevailed over obstacles to one's growth and maturing. The Wolins (1993) refer to this as "survivor's pride." It is a deep-dwelling sense of accomplishment in having met life's challenges and walked away, not without fear, even terror, and certainly not without wounds. Often this pride is buried under embarrassment, confusion, distraction, or self-doubt. But when it exists and is lit, it can ignite the engine of change.

Individuals, groups, and communities are more likely to continue development and growth when they are funded by the currency of their capacities, knowledge, and skills (Delgado, 2000; Kretzmann & McKnight, 1993). While the strengths perspective is powered by a similar belief, the observation of many who practice using a strengths approach is that many people who struggle to find their daily bread, a job, or shelter are already resilient, resourceful, and, though in pain, motivated for achievement on their terms. Kaplan and Girard (1994) put it this way:

> People are more motivated to change when their strengths are supported. Instead of asking family members what their problems are, a worker can ask what strengths they bring to the family and what they think are the strengths of other family members. Through this process the worker helps the family discover its capabilities and formulate a new way to think about themselves. . . . The worker creates a language of strength, hope, and movement. . . . (p. 53)

3. ***Assume That You Do Not Know the Upper Limits of the Capacity to Grow and Change and Take Individual, Group, and Community Aspirations Seriously.*** Too often, professionals assume that a diagnosis, an assessment, a profile, or a demographic characteristic sets the parameters of possibility for their clients. In our personal lives, looking back, we sometimes marvel at the road we traveled—a road that we, at the outset, might not have even considered taking—and the distance that we have come. For our clients, too often, we cannot imagine the prospect of similar dizzying and unanticipated destinations. The diagnosis or the assessment becomes a verdict and a sentence. Our clients will be better served when we make an overt pact with their promise and possibility. This means that we must hold high our expectations of clients and make allegiance with their hopes, visions, and values.

It is becoming increasingly clear that emotions have a profound effect on wellness and health. Emotions experienced as positive can activate the inner pharmacoepia, those chemicals that relax, help fight infection, and restore. This is undoubtedly part of our evolutionary success; our ability to adapt to situations, even highly toxic ones, that were not foretold in our genome (Damasio, 1994). When people believe that they can recover, that they have prospects, that their hopes are palpable, their bodies often respond optimally. That does not mean that people do not get sick. It does mean that when people are sick, healers can make an alliance with the body's regenerative powers and augment them with real but nonetheless fortifying and uplifting expectations (Weil, 1995). Roger Mills's (1995) community empowerment projects are based on similar principles (see Chapter 13). Mills's idea is that everyone has innate wisdom, intelligence, and motivating emotions and that these, even if muted by circumstance, are accessible through education, support, and encouragement. The goals of his projects are to "reconnect people to the [physical and mental] health in themselves and then direct them in ways to bring forth the health of others in their community. The result is a change in people and communities which builds up from within rather than [being] imposed from without" (Mills, 1993, cited in Benard, 1994, p. 22). So it is that individuals and communities have the capacity for restoration and rebound.

4. *We Best Serve Clients by Collaborating with Them.* The role of expert or professional may not provide the best vantage point from which to appreciate clients' strengths and assets. A helper may best be defined as a collaborator or consultant: an individual clearly presumed, because of specialized education and experience, to know some things and to have some tools at the ready but definitely not the only one in the situation to have relevant, even esoteric, knowledge and understanding. Ms. Johnson knows more about thriving in a public housing project than anyone I can think of. Over the course of thirty-five years, she successfully raised eleven children. She maintained a demeanor of poise, and she demonstrated intelligence and vigor, even as her community underwent dramatic, often frightening changes. Her contributions to the community are, simply put, amazing. She has much to teach us and other residents of her community. I certainly would not presume to work *on* Ms. Johnson but would be privileged to work *with* her.

We make a serious error when we subjugate clients' wisdom and knowledge to official views. There is something liberating, for all parties involved, in connecting to clients' stories and narratives, their hopes and fears, their wherewithal and resources rather than trying to stuff them into the narrow confines of a diagnostic category or treatment protocol. Ultimately, a collaborative stance may make us less vulnerable to some of the more political elements of helping: paternalism, victim-blaming (or, more currently, victim-creating), and preemption of client views. It is likewise important to get the stories and views of clients out to those who need to hear them—schools, agencies, employers, local governments, churches, and businesses. This is part of the role of advocacy. The policies and regulations that affect many of our clients are crafted in the halls of Congress or the State House and are often far removed from their daily reality. Furthermore, these policies rarely take advantage of the wisdom and resources of their intended beneficiaries and recipients.

5. *Every Environment Is Full of Resources.* (See Chapters 12, 13, and 14.) In communities that seem to amplify individual and group resilience, there is awareness, recognition, and use of the assets of most members of the community (Kretzmann & McKnight, 1993). Informal systems and associations of individuals, families, and groups, social circuits of peers, and intergenerational mentoring work to assist, support, instruct, and include all members of a community (Schorr, 1997). In inclusive communities, there are many opportunities for involvement, to make contributions to the moral and civic life of the whole; to become, in other words, a citizen in place. No matter how harsh an environment, how it may test the mettle of its inhabitants, it can also be understood as a potentially lush topography of resources and possibilities. In every environment, there are individuals, associations, groups, and institutions who have something to give, something that others may desperately need: knowledge, succor, an actual resource or talent, or simply time and place. Such resources usually exist outside the usual matrix of social and human service agencies. And, for the most part, they are unsolicited and untapped. Melvin Delgado (2000), in his articulation of the capacity-enhancement approach to urban social work practice, describes the five critical assumptions of that approach: "(1) The community has the will and the resources to help itself; (2) it knows what is best for itself; (3) ownership of the strategy rests within, rather than outside, the community; (4) partnerships involving organizations and communities are the preferred route for initiatives; and (5) the use of strengths in one area will translate into strengths in other areas . . . a ripple effect" (p. 28).

Such a view of the environment, while seeming to comfort those who believe that people(s) should pull themselves up by their collective and individual bootstraps, *does not* abrogate the responsibility for working for social and economic justice. It does, however, recognize that while we await political transformation, there are reservoirs of energy, ideas, talents, and tools out there on which to draw. To regard the environment as only inimical or toxic moves us to disregard these resources or mistakenly judge them as disreputable. When it comes, the community that is aware of and employing its human and social capital to the degree possible is in a much better position to drink the cooling waters of social justice.

6. *Caring, Caretaking, and Context.* The idea that care is essential to human well-being does not sit well in a society beset by centuries of rugged individualism. Deborah Stone (2000) says that we have three rights to care. First, all families must be permitted and assisted in caring for their members. Second, all those paid caregivers need to be able give the support and quality care that is commensurate with the highest ideals of care without subverting their own well-being. Finally, a right to care boils down to this: that all people (and there may be 38 million children under the age of 10 who clearly need care and anywhere between 30 and 50 million adults who need some degree of care) who need care get it. We do have a horror of dependence. But, as Stone says,

> Caring for each other is the most basic form of civic participation. We learn to care in families, and we enlarge our communities of concern as we mature. Caring is the essential democratic act, the prerequisite to voting, joining associations, attending meetings, holding office, and all the other ways we sustain democracy. (p. 15)

In one sense, social work is about care and caretaking. Ann Weick (2000) makes the case that social caretaking as an activity is the profession's hidden (and first) voice; hidden because it is also woman's voice. Caretaking is, in a diffuse sense, also the work of the strengths perspective.

> Recognizing the capacity for toughness and tenderness, for clear reason and fluid intuition, for radical hope and dry-eyed reality brings us back to the challenges of caretaking. But rather than discounting its demands and possibilities, the lesson of our first voice tells us to pay attention to every dimension it encompasses. Social work is social caretaking. . . . We need to turn our attention to the humblest activities of social caretaking and offer our boldest ideas about strengthening the social web connecting us all. (p. 401)

Like social caretaking, and social work, the strengths perspective is about the revolutionary possibility of hope; hope realized through the strengthened sinew of social relationships in family, neighborhood, community, culture, and country. That contextual sinew is fortified by the expression of the individual and communal capacities of all. The strength of that sinew is also significantly dependent on the opportunities and barriers afforded by social policies—local, state, and national—that affect the quality of life and life chances for citizens.

SOME PRELIMINARY THOUGHTS

Social work has had something of a dissociative history with regard to building on client strengths. From its inception as a profession, the field has been exhorted to respect and energize client capacities. Bertha Capen Reynolds (1951) looked at the issue in terms of workers' obligations:

> The real choice before us as social workers is whether *we* are to be passive or active. . . . Shall we be content to give with one hand and withhold with the other, to build up or tear down at the same time the strength of a person's life? Or shall we become conscious of our own part in making a profession which will stand forthrightly for human well-being, *including the right to be an active citizen?* (p. 175, emphasis added)

The historical and continuing tension between the desire to become more professional, more technically adept, to focus on "function" rather than "cause" (Lee, 1929), to elevate social work to a new level of respect and comparability among the professions, and, on the other hand, to retain the interest in social action and the redress of social inequities seems to have been resolved recently in favor of the former. The writing, lexicon, and perspective of, say, clinical social work and those of social action or community development are quite different, maybe even at odds. While there is no implacable conflict between the interests of social work practice and social action, the infusion of psychodynamic thinking, the rise of private practice and vendorship, the mass appeal of DSM IV TR among other factors have driven social work toward a model of practice that is more heavily aligned with psychological thinking and psychopathology theories (Specht & Courtney, 1993). The theories that define such an alignment are typically oriented toward family and individual dysfunctions and disorders. While we must respect the impact of problems on the quality of life for our clients, we must also exercise extraordinary diligence to assure that the resources and positive attributes of clients draw our attention and define our efforts.

It does seem to be the case that group work has a long history of attention to the strengths and resources of group members and their neighborhoods. Andrew Malekoff (2001) puts it this way:

> There is so much talk today about strengths and wellness. This is hardly a new or revolutionary concept. But it has been neglected for too long. However, good group work practice has been paying attention to people's strengths since the days of the original settlement houses over 100 years ago, mostly without fanfare. (p. 247)

Although today's social work practice texts typically nod in the direction of client strengths but provide little guidance to the student or worker about how to make an accounting of strengths and how to employ them in helping, we are currently seeing movement away from the problem or pathology perspective. The solution-focused approach is one example. In essence, it regards clients in the light of what they have done well, those times that the problem has not been apparent, or those times when exceptions to difficulty have occurred. Furthermore, client goals and visions are the centerpiece of the work to be done. It is not unusual for solution-focused practitioners to ask how things would be positively different if a miracle occurred overnight and the problem no longer held (de Jong & Berg, 2001). The literature on resilience, discussed briefly earlier in this chapter, also provides conceptual and clinical ground for employing client strengths as a central part of the helping process. In the words of Benard (1994; see also Chapter 11), "Using resilience as the knowledge base for practice creates a *sense of optimism and hope.* It allows anyone working with troubled youth to, as poet Emily Dickinson urges, dwell in possibility, to have confidence in their futures and, therefore, to convey this positive expectation to them" (p. 4).

Finally, the research on the effectiveness of a strengths approach, although very preliminary, suggests that it may be an effective and economical framework for practice or case management (Rapp & Goscha, 2006). Related research on power of mind/health realization; resilience-based practice; solution-focused therapy; community building; and the research done on the critical factors in successful therapy provide some associated support for the elements of a strengths perspective that make a difference. Research actually done from the vantage point of a strengths approach includes the views and concerns of the stakeholders (subjects and clients) from the outset. The results of the research are to be used to achieve stated objectives of the stakeholders and/or to aid in the solving of identified problems.

In Chapter 15, I will discuss in more detail some of the converging lines of research and practice that are reinforcing the strengths perspective. I will also address some of the persistent and significant criticisms of it.

CONCLUSION

This edition of the book continues the effort to expand the conceptual, clinical, and practical elements of the strengths perspective. At its philosophical core, this perspective merely affirms or, rather, reaffirms, our dedication to understanding and revering the resources and resourcefulness that individuals, families, and communities bring to us when they seek our help. The central proposition of social work practice, as I see it, is to exploit the best in all of us; to work together to surmount adversity and trouble; to confront the appalling with all the tools available within us and around us; to wrestle distress and disillusionment to the ground with determination and grit; to grab the hands of others and march unwaveringly, even heroically, in the direction of hopes, dreams, and possibilities.

Let it be said once again. *The strengths perspective is not about ignoring trauma, problems, illness, and adversity.* While practitioners of the perspective disagree about the role of problems in the work that they do, all believe that this approach, at the very least, is about restoring some balance to our efforts—a balance that requires that we appreciate the struggles of an individual, family, or community but that more importantly we look at those struggles for hints and intimations, or solid evidence of strengths, capacities, and competencies. Jerome Groopman (2005), a physician, says this about his practice:

> Patients are awash in a sea of statements about the link between their emotions and maladies. For years I diverted or dismissed their inquiries because I did not know how to answer. Now my response is formed by the lessons taught to me by my patients and the stirrings of serious science. I . . . say we are just beginning to appreciate hope's reach and have not defined its limits. I see hope at the very heart of healing. For those who have hope, it may help some to live longer, and it will help all to live better. (p. 212)

The emphasis on problems and pathologies, no matter what we claim as a profession, surely is careening out of control. The medical/psychiatric/pharmaceutical/insurance cartel (and I use the term advisedly) has a tightening grip on the ways that we see and consider human nature and the human condition. It is de rigueur in popular culture, in the media, in clinics and agencies, even in personal relationships to allow what is problematic to seize our perceptions and interest. As social workers we are obligated to resist the siren call of the medical model in our work together with clients.

Duncan and Miller (2000) put it well:

> If therapists are to resist the pull to steer clients automatically toward diagnosis and medication, the belief in client capacity to conquer even extreme (and often dangerous) personal circumstances must go deep. Clients can use an ally in overcoming often dramatic obstacles to personal recovery. When professionals use their inevitable positions of power to hand power back to the clients rather than block client capacities, clients can even more readily reach their goals. (p. 216)

DISCUSSION QUESTIONS

1. In your view, what are the most significant contrasts between a strengths approach and a problem-focused one?

2. To assess your knowledge of your strengths:

   Take a piece of paper and make three columns. In one column, list those aspects of yourself that you think of as weaknesses or deficits. In the second column, record those qualities that you think of as positive attributes, talents, skills, and competencies. In the third column, write down those qualities that, with a little work, could become strengths. Now, ask yourself:

   Which of the lists was easiest to do? The hardest?

   Which of the lists is longer?

Which of the lists is more compelling or interesting?

Why did you answer the three questions above the way that you did?

REFERENCES

American Psychiatric Association. (2000). *Diagnostic and statistical manual of mental disorders (DSM IV TR)*. Washington, DC: American Psychiatric Association.

Becker, E. (1973). *The denial of death*. New York: Free Press.

Becker, H. (1963). *Outsiders: Studies in the sociology of deviance*. New York: Free Press.

Benard, B. (1994). *Applications of resilience*. Paper presented at a conference on the Role of Resilience in Drug Abuse, Alcohol Abuse, and Mental Illness. Dec. 5–6. Washington, DC.

Benard, B. (2004). *Resiliency: What we have learned*. San Francisco: WestEd.

Bledstein, B. (1978). *The culture of professionalism*. New York: Norton.

Clark, M. D. (1997, April). Strengths-based practice: The new paradigm. *Corrections Today, 165,* 110–111.

Cousins, N. (1989). *Head first: The biology of hope*. New York: Dutton.

Cullison, A. (September, 2004). Inside Al-Qaeda's hard drive. *The Atlantic, 294*, 55–70.

Damasio, A. R. (1994). *Descartes' error: Emotion, reason, and the human brain*. New York: Grosset/Dunlap Books.

deJong, P. & Berg, I. K. (2001). *Interviewing for solutions* (2nd ed.). Belmont, CA: Wadsworth.

Delgado, M. (2000). *Community social work practice in an urban context: The potential of a capacity-enhancement perspective*. New York: Oxford University Press.

Duncan, B. L. & Miller, S. D. (2000). *The heroic client: Doing client-directed, outcome-informed therapy*. San Francisco: Jossey-Bass.

Freire, P. (1973). *Pedagogy of the oppressed*. New York: Seabury.

Freire, P. (1996). *Pedagogy of hope: Reliving pedagogy of the oppressed*. New York: Continuum.

Fromm, E. (1973). *The anatomy of human destructiveness*. New York: Holt, Rinehart & Winston.

Gergen, K. J. (1994). *Realities and relationships: Soundings in social construction*. Cambridge, MA: Harvard University Press.

Glover, J. (2000). *Humanity: A moral history of the twentieth century*. New Haven, CT: Yale University Press.

Goffman, E. (1961). *Asylums: Essays on the situation of mental patients and other inmates*. Garden City, NY: Anchor/Doubleday.

Groopman, J. (2005). *The anatomy of hope: How people prevail in the face of illness*. New York: Random House.

Holzman, L. (2002, December). *Practicing a psychology that builds communities*. Keynote address. American Psychological Association, Division 27, Society for Community Research and Action Conference. Boston, Massachusetts.

James, W. (1902). *The varieties of religious experience*. New York: Modern Library.

Kaplan, L. & Girard, J. (1994). *Strengthening high-risk families*. New York: Lexington Books.

Katz, M. (1997). *On playing a poor hand well: Insights from the lives of those who have overcome childhood risks and adversities*. New York: Norton.

Kirsch, I., Moore, T. J., Scoboria, A., & Nicholls, S. (2003). The emperor's new drugs: An analysis of antidepressant medication data submitted to the U.S. Food and Drug Administration. *Prevention & Treatment, 5,* 5–23. It is an online journal: http://journals.apa.org/prevention/volume5/pre0050023a.html.

Kozol, J. (2000). *Ordinary resurrections: Children in the years of hope*. New York: Crowne Publishers.

Kretzmann, J. P. & McKnight, J. L. (1993). *Building communities from the inside out: Toward finding and mobilizing a community's assets*. Evanston, IL: Northwestern University, Center for Urban Affairs and Policy Research.

Langewiesche, W. (2003). *American ground: Unbuilding the World Trade Center*. New York: North Point Press.

LeDoux, J. (2002). *Synaptic self: How our brains become who we are*. New York: Viking.

Lee, P. R. (1929). Social work: Cause and function. *Proceedings of the National Conference of Social Work, 3*–20.

Malekoff, A. (2001). The power of group work with kids: A practitioner's reflection on strengths-based practice. *Families in Society, 82,* 243–250.

Mattingly, C. (1991). Narrative reflections on practical actions: Two experiments in reflective story-telling. In D. A. Schön (Ed.), *The reflective turn: Case studies in and on educational practice.* New York: Teacher's College Press.

Miller, S. D. & Berg, I. K. (1995). *The miracle method: A radically new approach to problem drinking.* New York: Norton.

Mills, R. (1995). *Realizing mental health: Toward a new psychology of resiliency.* New York: Sulzburger & Graham.

Parsons, R. J. & Cox, E. O. (1994). *Empowerment-oriented social work practice with the elderly.* Newbury Park, CA: Sage.

Pelletier, K. R. (2000). *The best alternative medicine: What works? What does not?* New York: Simon & Schuster.

Pinderhughes, E. (1994). Empowerment as intervention goals: Early ideas. In L. Gutierrez & P. Nurius (Eds.), *Education and research for empowerment practice.* Seattle, WA: University of Washington School of Social Work, Center for Policy and Practice Research.

Pransky, J. (1998). *Modello: A story of hope for the inner city and beyond.* Burlington, VT: NorthEast Health Realization Publications.

Rank, O. (1941). *Beyond psychology.* New York: Dover Books.

Rapp, C.A. & Goscha, R. J. (2006). *The strengths model: Case management with people with psychiatric disabilities.* New York: Oxford University Press.

Restak, R. (2003). *The new brain: How the modern age is rewiring your mind.* New York: St. Martin's Press.

Reynolds, B. C. (1951). *Social work and social living: Explorations in philosophy and practice.* Silver Spring, MD: National Association of Social Workers.

Rogers, C. R. (1961). *On becoming a person: A therapists view of psychotherapy.* Boston: Houghton Mifflin.

Saleebey, D. (1989). Professions in crisis: The estrangement of knowing and doing. *Social Casework, 70,* 556–563.

Scheff, T. J. (1984). *Being mentally ill: A sociological theory* (3rd ed.). New York: Aldine.

Schön, D. A. (1983). *The reflective practitioner.* New York: Basic Books.

Schorr, L. B. (1997). *Common purpose: rebuilding families and neighborhoods to rebuild America.* New York: Anchor/Doubleday.

Simon, B. L. (1994). *The empowerment tradition in social work: A history.* New York: Columbia University Press.

Specht, H. & Courtney, M. (1993). *Unfaithful angels: How social work has abandoned its mission.* New York: Free Press.

Stone, D. (2000). Why we need a care movement. *The Nation, 270,* 13–15.

Walzer, M. (1983). *Spheres of justice.* New York: Basic Books.

Weick, A. (2000). Hidden voices. *Social Work, 45,* 395–402.

Weil, A. (1995). *Spontaneous healing.* New York: Knopf.

Werner, E. & Smith, R. S. (1992). *Overcoming the odds.* Ithaca, NY: Cornell University Press.

Wolin, S. J. & Wolin, S. (1993). *The resilient self: How survivors of troubled families rise above adversity.* New York: Villard.

Wolin, S. & Wolin, S. J. (1996). The challenge model: Working with strengths in children of substance abusing parents. *Adolescent Substance Abuse and Dual Disorders, 5,* 243–256.

Wolin, S. & Wolin, S. J. (1997). Shifting paradigms: Talking a paradoxical approach. *Resiliency in Action, 2,* 23–28.

CHAPTER TWO

THE CHALLENGE OF SEEING ANEW THE WORLD WE THINK WE KNOW

Learning Strengths-Based Practice

ROBERT BLUNDO

Assumptions can be like blinkers on a horse—they keep us from straying from the road, but they block our view of other routes and possibilities along the roadside.
—Armand Eisen

In all affairs it's a healthy thing now and then to hang a question mark on the things you have long taken for granted.
—Bertrand Russell

You have been assigned a new case at your agency. The individual is a college student starting the third year at the local university where classes just began a little more than a week ago. Please read the following process recording and note your thoughts as you take in the information being presented. That is, please note the "data" or specific information that appears most important or significant to your beginning understanding. Now, even though you likely want more information, think of what immediately comes to mind in terms of how you would work with this person. What questions do you want to ask? What do you focus on as important information? How do you categorize or define the issue or issues being presented? Do you think of a possible diagnosis?

> Sorry I am late, had to give some notes to a friend. I called last week to make this appointment because I just felt that I was not going to make it. I felt so anxious and stressed at school the other day, I had to leave and did not attend my first class session. Actually, it was my first day back in school since taking a break last year. I had pushed myself too hard with work, school, and trying to keep the gay/lesbian/bi alliance going, I just couldn't do it any more. My drinking was getting worse and I was yelling at my partner so much I would have to leave to calm down. My dad would hit my mother and he drank a lot. Maybe I am just too much like him . . .

So, what do you think? What comes to mind when you think of what you have just been told? What gender is this young person? Do you need more information? What type of information or data do you think you would need? What thoughts do you have about treatment? If your social work background is similar to mine, you might be thinking about the multiple problems or maybe even a dual-diagnosis to start. Maybe you considered an evaluation of the drinking problem, obtaining more information about sexual orientation, family history of possible abuse, maybe an evaluation of suicide potential, possibly using the anxiety and/or depression scales, definitely treatment is needed, possibly couples work later on.

The material of this case is very limited, but for most social workers just a few pieces of information can get us started thinking and concluding, even though it is just preliminary at this point. What we usually see as most provocative are the "problems" apparent in the story being told. We look for what is going wrong, symptoms, what might be failings, underlying pathologies, and beginning histories to substantiate these early assumptions as we construct a mental picture of our client. It is the client's faults and weaknesses that we key in on as most significant in our listening. In actuality, we are rewriting or translating the story told by the client into our own professional language, a language grounded in theoretical models of pathological development and resultant problematic behaviors. We are seeing our professional versions of the person in terms of what is wrong and what then needs to be fixed through some form of intervention. Notice the belief that without much more information about the person's past and present problems we feel uncomfortable with attending to the problem or potential underlying problems. By the way, the young person is a woman.

Now for a moment try a second look at what was revealed in her story. Were you at all surprised that the young person was a woman? If so, what does that say about how "natural" our assumptions appear without awareness? Let's take a further look. It has been at least a week since the "incident" of anxiety at school and no reports of anxiety since then. In fact, it appears as if she is doing her work and has friends with whom she shares notes. Even though it is not clear, the vignette reveals that she missed the "first class session" on the first day back and appears to have made it to the other classes that day and the remaining classes during the week prior to seeing you. The comment about the drinking referred to a time last year while she was under stress. At least in this presentation there is no mention of a drinking issue at present or what she meant by "drinking too much." The individual demonstrated awareness of her provocative behavior with her partner and, importantly, addressed the issue by leaving so as not to provoke any further distress on the relationship that we only assume may have included threats of physical acts. Note, though, that physical acts were not actually mentioned at that point, only with regard to her father. The client handled her own previous stress by choosing to take time off from school to take care of herself and possibly her relationship. She also reports taking on a responsible effort with her gay/lesbian/bisexual organization on campus. She made an effort to help herself by calling for an appointment and has kept that appointment even though the anxiety level appears to have lessened. Finally, she shows a willingness to be open and to talk about herself with you.

If your experience was similar to mine at first reading, you too must have been struck by the contrast between the two interpretations or versions of the client's story. It is this contrast that is at the heart of shifting one's perspectives from a traditional pathology-based medical model perspective of practice to a strengths-based understanding of practice. Making this shift in practice is a considerable challenge for social workers like myself who have been educated and tutored in the traditional basic tenets of the profession's knowledge base and practice methods. It is additionally difficult for students just learning practice skills. Students come with a bias toward seeing problems and then trying to fix them by making suggestions to the client.

Unlike the additive approach to social work knowledge with the inclusion of more and more techniques, models, skills, and intervention protocols, taking on the challenge of learning strengths-based practice requires a more fundamental shift in how we understand and view the world. This requires a significant alteration in how we actually understand and think about those with whom we work, how we think about ourselves as professionals, the nature of the knowledge base for practice, and the process of social work practice itself. It is the fundamental nature of this shift that is the challenge to practitioners as well as students just learning the profession. This transformation of social work would shift knowledge building and practice to that of an egalitarian, collaborative working relationship that builds upon the strengths and resilience of individuals, families, and communities.

This chapter is about this transformative challenge in terms of the learning process of students new to the profession as well as practitioners who have been comfortably settled into the familiar world of pathology and deficit assessment and intervention. A review of the background and entrenchment of the medical/pathology/expert model of practice taught and practiced today will set the context of the challenges found in shifting perspectives. This will be followed by an exploration of some of the specific challenges that emerge when learning this new paradigm. Two specific issues—overcoming our natural predisposition to help by injecting our ideas and trained biases such as professional knowledge/expertise and professional practice traditions—will be explored by contrasting the traditional deficit-based assessment and problem-focused, expert-directed practice with the strengths-based assessment and a solution-focused, collaborative-based practice.

THE DEFICIT/PATHOLOGY KNOWLEDGE BASE BECOMES SYNONYMOUS WITH SOCIAL WORK

The preoccupation with problems, human deficits, with what is broken, gone wrong or failed, has dominated the attention of social work since its early development and exists today in the form of the taken-for-granted "problem-focused" practice models. Underlying this simple, innocuous looking model found in most social work texts and demonstrated in our practice generally is an entrenched foundation of assumptions about the human condition, models of helping, and a philosophy of science (Goldstein, 1997; Lubove, 1965; Rapp, 1998; Reid, 1995; Specht & Courtney 1994).

By the early 1900s, the work of organizations like the Charitable Organization Society (COS) and case workers such as Mary Richmond were moving the friendly visitor away from seeing poverty and human difficulties as merely moral failings in need of moral uplifting to one that viewed human suffering as something that could be rationally understood. The application of a "scientific" or rational study and analysis of problems and social conditions, supposedly free of subjectivity, could result in finding causes and applying treatments to mend the problem. Even though many early social work efforts had directed energies to changing the social conditions that resulted in human misery, the professionalization of social work, in particular social casework, began to purposely shift its focus toward intervention at the level of the individual and family. Five important elements coalesced and helped contribute to this shift: (1) the growing professionalization and training of the "friendly visitor"; (2) the growing fear of Bolshevism, the "Red Scare," following the Russian Revolution (1917–1918); (3) the integration of the medical model of practice into social casework; (4) embracing psychoanalytic and ego psychology theory and practice; and (5) faith in science and the leap to "scientifically based practice."

Professionalism and Education

As the twentieth century started, there was a growing "white collar" and professional middle class with many new occupations, including social casework, which was made up of mostly college-educated women and men. "Professionalization was a major social trend during this era" following the changes in the fields of medicine and engineering (Popple & Reid, 1999, p. 12). Charity Organization Societies started to organize in-service training classes with a focus on the "techniques" of social work. As the first schools of social work emerged in New York, Boston, and Chicago, the movement focused away from content on social issues, social reform, and social/economic inequalities and toward the practice techniques as used with families and individuals. Although some educators, such as Edward Devine of the New School of Social Work, did not support such a shift in emphasis, the movement grew. Abraham Flexner's speech at the National Conference of Charities and Corrections in 1915 sealed the direction when he proclaimed that social work was not a profession because it possessed neither a method of practice nor a specific social work knowledge base that could be taught as a standard format for social work practice. This reinforced the impetus toward education and training. Leaders in social work education encouraged the growth of training programs in university settings with an increasing focus on common techniques and methods of practice.

Bolshevism and Rising Fears

As social work moved away from addressing social inequities and social conditions, the national political agenda turned away from social reforms and issues of inequality. Fear of "foreigners" and fear of conflict created by obvious social class differences took center stage. Jane Addams (1930) described the reaction to this growing fear of social reform within social work itself: "Social workers exhibited many symptoms of this panic (Red Scare) and with a kind of protective instinct carefully avoided any identification with the phraseology of social reform" (p. 155). The national fears of collectivism and issues of social class further supported the movement away from addressing poverty and social conditions. Not only were social reforms neglected, social workers focused more on treating the pathologies of the families and individuals without providing financial or social assistance.

Medical Model and the Diagnostic School

Mary Richmond's practice text, *Social Diagnosis,* published in 1917, represented this shift of emphasis in rationality being directed toward the individual and away from social action and social reform. It offered to those in social work at the time a movement toward professionalism in terms of a transferable knowledge base and a model of practice that could be applied to a range of clients and situations. Importantly, it formalized the concepts of medical practice and brought them into a model of social work practice.

Mary Richmond specifically formulated the start of much of our present day social work language and thinking that was greatly influenced by the developments and innovations in community medical practice efforts of Dr. Adolf Meyer at Johns Hopkins University Hospital in Baltimore, Maryland, and the work of Dr. Richard Cabot at Massachusetts General Hospital. The use of the "study, diagnosis and treatment" model used in the emerging science of medicine was adapted to the practice of social work. Mary Richmond (1917) called the process "social diagnosis" and described the developing social work perspective in this manner:

> Social diagnosis is the attempt to arrive at as *exact a definition* as possible of the social situation and *personality of a given client.* The *gathering of evidence, or investigation,* begins the process, the *critical examination* and *comparison of evidence* follows, and last come its *interpretation and the definition* of the social difficulty. Where one word must describe the whole process, *diagnosis* is a better word than *investigation,* though in strict use the former belongs to the end of the process. (emphases added) (p. 62)

These fundamental "medical" constructs became the bases of social work practice within the developing schools of social work over the next decades and became the benchmark of good practice taught in the classroom and in social work practice texts. Thus began the diligence accorded lengthy process recordings and intake summaries focused on obtaining a broad spectrum of information believed necessary in constructing the diagnosis of the problem, a diagnostic process similar to that underlying understanding a physical illness.

Psychoanalytic Theory and Ego Psychology

Mary Richmond's (1917, 1922) efforts represented the start of a knowledge base for practice in terms of a model for gathering information, making an assessment and a social diagnosis. What was needed now was a theory or model of causality that would explain why individuals or families did what they did. In 1909, Sigmund Freud gave a series of lectures at Clark University and by 1915 *Good Housekeeping* magazine had published a series of stories popularizing psychoanalytic ideas (Heller & Rudnick, 1991). Psychoanalytic theory and practice methods were quickly embraced by American psychiatry as a "scientific" theory for understanding and treating a wide range of conditions.

Given the emphasis of the medical model on discovering the cause of illness and then prescribing a means to intervene in the cause and thus to cure the disease, social work was open to a means of understanding the cause of human suffering on an individual or psychological level. Psychoanalysis was embraced by many caseworkers working with children, the courts, medicine, and psychiatry as the knowledge base for understanding and intervention. Mary Jarrett (1918) commented, "We see case work about to pass into a psychological phase. . . . It is becoming evident that personality will become the leading interest in the future" (p. 287). A year later, Mary Jarrett (1919) proclaimed in her paper entitled "The Psychiatric Thread Running Through All Social Case Work" that it is the internal mental life of clients that would be at the heart of social casework (cited in Robinson, 1930). Social work was developing as a profession with a specific common method or practice to be called "social casework" and a body of knowledge and practice principles to support that work. The internal mental life of clients emerged as the focus for the knowledge base for future generations of social workers.

Faith in Science and Scientism

Scientism refers to the "exaggerated trust in the efficacy of a method" of inquiry that assumes objectivity or the ability to see the world independent of human thought, social context, or perspective (Merriam Webster's Collegiate Dictionary, 1994). This is reflective of a "modernist" approach to knowledge that assumes that what we think as being "reality" is singular, stable, linear, and knowable by observation. This is in contrast to a "postmodernist" approach that assumes "multiple realities conditioned by individual, social, and temporal factors" that places people within ever-changing contexts and expresses the uniqueness of human beings and their social circumstances (Neimeyer & Raskin, 2000, p. 5).

The early "scientific" and technical developments such as widespread utilization of electricity, the telegraph and the telephone, the prodigious feats in engineering (bridges, skyscrapers, flight, etc.) all had a profound effect on a growing faith in science to provide answers to human problems and to realize human possibilities. Freud was considered a scientist (as you may recall, he began his medical career as a neuroscientist) even though his observations about human nature and the human condition were not conducted as formal experiments. The medical community that welcomed Freud's theories considered themselves to be scientific and believed that their new field was built on a rational and objective understanding of human life. The idea of being "scientific" brought with it a sense of authority in that claims in its name were thought to be discoveries of a basic truth of nature.

This was a simplistic view of science and reflected an assumption that with diligence, careful observation, and analysis one could understand, predict, and treat any condition. Social casework came into being during this scientific age and incorporated the attitudes and beliefs of this time. The theories and methods of social casework practice reflected this faith in science and with it, scientific authority for its methods of practice. In the summer of 1918, Smith College hosted an eight-week training for social workers. One of the instructors noted that the "training of social case-work [is to] be based on scientific method rather than on philanthropic technique. . . . serious social work must . . . lift its eyes from the routine of simple fact-getting to . . . a more scientific method" (Chapin, 1918, pp. 591–592). The assumption was that a basic truth about human motivation and behavior had been or could be "discovered" and that the methods of "assessing, diagnosing and treating" these conditions had also been "discovered", as if a natural condition.

Reiteration and Entrenchment of Practice Principles

An early text by Margaret Bristol (1936) noted that although case records were needed for a wide range of necessary agency and educational functions, their most significant use remained the creation of the diagnosis. She believed that the very process of authoring a case record and diagnosis required "critical thinking and careful organization of material" and "compelled [the worker] to think through the situation and to make a diagnosis of the problem" (Bristol, 1936, p. 6). Gordon Hamilton (1946) referred to the social worker as a "trained diagnostician" who has the ability to "pluck from an unending web of social experience that thread of probable significance" (p. 134). Felix Biestek (1957) saw the diagnosis as central. It was developed as the "caseworker begins at once to formulate some notion of the *real nature* of the problem" (p. 45). We still see this assumed need reflected in the enormous amount of information social workers are encouraged to gather today with the ultimate goal of making an accurate diagnosis or assessment of the problem. The majority of present day social work practice texts used in schools of social work contain pages of assessment forms, inventories, and grids created to assist the social worker in gathering abundant amounts of information. Mary Richmond's (1917, 1922) translation of the medical pathology model of practice to social work is the primary process still used and taught today even though the language might be somewhat different. This orientation is at the heart of how most social workers think of practice today—focusing on the problem or what underlies the problem, looking for the cause of the problem by gathering evidence or data, assessing the data, reformulating the problem into a diagnosis (cause and effect) and developing a plan or intervention to address the "diagnosis" or problem as *understood by the social worker.*

Prior to embracing the psychoanalytic frame, client history and assessment consisted of social and family context in a sociological sense. The focus was on addressing the presenting situational problem. With Freudian theory, history and assessment became psychologically focused in terms of the dynamic interaction of the purported parts of the personality, the id, ego, and superego. Social work scholars and educators such as Florence Hollis, Howard Parad, Gordon Hamilton, Felix Biestek, Annette Garrett, and others were influential in further refining and reifying the psychodynamic model as social work practice through their texts and articles used to train social workers during the 1950s through the early 1970s. Remnants of these basic ideas are an integral part of our practice knowledge today and are reflected in most major texts on social work practice. The linearity of this psychodynamic model of practice kept social work practice focused on the internal life of the individual while the environment remained secondary. Little attention was given to the social, cultural, ethnic, and socioeconomic complexities of clients when direct interventions were being conducted. Gordon Hamilton (1957) stated that "the striking fact is that Freudian concepts were worked into casework practice so fully as to make casework a therapeutic process" (p. 15). For example, Hollis (1964) provided a glimpse of the complexity of social work thinking from an ego psychology perspective when she wrote that "in case work we are principally uncovering suppressed, preconscious material rather than unconscious material. Treatment holds as a major aim the improvement of the individual's functioning by seeking to gain more accurate and more complete understanding or previously hidden aspects of the individual's own feelings and behavior" (p. 84). The focus was on the psychological development of the individual within a family and the psychological dynamics assumed to be taking place within and between individuals. The presenting problem was translated into a failure in this intrapsychic dynamic. For example, unresolved parent–child relationships could be a manifestation of unresolved oedipal issues that needed to be addressed in order to intervene with the issues being presented. The social context and interpersonal relationships were merely manifestations of these inner drives and instincts.

Ego psychology, built on the work of Sigmund Freud (1923), Anna Freud (1936), and Heinz Hartmann (1939) with its notions of defense mechanisms such as repression and denial and the central construct of "transference," moved social work practice into the realm of managing the interplay of instincts, social conscience, environmental forces, and the ego's defenses against various forms of anxiety that were at the heart of client struggles. Howard Parad (1958) described the reliance of social work on ego psychology as resulting in social worker's increased "diagnostic acumen" and "firmer grasp of the fundamentals of human motivation and behavior" (pp. 3, 6). Hamilton (1958) noted that with the shift of focus to ego psychology, "casework stopped digging for 'undistorted id impulses' and began to work with the derivatives of the unconscious, with impulses as disguised and modified by ordinary concerns, relationships, activities, attitudes, and behavior" (p. 23).

This continues in a different form today. The seventh edition of *Direct Social Work Practice* (Hepworth, Rooney, Rooney, Strom-Gottfried, & Larsen, 2006) describes how the "problem" must be understood in depth by maintaining a "focus on the problems until [the worker has] elicited comprehensive information [and] possesses sufficient information concerning the various forces . . . that produce the problems" (p. 50). The worker's success is dependent on having the "skills needed to explore problems thoroughly, because success in the helping process depends on [his or her] ability to obtain clear and accurate definitions of the problems . . . in-depth (Hepworth et al., 2006, p. 150). It is the social worker who remains central in this process. The worker is responsible for interpretations and finding causes to which he or she must now match an intervention technique that matches the "problem" as understood by the social worker. For example, if a client is fearful or expresses some anxiety about an undertaking, the worker's responsibility is to "elicit the problematic emotions, to identify their cognitive sources, and to assist clients in aligning their thoughts and feelings with reality" (Hepworth et al., 2006, p. 373). But, it is the worker's "reality" that is now the goal for the client. Social work practice as described in these and other practice texts is generally a very complicated process of understanding the problem, interpreting the manifestations of deeper issues only the social worker can uncover, and then applying approaches not on the basis of this particular client but on the basis of an assumed diagnosis and the selection by the worker of an "evidence" -based practice used to address this type of problem. It is hard to think in terms of self-determination, empowerment, social justice, diversity and uniqueness, and individual and community strengths when social work practice is described in this manner, even though these social work values are seemingly promoted throughout this and other similar practice texts. As with many texts, these values become accumulative add-ons to the foundation of pathology and worker expertise in diagnosing and selecting treatments.

These traditional practice texts continue the established practice of focusing on understanding problems in terms of what is wrong or defective and requiring the social worker to understand the deeper meanings and underlying dynamics that might be causing this problem and then deciding on an intervention. Such practice reflects what Leslie Margolin (1997) describes as "social workers inserting themselves into client's lives, initiating actions, judging outcomes, controlling technologies and meaning" (p. 119). According to Margolin (1997), traditional social work practice is *disempowering* as workers use technical skills such as confrontation, overcoming resistance, and managing the manipulative client while at the same time manipulating the relationship to enhance the compliance with professional decisions. Merely interjecting content into social work texts that state that clients have strengths and suggesting that clients be asked about strengths is not strengths-based practice.

What is most problematic with the inclusion of strengths talk in social work conversations is that the insertion of the strengths and empowerment lexicon into a traditional frame or perspective gives a false sense of understanding to those learning and engaging in practice. Social workers have thus managed to use the language of strengths and empowerment while maintaining the "prerogative to plan and strategize, direct and control" the process while convincing themselves that they have "empowered" the client (Margolin, 1997, p. 122). Margolin (1997) has referred to this as the "central paradox" of mainstream social work practice conceptualizations of strengths and empowerment. That is, "to become who one truly is, and to do what one truly wants, one has to absorb [the social worker's] definitions, interpretations, and prescriptions" (Margolin, 1997, p. 124). Therefore, to learn the strengths perspective, one must seriously challenge the basic foundations of practice knowledge, the eighty years of variations on a basic theme of "disease and expertise" as it is taught and practiced today. Anything less is a distortion of the meanings employed in a practice from a strengths and empowerment perspective.

Alternative Roads Not Taken and Missed Opportunities

A common occurrence for human beings is the inability to predict or see into the future because we are so absorbed in what we know in the present. Taleb (2007) states that "human beings are cognitively wired to learn specific facts and in particular things we already are familiar with without assuming that this 'world' might be subject to dramatic change" (p. 173). In retrospect, looking from the present strengths perspective, one can now see elements of what might have taken social work down a different path. For example, even though Mary Richmond's (1917) work provided the framework for what would become the diagnostic school of social work practice, she had serious reservations about the psychoanalytic focus on the individual that social casework was taking. Richmond had developed her ideas, in part, based on the work of George Herbert Mead and John Dewey and "emphasized the social construction of identity, [and] called for assessing the problems of individuals in their social contexts" (Agnew, 2004, p. 168). In her later work, *What Is Social Case Work?* (1922), Richmond challenged the elitism of professionalized social work and called for an appreciation of the uniqueness of individuals and a respect for the self-determination that was a part of every human being. One obvious note is that her first book was titled *Social Diagnosis,* referring to her belief in understanding the social context of an individual's problems.

Mary Cannon (1935) supported the idea that the intent of social case work practice was "strengthening environmental support on the one hand and releasing resident energies in the individual on the other" (p. 112). Jessie Taft (1944) reminded social workers that "The client, in our belief, is not a sick person whose illness must first be classified, but a human being, like the worker, asking for a specific service" (pp. 7–8). Taft represented a different approach identified as the functionalist school, representing a serious but momentary exception to the dominance of the diagnostic school's psychoanalytic perspective. The brief ascendancy of the functionalist school in social work developed a conception of practice that came to be overshadowed by the dominant medical model of practice, the diagnostic school. The functionalist viewed "clients" as having potentials and strengths and not as broken and diseased. Jessie Taft (1944) believed that the use of diagnosis and treatments as construed within medicine, psychiatry, and the diagnostic school of social case work were "fundamentally antagonistic" to the principles of social work. She called for embracing the psychology of "growth" rather than "disease" (Taft, 1944, pp. 7–8). Bertha Reynolds's (1975) narrative on the philosophy of social work practice originally published in 1951 asked if social case-workers might do better to shift from asking about the problem that brought clients to seek help to first asking them "You have lived thus far, how have you done it?" (p.125).

Gordon Hamilton (1958) recalled her own experiences during the Depression era and the extreme economic and social stress confronting many people. She recalled how the experience had helped social workers "rediscover those inner resources of character [in clients] to which social casework had always been attuned" (p. 22). She went further by acknowledging that it is "part of man's (sic) heritage that under greatest pressures he seems to attain his greatest stature" (p. 22). This was understood as an example of "ego strengths" given the perspective of ego psychology emerging at the time. Hamilton (1958) understood these observed strengths in terms of the dominant social work theoretical framework and adjusted her observations to fit into the framework of her dominant construct, ego psychology and its mechanisms. Hollis (1958) described casework assistance as starting with knowing "what [the client] sees as his problem, what he has tried to do about it, what he wants to do about it" (p. 87). Then she quickly reveals the power of the dominant conceptual model by shifting to the expertise of the case worker and the theory that calls for evaluating the client's functioning in terms of ego capacity and the nature of his or her personality and adjustment as seen through the purported dynamics of the ego psychology model and interpreted by the case worker.

The problem-solving model developed by Perlman (1957) assumed a basic capacity for individuals to solve problems and intervention was focused in an educative manner to develop this capacity rather than to directly address the problem. She saw this as working with "ego strength" and therefore believed herself to be a part of the diagnostic school, even though she did not focus on ego derivatives of underlying instincts and infantile drives as did the diagnostic school dominant at the time in social work practice (Briar & Miller, 1971).

In each of these and many more instances a potential for seeing the world differently was lost as a consequence of the inability to see outside the dominant psychodynamic construct of the time. This inability to see a potentially different outcome or reasoning beyond the dominant trend continues given our "cognitive confinement" or reasoned allegiance to traditional medical models such as our focus on risk, damage, and pathology and the newer version of being scientific by means of evidence-based practice.

THE STRENGTHS PERSPECTIVE IN THE PRESENT CONTEXT OF SCIENTIFIC RESEARCH, EMPIRICALLY SUPPORTED TREATMENT, AND EVIDENCE-BASED PRACTICE

> *We like to think that prevailing educational systems and protocols of practice, perspectives on humanity, have evolved in rational ways, the consequence of dependable proofs and in accord with standards of technological growth. Not so. [The fact is that this story is not] a romantic account of battles of wills or revolutionary ideas but more of the helter-skelter influences of personalities, politics, transient fads, and ongoing empiricist-humanist debates.*
>
> —Goldstein, 1990, p. 32

The social work profession has a serious choice when confronted with its present urgency to be scientific in the form of evidence-based practice literature in social work. The challenge for social work is to become aware that the specific focus of some scientific research, specifically empirically supported treatment [EST] or evidence-based practice [EBP], is excluding a large set of well-founded scientific inquiry that challenges the most basic assumptions of EST and EBP research. In this process, social work knowledge is missing out on a wave of scientific research that supports much of the values and concepts of social work practice, in particular strengths-based practice.

Managed care and HMOs have driven the EST and EBP movements based on cost containment and therefore "interventions that achieve the defined treatment objectives in the most cost-efficient manner" (Bolen & Hall, 2007, p. 467). Based on the misguided notion of "treatment" or "intervention" narrowly defined as a specific set of skills or techniques used by a specific method of practice such as the cognitive-behavioral model, the forces of managed care and supporters within social work have been blinded to significant research that seriously challenges these assumptions. The point of inquiry in these research designs is the very specific techniques used to address pathological states as diagnosed according to the *Diagnostic and Statistical Manual* (American Psychiatric Association, 1994). Under the mantle of "scientific research," this effort purports to have irrefutable evidence that persons with a specific diagnosis should best be treated by a specific evidence-based treatment method. The irony is that there is considerable research that refutes these findings. Yet this scientifically rigorous research is consistently ignored. This is in addition to the problematic nature of the validity and reliability of making psychiatric diagnoses.

A large number of research efforts focused on practice outcomes found that "no particular treatment or approach is demonstrably superior to another, across disorders or within disorders" (Wampold 2001; Wampold, Minami, Baskin, & Tierney, 2002). Research by Jacobson et al. (1996) found that when the cognitive aspects of cognitive behavioral treatment for depression were removed, the changed treatment was as effective when compared to standard cognitive-behavioral intervention. Seligman and Peterson's (2003) review of the data on evidence-based research showed that "when one active treatment is compared to another active treatment, specificity [the techniques of a model that differentiate it from another model] tends to disappear or become quite a small effect" (p. 312). They concluded that the findings point to the fact that "no psychotherapy technique which we can think of . . . shows large, specific effects when compared to another form of psychotherapy or drug, adequately administered" (p. 312). The work of Lambert (1992) and Lambert and Bergin (1994) demonstrated that specific techniques are only responsible for less that 15 percent of the outcome in therapies in contrast to the "findings" suggested by the EBP or EST research that it is the specific technique of a model that determines the outcome. Of greater interest is the fact that Lambert's (1992) research demonstrated that 40 percent of the outcome resulted from factors or qualities that were a part of the client's makeup and environment such as social support, personal and social resources and assets, and fortuitous, contingent events, all of which he identified as "extratherapeutic change," or change that was related to factors outside the typical therapeutic work. The second most significant factor was the "relationship" or the client's perception that the practitioner was understanding, warm, accepting, and encouraging. Hope and placebo effects were as effective as specific techniques.

Goldstein's 1990 review of practice research revealed the central importance of the relationship and the alliance in practice. The optimal therapeutic relationship is marked by "collaboration, the sharing of initiative and responsibility, and the avoidance of dependency and authority. . . . the therapist's self-investment, affirmations, genuineness, and empathy also contribute to the quality of the helping relationship" (p. 38). Supporting these conclusions, what does remain across techniques is what Seligman and Peterson (2003) call "deep strategies" such as instilling hopefulness, optimism, interpersonal skills, and authenticity.

Seligman and Peterson (2003) find that what is significant in terms of practice are these "deep strategies" or themes that seem to appear over and over in successful work. Some of these strategies are a collaborative relationship that "instills hope" and builds "buffering strengths" (p. 312). These authors view strengths as consisting of such qualities as "courage, interpersonal skills, rationality, insight, optimism, authenticity, perseverance, realism, capacity for pleasure, future-mindedness, personal responsibility and purpose" (Seligman & Peterson, 2003, p. 313). They view practice as a process of building client strengths rather than "delivering specific damage-healing techniques" (Seligman & Peterson, 2003, p. 312). Wampold and Bhati's (2004) review of practice research demonstrates that it is the relationship or alliance between the worker and the client system that "predicts future improvement [and] . . . *it makes more sense to think of elements of the relationship as being empirically supported rather than particular treatments*" (emphasis added) (p. 567). Accordingly, "the ideal frame of reference would therefore be of the kind that encourages reflective and penetrating questions that deepen understanding. They preserve rather than simplify the complexity of the human event. Rather than categorizing, [practice takes] into account the variability of human situations" (Goldstein, 1990, p. 38).

Trinder (2000) describes social work practice as not fitting into a model based on medical treatment. Human issues are significantly more complex, and intervention requires a human relationship more than ingesting a particular drug or undergoing a particular physical procedure. Trinder (2000) recognizes that both the social worker and the client come into a human relationship with "their own histories and understandings, and are embedded in continuing social relationships, with family, friends, and colleagues, outside of the context of the intervention" (Trinder, 2000, p.149).

Given the extensive and growing evidence that specificity of a treatment such as promoted by supporters of EST (empirically supported therapies) and EBP (evidence-based practice) is not a valid path to take, what alternative scientific research might social work build on and advance in terms of knowledge and practice? The answer lies in the emerging body–mind–culture research and its findings that support social work's most traditional ideas and further development of the strengths perspective as a guiding paradigm for understanding human development and behavior within the environment.

The strengths perspective is a larger view, a paradigmatic shift, rather than a specific technique. It represents a fundamental change in the way we think about those we work with and ourselves. As such, it is in line with the latest basic research in understanding fundamental human growth and behavior. The newest research is demonstrating that the biopsychosocial interplay that has been a hallmark for social work practice is being proposed anew. This research is looking at the body–mind–cultural connections and consequences in terms of the interplay between what we think of as physiology, psychology, and culture (Aspinwall & Staudinger, 2003; Benard, 2004; Csikszentmihaly & Csikszentmihaly, 2006; Kahneman, Diener, & Schwarz, 1999; Snyder & Lopez, 2007; Wexler, 2006). Human strengths or the capacity for "making it" through hard times is becoming one way of describing these findings. Human strengths are not isolated abilities or traits but one way of talking about the human capacity to continually move toward a sense of well-being. This sense of strengths or well-being emerges "from active encounters with life's challenges, setbacks, and demands, not from blissful, conflict-free, smooth sailing" (Ryff & Singer, 2003, p. 279). For social workers to further understand human strengths requires a recognition of the "dialectic between pain and pleasure, between what is high-minded and inspiring and what is painful, debasing, and cause for despair. Human well-being is fundamentally about joining of those two realms" (Ryff & Singer, 2003, p. 279). Resiliency, in terms of human development, brings these two realms together over the life span and can offer social work a way of understanding that supports building a social work practice focused on enhancing strengths rather than decreasing deficits given life's continuous challenges and difficulties.

Future directions within social work need not be in the form of evidence-based techniques focused on personal pathology but in the direction of more basic transdiciplinary research uniting biology, psychology, neuroscience, and the social sciences. These important new directions of research are pointing to what social workers have long described as the biopsychosocial dynamic. The merger of neurobiology, social psychology, cognitive sciences, and cultural studies is shifting the way we might understand the interplay of mind, body, and society in daily functioning. For example, one of many studies demonstrates that people who lived in persistently low economic conditions but had good quality social ties during their lives were significantly less likely to have biological, psychological, and socially negative consequences (Singer & Ryff, 1999). Subjects were more likely to attend and complete schooling, have better health and present with less mental health issues. Strengthening social ties for youth living in serious economic conditions is one way of assisting them in having a better life. Obviously, poverty must be addressed in the long run, but this research points to measures that might be taken as prevention or building immunity while poverty continues to exist. Having strong social ties is a human strength and reflects the idea of the strengths perspective, which sees people as members of a community, in relationship with others.

The strengths perspective recognizes both the complexity and uniqueness of each human life. It recognizes the context and mutuality of human interaction as always changing and having potential for growth. Rather than look for "damage and making judgments about limitations, the strengths perspective seeks the individual and communal resources from which the [person] can draw in shaping [his or her own life]" (Weick, Rapp, Sullivan, & Kisthardt, 1989, p. 352). The focus shifts from the internal psychological dynamic to the reciprocal interactions of individuals with others and their community. It is this relational nature of human development and behavior that the social worker enters and collaboratively works at recognizing and manifesting the resiliency and strengths of this particular person, family, agency, or community. The issue for social workers is how to shift the attachment to the dominant pathological themes of knowledge and practice that are still pervasive and rarely questioned.

SHIFTING THE FUNDAMENTAL FRAME
OF PRACTICE

It is the tenaciousness with which we humans attach ourselves to the meanings we create about our world that is at the center of the challenge of learning the strengths perspective. Our professional training and practices have been for the most part a set of traditions handed down and reified. These traditions are like lenses or blinders that keep us focused on a particular path but keep us from seeing other possibilities. Erving Goffman's (1974) concept of "frames" captures this ongoing process within each of us as individuals and as we come together to create a "profession." The notion of living within a frame refers to the constructed meanings or definitions we share with others that provide us with "models" of daily interactions and practices. For example, when we enter a restaurant, we have little to think about other than what we might want to order. Unless we have never been in, read about, or heard about a restaurant, most of the activity will seem very natural and seemingly without thought about the process itself. Everyone participating in the "restaurant" experience knows what he or she is expected to do. There are numerous rules and roles to be played out in getting a quick bite. It is only when someone does not follow the script that we are aware of the frame or process. Most often the frame breaker is seen as rude or inappropriate. Similarly, once ensconced within the world of constructed meaning shared by others in the social work profession, doing things differently is usually met with suspicion, and attempts are made by others to maintain the predominant frame. To suggest changing the frame is very difficult. It is like being asked to change "reality" as we live it out day to day in our professional relationships. The frame is so reified that to question it seems unrealistic.

In contrast to the continuing adherence to traditional constructs identified with the profession, the strengths perspective offers the profession an opportunity to change frames and learn to collaborate with individuals, families, and communities in a more egalitarian working relationship based upon strengths and resilience. The client as well as the client's support system or environment would move into a central role in the entire social work process. In a frame-challenging, mind-bending example of family practice, a social worker enters a family residence, and the first question she asks is "What is working well that you want to see continue?" (Miley, O'Melia, & DuBois, 1998, p. 4). Needless to say, the family members who were very familiar with professional techniques and attitudes (professional clients) were taken aback as well as those professionals reading this for the first time. The social worker's intervention did not and could not eliminate the inherent inequality of the relationship but did challenge the preeminence of the worker as sole determiner of what should be going on and how this family should be living its life. In many ways the social worker's effort was reflective of the latest research on psychotherapy and counseling that is seriously challenging the traditional practice relationship, as well as the processes (Lambert, 1992; Lambert & Bergin, 1994; Ryff & Singer, 2003, Seligman & Peterson, 2003; Wampold, 2001; Wampold et al., 2002). What prevents us from transforming our standard knowledge and practice?

A consequence of constructed realities is that each of us selectively attends to that which matches our worldview. We therefore see a world as we have imagined it and in a way that our theories and actions reinforce the sense of its existence out there in the world. This frame or constructed reality being shared by others with whom we work and live, shared and reinforced by our profession in terms of its teachings and socialization processes, is comfortable and real as if a natural phenomena. Feeling so real, it is often hard to become even aware of the existence of our frames and constructed meanings. It is only when something unexpected or unimagined shakes up the process that we become aware of being engaged in a set of expectations, rules of action, and modes of thought. Even under these contradictions or evidence that our frames might not be the whole story, we are very persistent in maintaining our perspectives and beliefs. The "primacy effect" and "belief perseverance," among other concepts in the study of human inference, demonstrate that people are very resistant to changing or altering their initial beliefs (Kirshner & Witson, 1997; Lord, Ross, & Lepper, 1979; Nisbett & Ross, 1980). Importantly, once this belief or theory is in place, individuals are very resistant to any conflicting evidence. In the face of alternative evidence, individuals selectively choose that evidence that substantiates their original idea or theory.

We are not as "free" as we would like think we are to evaluate and weigh different ideas and constructs. The neurological facts are that we are even less likely to be innovative and changeable as we age (Wexler, 2006). Human beings have not only a cognitive but a neurologically based biasing process that determines what they see and understand. Wexler (2006) describes this as an "internally driven prejudgment of what is to be perceived" (p. 152). When we have been inundated with constructs and knowledge that purport to explain human development and behavior, we are not likely to shift our perspective. When trained in a profession that socializes you to a rather specific perspective on viewing clients and engaging them in practice and this is followed by continued reinforcement from colleagues, supervisors, trainings, and policies, ideas that challenge this view are experienced as odd and mistaken. In fact, according to neurological and cognitive studies, "experienced-dependent, learned internal structures [cognitive models or thematic constructs] filter [out], select [parts of what is being experienced], and otherwise alter our perception and evaluation of sensory inputs" (Wexler, 2006, pp. 154–155). Obviously, humans are not aware of this process, and it appears to be merely the ability to understand an experience as if everyone would do it the same way, as with the restaurant frame. This notion of a natural ability to see and understand something as if real can be challenged by others having different experiences with the same occurrence. Most often the alternative description is disregarded, and selective attention keeps the original perception intact. For example, although eugenics is now seen as an anathema, social workers once embraced it as a reasonable alternative for the "care" of certain individuals in our society and as a way of addressing some social issues. It was considered a scientifically based practice founded on the science of evolution and genetics. It took more than ninety years before the last vestiges of the sterilization were stopped only thirty-five years ago. It is hard to imagine something as extreme as this being a part of our accepted practice. The problem is that it is even more difficult to see potential issues with much less extreme ideas such as we might practice in social work. In professional settings, the dominant knowledge base is supported by repetition and by socialization within the organization and profession. In this way, the dominant constructs and perspectives take on a sense of truth and are defended rigorously when challenged. Through selective attention we reinterpret and reinvent our comfortable and familiar ways in order to hold onto them and feel reassured about our professional and personal selves.

SHIFTING FRAMES TO A STRENGTHS PERSPECTIVE

The strengths perspective is a significant alteration of thinking for traditional social workers as well as students just learning social work practice. Dennis Saleebey (1997) strongly emphasizes that "everything you do as a social worker will be predicated, in some way, on helping to discover and embellish, explore and exploit client's strengths and resources in the service of assisting them to achieve their goals . . ." (p. 3). The emphasis shifts from problems and deficits defined by the worker to possibilities and strengths identified in egalitarian, collaborative relationships with clients. Saleebey (1997) describes the frame of the strengths perspective as reflected in three basic principles:

- Given the difficulties they have, and the known resources available to them, people are often doing amazingly well—the best they can at the time.
- People have survived to this point—certainly not without pain and struggle—through employing their will, their vision, their skills, and, as they have grappled with life, what they have learned about themselves and their world. We must understand these capacities and make alliance with this knowledge in order to help.
- Change can only come when you collaborate with client's aspirations, perceptions, and strengths, and when you *firmly believe* in them. (p. 49)

But these inspiring words are not an easy task to undertake as my initial example hopefully demonstrated. To make them more than words, to translate them into practice is a significant challenge.

One of the most important steps in meeting this challenge is what Saleebey (1997) has referred to as "suspending disbelief" in the client's understandings and explanations and desired outcomes. Unlike the advice of Hepworth and Larsen (1993), who caution the worker to "avoid the tendency to accept client's views, descriptions, and reports as valid representations of reality," the strengths perspective embraces the worldview of the client (p. 197). It is truly "starting where the client is" rather than "starting where the theory is." Duncan, Hubble, and Miller (1997) describe it this way:

> We have learned to listen more, turn off the intervention spigot, stay still, and direct our attention to them [the client]—recalling, as Ram Dass once said, "The quieter you become the more you will hear." The greater success we have experienced in doing this, the more room clients have had to be themselves, use their own resources, discover possibilities, attribute self-enhancing meanings to their actions, and take responsibility. (p. 207)

De-Centering: Turning "Facts" into Hypothesis

But how do you shift such habits that seem part of our social understandings as well as the traditional doctrine of social work professionalism? I am speaking of a real shift in orientation or basic viewpoint rather than merely adding on a component as I have mentioned above. This shift is similar to altering what Aaron Beck (1972) refers to as "automatic thoughts" in that our professional habits of the mind or frames occur without recognition on our part. Yet, these frames are the lens through which we perceive and interact with clients. It is this accustomed or habitual professional thinking that guides our perceptions, thinking, and understanding that must be "de-centered," as the cognitive therapist would say, or "externalized" in terms of its dominant traditional social work narrative, as White and Epston (1990) refer to a similar process in narrative therapy.

Following the mode of cognitive therapy, all of us would need to distance ourselves from the automatic thoughts. That is, in order to shift perspectives from our traditional medical model to a strengths perspective, it would be necessary to first recognize the frame and then to view our professional conceptualizations as hypothesis rather than fact. This would permit dissociating oneself from the constructs we operate from and to examine them from a different point of view. We each would suspend our traditional professional constructs and look at the client from the perspective of strength and resilience.

De-Centering and Shifting Frames: Some Examples

Working with students just entering into social work training has been very helpful in my own de-centering process. The students come with a natural affinity or bias for looking at what is wrong or broken and quickly setting about to offer suggestions or answers for the client to follow. The students and I have explored the strengths perspective from within solution-based conversations held during class. In doing so, both the students and I have been confronted by our own assumptions or frames. The "clients" (actually students who are being interviewed in class and talking about real issues or challenges such as a roommate problem that they are dealing with at the time) reveal that they have actually been successful in addressing their issue in ways none of the members of the class or myself would have guessed or suspected. Being confronted with awareness of our own automatic perceptions and assumptions—mine being professional training and theirs the natural desire to do something—holds us back from listening to the issues as described by the client and brings a sense of uneasiness to all of us in the classroom.

For all of us to develop trust in the experiences, the students and I began to purposely eliminate any questions about background or about the problem. In its place, we went straight to the type of question often used by solution-focused practitioners such as Insoo Kim Berg (1994): "If six months from now you were to believe strongly that our work together was successful or it had a made a difference, what would be different then that would let you know that our work here was successful?" With some clarification and checking out our assumptions about the answers, a clearer and specific goal often emerged that was something much different than anyone in the class would have suggested. These goals were inclusive of support systems and cultural values and reflected reasonable expectations and outcomes on the part of the "client." Steps taken to make the goal more likely successful were likewise straightforward and specific as described by the "client." As a matter of fact, many times the "client" had actually accomplished the goals in the recent past. Strengths- and solution-oriented helpers think of these as "exceptions," similar to White and Epston's (1990) narrative notion of "unique outcomes" or lived experiences that are outside the dominant story, not part of the problem-saturated talk. These are the alternative stories or outcomes that represent possibilities or strengths from which goals and changes are possible. The results of our experiment usually left the students, the "client," and myself energized, hopeful, and surprised by what had happened time and time again. In one moving story, a student revealed that she had had a life of considerable turmoil and pain (she did not share the details in class).

From a strengths perspective, it was obvious that she had somehow made it to this point, obviously not with out pain and scars, and was with us in class and working on her degree. As we asked a strengths-based question about how she had managed to do this, she revealed that a family with whom she was a friend had taken her into their home to live (without the involvement of social services). Thinking from a strengths perspective, it was recognized that she must have done something to create such caring on the part of this family. That is, there was recognition that she must have had certain qualities that had led to such a meaningful relationship. The student had never considered her own qualities. As a matter of fact, she generally had very negative opinions about herself. Subsequently, the student reported how meaningful this awareness had been for her and how she had used it to help herself during some rough times during the semester.

It is often the simplest comment that goes unnoticed by my students and myself as we strain to "hear strengths" over the noise of "problems" being searched out by our minds. In one case, a student reported that he had been driving a friend who had serious drug problems when the friend revealed that he had just "shot up" for the first time in several weeks. The student, who had considerable experience working in traditional drug treatment facilities, was ready to challenge his friend's actions and thought of making him get out of the car. Then, the student considered what we had been talking about in class. He said "what the heck" and asked a strengths-based question: "How did you stay clean for so many weeks?" The student could not remember such a long conversation with his friend about what he was doing to stop and how he had been successful for such a length of time. The student learned a great deal more about his friend's struggles and his successes.

In another example of hearing strengths through the noise of problem-drenched talk, my students and I watched a video demonstrating Insoo Kim Berg's (1994) work with a couple. The man did not really want to be in counseling, and the woman had already gone to see a lawyer about a divorce. My students are always caught up with the fact that the husband is not wearing a wedding ring. They always want to ask "why?" and want to ask the wife how she must feel. They quickly deduced that he must be having an affair. They are so caught up in problem-saturated thinking that they often miss the work that Berg and the couple are doing together. The students are asked to speculate as to the outcome of the first interview. They have a hard time imagining anything productive happening. Some have strong beliefs that the issue of the ring needed to be addressed, and some wanted to hear more about feelings and past histories. When the second interview is shown, Berg herself is surprised by the turn of events when the couple returns two weeks later for the second interview. They have engaged in changes in their lives that neither Berg nor my students could have conceived or suggested. The students had missed the strengths, resilience, and unique outcomes possible when clients direct their own lives. It was those "extratherapeutic" factors, combined with Berg's asking for directions in terms of what *they wanted* different, that played out in the significant shift that emerged. It was the choices made by the couple together outside of the sessions that had resulted in the shifts they made. The problem as presented initially by the couple did little to predict the outcome. The fundamental point for the students was the challenge this process presented to their assumptions of something being broken and needing fixing by the expert. The same easily holds true for professionals and habitual ways of working where the theory and technique direct the work.

CONCLUSION

The strengths perspective is a paradigm shift or transformation of social work knowledge and practice. It is manifested in a deep change in attitude and frame from which to understand and engage those with whom we are working. The strengths perspective shifts our orientation from a worker-directed effort to a client-directed effort in collaboration with the professional. Professional knowledge is about how to be available in a different way; that is, in a way that exploits the strengths and resilience of the client and believes in this process.

For a professional practitioner to fully appreciate the implications of the strengths perspective, it is necessary to engage in a personal analysis just as if attempting to shift "automatic thoughts" or to engage "unique outcomes" as alternative narratives to the dominant professional perspective. It is only in the de-centering or recognition of the traditional frame that any shift can be made. For my students and me, de-centering comes in the form of surprise and uneasiness. When the "client" is made the center of practice in a true sense, uncertainty and not knowing take center stage. A truly mutual/collaborative dialogue takes place, resulting in unique outcomes unanticipated by the clever professional or the eager student. But, what always follows is a mistrust of our own experiences. It is the uncertainty, the not knowing, and maybe the unfamiliarity of relying on the client to take the lead, in giving direction to the work to be done, that is so uncomfortable. Isn't it the job of the social worker to "treat" the client with an intervention based upon empirically grounded expert knowledge about how lives are to be lived? What about the unconscious motivations and defenses that must be understood and overcome? These expectations on the part of the professional's habit and the student's eagerness to help need to be challenged again and again until an actual shift in frame takes place and becomes an active part of strengths-based practice. Once the frame is shifted, it is easier to then integrate the necessary and appropriate process demanded by agencies and funding sources and, more importantly, that will enhance the collaborative effort toward client-directed change. The professional knowledge shifts from pathology to that of human development in terms of resiliency and the self-righting process: How do people make it and in what way is life context a part of that process? Social work research shifts to the biopsychosocial elements that are emerging in biological and social sciences and the manner by which people can and do make it through life. How we might practice to collaborate with the human potential becomes the focus of research rather than focus on a specific technique.

The strengths perspective challenges our professional conventions, our habits of the mind. Thinking in terms of strengths and resilience confronts our Western European cultural tradition that assumes that "truth" is discovered only by looking at assumed underlying and often hidden meanings, making causal links in some sequential order leading to the "cause" of it all. Duncan and colleagues (1997) note, "traditions are important in all human pursuits, but they can also have inhibiting and damaging consequences. The source of [social work practice] traditions are [sic] mainly grounded in theory, not fact, and yet they often assume the status of fact" (p. 7). Adherence to pathological models of human development and practice imposes an agenda onto those with whom we work. It can blind us to seeing the possibilities, resilience, and strengths of people caught up in often difficult and complex issues. Challenging this cultural and professional tradition as well as a process that has become synonymous with the social work profession is a serious task that needs to be undertaken if social work is to embrace a belief in human resilience, possibilities, and strengths.

It is important for practitioners as well as students to recognize that the strengths perspective is a very different paradigm that informs practice across many levels of practice. A recent example is our work with a local elementary school, which provides a sense of the manner by which my students and I are starting to engage agencies and clients from the strengths perspective.

A small elementary school where 85 percent of the students are from the local city housing project was the site of a brainstorming session on how to address a long list of problems facing the teachers and staff who wanted to make a difference in these kids' lives. Social workers from the Department of Social Services, a few of my students, and I were called in by the principal to address the daily problems teachers and students were encountering in the classrooms. The list of issues covered lack of parental participation, teacher burnout, disruptive kids, difficulty teaching, and poor community relations. The conversation became overwhelming as more and more problems began to saturate the room. The principal wanted to take action right away and suggested that all the teachers be surveyed about the most serious problems they were having so that the professional group could then plan on how to address these problems. A social worker thinking from a strengths perspective used a solution-focused skill to shift the conversation. The social worker wondered if the teachers could be asked "if a miracle took place" and their teaching experience was the best they could imagine in this school, what would that look like? What would they and their students be doing differently? Importantly, had any part of the miracle happened in the classroom, just a little bit, over the past three weeks? The atmosphere in the room of professionals changed immediately. The contrast between a traditional problem focus on fixing a problem or eliminating a risk factor and a strengths perspective that focuses on building resilience became a powerful tool for transforming the dialogue and the feelings of all the participants at the meeting. Nothing had taken place except for a shift in perspective away from problem-saturated talk and trying to eliminate problems to thinking in terms of strengths, what appears to be working, and desired possibilities. The shift literally lightened the room. The gloom of being overwhelmed with problems and risk factors gave way to hopefulness and thinking of finding goals to build toward and strengths to build on.

Implementation of this simple process has resulted in a very different attitude and process on the part of administrators and teachers. They are really enjoying their sessions and learning a great deal about themselves and what possibilities there might be for their teaching and connecting with the community. A lengthy list of what students and teachers are already doing that is working and new possibilities to shift the learning experience to one of enjoyment and productivity has taken hold in the consultation sessions and is being initiated in the classroom.

Human beings are always in a process of changing within themselves as they exist within a constantly changing world. The strengths perspective builds on the potential for change that is already present. It does not ignore or try to eliminate a problem or risk factor; it creates a collaborative condition for building alternative possibilities. The worker cannot make poverty, racism, fear, dangerous surroundings, failures, and bitterness on the part of students and parents go away, but he or she can help provide an opportunity for a different present moment and future in some small ways that can have life-changing effects. When a teacher recognizes the strengths and potentials in a child who has managed to stay attentive for an hour during the day and acknowledges that with the child and with a note home about how well he or she had done, a change has taken place in that child's own sense of self and the world around him or her. Importantly, building on what had made that possible, the strengths and resiliency of the child, creates a more hopeful present moment and better future possibilities. It is not possible to overthrow poverty and racism in this situation. It is possible to build on the strengths and resiliency present in this context if they can be recognized, exploited, and expanded to support a life that can then more likely confront the serious challenges.

DISCUSSION QUESTIONS/EXERCISES

1. What are the historical circumstances that helped entrench the exclusive problem-based and deficit-dominated perspective in social work?

2. How might you explain the fact that social work practice tends to follow the new version of being "scientific," in the form of evidence-based practice, while ignoring the growing evidence that challenges this "one-size-fits-all" construct?

3. How might you go about providing a strengths-based alternative to the traditional or conventional problem and deficit-dominated discourse in your agency?

4. What is the challenge for you in considering to practice from a strengths-based perspective?

5. What makes it so hard for a profession like social work to shift its fundamental perspective of practice?

6. A: Take a moment and write down everything that has gone wrong over the past two days. Make sure you describe what went wrong and how you felt or might still feel about the occurrence. This is what we often ask our clients to do for us when asking about their problems. How does it leave you feeling? Do you feel hopeful? Do you feel motivated?

    B: Take a moment and write down everything that went well over the past two days, even if just a little bit. Make sure you describe what went well and how much better you felt at the time or still feel thinking back. How does this leave you feeling? Do you feel more hopeful? Do you feel more motivated?

    When talking with clients, considering what has gone well, even if a little bit, as they are trying to address life's challenges shifts the energy into a direction of hope and motivation most of the time. As workers, we have the opportunity to help create different moods and contexts for our work. Which of the previous two moods would be more helpful in trying to consider answers to life's challenges?

REFERENCES

Addams, J. (1930). *The second twenty years at Hull-House.* New York: The Macmillan Company.

Agnew, E. N. (2004). *Mary E. Richmond, and the Creation of an American Profession.* Champaign, IL: University of Illinois Press.

American Psychiatric Association. (1994). *Diagnostic and statistical manual of mental disorders,* (4th ed.). Washington, DC: Author.

Aspinwall, L. G. & Staudinger, U. M. (Eds.). (2003). *A psychology of human strengths.* Washington, DC: American Psychological Association.

Beck, A. T. (1972). *Depression: Causes and treatment.* Philadelphia: University of Pennsylvania Press.

Benard, B. (2004). *Resiliency: What we have learned.* San Francisco, CA: WestEd.

Berg, I. K. (1994). *Family based services: A solution-focused approach.* New York: W. W. Norton & Company.

Biestek, F. P., Jr. (1957). *The casework relationship.* Chicago, IL: Loyola University Press.

Briar, S. & Miller, H. (1971). *Problems and issues in social casework.* New York: Columbia University Press.

Bristol, M. C. (1936). *Handbook on social case recording.* Chicago, IL: The University of Chicago Press.

Chapin, F. S. (1918). A scientific basis for training social workers. *Mental Hygiene, 2* (3), 590–592.

Csikszentmihaly, M, & Csikszentmihaly, I. S. (Eds.). (2006). *A life worth living: Contributions of positive psychology.* New York: Oxford Press.

Duncan, B. I., Hubble, M. A., & Miller, S. D. (1997). *Psychotherapy with "impossible" cases: The efficient treatment of therapy veterans.* New York: W. W. Norton.

Freud, A. (1936). *The ego and the mechanisms of defense.* New York: International University Press.

Freud, S. (1923). The ego and the id. *The standard edition of the complete psychological works of Sigmund Freud.* 24 vols. Edited by James Strachey. London: Hogarth, 1953–66.

Goffman, I. (1974). *Frame analysis.* Cambridge, MA: Harvard University Press.

Goldstein, H. (1990). The knowledge base of social work practice: theory, wisdom, analog, or art. *Families in Society 71* (1) 1990, 32–43

Goldstein, H. (1997). Victors or victims? In D. Saleebey (Ed.), *The strengths perspective in social work practice* (2nd ed., pp. 21–35). New York: Longman.

Hamilton, G. (1946). *Principles of social case recordings.* New York: Columbia University Press.

Hamilton, G. (1958). A theory of personality: Freud's contribution to social work. In H. Parad (Ed.), *Ego psychology and the dynamic casework.* New York: Family Service Association of America.

Hartmann, H. (1939). *Ego psychology and the problem of adaptation.* New York: International University Press.

Heller, A. F. & Rudnick, L. (1991). *1915, the cultural moment.* New Brunswick, NJ: Rutgers University Press.

Hepworth, D. H. (1993). Managing manipulative behavior in the helping relationship. *Social Work, 38,* 674–682.

Hepworth, D. H. & Larson, J. A. (1993). *Direct social work practice* (4th ed.). Pacific Grove, CA: Brooks/Cole Publishing Company.

Hepworth, D. H., Rooney, R. H., Rooney, G. D., Strom-Gottfried, K., & Larsen, J. (2006). *Direct social work practice: Theory and skills* (7th ed.). Belmont, CA; Thomson.

Hollis, F. (1964). *Casework: A psychosocial therapy.* New York: Random House.

Hubble, M. A., Duncan, B. L., & Miller, S. D. (1999) *The heart and soul of change: What works in therapy.* Washington, DC: American Psychological Association.

Jacobson, N. S., Dobson, K. S., Truax, P. A., Addis, M. E., Koerner, K., Gollan, J. K., et al. (1996). A component analysis of cognitive-behavioral treatment for depression. *Journal of Counseling and Clinical Psychology, 64,* 295–304.

Jarrett, M. C. (1918). Psychiatric social work. *Mental Hygiene, 2* (2), 283–290.

Kahneman, D., Diener, E., & Schwarz, N. (Eds.). (1999). *Well-being: The foundations of hedonic psychology.* New York: Russell Sage Foundation.

Krishner, D. & Witson, J. A. (1997). *Saturated cognition: Social, semiotic, and phychological perspectives.* NJ: Lawrence Erlbaum.

Lambert, M. J. (1992). Psychotherapy outcome research. In J. C. Norcross & M. R. Goldfried (Eds.), *Handbook of psychotherapy integration* (pp. 94–129). New York: Basic Books.

Lambert, M. J. & Bergin, A. E. (1994). The effectiveness of psychotherapy. In A. E. Bergin & S. L. Garfield (Eds.), *Handbook of psychotherapy and behavior change* (4th ed., pp. 143–189). New York: Wiley.

Lord, C., Ross, L., & Lepper, M. R. (1979). Biased assimilation and attitude polarization: The effects of prior theories on subsequently considered evidence. *Journal of Personality and Social Psychology, 37,* 2098–2109

Lubove, R. (1965). *The professional altruist: The emergence of social work as a career.* Cambridge, MA: Harvard University Press.

Margolin, L. (1997). *Under the cover of kindness: The invention of social work.* Charlottesville: University Press of Virginia.

Merriam-Webster's collegiate dictionary (10th ed.). Springfield, MA: Merriam-Webster.

Miley, K. K., O'Melia, M., & DuBois, B. (1998). *Generalist social work practice: An empowerment approach* (3rd ed.). Boston: Allyn and Bacon

Neimeyer, R. A. & Raskin, J. D. (2000). On practicing postmodern therapy in modern times. In R. A. Neimeyer & J. D. Raskin (Eds.), *Constructions of disorder: Meaning-making framework for psychotherapy*. Washington, DC: American Psychological Association.

Nisbett, R. & Ross, L. (1980). *Human inference: Strategies and shortcomings of social judgment*. Englewood Cliffs, NJ: Prentice-Hall.

Parad, H. J. (Ed.). (1958). Introduction. In H. Parad (Ed.), *Ego psychology and the dynamic casework* (pp. 1–9). New York: Family Service Association of America.

Perlman, H. H. (1957). *Social casework: A problem-solving process*. Chicago, IL: The University of Chicago Press.

Popple, P. & Reid, P. N. (1999). A profession for the poor? A history of social work in the United States. In G. R. Lowe, & P. N. Reid (Eds.), *The professionalization of poverty* (pp. 9–28). New York: Aldine De Gruyter.

Rapp, C. A. (1998). *The strengths model: Case management with people suffering from severe and persistent mental illness*. New York: Oxford Press.

Reid, P. N. (1995). American social welfare history. In R. L. Edwards (Ed.), *Encyclopedia of social work* (19th ed., Vol. 3, pp. 2206–2225). Washington, DC: NASW Press.

Reynolds, B. C. (1975). *Social work and social living*. Washington, DC: National Association of Social Workers. (Original work published 1951.)

Reynolds, S. & Trinder, L. (2000). *Evidence-based practice: A critical appraisal*. Oxford, UK: Blackwell Science Ltd.

Richmond, M. E. (1917). *Social diagnosis*. New York: Russell Sage Foundation.

Richmond, M. E. (1922). *What is social casework? An introductory description*. New York: Russell Sage Foundation.

Robinson, V. A. (1930). *A changing psychology in social casework*. Chapel Hill: The University of North Carolina Press.

Ryff, C. D. & Singer, B. (2003). Ironies of the human condition: Well-being and health on way to mortality. In L. G. Aspinwall & U. M. Staudinger (Eds.), *A psychology of human strengths*. Washington, DC: American Psychological Association.

Saleebey, D. (1997). The strengths approach to practice. In D. Saleebey (Ed.), *The strengths perspective in social work practice* (2nd ed.). New York: Longman.

Seligman, M. E. P. & Peterson, C. (2003). Positive clinical psychology. In L. G. Aspinwall & U. M. Staudinger (Eds.), *A psychology of human strengths*. Washington, DC: American Psychological Association.

Singer, B. & Ryff, C. D. (1999). Hierarchies of life histories and associated health risks. In N. E. Adler, B. S. McEwen, & M. Marmot (Eds.), *Socioeconomic status and health in industrialized countries. Annals of the New York Academy of Science, 896,* 96–115.

Snyder, C. R. & Lopez, S. L. (2007). *Positive psychology: The scientific and practical explorations of human strengths*. Thousand Oaks: CA: Sage Publications.

Specht, H. & Courtney, M. (1994). *Unfaithful angels: How social work has abandoned its mission*. New York: Free Press.

Taft, J. (1944). Introduction. In J. Taft (Ed.), *A functional approach to family case work*. Philadelphia: University of Pennsylvania Press.

Taleb, N. N. (2007). *The black swan: The impact of the highly improbable*. New York: Random House.

Wampold, B. E. (2001). Contextualizing psychotherapy as a healing practice: Culture, history, and methods. *Applied and Preventive Psychology, 10,* 69–86.

Wampold, B. E. & Bhati, K. S. (2004). Attending to omissions: A historical examination of evidence-based practice movements. *Professional Psychology: Research and Practice, 35*(6), 563–570.

Wampold, B. E., Minami, T., Baskin, T. W., & Tierney, S. C. (2002). A meta (re)analysis of the effects of cognitive therapy versus "other therapies" for depression. *Journal of Affective Disorders, 8,* 159–165.

Weick, A., Rapp, C., Sullivan, W. P., & Kisthardt, W. (1989, July). A strengths perspective for social work practice. *Social Work, 350*–354.

Wexler, B. E. (2006). *Brain and culture*. Cambridge, MA: MIT Press.

White, M. & Epston, D. (1990). *Narrative means to therapeutic ends*. New York: W. W. Norton & Company.

CHAPTER THREE

THE OPPORTUNITIES AND CHALLENGES OF STRENGTHS-BASED, PERSON-CENTERED PRACTICE

Purpose, Principles, and Applications in a Climate of Systems Integration

WALTER E. KISTHARDT

The essential political problem is that of ascertaining the possibility of constituting a new politics of truth . . . not changing peoples' consciousness, or what's in their heads—but the political, economic, institutional regime of the production of truth.
—Michel Foucault

The strengths perspective, and concomitant strengths-based practice, continues to interest, intrigue, and challenge front-line workers, policymakers, funders, and those who administer a wide range of programs designed to assist people in achieving their goals (Anderson & Carter, 2003, Glicken, 2004, Krogsrud-Miley, O'Melia, & Dubois, 2004; Pulin, 2005). For many, the dilemma has been finding ways to integrate a strengths approach with prevailing medical and problems-based frameworks related to medical necessity and funding. For others, the challenge has been to develop and deliver training curricula that capture the complexity of what initially appears to be a straightforward and simplistic approach to practice. In recent years the purpose and principles of strengths-based, person-centered practice have been embraced as a potential "truth" that may serve to foster true integration of multiple service systems on behalf of each service participant.

In this chapter I identify key concepts regarding the nature of our ultimate purpose in entering the collaborative helping process. What do we want to happen? What do our programs want to happen? How do we measure success? By counting units of service or by documenting social outcomes realized by those who are disenfranchised? These are at the heart political questions. I shall illustrate diverse practice applications and propose six core principles of strengths-based, person-centered practice that may serve to guide and direct the efforts of multiple stakeholders and diverse systems of care. I will draw upon my collaboration with a wide range of programs interested in implementing the strengths approach and achieving systems integration in their work with service participants. These populations include people living with HIV/AIDS, adults with persistent mental illness, adults with developmental disabilities, and persons struggling with substance abuse/addictions or co-occurring disorders. I then examine some practical applications that seem to promote a collaborative power-sharing, interpersonal helping relationship. I conclude with some reflections regarding the current trend toward service and systems integration and what challenges lie ahead.

THE PURPOSE OF THE STRENGTHS APPROACH

In order to be effective, efficient, and responsive practitioners, a clear understanding of the purpose of our helping efforts is essential. I have used the following statement of purpose with my social work graduate students and providers across the country in training seminars (Kisthardt, 2002, p. 164).

> To assist individuals, families, and communities within the context of a mutually enriching, collaborative partnership, to identify, secure, and sustain, the range of resources, both external and internal, needed to live in a normally interdependent manner in the community.

There are several key contrasts that this statement of purpose suggests to providers. First, we strive in a strengths approach to "help" people achieve the goals that they *want* to achieve, not the goals that someone else believes they *need* to achieve. Second, the strengths approach does not suggest that "anything goes"—that whatever the service participant wants is agreed with and used to fuel the helping plan. This is where the notion of "normal interdependence" becomes crucial.

The strengths-based practitioner is keenly aware of the social/cultural/legal constraints on individual behavior within a given community. Behavior that is normally interdependent (and I use the term "normally" sociologically) is tolerable, acceptable, and ultimately, legal. The provider who embraces the concept of normal interdependence seeks to influence others, within the context of the professional helping relationship, to make choices that are likely to be healthier for them, and that are respectful of other citizens. If our focus is upon the "problem" this begs a very important question: What problem do we focus on first? Medical management and adherence to the medical regimen for symptom management? Mental health diagnosis and compliance with psychoactive neuroleptics? The problematic use of alcohol as indicated by the person's score on the addictions severity index? Consider the following situation:

> Let's say that you have asked a service participant, who happens to have co-occurring diagnoses of mental illness and substance abuse, and who also is living with AIDS, "what do you want in your life?" The person states that he wants to work, but that his anti-retroviral medication is causing nausea. He notes that one of the ways he copes with his illness is by using alcohol. He has been arrested once for driving under the influence. His probation plan requires that he completes a residential substance abuse treatment program. He tells you that he has "been down these roads before" and that what he really wants is to get a job so that he can get his own place and get on with his life. How do you respond?

This example typically engenders much discussion and even heated debate. Treatment providers will tend to have different viewpoints that appear to be related to their training and experience. Some may say that the initial focus should be on the substance abuse, as this is the core problem that will continue to negatively affect all other aspects of this person's life unless it is directly confronted and addressed through planned intervention. Others will suggest that the substance abuse is related to clinical depression and that once the depression is understood and treated, the use of substances as a self-medicating mechanism will no longer be needed. Others will argue that we must develop programs to treat both of these disorders simultaneously in order to be effective. Still others will suggest that due to the diagnosis of HIV/AIDS, the person should be referred to the Ryan White case management program for initial evaluation and brokerage case management services.

This example illustrates the systemic fragmentation and multivariate and complex nature of peoples' lives demanding the attention of advanced generalist social work practice (Derezotes, 2000). By developing approaches that place the person not the problem at the center of our deliberations, we are more likely to meet the person in the middle and to discuss and develop a plan that both provider and service participant can live with. This requires that strengths-based practitioners, regardless of their theoretical and methodological stance, ask the following question:— "How am I contributing to the *social* outcome that has been articulated by the person?" I submit that medical, behavioral, and psychological outcomes (medication adherence, sobriety, insight, and cognitive restructuring) are incomplete without concomitant changes and gains in one's social world. Examples of these outcomes might include meaningful employment, increased social support network, achieving a permanent home of one's choosing, gaining opportunities for leisure, and having opportunities for spiritual growth and connectedness.

The concept of normal interdependence should ultimately determine whether we affirm and support each person's own aspirations. I argue that if we choose not to help someone with a goal that is normally interdependent, then this reflects a stance of oppression and a fundamental difference of opinion regarding values (Foucault, 1980). In a strengths-based approach, our task becomes helping others engage in behaviors that respect the wants and needs of other citizens in the community, while at the same time promoting personal gratification, satisfaction, and sense of accomplishment. As a Supreme Court judge once ruled, "individual liberty ceases, where public peril begins." In the spirit of eco-systemic theory, this perspective involves "the creation of structural conditions under which people can choose to give to their community as well as to take from their community" (Breton, 1994, p. 29). The treatment or helping process should enrich a sense of citizenship, inclusion, and meaning; a sense of autonomy and social responsibility, a shift from valuing independence to affirming and valuing interdependence (Capra, 1996).

The strengths perspective challenges us to move beyond narrow notions that serve to ostensibly explain "problematic" human behavior in the social environment. For example, in my work with substance abuse providers in Kansas I have used a framework (see Figure 3.1) to help them understand how the strengths perspective may help us to expand (not eliminate) more conventional bio-neurological foci and consider a range of other factors that converge to influence decisions at any given point in time.

Several points are emphasized as we review this framework. First, this does not suggest in any way that the decision to drink is not totally influenced by biological and psychological cravings and the fact that the person has been designated to have an "illness." If

FIGURE 3.1   **How Do Providers Understand and Respond to Substance Abuse and Chemical Dependency Behaviors? Contrasting an Illness Perspective with a Strengths Perspective**

ILLNESS PERSPECTIVE	STRENGTHS PERSPECTIVE
The problematic behavior, i.e.,drinking, is a function of the illness. The person drinks to excess because he or she is an alcoholic, a medical disease that is rooted in human biology. It is only through total abstinence that one is able to cope effectively with this illness, as it is a life-long affliction.	Decision to drink or not to drink is a conscious choice. There is a personal agenda, desire, that is related to the use of a particular substance. Key is to discover what the addictive behavior means to each unique person, placing the behavior in social context.
When a person suffers from co-existing disorders of chemical dependency and mental illness, there is difference of opinion regarding what to focus on first. One theory suggests focusing on treating the addiction first, the other holds that the mental illness must be addressed first. Others suggest that treatment addresses both simultaneously.	When a person struggles with mental illness and substance abuse/chemical dependency, the focus is on the person, not the problems. The outcomes, desires, aspirations of the person drive the helping activities. The needs as identified by the provider may or may not be relevant in achieving these person-centered helping outcomes.
Key concepts in treatment include limit setting, boundaries, recognizing and managing, manipulative behavior, confrontation, denial, minimizing, rationalizing, enabling as a process that promotes and contributes to pathology, abstinence as goal of treatment	Key helping concepts include partnership, collaboration, mutuality, power sharing, graduated disengagement, normal interdependence, reduced harm, abstinence encouraged but not a prerequisite for helping.

PROPOSED THEORY TO BRIDGE THE GAP BETWEEN THESE PERSPECTIVES

For people to modify their use of chemical substances they must come to a point in their lives where they want to change, or realize that they need to change in order to achieve and/or sustain something that holds more meaning and value for them than does the substance. *People* choose recovery... people are not powerless. The capacity to make and act on choices that promote wellness is an inherent strength.

we follow this logic, that the "illness" or "disease" is primarily the casual factor for substance abuse/dependency (consider that relapse is assumed to be a natural part of the recovery process), then we would probably have precious few people who sustain long periods of sobriety. Second, all behavior takes place within a social context and is profoundly impacted by the social realities of the moment. The decision to remain substance free must be reinforced by social, relational, economic, and material gains. I prefer to refer to these gains as "payoffs." If the person experienced payoffs for the use of a substance, and they are no longer experiencing payoffs for choosing sobriety (a lack of employment opportunities, discrimination, oppression, homelessness, etc.), then is it reasonable to expect that this decision will be sustained over time? This is why advocacy and attendance to social justice issues must be an integral part of treatment at the inception of care. Currently, I am involved in a project in Kansas where substance abuse counselors are being trained in strengths-based, person-centered case management. This will expand the range of their care and intervention and will encourage them to focus on advocacy and resource acquisition priorities. A wise juvenile judge once shared with me this observation, "Why should we expect these youth to change when they have nothing to lose?"

The six principles of strengths-based practice serve to guide and direct the range of helping efforts related to this purpose. I have found that there is often disagreement on one or more of these principles not only between different systems, but within different components of the same agency. If providers are not able to agree on these principles, integration, consistency, and continuity of care become far more difficult, if not impossible to achieve. We now examine these principles, incorporating examples from programs where I have provided training and/or technical assistance.

THE SIX PRINCIPLES
OF STRENGTHS-BASED HELPING

1. The initial focus of the helping process is on the strengths, interests, abilities, knowledge, and capabilities of each person, not on their diagnoses, deficits, symptoms, and weaknesses as *defined by another.*

The human beings who enter your life as a service provider are so much more than a collection of symptoms and an amalgam of problems. They are survivors. They are exceptionally adaptive. Despite the effects of poverty, oppression, discrimination, illness, disappointments, public apathy, and even at time hostility, people who are described as being at risk and/or vulnerable still resolve to live each day as best they can. They are creative, resilient, persistent, and courageous. They have not given up but have decided to press on despite external challenges and internal conflict and pain.

This principle suggests that people decide for themselves what they want in life. Even if this statement is something as basic as "I want to live," to be able to express one's personal aspirations and desires is an important strength. Once this statement is made, then attention to deficits and various other needs assumes meaning for them. For example, I have reviewed many treatment plans that list the goal as "medication compliance." Whose goal is this? In many instances, it is the providers' goal. They are focusing on what they believe the person "needs." Most service participants I speak to would rather not take their medications. A person may ultimately decide to take medication because it helps that person to achieve something desired. Medication, therefore, is viewed as a means toward some other socially oriented end. One person once shared, "I want to keep my job. I really love it, and I know I need to take my medications to help me stay healthy." Still another person told me "I didn't want to work any more, so I went off my medication, and I lost the job." If the fact that this person no longer wanted to work had been identified, he could have been counseled to leave the job in a normally interdependent manner, giving notice and getting a letter of reference. What happened, however, was that his "illness" and "medication non-compliance" were cited as the reasons why he "lost" his job.

This principle challenges us to assume a stance of respect and admiration for people. We are challenged to assume the role of "student" interested in learning about this person's

hopes and dreams, rather than as the "expert" who purports to know more about what motivates a person than the person does (Miller & Rollnick, 2002). We are committed to get to
know all persons as unique and valuable beings, to learn what things they want in their lives,
what holds meaning for them, and to then collaborate on what needs to happen in order for
them to be successful. One service participant remarked:

> Mary (social worker) was the first person I ever worked with who asked me what I wanted to
> do. She told me that she admired me because of how I have been able to cope with my mental
> illness and still get what I need each day. She told me she had a lot to learn from me. She said
> I have a lot of strengths, and I guess she's right . . . but I didn't see them as strengths . . . but
> I do now.

A focus on strengths does not mean one ignores or deliberately turns a blind eye to
the realities of decisions people make regarding behaviors that may indeed not be conducive
to their wellness and/or the wellness and safety of others. In the era of managed care the challenge is to balance attention to symptoms, problems, deficits, and medical necessity with
attention to the development of individualized plans of care that demonstrate evidence that
the intervention is making a difference. This principle reminds providers that every helping
intervention is grounded in the meaning ascribed to the process by each individual (Finn &
Jacobson, 2003). As these authors suggest, practice rooted in a social justice framework
must integrate meaning, context, history, possibility, and power. This principle is summed
up nicely by a young woman who shared "the first thing is to get to know me . . . I am not
a collection of problems, pathology, and failures . . . I have hopes and dreams and visions
for what I want in my life . . . you are not living my life . . . I am different from everyone
else you will encounter . . . show respect for that difference, honor it . . . and I'll let you in
. . . ignore it, or come off like you know more about me than I do, and it will do no more
than to frustrate us both."

2. The helping relationship becomes one of collaboration, mutuality, and partnership. Power with another, not power over another.

Power is a sociopolitical construct (Anderson & Carter, 2003). Foucault (1980) has suggested that power is "co-extensive with the social body . . . that power is relational, and that
relations of power are interwoven with other kinds of relations for which they play at once
a conditioning and conditioned role" (p. 142). Power is expressed through influence. It is
"the ability to get things done the way one wants them done . . . the ability to influence people" (Shafritz & Ott, 1996, p. 354). For example, professors may feel powerful when students share that their comments have influenced them to reconsider some notions they have
held regarding a certain group of people. In a like manner, students may feel powerful when
they suggest an alternative assignment that will help them to more fully experience and
learn about a given concept and the proposal is accepted by the professor. How do we
respond when a "client," "patient," or "consumer" suggests that what we have recommended
is not what he or she wants or believes that he or she needs at this time? I have frequently
used the example that if professionals recommend a certain set of protocols in an attempt
to influence a service participant, it will likely be thought of as "assessment and treatment."

Whereas, if the person disagrees, and shifts the attention to some other set of protocols that they believe will be helpful, this may be interpreted as "manipulation." This double standard runs antithetically to a true notion of mutual influence, true collaboration, and power sharing (Mattaini, 2001). Relationships where power, as reflected in influence and decision making, is skewed disproportionately in one direction, may eventually lead to oppression. As Friere suggests, human beings are not liberated through revolution, but through "communion" with each other (1994, p. 114).

This principle challenges us to develop helping plans *with* people not *for* them. It challenges us to share power and decision making as we journey with another human being. The challenge of implementing this principle in practice demands that we expand the boundaries of the helping enterprise. Who decides where meetings take place? Who decides what the treatment goal is to be? Who decides how long the meetings take place? Who decides if there can be communication between regularly scheduled meetings? Who decides which questions are "appropriate" and which are not? Who decides whether there will be "self-disclosure" on the part of the provider? These are but a few of the important questions to ask as we strive to make the helping relationship more collaborative and more strengths based. A service participant shared these thoughts with me regarding the power of this type of relationship:

> My case manager was more like a friend than other workers in my past. She really seemed to care about me, and she did not force me to do things. We talked about our mothers, we smoked and laughed together. She helped me get my own place and she came to AA meetings with me. Now I go without her. She has been a gift from heaven, a real miracle in my life. When I think about drinking now . . . and I do, pretty much every day . . . I realize I want to keep my apartment more than I want to drink and I get busy with other things that bring me a sense of joy . . . if I was still living with my mother I'd probably resort to drinking again. She helped me to get something in my life I didn't want to lose."

Strengths-based practitioners have realized the importance of expanding traditional "boundaries" of the helping relationship. As Derezotes (2000) notes, "in a reciprocal relationship, the client and worker share co-responsibility for the work process . . . the worker and client view themselves as equals . . . (they) co-create the practice goals, objectives, and tasks" (p. 79). The ideal situation in any helping encounter is when both workers and service participants, having been guided by the wants and needs of those helped, come away from the process enriched. Strengths-based practitioners do not have more invested in the process and outcomes than do service participants. There is a belief in the resourcefulness, determination, and resiliency of all people, regardless of illness, disability, or personal history.

3. Each person is responsible for his or her own recovery.
The participant is the director of the helping efforts.
We serve as caring community living consultants.
The healing process takes place on many levels.

People constantly make decisions. Do I take one drink or not? Do I change the baby now or wait until later? Do I take my medications? Do I get out of bed today? A strengths perspective recognizes that decisions are being made. The question here is not whether someone is conscious that he or she is making a decision. Behavior becomes a *de facto* indication of the decision that has been made. If we are to influence and promote other decisions that are more normally interdependent, the first step is to help people realize that they are in fact making these decisions, and that if these decisions continue, they may not attain the goal they have articulated. This view certainly recognizes that bio-neurological realities affect human behavior. It suggests, however, that this variable is not exclusively the "cause." Environmental, cultural, spiritual, economic, psychological, and ethnocultural factors also warrant the strengths-based practitioner's attention and consideration.

The example of the young single parent who refuses to get help for a chemical addiction is a prime example. She has stated that she *wants* to be reunited with her infant who has been placed in foster care. This goal becomes the ultimate focus of the work. She refuses, however, to participate in treatment, and the providers, who have a duty to the baby and the larger community, petition to terminate parental rights. The young parent may "blame" social services for "taking" her baby. In point of fact, her decisions, as reflected in her behavior, suggest that competing desires are at play. She directed and determined the course of events, the workers responded. I have spoken with many providers who were convinced that what some of these young people may truly have wanted was to not be a parent. By making certain decisions, they accomplished that goal in a manner where the responsibility and blame could be shifted to the state department of children and family services.

A recent collaboration with a residential treatment facility for people struggling with chemical addictions provided me with renewed insights regarding the nature of recovery and the compatibility of this concept with strengths-based practice. After providing a two-day training on strengths-based, person-centered care, I spent time at the facility observing intake and a wide range of psychoeducational treatment groups. It seemed clear from my observations that tasks tended to be "assigned" by counselors, not generated from a discussion of a range of options relating to the social goals that each person held for him, or herself. As the staff began to implement person-centered strengths assessments, and personal wellness plans, they reported increased enthusiasm and follow-up on the part of those receiving treatment. They also reported feeling less pressure to constantly generate treatment plans and tasks for people. As one counselor stated, "you have really challenged me to get out of my box . . . it's not comfortable . . . I like staying in my box, it's what I know and what I believe . . . but I realize how this approach is actually freeing and healthier for me . . . if they don't own it, it's not going to work."

As a result of this process, service participants began to attend and participate in the staff discussion of their plans where they had not been involved before. The idea was generated that each person who received care should leave the facility with his or her own "Personal Recovery Plan," which had been developed at the residential facility. The community case manager had also been involved in the training and was in a much better position to continue the process as each person was discharged from the facility.

4. All human beings have the inherent capacity to learn, grow, and change.

The human spirit is incredibly resilient. Despite the hardships, trauma, experience of repeated psychiatric hospitalizations, years of living on the streets, years of experiencing the negative effects of poverty, physical or neurological disability, structural oppression, stigma and discrimination, each person, at the time you begin the collaboration, may be on the verge of making important changes in his or her life (Prochaska, DiClemente, & Norcross, 1992). This principle challenges us to harness the motivating power of positive expectations—the healing power that often is the product when the faith, hope, and love conveyed by one person ignites the fire of potentials and possibilities for another.

I have encountered service providers in training seminars who suggest that this principle is fine for those who are "higher functioning," but the majority of the people they work with have "severe disabilities" and may not even be able to tell you what they want. In these types of situations it becomes important to shift our focus from asking questions to patiently observing. A strengths perspective suggests that people will indicate their preferences by their behavior. Moreover, we should constantly attempt to try something new and different with people who may seem to have very little potential to accomplish new tasks or to engage in certain behaviors. The following experience illustrated the essence of this principle, and it is an image I will never forget.

> I was providing two days of training for staff at Tachachale, a residential treatment facility in Gainesville, Florida. Prior to the training, the staff was taking me on a tour of the cottages. In one cottage was a young man who was lying in a hospital bed face down and reclined at a 45-degree angle, with his head about two feet from the floor and his feet elevated. He was not able to speak, as he had experienced significant neurological impairment due to traumatic brain injury. This position assisted with postural drainage. As the staff stopped to introduce me he began to make low guttural vocalizations. It seemed clear that he heard the staff member and was responding as best he could. Acting on an impulse, I lay down on the floor where he could see my face and said, "Hi Jimmy, it's nice to meet you." At which point Jimmy began to make much louder vocalizations which the staff agreed was laughter! They stated that they had never heard him respond in this manner. I asked them if they had ever lain down on the floor to talk to him when he was in this position. They had not. They decided that they would start doing this, especially on those days when it seemed to them that he was having one of his "off" days.

If we believe that all people possess the capacity to learn, grow, and change, then we will constantly be seeking new and different strategies to create opportunities for this growth to occur. At every helping session we should strive to learn something about the service participant(s) that we did not know before. In a sense, then this is our opportunity to learn, grow, and change. Each new piece of information may serve as a key that unlocks the potential that resides in all people. Sometimes when staff has worked with a person for several years, they may get to the point where they think they know "everything" about the person. Many times, when I have done an actual demonstration of engagement, strengths assessment, and planning with a current service participant at a particular program, I have learned things about them in 20 minutes that no one at the agency knew. The following example illustrates this point.

> At a recent training in Iowa, I spoke with a man at a workshop in Fort Dodge who has a developmental disability. There were over 100 people at the seminar, and this gentleman agreed to come up front and work with me to demonstrate the engagement and strengths assessment process. During our conversation, I asked him if spirituality was an important part of his life. He hesitated, looked around the room, and then shared that he wanted to get baptized into the Lutheran faith. There was a marked buzzing in the room, and it became clear that this desire had never been shared with anyone at the program. I asked him if his family (especially his father who was his legal guardian) would be supportive of this. He said that

he told his grandmother and she thought it was a good idea, but that he was afraid to ask his father as he was not sure how he would react. The staff later said they would work with him on a plan to share this desire with his father at his next circle of support meeting.

As I said, when we work with people day in and day out, for a period of many months or even years, we may come to believe that we know everything about them. Coming to this conclusion serves as a barrier to integrating a strengths perspective in our work. There is always something new to learn. There is always a different question to ask. We must assume the perspective of an explorer, and enter into a voyage of discovery. The more we learn about the uniqueness, talents, skills, accomplishments, desires, and knowledge people possess, the more creative we may be in mutually developing helping plans that are truly individualized and hold particular meaning for them.

5. Helping activities in naturally occurring settings in the community are encouraged in a strengths-based, person-centered approach.

Models of community care with vulnerable and multiply challenged populations suggest that working with people in naturally occurring settings whenever possible is an effective component of effective and efficient practice (Bentley, 2002). A common characteristic of each of these models is the fact that case managers as well as therapists are expected to work with people in various locations in the community as well as in their homes whenever possible unless there are legitimate concerns regarding safety. In this manner, providers may observe skill sets not demonstrated at the program or agency. In addition, the environmental strengths in terms of natural helpers, employment opportunities, and a range of other potential connections may be discovered.

In my conversations with providers, several benefits of meeting with people outside of the mental health center or program building are frequently noted. First, we are able to observe firsthand some of the realities of the person's day-to-day living circumstances. Second, people often feel more comfortable and share more detailed personal information in the context of completing tasks together in the community. Third, people with disabilities are more visible in the community, and this serves to break down myths, stereotypes, and the discrimination that is often a result of these biases. In addition, many case managers state that they would much rather be out of the office, so there is a feeling of satisfaction and even joy that accompanies the challenges of holistic, comprehensive helping. Finally, providers often report a marked change in people's behavior when they are in naturally occurring settings in the community. People behave less like "patients" or "clients" (Mead, 1934) and more like collaborators and partners in completing the helping tasks. The goals related to community activities should always be documented on the Person Wellness Plan with the service participant or guardian signing off, thus reflecting informed consent (Hepworth, Rooney, & Larsen, 2002, p. 69).

Strengths-based practice rekindles and invites even further application of ecosystems theory in our work with people. As we discover the desires, talents, and interests of each person, we discover locations in the environment where the goal is to enhance the "reciprocal interactions" (Krogsrud-Miley et al., 2004, p. 30). The focus of our efforts shifts from seeking to promote some sort of "change" within the person or within environments. We hone our skills in recognizing, appreciating, valuing, and utilizing that which is already there. In a sense, we co-create with individuals and various social settings a mutually enriching partnership and exchange. Indeed, there may be aspects of the person and aspects of environments that may suggest change and transformation. Greif views this transformation as a "dynamic process between people and their environments as people grow, achieve competence, and make contributions to others" (Krogsrud-Miley et al., 2004, p. 30). Principle 6 expands upon these points.

6. The entire community is viewed as an oasis of potential resources to enlist on behalf of service participants. Naturally occurring resources are considered as a possibility first, before segregated or formally constituted "mental health" or "social services."

This principle challenges providers to avoid the "knee-jerk" reaction that sometimes accompanies the planning and referral process. For example, the person sets a goal of finishing her or his high school equivalency (GED), and the provider refers the person to a GED study group at the "partial hospital" day program. Before this referral should be made, the provider might encourage enrollment in a review course offered by the local junior college or see if there is a mentoring program where the participant may study one-on-one with a retired teacher who is willing to volunteer his or her time. This may actually be more comfortable for those who do not do well in formal classroom-like settings. Seeing the entire community and the potentials and possibilities for resource development is an essential perspective of the strengths-based practitioner. The strengths perspective transcends the individual, to draw in neighborhood, organization, and larger community resources (Sullivan & Rapp, 2002).

One major disincentive to implementing this principle in mental health practice has been the prevailing policy of fee for service. If the center is billing for services provided at its program and it cannot bill for services provided by a natural helper, the choice for administrators is fairly clear cut. If they are to achieve their goal of sustaining the program, revenues are needed. The landscape of funding services for people with persistent mental illness, however, has shifted markedly in recent years.

The onset of managed care, capitated financing schemes, and case management options through Medicaid now provide incentives for providers to expand traditional notions of "therapeutic" and "clinical" care (Maguire, 2002). For example, in a capitated arrangement, providers receive a set annual dollar limit for each person who meets the criteria of persistent mental illness. Person-centered outcomes will drive the work. How each individual meets the needs related to these outcomes will vary. The point is—providers will be more likely to use a wider range of natural supports if their funding is not totally dependent on formally constituted clinical services.

The onset of "supportive housing" is another example of this principle (Ridgeway & Zipple, 1990). Often a person desires to secure his or her own apartment and others, family and/or treatment team, see this goal as "unrealistic." A plan is then suggested where the person lives in a group home or other supervised housing arrangement as a transitional step. For some individuals, this approach works well. For others, however, it is not effective and often leads to acting-out behaviors. Anyone who has ever lived in the same space with six or more non-relatives for a period of time knows firsthand how stressful congregate living may be.

This principle challenges providers to creatively and directly identify and strive to remove barriers so that each person may live where he or she wants to live. As one service participant shared: "I was in a group home and I couldn't take it. I can't be around people. I don't like people. I went back to the hospital (state psychiatric hospital), I had more freedom there. My case manager helped me to get my own place. It's not much, just one room, but it's mine." Having a place to be and become is important for us all.

Each of these principles serves to guide and direct strengths-based, person-centered helping. By identifying and honoring individual aspirations, skills, resiliency, resourcefulness, and potential for growth, we gain a fuller picture of the person. As Sir William Osler, pioneering physician once said, "it is more important to know what sort of patient has the disease, than it is to know what sort of disease the patient has." By realizing that there is more in our shared experience as human beings that make providers more like participants than different from them, we gain the courage to be warm, caring, empathic, and genuinely affirming of people's own visions (Kisthardt, 1996). In this spirit of connection, we expand the boundaries of "therapy" and strive to assist in ways that are "therapeutic." When this happens, both provider and participant come away from the process enriched, fulfilled, and gratified. One participant became tearful as he shared his experience with his provider:

> He's like a brother to me. I know he care (sic) about me. He checks on me, comes to my place, makes sure I get my medicine . . . he send me a card at Christmas. I never got a card at Christmas . . . it meant so much. . . . I showed it to my mom. I'm gonna keep the card forever . . . Tom's (provider) gone now, but I'll never forget him.

A strengths-based practitioner understands that people we work with make decisions. The essence of helping is to help people bolster their internal and external resources so that more choices may be available to them. We strive, through the collaborative partnership and caring relationship, to influence decision making that may lead to healthier, more satisfying lives. We recognize that the first meetings play an important role in whether people choose to work with us. My research on the service participant perspective regarding the factors that promote effective engagement suggests the following strategies.

STRATEGIES THAT PROMOTE EFFECTIVE ENGAGEMENT FROM THE PERSPECTIVE OF THE SERVICE PARTICIPANT

We are now well into the era of "targeted populations." For example, people with the coexisting disorders of mental illness and substance abuse, people who are receiving TANF (Temporary Assistance for Needy Families), people with developmental disabilities, people who are homeless, people who have been diagnosed with HIV/AIDS, or people who are mandated to receive services by order of the correctional system may become the focus of helping efforts. Engaging these individuals, who are confronted with many challenges, not the least of which are related to poverty and structural discrimination, is not an easy task.

By talking to people who receive services as well as to experienced community care providers across the country, the following strategies appear to contribute to effectively engaging people in the helping process. I will use examples from work with many different populations. These experiences were shared during time I spent at different service agencies providing training and technical assistance in the strengths model.

Focus more on conversational skills than interviewing skills

Service participants seem to respond more fully to providers who come across as real people. It is not possible to have a conversation with another person if I am not willing to self-disclose. I have heard from many providers who share that they have been trained not to self-disclose to a patient, client, etc., and indeed, that many of their programs have policies that prohibit such activity. Despite this reality, many seasoned providers have learned that they will get much more information if they are willing to share personal information that is timely, relevant, and designed to foster trust and collaboration. The following example from a training session I conducted for the staff at the Department of Corrections in Kansas illustrates this point:

> After an exercise where the people at the training were asked to spend a few minutes with a colleague identifying as many things as they could that they had in common, we reconvened. One of the uniformed corrections officers (complete with standard issue sidearm neatly holstered by his side) stood up and said, "if you are asking us to do this type of thing with prisoners, we would be in direct violation of the Department of Corrections Policy and Procedures Manual, which clearly states, "at no time disclose personal information to any of the inmates." After I thanked him for sharing this information, I said, "now, given that reality, may I ask if you have ever shared something about yourself with an inmate?" He hesitated, and then said "yes, I have." I then asked all of the other uniformed officers in the room if they had ever self-disclosed in their interactions with inmates. All of their hands went up. Our discussion then centered on how they made decisions regarding what specifically might be shared, under what circumstances, and to whom. One officer summarized our discussion by saying "we're much less likely to have trouble with inmates if we treat them with respect, like human beings, and to affirm that we may have common interests as human beings."

Send a clear message that you are not there to make negative judgments, to try to change them, but rather to affirm their own aspirations and work together toward making those dreams a reality

This is accomplished by integrating questions from a Person-Centered Strengths Assessment right from the start of the work (see Figure 3.2). This process seeks to identify what people want in their lives, before identifying what they need in their lives from your perspective. The shift from focusing on what someone else thinks the person needs to the person's own motivation (what he or she really wants) seems to be an essential component of effective engagement. The following example from a case manager working with a person with coexisting disorders clearly illustrates this shift. He shared this with me six months after going through the strengths perspective training at his agency.

**FIGURE 3.2   Strengths-Based, Person-Centered, Assessment Relating to Decision
to Use Substances**

Participant: _____ I.D.: _____

Date: _____ Primary Counselor/Therapist/CM: _____

Gender: _____ M _____ F   D.O.B.: _____ Years since initial diagnosis: _____

Number of previous admissions for substance abuse treatment: _____

Highest grade completed in school: _____

Previous involvment with the criminal justice system: _____ Y _____ N

In your own words, describe the circumstances leading to your being here at this time.
(use back if necessary)

What is your drug of choice? What is it about this substance that most appeals to you?

When you reflect upon your use of substances, what are the things that motivate you to decide
to use?

Describe your patterns of use . . . for example, what time of day, alone or with others, at a bar, at
home, or somewhere else in the community, etc.

What happens to your mood and behavior when you use?

Why have you decided not to stop using before now?

What are the things that you do in your life that help you feel good about yourself and happy that do not involve the use of substances?

What would you stand to gain if you decide to stop using?

What do you stand to lose if you stop using?

Who are the most important people in you life?

What are the three most important material possessions in your life?

What are the things you are most afraid will happen if you stop using?

What are the things you are most afraid will continue to happen if you continue to use?

What are the three things that are most important for someone to know about you in order to better assist you in getting what you want and need in your life?

(continued)

FIGURE 3.2   Continued

What are the three barriers or obstacles that must be overcome for you to achieve your goal of daily sobriety?

Please add any other information that you believe is important in better understanding you and you situation.

> I started working with a guy who had a long history of mental illness and substance abuse. At our first meeting I asked him if he was still drinking, and he said "occasionally." I asked him if he would be willing to accept a referral for in-patient detox after which we could start working on some other things in his life. He said, "I can handle it, I don't have a problem with it." My first thought was that he was clearly in denial. I then thought about shifting the focus and I said, "OK, you don't want to work on that and you don't think you need to, what is it that you do want?" He said, "I want my own apartment." I asked him to write that goal on the top of the personal wellness plan. He did. Then we talked more specifically about finances, location, etc. I agreed to meet him the following week to begin to develop the plan to achieve this goal. I then said, "OK, our meeting is at 11 a.m. You need to know that I will be sober when I get there. I also expect you to be sober, because this is your goal, not my goal, and if you really want it you have got to make some important decisions about your drinking. If you have been drinking before I get there, I'm going to leave." He agreed. When I showed up, he was ready and indeed had not been drinking. This was the first time in a long time that he had not taken a drink before noon. The weeks went by and he worked hard to complete the short-term goals related to getting an apartment. When he moved in, he was so proud and said he had never really had his own place. I said, "if you want to keep it, you might think about watching how much you drink." It would have been better, I believe, if he would not be drinking at all and working on sobriety. This however, was not his goal yet. He has been in the apartment for three months and seems to be doing well. He reports that he is still taking a drink every now and then, but that he has "really cut down, because I don't want to get sick again and lose this great apartment."

Engage in activities you both enjoy

Providers who work with children have known for years how important it is to get on the floor with kids and engage through games and activities that the children enjoy and that make them comfortable. What happens to that strategy when we are working with adults? Why is it sometimes considered "unprofessional" or even "unethical" to engage in activities with a participant that are enjoyable, while at the same time doing an assessment, getting ideas for possible helping plans, monitoring and evaluating their progress, etc.? When we ask people where they would like to meet, if they would like to walk while we talk, if they would like to throw a ball back and forth while we get to know each other, these are truly examples of starting where the client is. The following vignette, shared by an income maintenance case manager/advocate from Kansas City, is still the best example I have heard of creative use of self in an effort to engage an assertively reluctant participant.

> A case manager was working with a program to attempt to engage with noncustodial fathers (The Futures Connection) throughout the city. Each time the case manager found this particular gentleman, he was not willing to talk at any length and would not remain very long. The case manager sometimes spent hours just trying to find him, and often he did locate him at the neighborhood basketball court, where he was known for his skill. The case manager then got an idea. He told the man that he had a proposition for him. They would play one-on-one to 21 points. If the participant won, the case manager would "not bother him" any more. But, if the case manager won, the participant would become involved in the program. The person agreed. The case manager won the game! The participant, bound now by the agreement made on the basketball court, was true to his word and became involved in skill training, job readiness, and case management. When the participant completed the program, he got a full-time job, with benefits, driving a Pepsi truck and making $14.00 per hour. He had re-established contact with his children, and was regular in his child support payments to their mother.

Be sensitive to cultural factors . . . honor diversity and seek to assist people in involvements that hold meaning for them

The strengths approach, by its very nature, attempts to be sensitive to the importance of culture in people's lives. A strengths-based practitioner is like an ethnographer. The goal is to learn about one's lived experience, meaning, and future visions that hold meaning and value (Anderson & Carter, 2003). When we gain an appreciation for a worldview that is different from ours, we will join people in generating plans that reflect outcomes that resonate on multiple levels. The following example shows the power of culturally sensitive engagement.

> A social worker who was a case manager at a community support program for people with persistent mental illness was attempting to engage with a young man by doing outreach in Lawrence, Kansas. During the first few visits the case manager's agenda was to influence the young man to come into the mental health center for intake, evaluation, and to become involved for "socialization" at the partial hospital program. The young man was cordial and polite, but refused to go to the center. As the case manager grew to know him better, they talked of his Native American roots. They talked of things he had done in the past related to the culture of his people. He shared that he used to get much from attending sweat lodge ceremonies. The case manager then got the idea of connecting him with some people at the Haskell Indian School located in Lawrence. He said he would agree to this plan. They both went to meet some students at the school, and he quickly became involved in a regular sweat ceremony. He also eventually became more involved with the services the mental health center had to offer.

Seek to incorporate humor, joy, and laughter into the helping process

To be sure, many people we attempt to help are in very serious situations and struggle with the harsh realities of poverty, illness, addiction, sadness, and loss. Our field is becoming increasingly aware of the healing power of humor, joy, and laughter. As Sigmund Freud once said, "Like wit and the comic, humor has a liberating element. It is the triumph of narcissism, the ego's victorious assertion of its own vulnerability. It refuses to suffer the slings and arrows of reality" (1905). It is somewhat unfortunate that many service providers equate the presence of humor and laughter in the helping process with being callous, uncaring, heartless, and indifferent. I recently spoke to an emergency room nurse who was written up because her supervisor heard her laughing, and the ER was "no place for laughter."

It seems clear from feedback I have gathered from people on the receiving end of our ministrations that a sense of humor, honesty, and joy are perceived as important characteristics of people who would attempt to help them. And, as one participant shared with me, "this does not mean they try to do a ten-minute monologue to try to make me laugh, and it does not mean that they use humor as a substitute for knowledge, skills, and professionalism."

It seems clear that a strengths perspective dictates that we balance our notions of the "truth" as "experts" in the field with the service participants' notion of truth and the meaning they ascribe to their lives. I have a developed a strengths assessment designed to capture the essence of this lived truth. This tool has been utilized in the Kansas project, and the feedback from both providers and participants has been quite positive (see Figure 3.2).

During the engagement process providers gather data and seek to begin documenting the helping/service plan. Many providers are now incorporating the Person-Centered Strengths Assessment and the Personal Wellness Plan in their daily work with participants. The last section of this chapter examines these helping tools in greater detail.

THE PERSON-CENTERED STRENGTHS ASSESSMENT AND PERSONAL WELLNESS PLAN

There are several important points regarding the Person-Centered Assessment in Figure 3.2. First, this assessment was completed by the service participant, not the provider. It is recorded in the first person and written using language and with a perspective that provides a window to the soul. It opens up multiple avenues in the helping dialogue. Second, it provides the service participant with an active and leading role in the helping partnership. The information that is shared on this tool leads to creative and individualized plans as reflected on the Personal Wellness/Recovery Plan (see Figure 3.3). Staff reported that once this individual recorded this information and it was shared and discussed with her team, the helping process proceeded in a very different manner than it had in the past. She was included in all clinical meetings where in the past she had been excluded. They began to work on specific goals with the agency also contracted by the state to work on reunification with her children, which provided to be her primary motivation. Finally, the staff began to focus on preparing her for employment by assisting in updating her resume, obtaining references from prior employers, and working with a counselor who had been certified to provide strengths-based, person-centered case management so that she could begin the interviewing process while still in

FIGURE 3.3   Person-Centered/Community-Based Wellness/Recovery Plan

Participant: _____ Therapist/CM: _____

Participant's aspiration: (motivation . . . may be concrete or abstract)

Intermediate concrete goal related to aspiration: (three to six months time-frame)

Short-term goals: (What NEEDS to get done to accomplish the above)

Goal/Task/Objective: **Target Date—Date Achieved**

_____   _____   _____

        PARTICIPANT   PROVIDER   SUPPORT PERSON

residential treatment. In the past, these activities were not considered to be a part of treatment but rather as a part of reintegration and aftercare.

    1. *Both documents must reflect the dynamic nature of the helping process.* Many programs have become accustomed to writing a treatment plan for a service participant that often is not reviewed until some time in the future. In some programs it is an annual review. Seasoned clinicians know that gathering relevant information (assessment) and working toward goals the service participant has articulated occurs at each and every helping session. Therefore, new information regarding the person's life should be documented as the helping process evolves. Moreover, shifts in the service participant's priorities and incremental gains made toward stated goals should be recorded at each visit. I have suggested that both these tools be used when meeting with the person. Many clinicians do their paperwork after the person has left the office. Providers who have begun to use the person-centered strengths assessment and personal wellness plan at each meeting report that this is an effective strategy to draw the person into the collaborative helping partnership. Some providers have shared that they now complete their progress notes in the presence of the service participant. One provider shared, "this really helps me to be more descriptive and less jargony . . . I also tend to use more strengths-based language . . . rather than stating the client is resistive, manipulative, nonamenable to treatment . . . I will say . . . client continues to have strong feelings about what he wants and needs and has remained steadfast in his decision not to follow through on my recommendations."

2. *These documents are designed to be "user friendly." Therefore, service participants should be encouraged to actually write the information and record the plans.* I have suggested that providers give people a copy of the assessment to take home with them to work on at their own pace. Many providers have reported being "amazed" at how much information people write when they have a chance to take the form with them. I recall an experience I had doing training at a state hospital in Kansas. A patient from one of the wards volunteered to join me in a demonstration of how I would conduct the first meeting using a strengths approach. At the conclusion of our conversation, I showed him a copy of the Person-Centered Strengths Assessment. I pointed out that I had asked him many of the questions during our talk just as they appear on the assessment. I invited him to take the form back to the ward, and I encouraged him to work on it if he felt up to it. I then asked him to consider sharing it with his treatment team next time they met. The following day at the training the group had quite a surprise. The young man had finished the entire assessment and had asked one of the nurses if he could come to the training building again to show me how well he had done. As I shared some of what he'd written, the treatment team was quite impressed by the fact that he was able to concentrate for this period of time and that he had recorded meaningful information that was not included on their diagnostic, problems-based intake assessment.

3. *These documents honor and document the person's wants, desires, and aspirations first. Once this data has been gathered, the needs are discussed and negotiated in the helping process.* As you can see as you examine the strengths assessment, it does not focus on what someone needs from another person's perspective. It focuses on what people have going for them now, what they *want* in the future (some people write, "I want to keep things just the way they are"), and what people have accomplished in the past. The areas of people's lives, or life domains, provide a holistic, comprehensive picture of person and environment. If the person is not able to write, I encourage the provider to record responses in the person's presence, using his or her own words. If the person is not able to talk, I have encouraged providers to record observations in each of these areas, as people will tend to gravitate to activities that are enjoyable or pleasant for them.

One of the most frequently noted barriers to using a strengths approach, especially in work with people who suffer from neurological impairments or other developmental disabilities, is the question of safety. The following example from a workshop I provided in Indiana illustrates how we can negotiate with people around this concern once we have affirmed their agenda and motivation.

> A 27-year-old woman with a developmental disability agreed to work with me to demonstrate the strengths approach in front of over fifty of the staff as well as her mother (her legal guardian) who attended the training. I asked her what she really liked to do during the day. Before she answered, she slowly looked around the room, smiled, and then said with some conviction "I like to go to Scott's grocery store." I heard a bit of rumbling in the room and bits of comments shared between the staff in the room. I then invited her to write that down on the assessment. The rumbling grew a bit louder. She agreed, and I gave her the letters and she wrote them on the assessment. She talked about how she likes the people at Scott's, how they make her laugh, and how she buys Twinkies. She then said, "I take the Twinkies back to my room, and eat them before my program manager gets there!" Now the group was laughing loudly. As I learned in processing this encounter, the staff was actually trying to keep her from going to Scott's through a contingency management plan. They thought it was not safe, and they were concerned that she was overweight and they knew she liked to get Twinkies. What took place was rethinking her plan, and making a deal with her that they would not try to stop her from going to Scott's if she agreed to buy one Twinkie, not three, and to buy one apple. She happily agreed to this plan. I heard from the staff at this program some months later that they were working on helping her to get a part-time job at Scott's as she was unhappy at the sheltered workshop and shared that she wanted a "real job."

CONCLUSION

This chapter has briefly examined a statement of purpose, six principles, and practical tools to aid in the integration of a strengths perspective in interpersonal helping. Concepts such as normal interdependence, personal autonomy, personal freedom, citizenship, account-ability, reciprocity, community resources, the fundamental difference between what we want in our lives versus what we truly need in our lives, negotiated plans, partnership, collabo-ration, and mutual enrichment (provider and service participant) become essential to con-sider as we become more strengths based and person centered. For some providers, this process entails some profound shifts in perspective and practice. For others, however, these notions have served as a welcome affirmation of beliefs and helping activities that have long been integral components of their community-based helping efforts.

Policymakers and funders are challenging providers to integrate and coordinate their services on behalf of people who are involved with multiple systems. People are frequently involved with corrections, addictions, mental health, social welfare (TANF), etc. The strengths perspective has been suggested as a philosophical and conceptual bridge that may serve to span systems. I was involved with a recent yearlong SAMHSA study in Oklahoma that demonstrated that providers from different and often disparate theoretical perspectives can achieve consensus on a common purpose and set of practice principles. The growing research and anecdotal evidence suggests that further refinement, development, and evaluation of a strengths-based model is indicated. If service participants are welcomed as key informants and legitimate stakeholders in this enterprise, we will generate deeper and more valuable knowledge.

One of the most common concerns I have heard regarding strengths-based, person-centered practice is that of safety and potential liability. Providers and agency administrators often express a fear that affirming a goal that engenders some risk for the participant may leave them open to litigation should some harm or injury take place during the helping process. Concepts such as informed consent, inclusion of guardians, wraparound services, incremental short-term goal attainment, risk assessment and risk management, harm reduction, experiential learning, and individual guarantees and rights under the Constitution all need to be continuously explored and considered as we engage more fully in person-directed, strengths-based helping approaches.

We will be challenged to continue to gather data from multiple sources through research, both qualitative and quantitative methods, that provide evidence regarding the effectiveness of innovative, creative, strengths-based models. As practitioners we must continue to view ourselves as researchers, and every helping situation represents the opportunity to contribute to the knowledge base of the profession. Some may design large experimental studies with random assignment to determine effectiveness. Others may use strengths assessments and personal wellness plans from one helping situation to contribute to our understanding of the helping process. We must also never discount each service participants' own perspective as a contributing expert in striving to more fully understand what works and what does not (Brun & Rapp, 2001; Kisthardt, 1993).

We must continue to work with and educate funders who may tend to operate from a medically oriented treatment paradigm about the nature of strengths-based work and the rationale behind a broader range of creative community based initiatives. Current trends suggest the importance of tying funding to performance and outcomes rather than funding provision of services. If this is to be accomplished, all stakeholders must share a common vision regarding the goals and principles that guide and direct our helping efforts. Toward this end more counties are developing cross training, where all levels of the system gather to engage in a conversation regarding their desires for people with disabilities and how best to maximize resources to provide services in a more integrated, efficient, and effective manner. For example, at a recent training on strengths-based, person-centered practice in Indiana, in attendance were mental health case managers, vocational rehabilitation counselors, probation officers, the chief of police, substance abuse counselors, family members, service participants, teachers and school principals, therapists, and state planners. I have had similar experiences in Florida, Iowa, North Carolina, and Oklahoma. True integration can only take place when different systems come together and engage in critical dialogue and come to some consensus regarding outcomes and value-based concepts related to services and treatment.

This chapter has attempted to identify and clarify some key concepts related to strengths-based, person-centered practice. This discussion has certainly not been exhaustive. My hope is that your reading has generated thoughts and feelings regarding your work with people and how you respond to each unique person and situation. Consider the following poem from my book *You Validate My Visions: Poetic Reflections of Helping, Healing, Caring and Loving* (1996) and the questions for discussion that follow.

WHAT IS PERSON CENTERED?

What is "person centered"? an important question today.
As we strive to help another, as she travels on her way.
As we try to know the spirit that makes people what they are.
As we encourage one, whose arms are weary, to reach for one more star,
Person-centered is seeing beyond labels which have been worn.
A person is more than symptoms, and the problems he has born.
A person cannot be fully understood, by calling her a name.
Schizophrenic, Borderline, or Bi-Polar . . . people are not the same.
To be person-centered is a challenge; it is not an easy task.
The nature of our sharing, the questions that we ask.
What are your gifts? What are your joys? What holds meaning on your quest?
What are your dreams? What makes life real? What is it you request?
A person is a producer, a person also consumes.
A person may have more potential than prognosis may assume.
A person is entitled to express his own opinion,
Without fear of reprisals, when another holds dominion.
A person has the right to fail, as she risks something new,
Without another telling her "that goal is unrealistic for you."
A person is a fluid being, ever changing, ever free.
A person makes his own decisions, though others may disagree.
A person is a spirit, whose energy is divine.
A person is a work of art, that the brushes of life refine.
More than a "stage," more than a "phase," more than "old" or "young."
More like a song, drifting on the wind, both singer, and that which is sung.
A person may make plans one minute, and then decide to change them.
A person may order things a certain way, then turn, and rearrange them.
A person may not grasp some things, while with others, they are clever.
A person is the moment . . . a person is forever.
Person centered is being grateful, for the gifts that others share.
Person centered is valuing the opportunity to care.
Person centered is cherishing the wonder of each being.
Person centered is joyful, it is enriching, and it is freeing.

DISCUSSION QUESTIONS/EXERCISES

1. Consider the assessments used at your agency. To what extent are they oriented toward the interests, desires, talents, skills, and knowledge of each person? If you only had five questions to ask someone as you begin work with him or her, what would you ask?

2. Examine the policies of your agency. In what ways do you think these policies promote strengths-based, person-centered work? For example, is there a policy that workers cannot accept gifts from clients. What if a part of that person's culture is to share something with another who helps them, and she bakes a loaf of bread for you? What if the client invites you to his home to share a meal? How do we respond? Why?

3. Identify strategies your agency has in place currently to meet regularly with providers from other systems who are also involved with people your agency is working with. To what extent has service integration occurred?

4. You are sitting in your office and the service participant states that she would rather meet outside at a picnic table to talk about her situation as she does not like closed spaces. How do you respond? Why? How is your response "person-centered"?

5. Listen and observe a staff meeting where a person or family's situation is being discussed. To what extent is the conversation balanced between problems, deficits, needs, and person-centered goals, skills, accomplishments, etc.?

6. What does power-sharing mean to you? In a small group share examples of times when you have not been in a power-sharing relationship and times when you have been. Discuss the difference.

REFERENCES

Anderson, J. & Carter, R. W. (2003). *Diversity perspectives in social work practice.* Boston: Allyn and Bacon.

Bentley, K. J. (Ed.). (2002). *Social work practice in mental health care.* Pacific Grove, CA: Brooks/Cole.

Breton, M. (1994). On the meaning of empowerment and empowerment-oriented social work practice. *Social Work with Groups, 17,* 23–37.

Brun, C. & Rapp, R. C. (2001, July). Strengths-based case management: Individuals' perspectives on strengths and the case manager relationship. *Social Work, 46* (3), 278–288.

Capra, F. C. (1996). *The web of life.* New York: Doubleday.

Derezotes, D. S. (2000). *Advanced generalist social work practice.* Thousand Oaks, CA: Sage.

Finn, J. & Jacobson, M. (2003). *Just practice: A social justice approach to social work.* Peosta, IA: Eddie Bowers Publishing.

Foucault, M. (1980). *Power/knowledge: Selected interviews and other writings.* (C. Gordon, ed.) New York: Pantheon Books.

Freud, S. (1905). *Jokes and their relation to the unconscious.* (J. Strachey, trans.) New York: Norton. (Original work published 1960)

Friere, P. (1994). *The pedagogy of the oppressed* (rev. ed.). New York: Continuum.

Glicken, M. D. (2004). *Using the strengths perspective in social work practice.* Boston: Allyn and Bacon.

Hepworth, D. H., Rooney, R. H., & Larsen, J. A. (2002). *Direct social work practice: Theory and skills* (6th ed.). Pacific Grove, CA: Brooks/Cole.

Kisthardt, W. E. (1993). An empowerment agenda for case management research: Evaluating the strengths model from the consumers' perspective. In M. Harris & H. Bergman (Eds.), *Case management: Theory and practice* (pp. 165–182). Langhorn, PA: Harwood Academic Publisher.

Kisthardt, W. E. (1996). *You validate my visions: Poetic reflections on helping, healing, caring, and loving.* Kansas City, MO: Author.

Kisthardt, W. E. (2002). The strengths perspective in interpersonal helping. In D. Saleebey (Ed.), *The strengths perspective in social work practice* (3rd ed., pp. 163–185). Boston: Allyn & Bacon.

Krogsrud-Miley, K., O'Melia, M., & Dubois, B. (2004). *Generalist social work practice: An empowering approach* (4th ed). Boston: Allyn & Bacon.

Maguire, L. (2002). *Clinical social work: Beyond generalist practice with individuals, families, and groups.* Pacific Grove, CA: Brooks/Cole.

Mattaini, M. A. (2001). The foundation of social work practice. In H. Briggs & K. Corcoran, (Eds.), *Social work practice* (pp. 15–35). Chicago, IL: Lyceum Books.

Mead, G. H. (1934). *Mind, self, and society.* (C. W. Morris, ed.) Chicago, IL: University of Chicago Press.

Miller, W. R., & Rollnick, S. (2002). *Motivational interviewing: Preparing people to change addictive behavior* (2nd ed). New York: Guilford.

Prochaska, J. O., DiClemente, C. C., & Norcross, J. C. (1992). In search of how people change: Applications to addictive behaviors. *American Psychologist, 47*(9), 1102–1114.

Pulin, J. (2005). *Strengths-based generalist practice* (2nd ed). Belmont, CA: Brooks/Cole-Thompson Learning.

Ridgeway, P., & Zipple, A. M. (1990). The paradigm shift in residential services: From the linear continuum to supported housing approaches. *Psychosocial Rehabilitation Journal, 13,* 11–31.

Shafritz, J. M., & Ott, J. S. (1996). *Classics of organizational theory* (5th ed). Fort Worth, TX: Harcourt College Publications.

Sullivan, W. P., & Rapp, C. A. (2002). Social workers as case managers. In K. Bentley (Ed.), *Social work practice in mental health* (pp. 180–210). Pacific Grove, CA: Brooks/Cole.

CHAPTER FOUR

CHRONIC ILLNESS
AND TRANSILIENCE ALONG
MY SPIRITUAL PATH

EDWARD R. CANDA

This chapter is a personal account of how I live with a chronic illness, cystic fibrosis (CF), within the context of a spiritual path that transforms and transcends adversity. I hope that readers can adapt what might be of value and learn from my mistakes and peculiarities. Therefore, I will scrutinize my experiences, offer advice, and disclose personal life details. I will attempt to balance the idiosyncrasies of my life with a systematic and rigorous approach to introspection and reflection on results from other studies of health and resilience.

Cystic fibrosis is one of the most common genetically based terminal illnesses in the United States, mainly among those of European descent, occurring in one out of 3,900 live births (Cystic Fibrosis Foundation, 2007; Ellmers & Criddle, 2002). There are about 30,000 people with CF in the United States and about 70,000 worldwide. Until recently, CF was considered a childhood disease because people with CF did not often live into adulthood. However, due to rapid advances in diagnosis and treatments, the median age of survival has risen to 36.8 years, and about 40 percent of people with CF are age 18 or older. The most serious and life-threatening symptoms of CF involve impairment of lung and pancreatic functions. Most people with CF require some combination of daily respiratory clearance therapies, antibiotics (oral, inhalation, or intravenous), vitamin supplements, and digestive pancreatic enzyme supplements. For some people, all of this is necessary from birth. For others, symptoms emerge later. There are more than 1,000 genetic variations of CF, which influence a wide range and course of severity. Perhaps reflecting this dire clinical picture, the social-work-based studies by Coady, Kent, and Davis (1990) and Widerman (2004) emphasized psychosocial difficulties of people with CF and their social workers. Since CF is a treatable but incurable and terminal chronic illness, usually requiring a heavy daily treatment regimen, it is pertinent to strengths-oriented research to explore how people with CF cope, hope, survive, and thrive in the face of adversity. Several studies have shown that adults with CF have a similar level of psychosocial functioning or mental health as the general population (Abbott, 2003; deJong et al., 1997; Shepherd et al., 1990). As Abbott said, "People with CF demonstrate a remarkable psychological resilience" (p. 45).

There are a few reasons that persuade me that there might be something to learn from my experience. Through my studies to be explained below, I realized that while I shared many attributes with other adults with CF for whom spirituality is important, I am also rather unusual. Unlike many other adults with CF, I rarely have hospitalizations or debilitating health crises, my symptoms are relatively moderate, and I employ an extensive number and variety of spiritually based practices that support (in my view) a resilient response to the challenges of CF. I am now 53 years old and thriving in my personal life and profession. When I was born, the median age of survival for a person with CF was about 5 years. My older brother Tom died of complications related to CF when he was 41 years old. I have often asked myself, and others have often asked of me, "Why am I still surviving and thriving? Do my spiritual activities and way of life contribute to this?"

Of course, I cannot answer that definitively based on my limited experience and self-reflection. My subjective impression is that my spiritual way of life is central to my well-being, including the practical physical aspects of health and overall sense of life satisfaction. Further, the body of empirical research on spirituality and health suggests that spiritual practices likely contribute to resilience (e.g., Koenig, McCullough, & Larson, 2001). However, there is very little available information about the details of how and why this may work from the standpoint of people with CF. Even qualitative studies tend to give only brief snippets of individuals' experiences.

So in this chapter I will provide a brief summary of related research on spirituality, health, and resilience, including my own studies, in order to set a context for my personal account. Then I will present a detailed introspective account. Finally, I will offer some considerations of how my story might be relevant to other people with chronic illness and the social workers, researchers, and other helping professionals who work with us.

SETTING THE CONTEXT

In the past twenty-five years, in North America, the topic of spirituality has emerged from near complete neglect in social work, counseling, medicine, nursing, and related helping professions to become much more widely discussed, debated, researched, and taught (e.g., Canda, 2005; Graham, 2006, Koenig, 2007; Miller, 2003, O'Brien, 2003). In particular, hundreds of studies pertaining to health and mental health show that a strong sense of life meaning and purpose as well as participation in religious communities and use of spiritually based healing activities, such as prayer and meditation, tend to be associated with higher levels of self-reported well-being; lower levels of depression and anxiety; lower frequency of suicide, substance abuse, and family violence; faster recovery from illness or surgery; better mental health recovery; and greater longevity (Fallot, 1998; Koenig et al., 2001; Sidell, 1997; Van Hook, Hugen, & Aguilar, 2001). Literature on positive coping, resilience, and strengths make the general point that spirituality and religion can serve as important sources of inner and outer supports for people dealing with adversity and illness (Dunbar, Mueller, Medina, & Wolf, 1998; Hawks, Hull, Thalman, & Richins, 1995; Snyder & Lopez, 2007; Young & McNicoll, 1998).

Controversies remain over the rigor of research methodologies, contrary evidence, the difficulty of operationalizing spirituality and religion for research purposes, applying spiritually based approaches to helping in social work and healthcare settings, and the possibility of harmful effects of religious practices and beliefs (Canda & Furman, 1999; Powell, Shahabi, & Thoreson, 2003; Sloan, Bagiella, & Powell, 1999; Sloan, Bagiella, VandeCreek, & Hover, 2000; Thyer & Walton, 2007). Yet it is clear that spirituality (in both religious and nonreligious forms) is regarded by many people in the general population, as well as by some helping professionals and researchers, as a major source of resilience and strength. A spiritual search for meaning, life purpose, and moral ways of relating with the world, including engagement in religious communities' practices and beliefs, can assist resilient response to illness and adversity through an enhanced sense of understanding, greater encouragement, more consistent self-care, logistical and social support from family and friends, and the sense of support from sacred or transpersonal beings and forces (such as God, Buddhas and Bodhisattvas, angels, ancestors, helping spirits, and vital energies like qi or kundalini).

Several quantitative and qualitative studies of spirituality in relation to people with CF show that positive spiritual and religious coping can be significant in encouraging adherence to medical treatments, promotion of hope, and supporting psychological well-being (Abbott, 2003; Abbott, Dodd, Gee, & Webb, 2001; Burker, Evon, Sedway, & Egan, 2004; Gee, Abbott, Conway, Etherington, & Webb, 2000; McNeal, 2002). A qualitative exploration of religious/spiritual coping among twenty-three children with CF revealed eleven strategies of coping, such as demands or requests for God's help, belief in God's support and intervention, finding support through prayer and religious community participation, or discontent with God and congregations, sense of God as punisher, and belief that God is irrelevant (Pendleton, Cavalli, Pargament, & Nasr, 2002). In general, these studies suggest that positive appraisals of God's involvement in one's life; sense of social support from religious participation; sense of hope, purpose, and meaning in life; and feeling that medical providers and medicines are congruent with their spirituality tend to be associated with psychological well-being and treatment compliance. Widerman (2006) recommends that people with CF should assess the effectiveness of their coping approaches, including spirituality, and that social workers and other mental health professionals may be able to assist this process.

My own studies of spirituality as a source of resilient response to the chronic illness of CF gave vivid examples. I co-authored a quantitative survey report that included all 402 patients of all ages at a major CF treatment center to explore to what extent patients utilized nonmedically prescribed treatments (Stern, Canda, & Doershuk, 1992). We found that about 60 percent of patients or their guardians reported patients using spiritually based healing activities such as group prayer, faith healing, use of religious objects (such as a medal), pilgrimage, meditation, and others. Most respondents reported benefits such as amelioration of symptoms and providing feelings of care and support. No injuries or significant costs were reported. However, this study was not able to measure effects of these activities or to inquire deeply into the participants' specific spiritual practices, their meanings, and life contexts.

In order to explore the latter, I followed up with individual interviews of sixteen adult participants from the original survey who had demonstrated a high level of interest in their faith (Canda, 2001, 2006). This study revealed that these adults viewed having CF as a challenge that can be infused with a sense of life meaning and purpose and that can be met well through diligent use of medical and spiritually based healing practices with the loving support of family, friends, and sacred sources of strength. All of these participants viewed their lives as spiritual developmental processes that involved searching for a sense of meaning and purpose regarding having CF, drawing on various religiously and nonreligiously based spiritual activities for healing, and connecting with sacred sources of healing and helping power (e.g., God, Jesus, angels, nature, and healthcare providers as conduits for divine help). These observations were further amplified by a review of autobiographical accounts of people with CF and checking of findings with others through online discussion groups for people with CF. McDonough's (2002) essays on creative and spiritually attuned ways of living with CF were especially helpful.

In order to develop this chapter, I have gone through an extensive, lengthy, and systematic process of reflection and introspection. My survey and interview studies above included my involvement as both researcher and interviewee participant, which were developed, implemented, and reported over a period of about fifteen years. Further, in preparation for the current writing, I re-examined the fifty-nine single-spaced pages of the transcript from my interviews of 1996, with the advantage of eleven years of hindsight and some emotional distance, and with special attention to my account of the spiritually based activities and way of life that I said contributed to my resilient response to CF. The transcript was based on two interviews with me (total about 4 hours) conducted by a research assistant whom I trained in the use of my interview guide. My current reflection on that transcript reminded me how that original interview was like a snapshot of my self-description at one point in time. So I approached my reflection on the transcript with five questions:

1. What were the spiritual practices and qualities that were important to me then?
2. To what extent are these relevant to me today (2007) and what should I add to expand insights based on eleven years of additional experience?
3. Given these reflections, what lessons have I learned that might be of use to others?
4. What is peculiar or idiosyncratic about my spiritual approach and life situation that would limit relevance to others with CF and other chronic illnesses?
5. Considering my experiences in the light of other studies, what are some implications for social work?

The sequence of my studies on CF and spirituality started with a broad view survey, including many people but with few details, then went into greater depth and detail about sixteen people's self-portrayals, and now focuses down onto one of these people, myself. This systematic process of inquiry and introspection has intersected with my ongoing spontaneous and informal introspections that began when I was diagnosed as having CF at the age of 18.

In order to answer question 1 above, I will present a summary of the opinions and insights from my transcript of eleven years ago that illustrates my ways of utilizing spirituality for resilient response to the challenges of CF, according to two themes: my understandings of spirituality and the nature of explicit spiritually based activities that support my well-being. In response to question 2, for each of these themes, I will reflect on current relevance and lessons learned over time. I will also consider pertinent issues related to questions 3 and 4. Accordingly, in the following section, I will present my views on each theme with summaries and quotes from the original transcript, followed by current reflections. In the implications section, I will respond more extensively to questions 3 and 4 in connection with question 5.

CHRONIC ILLNESS AND MY SPIRITUAL PATH

The Meaning of Spirituality

In the transcript, I defined spirituality consistently with the formal definitions I have developed for social work, based on the insights of many other scholars (Canda, 1988; Canda & Furman, 1999). I said that, in a narrow sense, spirituality is an intrinsic aspect of all human beings that involves a search for a sense of meaning, purpose, and moral standards for relating with ourselves, other people, and the rest of the universe. This is complementary to the physical/biological, mental, and social aspects of a person, and it gives meaning to them. In a holistic sense, spirituality is the totality of the person that cannot be reduced to any name, role, or function. It sets the context of all our aspects and helps bring them to completion. I added that spiritual traditions often recognize the mysterious aspect and wholeness of the person by positing a soul, spirit, or irreducible consciousness.

I defined religion as institutionalized patterns of belief, behavior, and ritual that have a basic concern with spirituality and are shared by a community over time. Spirituality can be expressed through religious forms or not. For me, spirituality was expressed through my affiliations with the Roman Catholic Church (especially the contemplative and social justice aspects) in which I was raised, with Zen Buddhist meditation practice that I learned as an adult, and through my studies and experiences in Confucian, Taoist, shamanistic, and other religious systems. For me, all of these religious involvements were compatible; they offered insights and spiritually based healing practices helpful to dealing with CF.

Faith was for me a concept related closely to spirituality and religion. I said that faith involves one's fundamental beliefs, commitments, convictions, and understandings that relate to the nature of reality. Formation of my faith includes sensory experiences, critical reasoning, and scientific evidence. But there is also a mystical aspect of my faith that passes beyond ordinary rational understanding. I said that, for me, mature and authentic faith needs to be based on many kinds of experiences. It should not be based simply on uncritical acceptance of hand-me-down religious conventions. "Authentic faith to me means something I develop through a very persevering, continuous process of self reflection and reflection on the world that searches out the meaning of my life, my purpose, and the nature of reality." I described faith as a dynamic process of ". . . direct experiential searching for the divine, for ultimate reality, and the nature of oneself, and not to accept anybody's answers for that."

My experiential approach to spiritual exploration can be illustrated from the transcript by a story of a transpersonal experience and its significance for my life. (See also Canda & Furman, 1999) "Around my sixteenth birthday I was reading the philosophical manuscripts of Karl Marx. . . . I was really impressed with Marx's ideal of the utopian society of justice for everyone, in which there would be no alienation between any person or between people and nature. So one time when I was meditating, I was posing this question to myself: What would it mean to eliminate all forms of alienation or separation? Suddenly my sense of separateness as an ego-bound being disappeared and I felt one with the universe. That was a very powerful, overwhelming experience that opened up my life path. . . . That mystical visionary experience gave me a direct awareness of the ontological condition [of no separateness] and showed me that my life was supposed to be about making the existential level [of people living with separateness and alienation] closer to the ontological."

I explained that this root experience led me into a heightened sense of empathy and compassion, a sensitivity to suffering, and an intention to dedicate my life to service. It also prepared me to realize, once I knew I had CF, that my suffering could be placed within a transformational process of growth. My Catholic upbringing helped give me a model for this. "Like I learned growing up, you can offer up your own suffering along with Christ's suffering. Then, along with his death and resurrection, there's a transformation. Christ's death and resurrection were a gift to everyone. So if I incorporate my suffering into that kind of process, then it's not just me dealing with an illness, but it's me together with everything else moving through challenges and supporting each others' transformation. . . . That's just the ordinary human being job description."

Current reflections.   As I look back on these ideas, it is not surprising that the definitions of spirituality and religion are so close to what I have published for social work professional purposes. Insights from the social work scholars whom I interviewed to develop the definitions made a significant impact on my personal thinking. Further, my previous academic study of religions helped me to pull together these scholars' ideas. These definitions remain relevant and useful to me now.

These definitions have import specific to my personal spiritual path in life and the way I approach the challenges of chronic illness. Ever since early elementary school until now, I have been prone to probe deep questions about life and the nature of reality, to question religious and social conventions, and to search out answers through many cultures, religions, and personal experiences. Both scientific and mystical means of inquiry (such as meditation, prayer, and contemplation) have remained important to me. Naturally, then, it follows that once I was diagnosed as having CF, I would apply the same approach to its challenges. What is the meaning and purpose of CF in my life? What wise insights and healing practices can I learn from diverse spiritual traditions and conventional medicine that can promote my health and well-being? The process of exploring this remains as pertinent as ever for me, and in some ways it becomes more pressing at an age that is considered "middle" for most people but is considered "old" in terms of CF mortality statistics.

My spiritual perspective draws on many philosophies, scientific studies, and religious traditions in a continuous quest. Some people, religious and nonreligious, might not be comfortable with my approach to spirituality and health, given its predication on an unusually intense and varied spiritual propensity. So it is important to emphasize that I do not wish to impose it on others. I only hope that my example might suggest possibilities and that each person find a way that best suits her or his life perspective and commitments.

Like all the other interviewees in my study, transpersonal experiences of intimate connection with God, angels, nature, and healing energies gave me affirmations, insights, and a vivid sense of support by sacred beings and forces (Canda, 2001). For some of the participants, this was mainly a matter of a profound sense of personal relationship with God. For others, this also included revelatory visions and dreams and other intense peak experiences. For all of us, the transpersonal experiences intensified and deepened our lives. They fueled our motivations for promoting the well-being of ourselves and others. As I look back over the years, this seems a very important point. If a person's spiritual beliefs are merely a matter of superficial conformity, unexamined assumptions, or ideas stuck in one's head, they may not be able to meet the test of adversity and /or to respond to the serious questions about the nature of suffering and mortality that frequently arise with chronic illness.

Spiritually Based Healing Practices

According to the transcript, by spiritually based, I meant that the healing practices were tied explicitly to my sense of life meaning and purpose and often derived from various religious traditions. But as will become clear, I view my entire life as a "spiritually based activity," that is, an intentional movement along a spiritual path of well-being and well-becoming. In order to make this vivid, I will summarize the range of activities I employed along with some examples.

I explained that I frequently engaged in types of prayer. Following a Catholic contemplative view (Canda, 1990), I distinguished forms of prayer as petitionary (asking for divine help), devotional (praising or thanking God), reflective scripture reading, silent contemplative prayer or meditation (without attachment to thoughts, images, or feelings while simply abiding in God's loving presence or ongoing mindful awareness of each moment), participating in communal religious activities of prayer and meditation (mostly Catholic and Zen, but also including other varieties, such as invited participation in other religion's rituals), and practicing moment-to-moment clear awareness during ordinary activities throughout the day. I felt that all of these practices helped to alleviate particular symptoms of illness and distress and also to enhance my overall sense of well-being.

I said that I rarely used petitions for divine healing because I wanted to avoid making egoistic demands. However, sometimes during times of stress, I offered a plea for help, open to the will of God. But I did not do this with an expectation of literal cure. It was more a dialogue with God. Usually, when receiving a new batch of prescribed medications or herbal medicines prepared by friends, I would take a moment to give thanks to God and to relate to them as sacred gifts. This relieved a sense of medications as inconvenient artificial intrusions.

I engaged in silent contemplative prayer, meditation, and practicing moment-to-moment clear awareness to some extent nearly every day, usually multiple times. For example, during daily activities such as house chores or business meetings, I often repeated an inner silent mantra (a significant phrase to assist with focusing and clearing awareness). I nearly always kept with me small religiously significant objects (such as Buddhist prayer beads or a Catholic medal) to help remind me to live mindfully. During my daily respiratory therapies, I often used meditation, mindful breathing, or healing visualization techniques to relieve stress and physical strain, to enhance awareness of subtle physical cues, to keep aware of the supportive presence of God, and to enhance therapeutic effects. Most days, while walking on campus, I would be aware of myself placing each step, enjoying each moment, and appreciating the earth and all around me for beauty and support. When I did physical exercise, I tried to do it in a meditative way. Usually at night, I would do mantra practice while falling off to sleep.

Another frequent visualization practice was to relate to water as a healing gift of God's grace. For example, during a morning shower, I would focus on enjoyment of the water flowing over my body, cleansing me physically and spiritually, and waking me to the possibilities of a new day. When I took the first sip of water in the morning, I would hold up the glass and look into the clearness of the water, being grateful for the water upon which all life depends, and looking around at my home with thankfulness for being alive on a new day.

Nearly every week, a friend would visit my home to do foot reflexology treatment for me. In her practice, she meditatively massages points on the feet that are intended to soothe and strengthen corresponding areas of the body. While she did this, I gave myself permission to just relax, to let go of pains, preoccupations, and distractions, and to let myself enjoy repose.

I also organized and maintained a group of friends to meet nearly every month for a session of vigorous, meditative, and energetic group performance with a variety of drums, gongs, rattles, bells, and other percussion instruments. I practiced meditative drumming, sometimes including a drum/dance that I had learned in Korea, at least a few times each week. I felt that this percussion practice strengthened my vital energy, helped to support my over-all physical stamina and immune system resilience, and was simply enjoyable. In addition, friends and family frequently prayed for me, giving me a sense of support. I frequently took herbal medicines that were prepared by an herbalist friend through a process that was respect-ful of the plants as sacred beings and that set an intention for my good health.

Occasionally, I engaged in pilgrimages to places considered to be sacred or to have healing properties in Catholic, Buddhist, Indigenous, or Korean shamanistic traditions, given my good fortune to do extensive international travel. Other occasional practices included spir-itually focused discussions with family and friends about chronic illness; acupuncture based on traditional East Asian medicine; and meditation retreats and practices to deepen a com-fortable awareness of mortality and to prepare for death.

Given all these spiritually based healing activities, a typical day was full of practices designed to yield specific benefits and to support a general sense of well-being and resilience. I incorporated medically prescribed healing activities within a spiritual context of meaning and purpose and complemented them with many nonmedically prescribed spiritually based healing practices.

I emphasized that all of these activities need to be done in a consistent and persistent manner, while varying the details based on the fluctuations of one's situation and spiritual characteristics. "This requires ongoing daily self observation. The problem that I have some-times is just getting tired out of doing these things and then slacking off. . . . So it shouldn't be varying what you do out of laziness or discouragement or procrastination or inconsistency. It should be varying . . . to what is appropriate at the time. . . . If you know how to perform a certain musical piece, once you really know how to do that well, then you can vary it and improvise on it."

I described this daily self observation as a form of mindfulness, based on the Zen tra-dition. "Mindfulness means . . . having a clear awareness of oneself and the situation moment to moment. And out of that clear awareness there is a natural arising of a sense of the spe-cialness and significance of each moment . . . and the natural intent to relate in a compas-sionate manner."

Current reflections.   In retrospect, I notice that the pattern of variety, frequency, and pervasiveness of spiritually based healing activities has not changed until now. The details, though, shift on a daily basis. Over extended time periods some major details change. For example, on a daily basis, the specific activities I use vary according to medical advice and my changing needs, goals, mood, and patience level. Over the course of many years, certain practices waxed and waned. I also learn new activities and try them out for periods. If they work well for me, I continue.

All of these practices take their full significance and effect from their integration within an approach to life as a journey on a spiritual path of continual learning and growth. Every occasion for grief, joy, fun, boredom, inspiration, and challenge becomes an opportunity for stretching beyond one's limits, moving toward fulfillment of one's full potential, nurturing loving relationships, and contributing to the wider good of the world.

For many years now, I usually begin each day, and sometimes also the day's first visit to my office, with a silent prayer of thankfulness and dedication. I stand erect, clear my awareness, and put my palms together. Then in my mind's voice I say, "This day is for you, God, and for the well-being of all." As I say this, I bow with palms together. As I raise myself up, I extend my arms open wide to embrace the world. As I return to erect posture, I bring my hands toward my body until they touch palms down upon my chest, above my heart and lungs. Finally, I bow again. This signifies a full circle of connection and unity between me, all beings, and God within an intention to live for the benefit of all.

An important underlying principle is consistency with flexibility. It strikes me as crucial to my health that I remain consistent in my prescribed medical practices with close to 100 percent compliance. I measure this by self-monitoring, discussions with physicians, results of health status tests (such as lung function), and keeping schedule for prescription renewals. The details of conventional medical practices also fluctuate in response to such things as severity of symptoms, development of antibiotic resistant strains of bacteria, and treatment innovations for CF. All of this presumes that I am proactive in discussions with medical providers, scrutinize their recommendations and explanations, and tailor a healthcare plan to my particular situation. It is also crucial for me to place the medical treatments within a spiritual context and to complement them with a variety of spiritually based healing activities, which themselves fluctuate.

There needs to be a harmony between consistency and flexibility. Too much consistency leads to unhelpful rigidity: Antibiotics stop working; certain spiritual activities are no longer relevant. Some healing activities (such as daily respiratory clearance or digestive enzyme supplements, and daily spiritual practices that feel crucial for one's health and well-being) cannot be interrupted without serious consequences. What any of those crucial activities are would depend on the person.

For example, on the first day of intensive writing for this chapter, I awoke after only 6 hours sleep (rather than my usual 7 or 8), feeling eager and energized to write. Many insights flowed into my mind. In order to meet my deadline and to maximize the sudden spurt of energy for creative writing, I showered and ate quickly, skipped my usual hatha yoga exercise, prayer, and meditation, did my respiratory clearance therapy, and then rushed into writing. During a rest break, I looked outside the bay window to my backyard and was stunned by the rare and beautiful sight of brilliant sunlight shining through a thick web of tree branches covered with gleaming ice. I opened the window to see more clearly. I could hear the many rain-like drops of ice melting off and the cracking of brittle branches. Suddenly, it hit me how lovely and precious was that moment.

That beauty had something to say about this topic. The beauty was present for only a short time. Like life itself, it was literally melting away in the very moment of enjoyment. It could only happen because of an ice storm that covered much of the plains states, causing extensive damage to trees and electric power lines and resulting in some deaths. Yet still the beauty could not be denied. This is like the beauty we can realize by being fully aware and appreciative of each moment, even in the midst of chronic illness.

So my routine was altered that day in many details. If I was not flexible, I would not be able to adjust to the demands and opportunities of a particular day. If I was not consistent in the general themes of approaching life as a continuous journey of learning, I may have missed the beauty of the melting web of ice. And if I go too far off my routine of healthcare practices, my health and well-being decline.

I must alter my routine in much more drastic ways when I do international travel, research, and teaching. Time zones change, and on long trips day and night reverse. Patterns of eating and sleeping change. I may not have easy access to my medications if they need to be replenished. I may be exposed to many kinds of viruses and bacteria as well as stressful situations. This means that I need to plan carefully, establish a good support system in the place to which I am going, and pay extra care and attention to how I adapt my healthcare practices during the travel and upon my return. In this way, I have been able to engage in professional work within many countries around the world.

Learning how to harmonize consistency and flexibility is like tuning a string on a musical instrument. If the string is too tight, it can break. If it is too loose, it has little sound. Within a certain range, we can adjust the exact tightness for the desired pitch.

Another principle that has stood the test of time for me is the importance of mindfulness for keeping this dynamic, flexible, and consistent stance of health promotion (Hahn, 1987; Kabot-Zinn, 1990). For example, I usually monitor my internal body sensations for feelings of hunger or light headedness and fluctuations of energy and stamina. Due to the fact that my pancreas does not produce sufficient enzymes to digest food properly, I must take pancreatic enzyme supplements with every meal. If I am not careful to eat snacks or meals at regular pacing, I can suddenly become weak, disoriented, headachy, and light headed. I have trained myself to be alert to subtle bodily sensations so that I eat on schedule or at the very early signs of hunger. I pay attention to every day's schedule for the timing of meals and opportunities for snacks. I must always remember to bring enough medications for my daily plan. My practice of meditation, contemplation, and mindfulness in religious contexts has helped me to develop this sensitivity, alertness, planning, and fast response to subtle bodily cues.

That does not mean I always succeed. Sometimes when I am distracted by intense work, fun, or prolonged conversations, I miss the cues and feel a sinking. But almost always I am able to recover quickly by a rapid response. Luckily, if I fail in that, usually my wife or a friend will notice and prompt me to eat. Further, if I eat mindfully, I can savor more profoundly the textures, colors, and tastes of food and I can enjoy any dining companionship more richly.

With the practice of mindfulness, I reap not only the practical benefits of health-promoting activities, but also the spiritual benefits of heightened empathic awareness of self and world, joy of life, and gratitude for the sacred gift of each moment. From such a viewpoint, all these healing activities usually seem to flow smoothly and naturally over the course of each day. They add to a sense of life enjoyment and spiritual fulfillment.

I noticed in my transcript that I did not talk enough about how I learn from mistakes on my spiritual path. Since then, learning from life mistakes has become an increasingly important theme for me. Of course, I make mistakes every day, occasionally dangerous and foolish blunders. I have tried to learn over the years how to be gentle and less judgmental with myself for my mistakes, how to improve, and how to make amends with others affected by my mistakes whenever possible. Mistakes that impinge on my health condition often have immediate or eventually obvious harmful consequences, so they actually are great occasions for learning, if I treat them as such. I would like to share one illustrative cautionary tale.

In March 2003, as the U.S.-led invasion of Iraq began, I developed an unexpected health crisis. One of the aims of my spiritual development has been to increase my empathy and sensitivity to human suffering. My own experience of chronic illness and its vicissitudes has impressed on me the need to pay attention to my own and others' distress and to respond helpfully. But if I am not careful, I can let empathy and sensitivity go too far into emotional enmeshment and hypersensitivity. So as the missiles flew and the troops deployed, I had a sharp sense of the destruction and death occurring to the military personnel of the United States and its allies as well as to the Iraqi military and civilians. Further, the earth itself was being ravaged. I became preoccupied with daily news coverage. I knew that I had no direct influence over the situation. The only way I could imagine to help was to watch the news, commiserate with the suffering, express my concerns, and pray for peace. Without realizing it, I linked my own body with the body of the earth and the bodies of the combatants. As I prayed, I inadvertently internalized the mass suffering. The havoc in the world thus injured my own body.

One night, I doubled over with terrible abdominal pain and uncontrollable nausea. I did not connect that to the war at the time. I rushed to the emergency room of the local hospital, where I was diagnosed with acute pancreatitis. Emergency room treatment and pain medication, along with meditation and healing visualizations, brought my nausea and pain under control. The condition shifted into a rare medical condition of very prolonged pancreatitis, with ongoing mild discomfort. This continued for more than two months.

Impairment of the pancreas due to CF certainly predisposed me to pancreatitis. It was not the first or most painful episode, but it was by far the longest. When I reflected on this episode in relation to my overall life context, I realized that the symptoms coincided exactly with the onset and early phase of the war. I realized that my empathetic connection with the suffering of humanity and the earth had become an excessive attachment that tore at my guts. I literally had an excruciatingly painful gut feeling.

Once I realized this, I was able to restore a more balanced awareness and concern that was not overly attached. On a practical level, I had to decide whether to go ahead with a study abroad course, scheduled for late May to mid June, when I would co-lead a group of social work students for three weeks of intensive travel and learning in South Korea. I knew that if I did not go, the students would lose this opportunity.

So, despite continuing symptoms of pancreatitis, I went to Korea with the students. Fortunately, the major change of environment and the pleasure of being in Korea with friends, colleagues, and students helped to break my excessive preoccupation with the war. Then, after several days, we were able to visit one of my favorite places, Horse's Ears Mountain, named after its shape like two giant horse's ears projecting up from the earth. That is a place recognized in Korean shamanistic tradition as having special healing energy. As soon as we arrived and throughout most of a day there, I could feel the nurturing mountain energy flow through my body. I sensed a deep soothing and healing. With each step, healing. With each breath, healing.

During that trip, I remained extra careful to meet all my health needs. The symptoms of pancreatitis disappeared. Even more valuable, I learned a significant lesson in how to keep empathic awareness of others' suffering and to express concern without taking on injury to myself. This experience illustrates how my spiritual approach to a health crisis, and to learning from mistakes, contributed to physical recuperation, spiritual insight, and greater degree of overall well-being.

My account of the importance of constant mindfulness, attention to body conditions, and frequent use of medically and spiritually based healing practices might give the false impression that my life is a constant preoccupation or sense of burden with CF. All the interviewees, including myself, indicated that they did not view their identities or lives simply in terms of CF. Many expressed indignation at helping professionals who view them only in terms of illness symptoms and statistics. Since the interview questions focused on the experience of living with CF, it followed that CF became the point around which all discussion revolved. If I were to tell the story of my life and spiritual path in a spontaneous way, then many situations and experiences would not directly involve CF at all, and CF would be a subsidiary theme that runs through the plot.

While CF is a significant aspect of my life, I seldom think about it during most days. I choose not to be preoccupied with it. I usually limit sharing about my having CF to occasions that might be helpful to others or to answer questions. I find that if I preoccupy with CF, and think of myself primarily in terms of CF, then I feel shrunk down to a fantasy of an illness with stereotypic implications for sickness, disability, and early death. Most of each day, I flow through my personal and professional activities, simply attending to what I need to do, fulfilling my goals and responsibilities. My healthcare practices continue usually with a sense of ordinary routine, like brushing teeth, taking a shower, or going to the restroom. These are the ordinary activities of daily self-care—that is, ordinary to me, even if they might seem otherwise to others. When I have especially difficult symptoms, I must focus attention on more extensive treatments. There are times when I feel discouraged, fatigued, anxious, or overwrought. Then I try to accept the feelings, regard them gently, and let them dissipate. If I do not become upset about being upset, then the upset resets to calm. Even the more difficult times become grist for the mill of spiritual growth work.

In my original interview, I did not emphasize enough the importance of fun and humor in good health. I love to laugh at myself and at the absurdities of life. I enjoy watching utterly pointless comedies. I have great fun telling stories and listening to stories. Many of my spiritually based healing practices are also great fun, such as drumming with my friends. I feel more light, free-flowing, and happy when I can make fun out of life and death. One of my favorite souvenirs is a small figure of death that I purchased in Mexico. Death is portrayed as a stark white skin and bones man, with a toothy grin, shaking two rattles, and wearing a hat in the shape of a happily smiling deer head. Every day I want to have fun, make art and music, or just relax.

I mentioned in the interview that relationships with family and friends have been very important. I am extremely fortunate to have a supportive circle of relatives, friends, and mentors. My wife, Hwi-Ja, is the most consistent and continuous source of support. Our relationship is integral to our spiritual paths and nearly every practical detail of daily life. Together, we have made a home that feels sheltering, nurturing, peaceful, and restorative. We remodeled our house and garden according to East Asian philosophical principles so that yin and yang energy qualities are harmonized, dynamic, and invigorating. Some of my relatives and friends join me in meditation, drumming, religious ceremonies, and stimulating conversations. We share helping for each other as needed and according to our various talents, skills, interests, and beliefs. Spiritual mentors and friends of many cultures and religions have shared advice, techniques, prayers, rituals, and ceremonies for my well-being. In addition, through work that matches my sense of life vocation, I have both intrinsic satisfaction and financial support.

This circle of mutual support extends into the healing embrace of nature, the planet, and the universe as a whole. I am acutely aware of the fact that my existence, like all beings, depends utterly on interconnectedness with all the plants, animals, myriad other creatures, stones, land, water, air, sun, moon, stars, and on and on. All my food and medicines, and my very body, derive from the web of life all around me. The more I am aware of my interbeing with all beings, the more gratitude I feel, the less stuck am I in a false sense of separate ego/body, and the more potent and enjoyable are all my medicines and foods. I experience all that is as an efflorescence of God's love and care and creativity. Words and theological formulae cannot really capture what I mean. It is wonderful to live within the sense of loving embrace of family, friends, all beings, and the divine within and beyond all this! In this context, all I am and do are inextricable from my spiritual path, including dealing with CF.

The participants in my interview study demonstrated that it is possible to grow in well-being even if and as one's physical health declines. For myself, this is because all aspects of life are infused and embraced in my spiritual path. Health resilience is not just a matter of accruing certain activities or supports; it is also a matter of living in a way that enfolds health promotion within an ongoing move toward ever greater wholeness, integrity, and fulfillment in oneself and in relation with all. Then even illness and death are opportunities for growth.

IMPLICATIONS

Caveats

I would like to forestall some possible misunderstandings of my suggestions for implications. In the introduction, I said that I and others have wondered if my spiritual activities and way of life contribute to my relatively good health. While this question is pertinent to study of resilience and strengths, it should not imply that someone's worth, quality of life, or spiritual attainment be measured by degree of physical health. Well-being can include and transcend good physical health. It is also not dependent on good physical health. Chronic illness poses difficulty to achieving well-being, but these same difficulties can be addressed as challenges and learning opportunities. We need a strengths-focused holistic view of social work practice that addresses the challenges of illness and socially imposed disabling barriers within the context of the whole person (Kim & Canda, 2006).

Further, I affirm the inherent dignity and worth of every person, irrespective of physical or other conditions. No one is more or less of a person, or a worthy person, based on health status. On a more cosmic scale, who can even know the whys and wherefores of when someone is healthy, ill, thriving, dying, or all of those at the same time? For example, my late brother Tom and I had intersecting but different life trajectories, purposes, and styles. He was like a path-finder, going ahead of me on the road of living with CF. He said that he hoped I would learn from his experience, including mistakes. In that way, even mistakes transform into good actions for others.

I encourage research and clinical assessment that evaluate the effectiveness of health-related complementary and alternative activities (Casey, 2006), including those that are spiritually based. I concur with Abbott's (2003, pp. 48–49) comment based on a review of studies about coping with CF: "We need to ask which strategies are adaptive/maladaptive for a particular individual against a particular outcome (psychological functioning, adherence to specific treatments)." But this should never lead to a sense of judging among people for worthiness or goodness.

In addition, I suggest that it is important to recognize the limitations of measuring effectiveness only based on outcomes. When people engage in spiritually based healing activities that are congruent with their beliefs and highest ideals, the activities are inherently, intrinsically satisfying, regardless of measurable outcomes. As one of my participants who had a lung transplant explained, she prepared herself for surgery to be at peace with loved ones and God, and she felt the supportive presence of God in her life (Canda, 2001). Therefore, whether the surgery resulted in death or longer life, she could accept that. Death during surgery might be counted as an outcome indicating failed prayer (and medical technique). But from her transpersonal view, a good relationship with God and her faith-based activities were inherently satisfying. She accepted any outcome because the process of her approach to living and dying were intrinsically fulfilling. Of course, it would be optimal to have both intrinsic satisfaction and beneficial health outcomes. But this is not always possible. Of course, everyone dies eventually; but this does not mean everyone is a failure.

Further Reflections on My Experience and Relevance to Others

My account of lessons learned emphasized several themes: life as a spiritual path; complementarity of spiritually based and conventional medical treatments; incorporating all healing activities within the context of one's spiritual path and infusing them with spiritual significance; mindful engagement in life and in particular healing activities through daily life; consistency, persistence, and flexibility of health-promoting activities; support from the circle of family, friends, the universe, and the divine; finding beauty in the midst of illness and adversity; learning from mistakes; rejection of ableist biases and dehumanizing illness stereotypes and labels; and growing in well-becoming and well-being throughout fluctuations of physical health and even in physical decline. I invite readers to question whether these themes might be relevant to your personal experience with adversity and to your professional practice and research regarding people with chronic illness. Koenig's (2007) suggestions for healthcare professionals can be very useful.

Given the wide range and large number of my healing activities, the pervasiveness of spirituality in my daily life, and my engagement in diverse religious traditions, my style might seem unfamiliar, daunting, or objectionable to many people. My style is most likely to be comfortable to people who are highly committed to both conventional medical and spiritually attuned practices and who see life as a spiritual journey. It is more likely to be

acceptable to people who are adventurous in exploring diverse cultures, religions, and healing practices. While the details of my spiritual beliefs and practices may not be applicable
to many people, their underlying spiritual path might be. I would like to propose that my spiritual way is crucial to my health and well-being, *because it is an authentic expression of who
I am and what my life is about,* not because it is a prescription suited to everyone. I suggest
that each person could work out her or his own authentic spiritual way, and the health promotion practices congruent with it, through continuous soul searching, introspection, dialogue with loved ones, and guidance from spiritual mentors and communities. For people
who are not religious, or even have no interest in matters explicitly spiritual, cultivating an
authentic life full of meaning, purpose, strength, and resilience can proceed without employing the language of religion, spirituality, or faith. This theme is consistent with studies that
show a sense of meaning and purpose is an important contributor to resilience (Benard,
2004; Snyder & Lopez, 2007).

I may be unusual in having a deep spiritual propensity since early childhood. I was
able to develop an approach to life as a spiritual path, as well as practical familiarity
with various spiritually based disciplines, such as contemplative prayer and meditation,
before I was diagnosed with CF at age 18. Erik Erikson referred to this as the style of
"homo religiosus" (Latin), meaning people who are precociously and consistently focused
on life as a quest for meaning (Erikson, 1962, 1969). I had a style of Catholic education
and family life that infused a sense of intrinsic spiritual propensity, that is, life pervaded
by self-reflective spirituality. In particular, I was close to my similarly spiritually inclined
older brother, who was diagnosed with CF not long before me, with whom I could discuss matters of spirituality, health, and mortality. This may have given me an advantage
because I accrued spiritual strengths, insights, and strategies that could be put into action
as soon as I had my CF diagnostic tests. Some researchers have suggested that adults with
CF might have some advantage in developing positive coping due to the longer period
of time to adjust and a sense that they have "beaten the odds," in contrast to sudden and
late onset severe illnesses (Burker, Carels, Thompson, Rodgers, & Egan, 2000; Burker
et al., 2004; Tracy, 1997). Further, some children with CF are likely to try to place their
experience and treatment of CF within the context of whatever spiritual beliefs they have
learned from family, religious communities, or the general public (Pendleton et al., 2002;
Stern et al., 1992).

This leads me to suggest that parents, teachers, religious community leaders, and mentors encourage children to explore their spiritual development, at each child's pace. Recently,
human service research and practice supporting children's spiritual development has begun
to increase (e.g. Crompton, 1998; Roehlkepartain, King, Wagener, & Benson, 2005). Perhaps this can guide social workers to recognize and support the spiritual development of children and youth—as consistent with the values of themselves, family, and community—both
for their own well-being and as a kind of immunization in preparation for adversity that can
occur at any time. This would be even more relevant for children who have been diagnosed
with chronic or acute illnesses.

I am rather introspective and introverted by personality, which inclines me toward
spiritual practices that rely on self-reflection, self-discipline, and time for quiet. People
who are more extroverted may not be so comfortable with this. But they could also learn
to incorporate mindfulness into daily activities that match their own interests and style.

For example, some people would agonize over a prolonged time of quiet meditation. But they could revel in a long mindful jog or walk in nature.

I have been fortunate to be surrounded since childhood with a loving and nurturing set of family and friends. I have had extensive and excellent educational opportunities that allowed me to explore different cultures and religions. I grew up in a working-class family, never lacking in necessities. I have since become established as a professional with secure income. I have been able to maintain good medical insurance throughout my life. I happened to grow up near a major CF world-class treatment center that was always on the cutting edge of medical research and treatments. I also have a genetic variant of CF that tends be associated with less severely life-threatening respiratory symptoms. People diagnosed with CF as adults tend to have less severe symptoms in childhood than those diagnosed early (Ellmers & Criddle, 2002; McCloskey, Redmond, Hill, & Elborn, 2000).

My good fortune in these respects leads me to wish for similar protective factors for everyone. Treatments that alter the genetic basis of CF-related symptoms are still in an early stage of development. In the meantime regarding CF, and for all time regarding everyone's health, I believe that social policies should promote universal access to affordable medical care. Social workers can advocate for such health-related social policies, insurance coverage, and disability rights. They can also do holistic biopsychosocial-spiritual assessments of clients with chronic illness in order to identify and support their full range of existing strengths and resources and to help fill in gaps (Eichler, Deegan, Canda, & Wells, 2006; Nelson-Becker, Nakashima, & Canda, 2007). Integrative theoretical models have been developed to help social workers think holistically about the personal and environmental issues involved in dealing with CF and disabilities (Kim & Canda, 2006; Robbins, Chatterjee, & Canda, 2006). In accord with social work and medical ethics, spiritually focused assessment and other helping practices should always be congruent with clients' beliefs, readiness, and goals for service; practitioners' competence; and available evidence about the efficacy of the practices (Canda & Furman, 1999; Canda, Nakashima, & Furman, 2004; Koenig, 2007; Lawrence & Smith, 2004). Interestingly, Lawrence and Smith use a case example of an adult man with CF, who has no formal religious involvement and no religious interest, as an illustration of when it is not appropriate to impose the topic of religion in medical care. All the participants in my interview study emphasized that professional helpers should show respect and interest for patients' spiritual beliefs and incorporate them when relevant, while never imposing their own religious or nonreligious beliefs (Canda, 2001, 2006).

Conclusion: From coping and resilience to transilience.   In my review of scholarly literature, I could not find a concept to encompass fully the spiritual way of living with chronic illness that I have observed in myself and the other interview study participants. *Coping* refers to a process of shifting behaviors, thoughts, and feelings that individuals use in interaction with their situations to avoid being harmed by life stressors (Abbott, 2003). An active and optimistic approach to monitoring and dealing with illness, including religious and nonreligious styles, has tended to be seen as generally beneficial in the CF research (Abbott, 2003; Burker et al., 2004; Pendleton et al., 2002). This concept of coping is helpful to get at how individuals respond to adversity, but it does not encompass the proactive (not only reactive) strengths of people and their supportive environments; nor do the research measures touch the encompassing way of life and how it may embrace and transform any particular coping styles and strategies in response to adversity.

Similarly, the concepts of *resilience* or *resiliency* involve a dynamic process of positive adaptation to significant adversity with positive developmental outcomes (Benard, 2004; Fraser, Kirby, & Smokolski, 2004; Luthar, Cicchetti, & Becker, 2000). This also assumes a stance of reactivity to adversity. The literal meaning of resilience is "to leap back," presumably to a pre-adversity condition. That does not capture the transformational and transpersonal possibilities of growing into newness through crisis. What of a way of life that proactively, preventively, and transformationally precedes, responds to, and transcends adversity?

Concepts of *quality of life* and *well-being* are useful to get at broader lifestyles and qualities of health. However, the measures typically used in medical research tend to be too structured, simple, and normative, equating level of physical symptoms (e.g., lung function) and mental health symptoms (e.g., anxiety and depression) with well-being. They do not shed enough light on the depth and detail of people's lives or spiritual paths, including the positive significance of spiritual crises and distress. For example, Gee and colleagues (2000) took a valuable step beyond usual practice to develop a validated health-related quality of life questionnaire specific to people with CF, based partly on their experience. This is excellent at identifying patients' ratings of the severity of CF specific problems in relation to physical, mental, and social domains of life. However, it does not include the spiritual domain. It also does not inquire about the positive possibilities for learning, growth, and enhancement of well-being that can occur when we address CF proactively and creatively. There is no assessment of strengths or resources for clients and healthcare professionals to build on.

The rubric of *strengths and resources* within the social work strengths perspective encompasses these ideas about coping, resilience, well-being, and good quality of life. It goes further by pointing to the wide range of possible intrapersonal, interpersonal, and wider environmental resources and ways of life that may be available to people to build their capacities and respond to adversities and oppressions (Saleebey, 2006). It also keeps a focus on people's strengths, capacities, goals, and resources, rather than reducing us to problems and pathologies. The strengths perspective is broadening and deepening to encompass the transformational and transpersonal possibilities identified in my studies of the way spiritually attuned adults relate to CF. Experiences of apparent weakness and fragility are themselves strengths if one realizes them as such. Dichotomous thinking about strengths versus weaknesses or pathology can be transcended.

I believe that all these concepts are useful for research and practice purposes, but they do not encompass the subtlety and profundity of life as a spiritual path that encompasses, infuses, vitalizes, transforms, and transcends the moment-to-moment details of living and dying. I have struggled with finding a useful concept for this. In my chapter for the 2006 edition, I followed established convention to use the word *resilience*. As I am no longer satisfied with the assumptions behind this word, I am improvising on it.

First, I considered the word **prosilience**. Prosilience literally means leaping forward. This has the advantage of avoiding the literal implication of resilience that people should react to adversity by springing back to a former condition. It captures possibilities of proactive living and moving forward in growth. But it still implies movement along a line of development. So in the interest of spurring further discussion, I would like to propose the term ***transilience***.

Transilience literally means a developmental leap of transcendence. I have been able to find only one use of this word in the literature related to resilience. Cook (1995) used this term in a grounded theory study of adult children of alcoholics in order to name the psychosocial process by which they moved to a new more positive state of life and reality. Based on my studies of spiritually focused adults with CF, I would like to define transilience as a whole person process of moving forward, backward, upward, downward, sideways, or back-around in a life committed to well-being and well-becoming. Transilience is not restricted to a linear idea of moving forward or backward on a line of health or quality of life indicators. It is not just a matter of reacting to problems or pathologies. It is not just a matter of building on strengths and resources. It encompasses coping, hoping, reacting, anticipating, preventing, promoting, and transcending. It is a leaping beyond health and quality-of-life indicators. It is a life of transformation that is not restricted to social conventional ideas about health, illness, fitness, strength, goodness, ability, or disability. When a person addresses all of living and dying, including adversity, within a spiritual path of growth and transformation, then mundane and profound events can generate growth into expanded consciousness, more profound intimacy with the world, and liberation from the constraints of body bounded selfhood. Transilience is a way of life that engages relationships with self, others, the universe, and the ground of being, however understood, in a spiritual (though not necessarily religious) path.

DISCUSSION QUESTIONS/EXERCISES

1. Using the author's self-reflections as an example, write your own account of your most significant spiritual beliefs, practices, and experiences (religious and/or nonreligious) in relation to your own dealing with issues of mortality, illness, disability, crisis, or adversity. You might ask yourself such questions as: How was spirituality, if at all, involved in my response to some important life challenge? How did my spiritual development up to that time help prepare me (and/or hamper me) to respond? Overall, what have been the most successful spiritually based strengths or resources that I have used in my life to gain a sense of meaning and purpose and to promote health and well-being? Are there any of these that I have discontinued that might be valuable to regain? Are there any new spiritual strengths and resources that I wish to explore?

2. In the first paragraph of "Further Reflections on My Experience and Reference to Others," on page 85, the author lists ten themes that emerged from his reflection about dealing with the chronic illness of CF. Consider how each theme might be relevant to your own development as a person and as a professional. Then consider how they might or might not be relevant to clients who have faced issues of chronic illness or other health challenges.

3. The author describes aspects of his background and personality that shape his spiritual way of life and dealing with chronic illness, including limitations and implications for others. Think about clients who may have different kinds of backgrounds from the author in terms of health status, cultural background, religious beliefs, personality, and availability of social supports and resources. Consider who the author's suggested implications might need to be adapted for.

4. In the final section of this chapter, the author considers the concepts of coping, resilience, quality of life, well-being, strengths, and prosilience. Review his reasons for stating that these are useful but insufficient to capture the full extent of what he calls transilience. Reflect on the distinctive qualities of transilience. Consider reasons you may agree or disagree that transilience is a useful construct. Have you observed transilience in the life ways of clients, colleagues, and acquaintances?

REFERENCES

Abbott, J. (2003). Coping with cystic fibrosis. *Journal of the Royal Society of Medicine, 96*(43), 42–50.

Abbott, J., Dodd, M., Gee, L., & Webb, K. (2001). Ways of coping with cystic fibrosis: Implications for treatment adherence. *Disability and Rehabilitation, 23*(8), 315–324.

Anderson, D. L., Flume, P. A., & Hardy, K. K. (2001). Psychological functioning of adults with cystic fibrosis. *Chest, 199*(4), 1079–1084.

Anonymous. (2002). Diagnosis review committee: New and revised diagnoses. *Nursing Diagnosis, 13,* 68–69.

Benard, B. (2004). *Resiliency: What we have learned.* San Francisco: WestEd.

Burker, E. J., Carels, R. A., Thompson, L. F., Rodgers, L., & Egan, T. (2000). Quality of life in patients awaiting lung transplant: Cystic fibrosis versus other end-stage lung diseases. *Pediatric Pulmonology, 30,* 453–460.

Burker, E. J., Evon, D. M., Sedway, J. A., & Egan, T. (2004). Religious coping, psychological distress and disability among patients with end-stage pulmonary disease. *Journal of Clinical Psychology in Medical Settings, 11*(3), 179–193.

Canda, E. R. (1988). Conceptualizing spirituality for social work: Insights from diverse perspectives. *Social Thought, 14*(1), 30–46.

Canda, E. R. (1990). An holistic approach to prayer for social work practice. *Social Thought, 16*(3), 3–13.

Canda, E. R. (2001). Transcending through disability and death: Transpersonal themes in living with cystic fibrosis. *Social Thought, 20*(1/2), 109–134.

Canda, E. R. (2005). The future of spirituality in social work: The farther reaches of human nurture. *Advances in Social Work, 6*(1), 97–108.

Canda, E. R. (2006). The significance of spirituality for resilient response to chronic illness: A qualitative study of adults with cystic fibrosis. In D. Saleebey (Ed.), *The strengths perspective in social work practice, fourth edition* (pp. 61–76). Boston: Pearson/Allyn and Bacon.

Canda, E. R., & Furman, L. D. (1999). *Spiritual diversity in social work practice: The heart of helping.* New York: Free Press.

Canda, E. R. Nakashima, M., & Furman, L. D. (2004). Ethical considerations about spirituality in social work: Insights from a national qualitative survey. *Families in Society, 85*(1), 1–9.

Casey, S. (2006). Beyond CF clinic recommendations: Integrated medicine. In A. McKenna and H. Goldswieg (Eds.), *Beyond lungs: Meeting the needs of adults with cystic fibrosis* (pp. 114–125). Hannover, Germany: Felsenstein CCCP.

Coady, C. A., Kent, V. D., & Davis, P. W. (1990). Burnout among social workers working with cystic fibrosis. *Health and Social Work, 15*(2), 116–124.

Cook, A. E. (1995). Wounds become gifts: The process of transilience in adult children of alcoholics. *Virginia Henderson Nursing Library.* Retrieved from www.nursinglibrary.org/Portal/main.aspx?pageid=4024&sid=10993

Crompton, M. (1998). *Children, spirituality, religion, and social work.* Suffolk, UK: Ipswich Books.

Cystic Fibrosis Foundation. (2007, June 5). *About cystic fibrosis.* Retrieved December 20, 2007, from www.cff.org/AboutCF

deJong, W., Kaptein, A. A., van der Schans, C. P., Mannes, G. P. M., van Aalderen, W. M. C., Grevink, R. G., & Koetter, G. H. (1997). Quality of life in patients with cystic fibrosis. *Pediatric Pulmonology, 23*(2), 95–100.

Dunbar, H. T., Mueller, C. W., Medina, C., & Wolf, T. (1998). Psychological and spiritual growth in women living with HIV. *Social Work, 43*(2), 144–154.

Eichler, M., Deegan, G., Canda, E. R., & Wells, S. (2006). Using the strengths assessment to mobilize spiritual resources. In K. B. Helmeke & C. Sori (Eds.), *The therapist's notebook for integrating spirituality in counseling: Homework, handouts, and activities for use in psychotherapy* (pp. 69–76). New York: The Haworth Press.

Ellmers, K. & Criddle, L. M. (2002). A new age for childhood diseases: Cystic fibrosis. *RN, 65*(9), 60–66.

Erikson, E. H. (1962). *Young man Luther: A study in psychoanalysis and history.* New York: Norton.

Erikson, E. H. (1969). *Gandhi's truth: On the origins of militant non-violence.* New York: Norton.

Fallot, R. (Ed.) (1998). *Spirituality and religion in recovery from mental illness.* San Francisco: Josey-Bass Publishers.

Gee, L., Abbott, J., Conway, S. P., Etherington, C., & Webb, A. K. (2000). Development of a disease specific health related quality of life measure for adults and adolescents with cystic fibrosis. *Thorax, 55,* 946–954.

Graham, J. R. (2006). Spirituality and social work: A call for an international focus of research. *Arete, 30*(1), 63–77.

Hahn, T. N (1987). *The miracle of mindfulness* (rev. ed.). Boston: Beacon Press.

Hawks, S. R., Hull, M. L., Thalman, R. L., & Richins, P. M. (1995). Review of spiritual health: Definition, role, and intervention strategies in health promotion. *American Journal of Health Promotion, 9*(5), 371–378.

Kabot-Zinn, J. (1990). *Full catastrophe living.* New York: Delta.

Kim, K. M. & Canda, E. R. (2006). A holistic view of health and health promotion in social work for people with disabilities. *Journal of Social Work in Disability and Rehabilitation, 5*(2), 49–67.

Koenig, H. G. (2007). *Spirituality in patient care: Why, how, when, and what* (2nd ed.). Philadelphia: Templeton Foundation Press.

Koenig, H. G., McCullough, M. E., & Larson, D. B. (2001). *Handbook of religion and health.* New York: Oxford University Press.

Lawrence, R. T. & Smith, D. W. (2004). Principles to make a spiritual assessment work in your practice. *The Journal of Family Practice, 53*(8), 625–631.

Luthar, S. S., Cichetti, D., & Becker, B. (2000). The construct of resilience: A critical evaluation and guidelines for future work. *Child Development, 71*(3), 543–562.

McCloskey, M., Redmond, A. O. B., Hill, A., & Elborn, J. S. (2000). Clinical features associated with a delayed diagnosis of cystic fibrosis. *Respiration, 67*(4), 402–407.

McDonough, L. (2002). *Lisa: The brief life of a writer.* Philadelphia: XLibris Corporation.

McNeal, G. J. (2002). End of life issues in a palliative care framework for a critically ill adult African American with cystic fibrosis: A case study. *Journal of Cultural Diversity, 9*(4), 118–127.

Miller, G. (2003). *Incorporating spirituality in counseling and psychotherapy.* Hoboken, NJ: John Wiley & Sons.

Nelson-Becker, H., Nakashima, M., & Canda, E.R. (2007). Spiritual assessment in aging: A framework for clinicians. *Journal of Gerontological Social Work, 48*(3/4), 331–347.

O'Brien, M.E. (2003). *Spirituality in nursing: Standing on Holy Ground* (2nd ed.). Sudbury, MA: Jones & Bartlett Publishers.

Pendleton, S., Cavalli, K. S., Pargament, K. I., & Nasr, S. Z. (2002). Religious/spiritual coping in childhood cystic fibrosis: A qualitative study. *Pediatrics, 109*(1), 1–11. doi: 10.1542/peds.109.1.e8

Powell, L. H., Shahabi, L., & Thoreson, C. E. (2003). Religion and spirituality: Linkages to physical health. *American Psychologist, 58*(1), 36–52.

Robbins, S. P., Chatterjee, P., & Canda, E. R. (2006). *Contemporary human behavior theory: A critical perspective for social work* (2nd ed.). Boston: Pearson/Allyn and Bacon.

Roehlkepartain, E. C., King, P. E., Wagener, L., & Benson, P. L. (Eds.). (2005). *The handbook of spiritual development in childhood and adolescence.* Thousand Oaks, CA: Sage Publications.

Saleebey, D. (Ed.). (2006). *The strengths perspective in social work practice* (4th ed.). Boston: Pearson/Allyn and Bacon.

Shepherd, S. L., Hovell, M. F., Harwood, I. R., Granger, L. E., Hofstetter, C. R., Molgaard, C., & Kaplan, R. M. (1990). A comparative study of the psychosocial assets of adults with cystic fibrosis and their healthy peers. *Chest, 97*(6), 1310–1316.

Sidell, N. L. (1997). Adult adjustment to chronic illness. A review of the literature. *Health and social work, 22*(1), 5–11.

Sloan, R. P., Bagiella, E., & Powell, T. (1999). Religion, spirituality, and medicine. *The Lancet, 353,* 664–667.

Sloan, R. P., Bagiella, E., VandeCreek, L., & Hover, M. (2000). Should physicians prescribe religious activities? *The New England Journal of Medicine, 342*(25), 1913–1916.

Snyder, C. R. & Lopez, S. J. (2007). *Positive psychology: The scientific and practical explorations of human strengths.* Thousand Oaks, CA: Sage.

Stern, R. C., Canda, E. R., & Doershuk, C. (1992). Use of non-medical treatment by cystic fibrosis patients. *Journal of Adolescent Health, 13,* 612–615.

Thyer, B. A. & Walton, E. (Eds.). (2007). *Research on Social Work Practice: Special Issue on Faith-Based Programs,* 17(2).

Tracy, J. P. (1997). Growing up with chronic illness: The experience of growing up with cystic fibrosis. *Holistic Nursing Practice, 12*(1), 27–35.

Van Hook, M., Hugen, B., & Aguilar, M. (Eds.). (2001). *Spirituality within religious traditions in social work practice.* Pacific Grove, CA: Brooks/Cole.

Widerman, E. (2006). Nourishing body and spirit: Challenges and coping strategies for adults with CF. In A. McKenna & H. Goldswieg (Eds.), *Beyond lungs: Meeting the needs of adults with cystic fibrosis* (pp. 126–133). Hannover, Germany: Felsenstein CCCP.

Widerman, E. (2004). The experience of receiving a diagnosis of cystic fibrosis after age 20: Implications for social work. *Social Work in Health Care, 39*(3/4), 415–433.

Young, J. M. & McNicoll, P. (1998). Against all odds: Positive life experiences of people with advanced amylotrophic lateral sclerosis. *Health and Social Work, 23*(1), 35–43.

ACKNOWLEDGMENTS

Thanks to my wife Hwi-Ja Canda and to my friends and colleagues Paula Duke, Kyung Mee Kim, Holly Nelson-Becker, and Dennis Saleebey, for reading my drafts and keeping me honest. I honor my brother Tom and my friend and consultant Lisa McDonough for being exemplars of people who used lessons from living and dying with CF to benefit others. Finally, I appreciate the encouragement and expert treatment of Robert C. Stern, my CF specialist physician for thirty-five years.

CHAPTER FIVE

THE STRENGTHS APPROACH TO PRACTICE

Beginnings

DENNIS SALEEBEY

The chapters in Parts Three and Four describe and discuss strengths-based practice with a number of different populations, in a variety of contexts and settings. These include among others: criminal justice; addictions treatment; gerontological social work; working with women who have been sexually abused as children; working with social workers on issues of professional resilience and risk; working toward economic human rights with disadvantaged populations; using health realization to tap into the innate health and wisdom of individuals and communities; and developing and using resources within the individual and in the social context in promoting mental health. While you will perceive differences among these approaches, you will see throughout the chapters a vital and unmistakable belief in the capabilities of individuals, groups, families, and communities. It comes across in many ways, but the following ideas are resoundingly clear from beginning to end:

- People who confront stress almost always develop some ideas, capacities, traits, and motivations that may subsequently be of use to them in the search for a better life. We have been much too energetic in looking for the impediments and injuries, the deficits and desolation rather than people's compensating and transformative responses to challenges.
- Even in the most demanding, tough, lean, and mean environments there is a bounty of natural resources—individuals, families, associations, institutions—available. While some communities are clearly more abundant than others, all neighborhoods have assets.
- Even though individuals may have labored for years under the blame and disapproving opinions of others, or self-criticism, habitual pessimism, or unfortunate life decisions, at some level, they almost always know what is right for them.
- As a species we surely have—or we would not have survived thus far—an innate capacity for self-righting and health.
- Healing, transformation, regeneration, and problem solving almost always occur within the confines of a personal, friendly, supportive, and dialogical relationship (Edward Sampson [1993] calls it "a celebration of the other."). Whether friend, intimate partner,

physician, social worker, shaman, or teacher, the more we entreat the power of a caring, egalitarian relationship with those we assist, the better for them and us.

■ All people have knowledge and talents, skills and resources that can be used for pressing forward toward a life defined in their own terms—toward their hopes and dreams, the solution of their problems, the meeting of their needs, and the invigoration of the quality of their lives—individually and collectively.

■ It is far more important to set one's gaze toward a better future, to traffic in possibility, than it is to obsess about the disappointments and injuries of a dank, dark past.

■ Even when people do injurious things to themselves and others, they are often trying to meet needs that all of us have—for respect, control, security, love, and connection.

To recognize the strengths in people and their situation implies that we give credence to the way clients experience and construct their social realities. We cannot impose from without our own versions (or those of the agency or other social institutions) of the world. This appreciation of context and construction is an acknowledgment of the special and distinctive social circumstances of each client or group (Saleebey, 1994). To hear the stories and narratives in a family or a community is one way to discover not only their preoccupations and challenges, but also to unearth their particular assets and abilities. Learning the language, the symbols, the images, and the perspectives that move clients—for good or ill—is to encounter their challenges and triumphs, over time. In discussing the recovery from chemical dependency from a transpersonal perspective, Moxley and Washington (2001) say:

> The person's journey in recovery [may] best be expressed as a personal narrative. Helping each person to express his or her story may be a potent way to help an individual understand a career of chemical dependency and to make sense of the social forces that shaped it. The construction of a personal narrative may be the most influential pathway to reveal the shadow and to illuminate the person's accommodation. (pp. 258–259)

You will see in the chapters that follow the high level of commitment and resolve that is required to get you into the client's life-world authentically and respectfully. Other themes that abound in the following chapters include the importance of genuine dialogue; forming positive expectations of clients; helping clients participate more fully in their world of people, institutions, and communities; identifying natural resources in the clients' world; and learning from clients. One thing becomes clear in reading these chapters: Operating from a strengths perspective is good, basic social work practice. There is nothing here that is not coincidental with the core of values that energizes and drives the profession. All that we can do in these pages is to give these principles more conceptual and practical vigor.

SOME BEGINNING OBSERVATIONS
ABOUT STRENGTHS-BASED PRACTICE

These observations are meant to answer some basic questions that have been asked over the years about generic practice from a strengths perspective. First of all, assume that it will take genuine diligence on your part to begin to appreciate and utilize client strengths in practice. The system is against you, the language and metaphors of the system are against you, consumers are sometimes against you because they have been inscribed with the cursor of disease, and, not insignificantly, the culture is against you. Pursuing the ideas that formulate and celebrate strengths, resilience, rebound, challenge, and transformation is difficult because they are not now natural to much of the social service, health, and mental health systems and their membership. Let us begin by examining some of the factors that are implicated consistently in salutary change and development.

The Core Conditions of Growth and Change

In their review and statistical analyses of studies done over the years on the factors that lead to constructive change in psychotherapy, Asay and Lambert (1999) concluded that there are four enduring components of such change. The four ingredients for change include factors in the matrix of clients' lives (their strengths and resources, contingent factors, etc.); the qualities of good helping relationships; positive expectations, hope and the placebo effect; and the technical operations and principles of theory. Barry Duncan and Scott Miller (2000) offer a precise and straightforward discussion of these factors in *The Heroic Client* (see pp. 55–62).

   What Asay and Lambert call extratherapeutic factors seem to promote the greatest degree of change. These include the strengths, assets, and resources within the individual, the family, and the ambient environment. Supportive kin, determination, insights gained from intimate sources, a rising sense of hopefulness, a lessening of stresses in the environment, and many other things may be involved here. Clearly important factors are contingent ones—luck, fortune, and the play of chance occurrences in one's life. All of these reflect the substance of individuals' or families' daily life—the web of resources in their surroundings, social support networks, their own wiles and wisdom, personal or collective traits and virtues, and the unforeseen in their lives. According to Asay and Lambert, the psychosocial matrix of a person's life may account for 40 percent of therapeutic change.

   For years, social workers have emphasized the importance of the helping relationship and the use of self as the medium of change and growth (Shulman, 1992). Half a century ago, Carl Rogers (1951) and his associates assured us that truly healing relationships bloomed from the qualities of caring, empathy, positive regard, genuineness, and respect. Over the last thirty years or so, Hans Strupp (1995) has been investigating psychotherapies of all kinds to mine the ore of real and positive change therein. He continually finds that the quality of the helping relationship is the single most important factor across schools of psychotherapy. Practitioners of the strengths perspective add to these the importance of collaboration—developing a mutually crafted project, meant to lay, brick by brick, a path to a person's or family's hopes and dreams. Charles Rapp, one of the most important figures in the development of the strengths perspective, defines the effective helping relationship as purposeful, reciprocal, friendly, trusting, and empowering (1998). Asay and Lambert (1999) reckoned that this factor might account for about 30 percent of the positive change in peoples' lives.

   Often forgotten, but truly important in promoting beneficial change are hope, positive expectations, and the placebo effect. My expectation that you can do better and prevail through your tribulations translates into the recrudescence of hope, the revival or birth of a dream—no matter how modest. A focus on possibility, an eye cast to a better future, and the creation of justifiable optimism all promote movement toward one's aspirations. Of all these, however, the most intriguing may be the placebo effect (see discussion in Chapter 1). Long known for its use in medical and pharmaceutical research, it has been virtually ignored as a force in bringing about change.

Michael Fisher (2000) reports that in the 1950s at the University of Kansas Medical Center, in order to test a new medical procedure for the treatment of angina, surgeons performed real operations on one group of patients with angina, and a placebo operation on the other group of men with angina. The placebo group was told that they were going to have heart surgery; they were given a local anesthetic, and incisions were made in their chests. But no operation was done, the surgeons just messed around a little bit, and the patients had the scars and postoperative pain to suggest that they actually had surgery. Seventy percent of the people who had the real surgery reported long-term improvement in their angina; but *all* of the placebo group did. Ethical problems with this study aside, the results are just short of amazing.

It is not at all uncommon in tests of psychoactive drugs for the placebo groups to show anywhere from 25 percent to 60 percent improvement (Arpala, 2000). As noted, the extent that the real drug is better than the placebo is thought to be the extent that the drug is effective. But it is unknown, for example, just how much the effect of the real drug is also a placebo phenomenon. In more recent years, people have been getting an active placebo in which they experience side effects—look at the drug ads in your magazines and check out the data. People are more likely to get better on active placebos because the experience of side effects convinces them that they are getting a real and powerful drug. Joseph Arpala (2000) reports that a study by Fisher and Greenberg revealed that in 30 percent to 40 percent of all the studies they reviewed of antidepressant drugs and placebos, the placebo was as powerful or therapeutic as the drug. Refer to Chapter 1 for a discussion of the study of the FDA's data on clinical trials of antidepressants.

So what is happening here? Many things no doubt. It could be—and many have proposed this—that when a person is sick and has an expectation, thanks to a procedure or pill, that he or she will get better, he or she mobilizes the healing systems within, whether it is the psychoneuroimmune system, endorphins (endogenous morphine produced by the body), relaxation response (which lowers, among other things, the level of cortisol, the production of which is related to stress), or some unknown process. But maybe even more important here is the expectation of the healer that you will get well, the mobilization of hope and possibility that things will be different in the future. We dissipate an awful lot of our possible goodwill, hinting or directly saying that things will not be better, that once stuck or hurt or disappointed or abused or ill, you will always suffer scars or the effects of these hurts will reverberate, in one way or another, throughout your life. It is not just the person's expectation that he will recover, rebound, do better, it is the unmistakable expectation of the social worker, physician, healer, minister, teacher, or parent that you will do better—the belief in you. As your social worker, I genuinely believe that you can make it, can leap that hurdle, climb that wall, escape that burden. You may need help, it may take time, but my belief in you is steadfast. As a child heretofore defined as at-risk, I define you, as Beth Blue Swadener (1995) suggests, as a child "at-promise." So the placebo effect harbors within it something of considerable persuasive authority.

Consider, too, that it may well be that even the group receiving a real medication may also experience a placebo effect—in some cases to the tune of 30 percent of its supposed efficacy (Brody, 2000). The emotional, nonverbal, and verbal messages that accompany the giving of a placebo appear to be extraordinarily important. Do they galvanize hope, mobilize positive expectations? Creating the expectancy of a healthy, efficacious response would seem to be a part of the potency of the placebo. But the message for practitioners is that you should never underestimate the sway of hope, the belief that things can improve. Such a prospect is vital to those individuals and groups who struggle against the tide of low expectations, little opportunity, belittled self-esteem, and thwarted justice. According to Asay and Lambert's inquiry, these factors may account for as much as 15 percent of positive, dynamic change.

That percentage is about the same as Asay and Lambert attribute to the effect of the technical operations and methods of a theory. These methods clearly are important. It is well known, for example, that cognitive behavioral techniques, and interpersonal therapy both, often in conjunction with antidepressant drugs, are effective in the treatment of moderate to moderately severe depression (Bentley & Walsh, 2001; Gitlin, 1996).[1] For people returning to the community after hospitalization for an episode of schizophrenia, the combination of a neuroleptic threshold dose[2] of antipsychotic medication and vigorous psychosocial and educational interventions is effective. It must be said, however, that in the absence of the first three factors, the techniques and methods of a theory or perspective hold less sway.

In many ways the strengths perspective builds on the mobilization of these factors, in particular the power of possibility and an unstinting and unqualified belief in the person's or group's capacity for change.

In a sense, this capacity, even propensity for change, is built into our very organism. If we view mind as a manifestation of the brain, consciousness and memory as the mind's twin foundations, and emotion as the energy that drives and engages these factors, we are constantly assessing and responding to the incessant beat of internal and external demands. Our brain, as we have seen, is defined, in part, by its plasticity, its moment-to-moment ability to change to register and respond to new information and stimuli. In a sense, then, our belief in the power of possibility is, in a metaphoric sense, making an alliance with the person's brain/mind.

In discussing the remarkable effects of "sham" surgery (in this case, on the knees), and the placebo effect, Groopman (2005) observes:

> Pain was the hurdle that prevented these patients from working to strengthen their muscles and ligaments. Once that hurdle could be overcome by the power of the mind, then the necessary rehabilitation could begin; hope offered a real chance to reach a better end. Hope helps us overcome hurdles that we otherwise could not scale, and it moves us forward to a place where healing can occur. (p. 177)

What Are Strengths?

Almost anything can be considered a strength under certain conditions, so this list is not meant to be exhaustive. Nonetheless, some capacities, resources, and assets do commonly appear in any roster of strengths.

---

[1]More evidence is mounting that the therapies without medication are quite effective.
[2]The smallest amount of medication that produces a beneficial effect.

What people have learned about themselves, others, and their world as they have struggled, coped with, and battled abuse, trauma, illness, confusion, oppression, and even their own fallibility. People do learn from their trials, even those that they seem to inflict upon themselves. People do not just learn from successes but from their difficulties and disappointments as well. In their recent book, *The Struggle to Be Strong* (2000), Al Desetta and Sybil Wolin report the narratives of adolescents who have been subjected to enormous challenges in their lives. Consonant with Steven and Sybil Wolins' theory that resilience is forged from seven traits and capacities[3] that one might learn in the struggle against adversity, these stories reproduce evidence of those. Youniqiue Symone, living in foster care, at the age of 16 wrote this about the relationship between her and her biological mother:

> I grew up when I realized this: My mother is not going to change because I want her to. She's only going to change when she wants to. I also know deep down in my heart that we are never going to be a real family. . . . I don't want to have children at a young age to show my mother what a "real mother" is. I want to break the cycle. If I don't, I might end up doing the same thing my mother did. (p. 14)

This is an example of more than ordinary insight in a 16-year-old coming to terms with a mother who, for whatever reasons, neglected her. Out of that realization and her particular understanding about its impact on her young life, Youniqiue has determined to walk a different path.

Personal qualities, traits, and virtues that people possess. These are sometimes forged in the fires of trauma and catastrophe, and they might be anything—a sense of humor, caring, creativity, loyalty, insight, independence, spirituality, moral imagination, and patience to name a few (Wolin & Wolin, 1993). These also are the products of living, the gifts of temperament, and the fruits of experience. Whatever their source, these skills and attributes might well become sources of energy and motivation in working with clients.

What people know about the world around them from those things learned intellectually or educationally to those that people have discerned and distilled through their life experiences. Perhaps a person has developed skill at spotting incipient interpersonal conflict or soothing others who are suffering. Perhaps life has given an individual the ability to care and tend for young children or elders, or it could be that a person could use an artistic medium to teach others about herself. Maybe personal experience has motivated an individual and shaped a keen ability to help others through the grieving process. Again, we have no way of knowing what it might be without observing and asking.

The talents that people have can surprise us sometimes (as well as surprising the individual as some talents have lain dormant over the years). Playing a musical instrument, telling stories, cooking, home repair, writing, carpentry (who knows what it might be?) may provide additional tools and resources to assist individuals or groups in reaching their goals. In addition, they may be assets that can be shared and given to others to foster solidarity, to strengthen mentorship, or to cement friendship.

---

[3]The seven possible elements of resilience are humor, insight, independence, relationships, creativity, morality, and initiative. People may develop any one or a number of these as they struggle with the challenges of their lives. They are also developmental, each undergoing maturation and sophistication with the passage of time.

> Writing is so easy for me because I can be as real as I want to be and not have to worry about being judged because of how I feel. I've written about forty poems. I write about love, hate, happiness, sadness, life, death, and friendship.
>
> Sometimes writing poetry is hard, so I write stories. Whether they're fiction or non-fiction, writing stories helps me. I write about everyday stuff. (Desetta & Wolin, 2000, p. 122)

Tamara Ballard, who wrote this at age 16, understands both her need to write and the gifts that her writing bestows on her.

Cultural and personal stories and lore are often profound sources of strength, guidance, stability, comfort, or transformation and are often overlooked, minimized, or distorted. It is now often told how the stories of women have been shrouded through domination but how they are, when recounted and celebrated, sources of profound strength and wisdom (Aptheker, 1989). Cultural approaches to helping, to cite another example—whether the sweat lodge, medicine wheel, drumming, chanting, or curanderismo—may be powerful sources of healing and regeneration. Cultural stories, narratives, and myths, accounts of origins and migrations, or trauma and survival may provide sources of meaning and inspiration in times of difficulty or confusion. The exploits of cultural heroes, fictional and real, may provide instruction and guidance.

Ian Frazier (2000) recounts this story, so instructive about cultural heroes. In the Pine Ridge reservation in South Dakota, a young woman, SuAnne Big Crow, had become a consummate and storied basketball player. In the dead of winter in South Dakota, basketball was and is a real happening. In the fall of 1988, SuAnne's team played a non-Native team in Lead, South Dakota, a place where the Lady Thorpes (her team) has usually been harassed with racial insults. In the locker room, before the game, the Lady Thorpes could hear the crowd getting louder and louder, yelling fake Indian war cries. They were also yelling nasty epithets like "squaw" and "gut-eater." Doni De Cory, who usually led the team out of the locker room because she was the tallest, where they then ran around the floor for two laps before going to the bench, did not want to go face that angry crowd. SuAnne said she would lead the team out onto the floor. She ran out on the court, dribbling the basketball, but when she got to the middle she stopped suddenly. She turned to Doni and tossed her the ball. She stepped into the jump ball circle at mid-court, unbuttoned her warm-up jacket, took it off, and began to do the Lakota shawl dance—a dance that shows the gracefulness and modesty of a young woman. She then began to sing in Lakota, swaying back and forth in the circle. The crowd fell silent. Then, when she had finished, she took the ball, dribbled around the court and went to the basket and made a lay-up. The crowd went wild (pp. 208–209). This story has many dimensions, not the least of which is the courage and creativity, the seizing of an improbable moment by a 14-year-old Oglala Sioux girl. This was serious risk-taking, which had profound and positive consequences for all involved. Frazier says that if there was a film of this hopeful, magical moment (there isn't), that he would run it "again and again for my own braveheart song. I refer to her, as I do to Crazy Horse, for proof that it's a public service to be brave" (p. 214).

Personal and familial parables of falls from grace and redemption, of failure and resurrection, of struggle and resilience may also provide the diction, the metaphors from which one may construct a more vibrant vision of the self and world.

People have pride as well; people who have leapt over obstacles, who have rebounded from misfortune and hardship often have what the Wolins call "survivor's pride." Sometimes this self-regard is buried under an accumulation of blame, shame, and labeling, but it is there waiting to be uncovered. "Pride drives the engine of change; shame jams the gears!" (Wolin & Wolin, 1994).

The community is a physical, interpersonal, and institutional terrain full of riches to be tapped into. The informal or natural environment is an especially fertile landscape, full of people and organizations, who, if asked, would provide their talents and knowledge in the service of helping and supporting others. The work of community development and organizing is, in part, dedicated to germinating the saplings of strength and resourcefulness in the community. The efforts of the Search Institute in Minneapolis in identifying those community strengths and assets that shore up the developmental infrastructure for all youth and help reduce risk behaviors is instructive in this regard. Among their many findings is that availability and vitality of community-wide institutions and neighborhood associations— youth groups, churches, synagogues, temples, ethnic associations, and schools—are critical elements of a responsive and working infrastructure for youth development (Benson, 1997).

The idea of *spirituality* is implicit, I think, in the discussions of and allusions to meaning-making. Ed Canda (see Chapter 4) has written with great wisdom about the nature of spirituality. Summarizing his perspective I would say it has three core assertions. First, spirituality refers to the essential, holistic quality of being that transcends the merely biological, psychological, social, political, or cultural but incorporates them all. This quality obliterates categorizations and dichotomies such as that between mind and body, substance and spirit (Canda, 1997). Second, spirituality reflects our struggle to find meaning, a working moral sensibility, and purposes that extend beyond selfish, egoistic concerns. Finally, spirituality refers to an essence that extends beyond the self, that defies ego boundaries, and allows us to join and revere the mysteries and complexities of life. This might be manifest in visions, peak experiences, cosmic revelations, experiences of the numinous and awe-inspiring.

But it is the hopes and dreams, the promise and possibilities of a better life, a different path, that spur many to action and the mobilizing of their resources and assets—often unused and forgotten. Many dreams and hopes have been disregarded, suppressed, distorted by circumstance or distress. But with help, positive expectations, and work they can be recovered, and made more vital.

For many individuals and groups, then, spirituality is a grand bulwark against the demands and stresses, both ordinary and inordinate, of life. It is also a means of discovering or creating meaning while confronting the vexing and sometimes seemingly incomprehensible events of daily life. Finally, it is a sense of the transcendent that can set the possibilities of the future in more hopeful compass.

How Do You Find Out About Strengths?

Sounds difficult, but the discovery of strengths depends on some simple ideas. Look around you. Do you see evidence of client interests, talents, and competencies?

Listen to clients' stories instead of zooming through an assessment protocol. Stories and narratives often contain within their plots and characterizations evidence of strengths, interests, hopes, and visions.

BILL

Bill was in his early forties, in and out of state hospitals since the age of 17 with a variety of diagnoses (chronic undifferentiated schizophrenia seemed to be the favorite). Single, living in a big city with no relatives nearby (or very interested in him), he worked as a dishwasher in a midtown bar and grill. He became hooked up with a community support program at the behest of a hospital social worker who was interested in keeping him out of the hospital. Bill was taking haloperidol. He was assigned a first-year MSW student as a case manager. The student was learning the strengths approach to practice and was anxious to try it. She began by encouraging Bill to "tell his stories"—how he got to be where he was, what interesting things he had done, and how he had survived with a serious illness. She learned many interesting things about Bill, and some of his stories clearly revealed a resourceful, motivated person. He had a serious problem with alcohol but quit drinking on his own. Yet he continued to frequent a local bar "because that's where all my buddies are," and being with his buddies was one outpost of connection and stability for him.

Bill also, on one occasion, saved enough money from his modest salary to take a trip to Oslo, Norway. He had seen some of Norway's marvelous statuary in an old *National Geographic* magazine and wanted to experience it for himself. He arranged and took the trip on his own. On his trek, he discovered a joy in flying. A dream began to form in his mind—he could see himself flying a plane.

He revealed his reverie to the social worker, who, given what she had come to learn about Bill, took it to heart. Together they began taking some modest steps toward his desire. In a few months, Bill got a job as a dishwasher at the airport, a busy international terminal, even though it involved an hour-long bus ride each way. He loved being around pilots and planes. At last account, Bill was working toward getting a job on the tarmac, perhaps as a baggage handler. Besides listening to his stories and searching within them for inklings of strength, character, and knowledge, the social worker did something else extraordinarily important to this kind of work: She let Bill know that she was genuinely interested in the hopes and dreams that he nurtured.

DAVID

In discussing her now 44-year-old son, David, who has struggled with a particularly virulent form of schizophrenia since his late childhood, clinical social worker and social work educator Mona Wasow (2001) said that it was only when they (parent, foster parent, doctor, and social worker) began to focus on his strengths and attributes that any significant change in his life took place. The change was not brought about by the new, more powerful medications but by a decision to encourage David to harness his talents (music and pottery making—both of which were immenent, not obviously present). She writes:

> A few years ago, at a regular . . . treatment meeting, one of the social workers was reporting on David's considerable deficits. The psychiatrist said, "I don't want to hear all that again. That's his illness and we have not been able to change that for years. Tell me about his strengths; we would do better to work with those."
>
> I remembered hearing David pick out parts of a Bach fugue on his guitar which is pretty good for a guy who has never had a music lesson. And his thoughtful foster mother had suggested pottery lessons because of an interest he seemed to have in a neighborhood pottery studio. My other children were artistic and musical; maybe David had talents, too?
>
> . . . After the first guitar lesson, the teacher said, "Hey, this man is talented!" Now that was worth taking a shower for [one of his symptoms was that he had no interest

in bathing]. Maybe the music teacher would say that again. Either way, these lessons would bring the continuing joy of learning to read music and of being able to produce some of those great tunes on the guitar. . . . Learn to ride the bus to get to the pottery studio? You bet. Even make a little eye contact with the friendly pottery teacher, who laughed with pleasure at David's newly created ceramic bear sitting in a canoe. The $215 he made in a pottery sale a year later produced even more eye contact. (p. 1306)

KAY

The psychologist and author Kay Redfield Jamison (1996) talks about her struggle with manic-depressive illness (she prefers that designation to bipolar because it more starkly reflects the reality of her suffering). Her struggle in part was over having to take the antimanic drug, lithium. She didn't want to because the medicine took the edge off her better manic moments (which she admitted almost always turned worse), and because of some of the side effects. It took years of suffering and pain for her to finally relent. But while lithium spoke to the molecular elements of her struggle, she says it was love that ultimately spoke to the narrative of her life.

But love is, to me, the ultimately more extraordinary part of the breakwater wall: It helps shut out the terror and awfulness, while, at the same time, allowing in life and beauty and vitality. . . . After each seeming death within my mind or heart, love has returned to re-create hope and restore life. It has, at its best, made the inherent sadness of life bearable, and its beauty manifest. It has inexplicably and savingly provided not only cloak but lantern for the darker seasons and the grimmer weather. (p. 215)

In trying to discover the strengths within and around, what sort of questions might one ask? There are several kinds of questions one might ask including:

Survival questions.   How have you managed to survive (or thrive) thus far, given all the challenges you have had to contend with? How have you been able to rise to the challenges put before you? What was your mindset as you faced these difficulties? What have you learned about yourself and your world during your struggles? Which of these difficulties have given you special strength, insight, or skill? What are the special qualities on which you can rely?

Support questions.   What people have given you special understanding, support, and guidance? Who are the special people on whom you can depend? What is it that these people give you that is exceptional? How did you find them or how did they come to you? What did they respond to in you? What associations, organizations, or groups have been especially helpful to you in the past?

Exception questions.[4]   When things were going well in life, what was different? In the past, when you felt that your life was better, more interesting, or more stable, what about your world, your relationships, your thinking was special or different? What parts of your world

---

[4]Thanks to the practitioners of solution-focused therapy for this terminology. We did not know what to call these kinds of questions (see De Jong, P., & Miller, S. D. [1995, November]. How to interview for client strengths. *Social Work, 40,* 729–736).

and your being would you like to recapture, reinvent, or relive? What moments or incidents in your life have given you special understanding, resilience, and guidance?

Possibility questions.   What now do you want out of life? What are your hopes, visions, and aspirations? How far along are you toward achieving these? What people or personal qualities are helping you move in these directions? What do you like to do? What are your special talents and abilities? What fantasies and dreams have given you special hope and guidance? How can I help you achieve your goals or recover those special abilities and times that you have had in the past?

Esteem questions.   When people say good things about you, what are they likely to say? What is it about your life, yourself, and your accomplishments that give you real pride? How will you know when things are going well in your life—what will you be doing, who will you be with, how will you be feeling, thinking, and acting? What gives you genuine pleasure in life? When was it that you began to believe that you might achieve some of the things you wanted in life? What people, events, and ideas were involved?

Perspective questions.   What are your ideas or theories about your current situation? How do you understand, what kind of sense do you make of your recent experiences and struggles? How would you explain these to yourself, to me, or anyone else?

Change questions.   What are your ideas about how things—thoughts, feelings, behavior, relationships, etc.—might change? What has worked in the past to bring about a better life for yourself? What do you think you should or could do to improve your status, your affairs? How can I help?

Meaning questions.   What are the primary ideas and values of your system of meaning system: those things that you utterly believe in and value above all? What are those transcendent, iridescent beliefs that give you a sense of purpose beyond the self? Where do they come from? Your experience? The culture? Some cosmic source? What part do they play in your everyday life?

These obviously do not exhaust likely questions. These questions are not meant to be a protocol, but rather they reflect the kinds of concerns and interests that might arise and direct your attention during conversations with clients or as you hear their stories, over the times that you speed with them.

What Are Some of the Elements of Strengths-Based Practice?

What follows is a representation of some of the stages and phases of practice. In truth, these steps may occur in a different sequence; they even might occur simultaneously. Practice of all kinds is a discursive kind of experience, not necessarily a well-staged and predictable stroll through a set of certainties toward an inevitable destination. What follows is a way to look at the process, knowing that it will be in some ways different every time you engage in helping an individual, or family, or working in a community.

In the Struggle—the Harbingers and Hints of Strength.   Clients (individuals, families, and communities) come to you because they feel, perceive, and/or experience discontent, stress, pain, and/or loss. This is their reality at the moment. They must speak to these. They want you to listen. Your professional creed also asks that you begin where the client is—that you hear and honor their story. So far, so good. But in practicing from the standpoint of strengths you also listen for what is almost surely there—as a leitmotif, or maybe swathed in the language of anguish—evidence of capacity, will, determination, and hope, however muted and hesitant. It is common for clients, even as they report their pains and predicaments, to mention decisions they have made, things that they have done that have been healthy or positive. Marshall, troubled by intermittent heavy drinking, said in passing that he did not drink during the week that his son (in the custody of his wife after a recent divorce and very important to Marshall) visited. Statements like this typically are not told to illustrate a strength but simply appear as a part of the recounting of a person's troubles. It is up to you to, at some point, reflect this exemplar of strength back to the individual or family because it does illustrate that people have some power to, at least momentarily, right themselves. You are always listening for the hints and murmurs of resilience and rebound.

Stimulate the Discourse and Narratives of Resilience and Strength.   There is often great resistance to acknowledging one's competence, reserve, and resourcefulness. In addition, many traits and capacities that are signs of strength are hidden under the rubble of years of self-doubt, the blame of others, and, in some cases, the wearing of a diagnostic label. Sometimes the problem of discovering strengths lies with the lack of words, sometimes it is disbelief, and sometimes it is lack of trust. The social worker may have to begin to provide the language, to look for, address, and give name to those resiliencies that people have demonstrated in the past and in the present (the Wolins' [1993] language of the seven resiliencies is helpful here). The daily struggles and triumphs of one's life as revealed in stories and narratives are useful (for example, what they have done, how they survived, what they want, what they want to avoid). At some point in this process, people do have to acknowledge their strengths, play them out, see them in the past and the present, feel them, and have them affirmed by the worker and others. In a sense, what is happening at this point is the writing of a better "text." Reframing is a part of this; not the reframing of so many family therapies, but adding to the picture already painted, brushstrokes that depict capacity and ingenuity, and that provide a different coloration to the substance of one's life.

The prompting of a discourse and the development of a personal dictionary of strengths and capacities depends on three factors. First, it is incumbent on the practitioner to provide the words and images of strength, wholeness, and capacity where they may be lacking. Second, it is important for the practitioner to be an affirmative mirror, beaming back to the client a reflection of that person's positive attributes, accomplishments, skills, and talents. Last, it is wise to carefully lay out with an individual what might be possible in her or his life—big or small things, it doesn't matter. And all of this must ring true to the person and be grounded in the dailiness of life.

Acting in Context: The Project.   The education continues about the capacities and resilient aspects of the self. Now these are linked up to the person's hopes, goals, and visions, and relevant external resources. The individual is encouraged to take the risk of acting on one's expectancies using the newly found or articulated competencies as well as already active ones. It is through action with the worker—collaborative and continuous—that individuals really begin to employ their strengths as they move toward well-formed, achievable goals. The collaboration with the social worker or practitioner to achieve desired goals using inner and communal resources is, in effect, a project—in the two senses of the word. On the one hand it is an undertaking, on the other it is a *launching of one's self* in the world of relationships, work, and/or play. This is precarious business for many people who have been through a figurative hell. But as they decide and act, they continue to discover and enrich their repertoire of aptitudes. They also discover the limits of their resilience and the effect of still-active sore spots and scars. But, in the end, it is their decision making and activity that lead to changes in thinking, feeling, and relationship that are more congruent with their goals and their strengths. It is also vital that the individual, group, or family begins to use naturally occurring community resources—from extended family to local associations and institutions—to move toward their goals.

For the social worker, this means advocacy in the form of discovering what natural or formal resources are available, accessible, and to what extent they are adequate and acceptable to the client (Kisthardt, 1993). The assumption here is that the environment is rich with resources: people, institutions, associations, families who are willing to and can provide instruction, succor, relief, resources, time, and mirroring. When people begin to plan fully to achieve their goals and to exercise their strengths, the effect is synergistic: They can do more personally, and they find themselves more connected to a community. For example, a receptionist at a physician's office begins to help an elderly woman complete her insurance forms, arrange transportation to and from the doctor's office so that she is more likely to keep appointments, and keep a level of health she believes is highly desirable. The synergistic effect is that the receptionist begins to do this for other elders as well and eventually finds other volunteers to assist them. For many of the older persons involved, this is an important support for the maintenance of relative independence—an important strength to be sure (see Chapter 9).

Move Toward Normalizing and Capitalizing on One's Strengths.   Over a period of time, often short, the social worker and client begin to consolidate the strengths that have emerged, reinforce the new vocabulary of strengths and resilience, and bolster the capacity to discover resources within and around. The purpose is to cement the foundation of strengths, to ensure the synergy of the continuing development and articulation of strengths, and to secure a place for the person to be. For many who have been helped through a strengths-based approach, one important avenue to normalization is teaching others what one has learned in the process. Finally, this is a process of disengagement for worker and client. Done with the assurance that the personal strengths and the communal resources are in place, disengagement is the ritual transition to normalization.

CONCLUSION

In summary, to assume a strengths perspective requires a degree of consciousness raising on the part of social workers and their clients—a different way of regarding what they do together. One thing is certain, however, from reports of many of those people who apply the strengths perspective in their professional work: Once a client is engaged in building up the strengths within and without, a desire to do more and to become more absorbed in daily life and drawn by future possibilities bursts forth.

At the end of her poetic and brilliant book on the human brain/mind, Diane Ackerman (2004) writes:

> Wallace Stevens was right, the body can be satisfied often and well, but the mind never. . . . Because mind is matter, we matter and we mind. We use words like small hand axes. We tele-vise alternate worlds. We scout the invisible. We practice the art of science. As songsters and sages have always said, we dream several dreams, only one of them during the night. For bet-ter or worse, we've become nature's way of thinking about itself, a brain for all seasons. (p. 258)

In the end, the ultimate source of our strength is that "enchanted loom"—the human brain.

People are always engaged in their situations and are working on them even if they just decide to resign themselves to their fate. Circumstances can overwhelm and debilitate. We know a lot about that. But dire circumstances can also bring a surge in resolve and the blossoming of capacities and reserves. We must know more about that.

DISCUSSION QUESTIONS/EXERCISES

1. With a friend or client, use some of the methods for discovering strengths described in this chapter. What was the outcome? How would you personalize such methods so they would be more useful to you?

2. Do you think that the way one goes about finding out about strengths has a different feel to it than methods for determining symptoms or problems? What, if any, is the difference?

3. What do you think of the role of luck and contingency in people's lives? How can it have an impact on your work with individuals, families, groups, or communities?

4. Do you know practitioners who approach clients from a strengths perspective? If so, what do you notice about their practice that is distinctive? Talk to them about how they came to practice in such a way.

5. How do you understand the placebo effect? Have you seen it at work in your professional or personal life?

6. What do you think of the role of hope in helping people create a more satisfying life for themselves?

REFERENCES

Ackerman, D. (2004). *An alchemy of mind*. New York: Scribner.

Aptheker, B. (1989). *Tapestries of life*. Amherst: University of Massachusetts Press.

Arpala, J. (2000, July, August). Sweet sabotage. *Psychology Today, 32,* 66–67.

Asay, T. P. & Lambert, M. J. (1999). The empirical case for the common factors in therapy: Qualitative findings. In M. A. Hubble, B. L. Duncan, & S. D. Miller (Eds.), *The heart and soul of change: What works in therapy* (pp. 33–56). Washington, DC: APA Press.

Benson, P. L. (1997). *All kids are our kids: What communities must do to raise caring and responsible children and adolescents.* San Francisco: Jossey-Bass Publishers.

Bentley, K. J. & Walsh, J. (2001). *The social worker and psychotropic medication* (2nd ed.). Belmont, CA: Brooks/Cole.

Brody, H. (2000, July/August). Mind over medicine. *Psychology Today, 32,* 60–65, 67.

Canda, E. R. (1997). Spirituality. In R. L. Edwards, I. C. Colby, A. Garcia, R. G. McRoy, & L. Videka-Sherman (Eds.), *Encyclopedia of social work* (19th ed., 1997 supplement). Washington, DC: National Association of Social Workers.

Desetta, A. & Wolin, S. (Eds.). (2000). *The struggle to be strong: True stories about youth overcoming tough times.* Minneapolis: Free Spirit Publishing Company.

Duncan, B. L., & Miller, S. D. (2000). *The heroic client: Doing client-directed outcome-informed therapy.* San Francisco: Jossey-Bass.

Fisher, M. J. (2000, October). Better living through the placebo effect. *The Atlantic Monthly, 286,* 16–18.

Frazier, I. (2000). *On the rez.* New York: Farrar, Straus and Giroux.

Gitlin, M. J. (1996). *The psychotherapist's guide to psychopharmacology* (2nd ed.). New York: Free Press.

Groopman, J. (2005). *The anatomy of hope: How people prevail in the face of illness.* New York: Random House.

Jamison, K. R. (1995) An *unquiet mind: A memoir of moods and madness.* New York: Vintage Books.

Kisthardt, W. E. (1993). A strengths model of case management: The principles and functions of a helping partnership with persons with persistent mental illness. In M. Harris & H. Bergman (Eds.), *Case management for mentally ill patients: Theory and practice.* Langhorne, PA: Harwood Academic Publishers.

Moxley, D. P. & Washington, O. G. M. (2001). Strengths-based recovery practice in chemical dependency: A transpersonal perspective. *Families in Society, 82,* 251–262.

Rapp, C. A. (1998). *The strengths model: Case management with people suffering from severe and persistent mental illness.* New York: Oxford University Press.

Rogers, C. (1951). *Client centered therapy: Its current practice, theory, and implications.* Chicago, IL: Houghton Mifflin.

Saleebey, D. (1994). Culture, theory, and narrative: The intersection of meanings in practice. *Social Work, 39,* 351–359.

Sampson, E. E. (1993). *Celebrating the other: A dialogic account of human nature.* Boulder, CO: Westview Press.

Shulman, L. (1992). *The skills of helping: Individuals, families, and groups* (3rd ed.). Itasca, IL: F. E. Peacock.

Strupp, H. H. (1995). The psychotherapist's skills revisited. *Clinical Psychology, 2,* 70–74.

Swadener, B. B. (1995). Children and families 'at promise': Deconstructing the discourse of risk. In B. B. Swadener & S. Lubeck (Eds.), *Children and families 'at promise': Deconstructing the discourse of risk.* Albany: State University of New York Press.

Wasow, M. (2001, October). Strengths versus deficits, or musician versus schizophrenic. *Psychiatric Services, 54*(10), 1306–1307.

Wolin, S. J. & Wolin, S. (1993). *The resilient self: How survivors of troubled families overcome adversity.* New York: Villard.

Wolin, S. J. & Wolin, S. (1994, October). Resilience in overcoming adversity. Workshop for Employee Assistance Program members, Kansas City, MO.

CHAPTER SIX

KEY DIMENSIONS OF THE STRENGTHS PERSPECTIVE IN CASE MANAGEMENT, CLINICAL PRACTICE, AND COMMUNITY PRACTICE

ANN WEICK

JAMES KREIDER

RONNA CHAMBERLAIN

In the long and proud history of social work, the profession has remained anchored in a seemingly simple proposition: that changing people's behavior cannot be accomplished by focusing only on their personal characteristics. In the early days of the twentieth century, as social work was forming itself into an organized effort to respond to the many challenges of industrialization and immigration, it became increasingly clear that people's life chances were powerfully affected by the social environment. Alcoholism, child abuse, domestic violence, and malnutrition caused great suffering among those affected but could not be dealt with in the absence of larger social factors such as poverty, health hazards, and violence. The awareness of both personal and social factors in understanding people's behavior became a linchpin in forming what has come to be known as the "dual focus" of social work.

Despite this powerful assertion of the interaction between people's personal characteristics and the social, political, and economic contexts in which they live their lives, through much of the twentieth century, bolstered by an evolving array of theories of human behavior, there developed a strong focus on identifying client or patient problems and making that the starting point of the helping process. Problems were believed to be lodged within the individual or family, largely unaffected by external factors. Theories of human behavior became increasingly sophisticated in developing ideas about causal factors for personal problems. The weight of psychologically based therapies often focused on individual behavior even when such factors as poverty, physical abuse, and discrimination clearly limited people's life chances.

The strengths perspective in social work, developed during the last decades of the twentieth century, represents a significant paradigm shift for the social work profession, as well as for other professions (Rapp, 1992; 1998, Rapp & Chamberlain, 1985; Rapp & Goscha, 2006; Saleebey, 1992; 1997, 2002, 2006, Weick et al., 1989). It rests on an understanding of human behavior that is radically different from the traditional pathology-based, problem-solving paradigm. It is based on the recognition that focusing on the problem does not solve the problem. Instead, it creates an even stronger affiliation with the problem and draws people more deeply into a retrospective view of how the problem came to be. In contrast, the strengths perspective asks people what they want and what they would like their life to be like apart from the problem. The channel through which change occurs is the uncovering of their aspirations, hopes, and dreams for a better life and the enlisting of their personal resources and the resources in their environment for moving more surely toward those goals. (See Chapter 1 for principles.)

One of the benefits of the strengths perspective is its application across fields of practice. There has been considerable work in extending this perspective across diverse populations. (For example, see earlier editions of *The Strengths Perspective in Social Work Practice* [Saleebey, 1997, 2002, 2006]). Based on this work, it seems useful to create an even broader analysis in order to more finely distill common elements that undergird and help further clarify the common denominators of the strengths perspective. Because practice is the ultimate test of the utility of this perspective, examples will be drawn from three practice arenas: *case management practice, clinical practice, and community practice.* Understanding the commonalities and differences among these practice areas can more sharply focus on essential strengths-based elements of practice and avoid the common misunderstanding that the strengths perspective is something to be simply added on to the traditional pathology-based, problem-solving paradigm.

CASE MANAGEMENT PRACTICE

The strengths perspective had its origins in the field of mental health, growing out of an attempt to work in a more constructive way with people who had severe and persistent mental illness. These were individuals whose problem of mental illness had taken over their lives through years of hospitalization, crises, and treatment by mental health professionals. Those who suffered with this condition were well-versed in their diagnoses, their symptoms, and their responses to medications and saw as dismal their chances for a normal life. They had, in fact, become their problem.

The strengths perspective grew from a kernel of a new idea: that work with people suffering from long-term mental illness should focus on what they wanted in their lives. It was based on the assumption that, despite their mental illness, they could build a new life beyond their problem. The bridge to this new life was a shift of focus from the problem of mental illness to a focus on their talents, assets, resources, and life goals. A key mechanism for exploring these life areas was the Case Management Strengths Assessment, developed by Chamberlain and Rapp (1983) and Rapp and Chamberlain (1985).

Because of its success in helping people accomplish this shift of focus, the Kansas Strengths Assessment instrument has changed little since its inception in 1982. The instrument contains seven life domains: Living Situation; Finances/Insurance; Vocation/Education; Social Support; Health; Leisure/Recreation; and Spirituality/Culture (Modrcin, Rapp, & Chamberlain, 1985). For each domain, individuals are asked to describe their current situation, recall any times when they experienced joy or satisfaction and to identify what interests and abilities they were using that contributed to the positive experiences. Next, they are encouraged to express their hopes, dreams, and aspirations for each area. Building on past success and specific dreams for the future, individuals are then asked to describe how they would like their life to be. Based on this assessment information, the case manager helps the client to establish their top priorities and they begin the process of developing achievable goals in the priority domains. With the act of completing the assessment, for most clients, the intervention has begun as the foundation for hope is laid.

In the years to follow, through the further development of strengths-based case management (Rapp, 1993, 2006), mental health workers were trained to focus on people's goals and aspirations and develop a strategy that would lead to success. This plan included not only personal aspirations but also the goal of helping people live in their communities rather than be separated from normal life by hospital walls. While it was always recognized that their medical condition would require some attention and management such as oversight of medication and perhaps even brief hospitalization, the problem of mental illness was seen as manageable. The person's own goals were the unchanging focus of the work.

Paul's story is a good example of this focus on goals, even ones not fully expressed. He was a 46-year-old man living in a board and care home in a small midwestern city. The referral to the mental health center reported that he was diagnosed with schizophrenia and was refusing to eat, shower, leave his room, or even talk to the staff or other residents. He was viewed as a suicide risk, but the state hospital was refusing to readmit Paul because he had not responded to treatment on a previous admission. Little was known about Paul except that he had lived all of his life with his parents on a farm in a distant rural area and had spent very little time in the hospital. Following the death of his parents, he had been sent to the city's hospital and subsequently discharged to the board and care home since he no longer had a home to which he could return.

As anticipated, Paul was also unresponsive to his new case manager. In a brainstorming session, the case management team concluded that, in the absence of a traditional strengths assessment, they would have to operate on the assumption that Paul's hopes, dreams, and aspirations would include being in a rural environment. Because that would not be available in a city, an approximation might be a riding stable. The case manager set to work and, after several emphatic nos, found a stable that would allow Paul to come there daily on a trial basis and to do chores if he was able.

Paul was soon mucking stalls and grooming horses and returning home with an appetite. While still a man of few words and one reluctant to shower, he began to seek the company of others and even enjoy social interactions. The stable owner was impressed with Paul's work, and he began receiving a salary. After a few weeks, his driver reported that it was common to find Paul sitting on the porch with the stable owner, surveying the landscape, looking contented, and exchanging the occasional word or two.

The example of consumer success in pursuing goals for a normal life was substantiated many times over through research, initially documented through four nonexperimental studies (Kisthardt, 1993; Modrcin, Rapp, & Poertner, 1988; Rapp & Chamberlain, 1985, Rapp & Wintersteen, 1989) and more recently included experimental studies, as reported in Rapp and Goscha (2006). The results of these studies showed that people who had previously been viewed as "hopeless" began to make improvements in their lives. Finding a job, making new friends, and shopping at a grocery store all became possible. The energy to make these changes came about through the power of their self-directed aspirations and hopes, aided by the ongoing assistance of a case manager who offered support, maintained focus on individual goals, and served as the connector with the rich array of human and physical resources available in the community. The training for strengths-based case management has now occurred in over forty-five states and in Japan, New Zealand, Australia, England, and Holland.

CLINICAL PRACTICE

Since its beginnings in social work in the early 1980s at the University of Kansas School of Social Welfare, the strengths perspective has been extended to many groups whose life circumstances make it difficult to use their own energy and dreams to fuel a significant change in their lives. While the field of clinical social work practice has broader and more complex goals than the pragmatic goals of case management practice with those suffering from mental illness, there is a clinical approach that is both compatible with and reinforcing of strengths-based practice. Like strengths-based case management, the development of solution-focused brief therapy (SFBT) grew out of a frustration with the predominant focus on pathology that had become deeply entrenched in therapeutic practice. The title of the book, *We've Had a Hundred Years of Psychotherapy and the World Is Getting Worse* (Hillman & Ventura, 1992) aptly expressed the consternation many clinicians felt when working with people from the "problem side." Like their counterparts in mental health, they learned a great deal about the nature of their problems but little about how to proceed to a better life.

In struggling to find an approach that did not spring from problems, Steve deShazer and Insoo Kim Berg, both social workers, along with several collaborators, became the original developers of the solution-focus brief therapy (SFBT) model. It had its genesis in the early 1980s when, while observing clients through the one-way mirror, they noted that the majority of people they saw in therapy did not need to know more about the problems they struggled with but rather more about potential solutions to these problems. In particular, this involved knowing more about what they wanted instead of their problems (i.e.,"solutions") and also when problems did not occur or were less ("exceptions to problems"). This simple shift in their approach to clinical practice resulted in both more rapid and more consistent resolution to client's presenting concerns. Solution-focused brief therapy began the movement away from traditional problem solving to solution building. Moving as quickly toward solutions as clients were able became the hallmark of the subsequent development of their approach at the Brief Family Therapy Center in Milwaukee.

By focusing both the worker's and the client's eyes on what the client wants to have happen as a result of their working together, an important process of bringing into consciousness the knowledge people have about their own life circumstances is initiated. This is in stark contrast to traditionally based approaches to helping where client's own knowledge is typically viewed as flawed, irrational, or distorted. Based on this traditional perspective, correcting those flawed, irrational, or distorted views is the logical response. By contrast, both solution-focused brief therapy and the strengths perspective assume that even severely challenged individuals have invaluable information about themselves and their lives. To trust what clients are saying about their current life—but more importantly, their hopes for a different life—establishes a radically different starting point for building a very deep sense of trust not only between clients and workers, but for clients in trusting themselves as having strengths and capacities worthy of attending to. Both strengths and solution-focused work intentionally create a partnership designed to explore in detail the shape of a person's life beyond the problem.

The solution-focused model of clinical practice offers a helpful corrective to the typical problem-solving approach that characterizes the practice of most of social work and other helping professions. It does so by accepting clients as the ones best suited to define both what they hope to achieve and who or what might help them reach their goals. It also adds useful extensions to the goal-oriented strategies of practice from the strengths perspective. Rather than plan and execute "interventions," the solution-focused model uses questions to guide conversations in a collaborative effort to explore and develop solutions. The use of questions as the primary technique or "intervention" reflects SFBT's postmodern assumptions noted in deShazer's comment, "Language constitutes the human world, and the human world constitutes the whole world" (Berg & deShazer, 1993). Consequently, SFBT uses questions to help people construct more useful "realities" rather than trying to correct their assumed to be flawed "reality." To guide this process, SFBT offers several types of questions that can help strength-based workers assist their clients in this solution building, as opposed to traditional problem solving. But doing so requires focusing and refocusing all eyes on solution building rather than on problem solving.

The SFBT practice of focusing on solution building rather than on problems is based on the assumption that in order to solve any problem, one needs to know more about possible solutions than about problems (deShazer, 1988). This assumption is supported by research from Milwaukee's Brief Family Therapy Center, where the solution-focused model was developed, finding less than a 5 percent correlation between client's problem descriptions and how they described their solutions to their problems (deShazer, 2004).

But what about clients who are very focused on their problems? Don't they need to "vent" about problems and the pain they feel as a result of their problems? These are common assumptions that trouble those new to SFBT. It is clear that not everyone is ready to shift from problem talk to solution talk immediately. This is where skill is required in terms of when and how to acknowledge the struggles people have so that they know we are hearing them, validate the feelings they experience so they know that we accept them and they can accept themselves, and offer an invitation to consider what they would prefer to have happen in their lives instead of the problem: that is, a potential solution. Those who are ready to accept the invitation will respond to our solution-building questions, and those who may still need more validation will let us know this by returning to problem talk. In that event, we not only "start where the client is at" but also "stay where the client is," returning to our listening carefully, taking him seriously, acknowledging that we hear and "get" him, and validating his feelings. Insoo Kim Berg was fond of referring to this as "leading from a half step behind." When people are ready to accept our invitation to engage in solution talk, then we can help them develop, describe, and define a solution that may become the goal to focus on and work toward. If, on the other hand, we assume clients must first engage in a good deal of talk about their problems, we are likely to ask questions that suggest that they *should* do so, and they are in turn likely to respond by assuming that sharing about their problems provides information we consider to be necessary (Miller, Hubble, & Duncan, 1995). By joining clients in "problem talk," we run the risk of unwittingly reinforcing the notion that doing so is an important first step in getting to solutions; for some it is, for most it is not.

Being able to focus on solutions rather than on problems can make a dramatic difference for our clients, helping them identify and reach for their hopes, dreams, and aspirations. Doing so, however, has far broader implications for quality of life than simply solving problems. It is often the first step in helping a person change her identity from one who is overwhelmed or disempowered by her problems to one who is capable of facing and solving her problems in living. When feeling both a sense of hope and of competence, people are generally much more willing to try new behaviors that may help them bring their solutions into fruition, as demonstrated by recent research in the areas of hope and positive psychology (Snyder & Lopez, 2007). Consequently, often the first step in leaving problems behind in solution building is simply not to focus on problems, but rather to focus on what people want instead of their problems. By focusing on the other side of the problem coin, which is how they will know the problem is resolved, clients often are greatly relieved to *not* have to recount their stories of confusion, pain, and failure but instead to be engaged by their helper in conversations around what they *want* in their lives instead of their problems.

Another typical consequence of asking the solution-building question, "What would you like instead of your problem?" is that a relationship is fostered that organizes around and affirms people's hopes and desires. Asking what people want to have happen also makes overt practitioners' beliefs that those they serve are capable and have the strengths, resources, and abilities that can be marshaled to improve the quality of their lives. This is a central assumption of strengths perspective practice (Saleebey, 2006, 1992) as well as of SFBT (Lipchik, 2002). However, if they are merely hollow words and workers do not convey this belief through their actions, clients may well doubt their own capabilities. In doubting their capacities, it is less likely that people will try to reach for their hopes and dreams.

Solution-focused practice skips the traditional broad "assessment" that invariably includes details about the history of problems, risks associated with problems, and symptoms caused by problems. Instead, SFBT invites conversations relevant to solution building. Following are some examples of ways to invite conversations that help clients move toward a discussion of solutions and away from problems.

"How will you know when your problems are behind you?"

"What will need to happen for you to be convinced that the problems that brought you in here are loosening their grip on your life?"

"How will you know when services are no longer necessary?"

"What will need to be different in your life in order for you to say our work together was successful?"

Gathering information about what solutions will look like early in the helping interaction often results in both client and worker becoming excited about constructing a better future, rather than reviewing a painful past. This excitement that both feel comes in part from a distinct contribution that SFBT can make to strengths-based practice. That is, "strengths" identified in solution-focused practice are *only* those relevant to the solution the client is working toward, rather than those from a list of isolated strengths that the worker and client then attempt to apply toward goals. In particular, strengths identified while asking about *exceptions* (when the problem doesn't occur and some of the goal related behavior does occur) are contextualized in relationship to clients' solutions so it is easier for clients to "own" their strengths and see them as viable resources in moving toward their goals. This offers a practical and useful option for the common challenge encountered by strength-based workers who list or map strengths without any idea of how to take advantage of them (Jacobson, 2001).

SFBT uses a variety of other questions to assist in solution-building in addition to goal-related questions. Perhaps the best known of these is from the *Miracle Conversation*, which is actually a series of carefully presented statements and questions. This conversation offers a very effective way to invite conversations about client's goals. In fact, deShazer stated that he found it so useful that he used the Miracle Question in nearly every first session since it was developed in the early 1980s (deShazer, 2003). Since the scope of this chapter will not allow a detailed discussion of the careful delivery necessary for the Miracle Question to be helpful, the reader is referred to De Jong & Berg (2008).

An example of a typical response to the question, "How will you know that the miracle has occurred?" illustrates the effects of SFBT's Miracle Question. Carl, who'd struggled with persistent obsessions since adolescence, responded to this question with a laugh, "Well, I'd act normal, for one thing!" Carl's response was typical of clients' initial responses to the Miracle Questions in that it was very vague and global, which means it will be hard to achieve, let alone know when he has achieved "normal." By waiting for him to elaborate, he continued, "Uh, I mean, I'd accept the fact that my mind can latch on to a worry that causes me to do weird things, you know, like the counting rituals I told you about. Instead of letting the worries dictate my actions, I'd just relate to whatever was happening in the moment and let the worries be like background noise that I can respond to or not. If I could, I'd get rid of my worries, but since I haven't been able to, I guess I'd just let them be and live my life as if they weren't the driver of the truck." To find evidence in Carl's life that he was capable of achieving his miracle, he was asked about *exceptions to problems*: "When is a recent time that you came close to your miracle happening (or when you experienced part of your miracle)?" *Exception questions* operationalize the assumption that all problems in social systems have exceptions, and those exceptions involve both personal abilities and strengths as well as environmental resources (Berg & Miller, 1992). When asked about exceptions, Carl thought, then responded, "Yeah, uh, I guess at my kid's ball game last week. One of those persistent thoughts got rolling that maybe he'd get really hurt playing out there and I couldn't do anything to protect him. It's like I benched the thought and went on watching his game. I'm glad I did, because he got his first home run that day! Normally, I'd be so wrapped up in my obsessing about things that I'd have had to leave the game or do one of my rituals to get my mind off my worries." Asking a *scaling question* further helped Carl in solution building: "If the Number 1 was as bad as it gets and Number 10 were your miracle happening, where would you rate yourself with what you did at your son's game?" Carl replied, "About a 7—no, more like an 8. That was pretty good: I decided what to concentrate on instead of my worries deciding for me." Solution-focused practitioners also ask *difference questions*. "What difference would that make in your life if you were to regularly bench the worries that try to overtake you?" Carl's enthusiastic response was, "Oh man! Huge difference! I waste so much time worrying about things that never happen!"

Carl was like the majority of people in his response to the series of related questions that comprise the Miracle Question and the other solution-building questions. By developing a detailed picture of what he defined as needing to be different for a more satisfying life, he quickly filled in how he would need to proceed in order to achieve the future he'd imagined. Since it was his plan, he viewed it as viable, was motivated to take action on his plan, and did indeed use his simple-sounding metaphorical solution ("bench the worries") to deal with long-standing and severe obsessions. In addition, and just as significant, he gained a sense of competence, dignity, and worth through experiencing his success. In this regard, he not only left his problem behind by achieving his self-defined solution, but his identity as a competent individual was also validated. Validation of one's strengths through direct experience is typically far more influential and empowering than when we try to provide validation or solutions for them.

Solution-focused brief therapy (SFBT) offers a valuable approach to of strength-based practice in clinical settings. SFBT is now practiced in clinical settings around the world: from mental health to criminal justice, from schools to medical settings, from children's residential to nursing homes, and from hospice to prisons, to name a few of the settings where the approach has demonstrated its usefulness. Its effectiveness is such that it is currently being reviewed as a "best practice" model.

COMMUNITY PRACTICE

While social work has maintained a long-term commitment to considering the social, political, and economic contexts within which people live their lives, the focus on individuals and families continues to be a predominant form of practice. However, lying close beneath the surface has been a small but lively interest in community building and all of its attendant possibilities and challenges. To consider the strengths perspective in relation to community offers a rich area of exploration and practice applications. From a historical perspective, social work planted itself within the community. In contrast to the individual and family focus of the Charity Organization Society, the founders of the Settlement House movement saw and acted on the need to establish themselves within neighborhoods and to see themselves as sharing the burdens and the possibilities of collective action to improve the lives of their neighbors. The need for mutual support and collective action continues to be a magnet that draws us into yet another opportunity to put the strengths perspective into action. The community projects at the University of Kansas School of Social Welfare have taken on this challenge in order to prepare students for community practice. (See also McMillen & Pransky, Chapter 13 and Rapp & Sullivan, Chapter 12.)

In the mid-1990s, the school partnered with community organizations to establish community practice programs in the urban core of Kansas City, Kansas. These projects have served a dual purpose including addressing issues identified as high priority by the community by implementing state-of-the-art practices and providing a rich and unique practicum experience to social work students. With the benefit of years of experience, two of these projects have developed significant value to both the community and the School of Social Welfare.

For the past eight years, a team of social work students and their practicum instructor have been placed at a local community development association, located in a neighborhood in Kansas City, Kansas. This community of 1,200 suffers from the social problems common to old, urban core neighborhoods: low income (i.e., median annual income of $16,000 with almost 25 percent of the population disabled); low educational rates (almost 40 percent of the population with no high school diploma or equivalency); neighborhood instability (over 50 percent of the housing stock is rental); and old, deteriorating housing stock and neighborhood infrastructure.

Despite the myriad problems faced by the community, its greatest strength lies in an active and engaged citizenry with a vision for what their community could be. Using a strengths model, the social work students have been instrumental in making some of these dreams become a reality. In collaboration with a strong local development association, local churches, schools, community police, businesses, neighborhood groups, a free clinic, and many neighborhood leaders, the student team identified youth as the area of greatest concern to the community. Concerns centered on poor academic achievement including high dropout rates, and the absence of any organized, out-of-school activities or safe places for youth to meet friends. Afternoons and weekends, many kids hang out on the streets and ultimately get into trouble with neighbors and police.

The social work team has developed numerous initiatives to assist the community's children. A youth academy was begun that focused on empowering kids to become a part of the community. The youngsters learn about the proud history of their community and learn to think about ways to make it better. After they have set a goal for improving their community, the social work team helps the youth identify the steps, work with community groups to get the necessary permission and resources, and carry through with the identified projects. The youth select projects of interest to them, such as painting school playground equipment, painting over graffiti, and cleaning up trashy areas near their homes.

A Freedom School, funded by the Children's Defense Fund was welcomed by the community this past summer. The school is focused on helping youth develop a love of reading, as well as a multicultural understanding of the community and social action. The social work team helped a local church write the successful grant application and helped neighborhoods organize fundraising efforts. Because of its relationships with schools and families, the social work team was indispensable in recruiting youth, obtaining parental permission, and setting up the administrative data tracking system. The school was successful and will continue next summer. Ninety-four children were enrolled and, on average, two-thirds attended daily. For six weeks of the summer, many of the area's youth were able to be in a safe, enriching environment, participating in extraordinary experiences, such as discussing children's healthcare with a member of Congress.

Another project included turning an inner city lot into a safe park for youth. The team and the local community development organization recruited neighbors and local businesses to clear the lot of debris, donate trees, bushes, flowers, sod, and wood for a deck, fence, and outdoor furniture. Churches and local grocers furnished food for the 74 volunteers, including many children, who arrived to turn an eyesore into a park in just one day. Significantly, the kids named the park, "Paradise."

The School of Social Welfare team is highly valued by the community. Over time, the team has built relationships and trust and is in a unique position to be helpful. In an area overwhelmed with unmet need, organizations and community leaders are so beleaguered with problem solving that they are rarely able to engage in proactive activities that would arise from applying strengths model. The team's activities grow out of strong relationships and understanding the shared vision—the hopes, dreams, aspirations—of the community. The team is able to play the same role with the community that the case manager plays with a client using the strengths model. The priorities and goals are derived from the community's vision and the team's job is to help actualize the goals. They organize the various community partners to collaborate on developing and implementing a plan. They fill in the gaps, contributing unique knowledge and skills and accessing resources.

Located in an adjacent neighborhood, a second community project offers an interesting counterpoint to the one described above. In this case, the community is a high school comprised of 1,200 students, the staff and faculty, the families of students, and the local organizations that possess resources needed by the families. For the past three years, a team of social work students and their practicum instructor have been placed at this inner city high school. The student body is multicultural (51 percent Hispanic; 25 percent African American; 23 percent non-Hispanic white; and 1 percent other). The fact that less than half of the teens starting high school actually graduate is of great concern to the community. Truancy, while a problem in and of itself, is also viewed as the most powerful indicator of youth who are likely to drop out. The social work team was asked to focus on the group of high school students who are truant.

The team has developed multiple strategies to approach this concern. Of particular importance to the team is to engage in activities that would empower teens to become part of the solution rather than identifying them as the problem. After surveying the teens to determine barriers to attendance, teen advisors were recruited to develop recommendations to the school that would address some of the most common barriers. One such advisory committee has been addressing the issue of school violence which causes some students to avoid school and others to be suspended. With the support of the social work team, the high school student advisory committee implemented the Students Advocating Against Violence (SAAV) project.

Implementing the SAAV plan, the entire student body was divided into two groups, by gender, which competed to achieve the most days without a fight. The advisory committee selected a succession of individual rewards for members of groups accomplishing each benchmark, beginning with five days. At the end of the school year, the boys were on a roll, having achieved more than sixty fight-free days. More importantly, students themselves had begun to mediate conflicted situations before they became violent.

The social work team also implemented a Mini-Grant program. Students who have an idea for improving the school write a proposal describing their idea, identify what materials they will need, and include how much the project will cost. The team helps students understand how to get the information that they need to complete their proposal and assists in getting the necessary permissions. The high school students do the work. The most popular projects that students have implemented have been aimed at improving the appearance of school grounds and to recognize student achievement by displaying honors in the school halls. All of these examples demonstrate the power that is experienced by youth who can set their own goals and participate actively in finding solutions to the problems they daily encounter. They become actors in their own lives, rather than being subjects who are acted upon.

COMMON DIMENSIONS OF STRENGTHS-BASED AND SOLUTION-FOCUSED PRACTICE

At first glance, the areas of case management, clinical practice, and community practice seem to require very different approaches. Imagining that people with severe mental illness, families and individuals with a stunning assortment of problems of daily living, and communities wracked with poverty, crime, and serious health problems could all benefit from a similar approach seems to defy the knowledge and experience of social workers and other professionals who work closely with them. The "problem-solving model" adopted by social work in the 1950s and its continuing prevalence in virtually all fields of practice suggests that one must start with the presenting problem(s) before moving on to a plan for "intervention" in the problem area. The language of "problems" and "intervention" has become firmly lodged in our assessment and diagnostic tools and requires us to find and stay with the problem until it is solved. However, strengths-based social work practice offers a very different vision.

A key dimension of the strengths perspective rests with the practitioner's willingness to adopt a radically different understanding of the worker–client relationship. Anyone familiar with social work knows that the quality of this relationship is the essential core of good practice. Meta-analysis of half a century of outcome data tells us that this is more than just a "nice" practice principle. Instead, a preponderance of evidence shows that a strong positive alliance is essential to successful practice (Miller, Hubble & Duncan, 1995). The presence of respect, compassion, and a nonjudgmental attitude are embellished with the skills of focused listening and marshaling needed resources. However, strengths-based practice requires another level of awareness. This begins with the worker's examination of her or his own biases about people whose life situations have made them "clients." To be a "client" is to be an "other." The term suggests that there is something lacking in that person that others, including oneself, do not lack. In the course of formal social work education, the personal biases that one may have regarding people who become "clients" (they are "lazy" or "damaged" or "sinful") may only gain new, professional vocabulary (they are "borderline" or "acting out"). Carrying those labels into daily practice does two things. It ensures that the practitioner will impose his or her own beliefs by believing that he or she knows what is best for them and also ensures that the worker will be in the "driver's seat." Unless social workers can consciously examine and adopt a view that places capacity, strengths, and hope in the center of their work, they will have difficulty supporting the fragile new beliefs of their clients.

To accomplish this, strengths-based and solution-focused practice requires a very different starting point. It asserts that every single person, no matter what his or her circumstances, is deserving of what we might call "radical respect." This respect is due, not just for what someone has done or not done, but for the amazing potential that sits quietly within each of us, waiting to be energized. The practitioner serves as a spark that lights up these possibilities within each person. In the midst of the vast array of problems that come with being human, we also have an incalculable store of promise and potential. It is this potential, as well as respect for the struggles people have encountered and surmounted, that requires us to step back and offer them radical respect. In this context, the focus on goals runs like a strong, shared cord through case management, clinical practice, and community practice.

Whether one is working with someone who is mentally ill or deeply distraught because of personal and family difficulties or struggling with impoverished community conditions, the place to start is by asking what the person/community wants instead of what the problem is. The formation of a goal about positive possibilities begins to engage a part of their minds that has been wrung dry by the worry and sense of failure they feel. To connect with their dreams and aspirations for a better life is the ignition switch that starts an entirely new avenue of engagement, energy, and hope. Both strengths- and solution-focused work intentionally create a partnership to design in detail the shape of a person's life beyond the problem. A relationship that builds on respect, trust, and support is, as with all social work, the means by which people gather the strength and hope to make changes in their lives.

The opportunity to name their own goals can be a powerful reinforcement for those whose problems have made them feel powerless and unworthy. In order for this new sense of power to be fully realized, there must be an intentional shift in the dynamics of power that are laced through every worker–client relationship. The "pathology paradigm" makes it very clear that the power to name the client's reality rests with the worker. However, strengths-based practice requires just the opposite. From the first encounter, the worker invites full engagement in the solution process by asking what the client wants to accomplish and how they can work together as a team to craft a better life beyond the problem. The deep respect for people's own self-righting abilities and their expertise on their own lives brings new meaning to our belief in self-determination. Whether it is in the clinic or community, success hinges on the intentional creation of a collaborative and hopeful relationship that helps unlock the natural store of reserves of strengths and aspirations of individuals, families, and communities.

Conclusion.   One of social work's strong suits is its skill in connecting people with needed resources. Identifying the supports necessary for an individual or group to move more surely toward their goals has helped put the "social" in social work. The complex networks of communication, resource tracking, and follow-up are daily fare for most practitioners. However, the role of resources expresses itself somewhat differently across case management, clinical, and community social work. For those suffering from serious mental illness, a wide array of resources are typically called into play in order for the person to find a comfortable niche in his or her community. As one can see from the Kansas Strengths Assessment tool (p. 3), the life domains cover everything from living situations to vocation/education, health, social support, recreation, and spirituality. As in the case of Paul, the social worker uses maximum creativity in linking the person with needed resources and supports. Community practice shares a similar expansiveness in identifying and connecting community groups with social service programs, city officials, policymakers, resident leaders, and funders in order to help the community group achieve its goals. The earlier descriptions of the neighborhood community project and the urban high school project help to demonstrate the collaboration with local churches, schools, local businesses, neighborhood leaders, and others that is required to use community strengths and assets in support of community goals. While solution-focused brief therapy, as with other clinical models, does not focus on environmental change, advocacy, and drawing on community strengths, it still offers very useful extensions to strength-based practice through its intense focus on the transformative potential of each person and through this, the shared commitment to collective empowerment at all levels of practice.

To ask someone how her or his life could be different begins the dream for a better future. The question itself tells us that the person experiencing the problem is the one who ultimately knows best. Acknowledging clients' expertise on their own lives creates a radically different dynamic in relationships, one which clearly conveys the trust, optimism, and respect of the practitioner. In contrast to problem- and pathology-focused approaches, long in use in social work and other fields, strength- and solution-focused practice is hope-inspiring practice. By attending to what people want in their lives instead of the problem, the ensuing goals and their renewed optimism give them new hope. This hope also engages and lifts the practitioner. The success of the relationship no longer rests completely on his or her shoulders. Instead, there is a collaborative partnership in which the practitioner can more fully express the values of radical respect, self-righting and hope that are the deep, true anchors of good social work practice.

DISCUSSION QUESTIONS/EXERCISES

1. How do you account for the growing popularity of solution-focused and strengths approaches to practice?

2. What are the key differences between solution-focused and strengths-based practices? What are their commonalities?

3. How do you get away from clients getting stuck on talking about their problems exclusively without your invalidating their "reality" or losing rapport?

4. What they want is the most important piece of information to be gained from clients. Why is that? What does that actually mean?

5. Can you see yourself practicing from these perspectives? If so, how? If not, why not?

6. If you were the "client," what difference do you imagine it would make for you if your worker practiced from the traditional problem, deficit, and pathology focus approach or from a strengths- and solution-focused approach?

REFERENCES

Berg, I. K. & deShazer, S. (1993). Making numbers talk: Language in therapy. In S. Friedman (Ed.), *The new language of change: Constructive collaboration in psychotherapy*. New York: Guilford Press.

Berg, I. K. & Miller, S. D. (1992). *Working with the problem drinker: A solution-focused approach*. New York: Norton.

Chamberlain, R. & Rapp, C. A. (1983). *Training manual for case managers in community mental health*. Lawrence: Kansas School: University of Kansas School of Social Welfare.

DeJong, P. & Berg, I. K. (2008). *Interviewing for solutions* (3rd ed). Belmont, CA: Thompson Brooks/Cole.

deShazer, S. (1988). *Clues: Investigating solution in brief therapy*. New York: Norton.

deShazer, S. (2003). The miracle question. *Internet article found at* http://grief-therapy.org/steve_miracle.htm.

deShazer, S. (2004). Personal communication.

Hillman, J. & Ventura, M. (1992). *We've had a hundred years of psychotherapy and the world's getting worse*. New York: HarperCollins.

Jacobson, W. (2001). Beyond therapy: Bringing social work back to human services reform. *Social Work, 46*(1), 51–60.

Lipchik, E. (2002). *Beyond technique in solution-focused therapy: Working with emotions and the therapeutic relationship*. New York: Guilford Press.

Kisthardt, W. E. (1993). The impact of the strengths model of case management from the consumer's perspective. In M. Harris & H. Bergman (Eds.), *Case management: Theory and practice* (pp. 165–182). Langhorn, PA: Harwood Academic Publishers

Miller, S., Hubble, M., & Duncan, B. (1995, March/April). No more bells and whistles. *Family Therapy Networker*, 53–63.

Modrcin, M., Rapp, C. A., & Chamberlain, R. (1985). *Case management with psychiatrically disabled individuals: Curriculum and training program*. Lawrence: University of Kansas School of Social Welfare.

Modrcin, M., Rapp, C. A., & Poertner, J. (1988). The evaluation of case management services with the chronically mentally Ill. *Evaluation and Program Planning, 11*(4).

Pransky, J. & McMillen, D. P. (2008). Exploring the true nature of resilience: A view from the inside out. In D. Saleebey (Ed.), *The strengths perspective in social work practice*. 5th edition, Boston: Allyn & Bacon/Longman.

Rapp, C. A. (1992). The strengths perspective of case management with persons suffering from severe mental illness. In D. Saleebey (Ed.), *The strengths perspective in social work* (pp. 45–58). New York: Longman.

Rapp, C. A. (1993). Theory, principles, and methods of strengths model of case management. In M. Harris & H. Bergman (Eds.), *Case management: Theory and practice* (pp. 143–64). Washington, DC: American Psychiatric Association.

Rapp, C. A. (1998). *The strengths model: Case management with people suffering from severe and persistent mental illness*. New York: Oxford University Press.

Rapp, C. A. & Chamberlain, R. (1985, September) Case Management Services to the Chronically Mentally Ill. *Social Work, 30*(5), 417–422.

Rapp, C. A. & Goscha, R. J. (2006). *The strengths model: Case management with people with psychiatric disabilities.*, New York: Oxford University Press.

Rapp, C. A. & Wintersteen, R. (1989). The strengths model of case management: Results from twelve demonstrations. *Psychosocial Rehabilitation Journal, 13*, 23–32.

Saleebey, D. (Ed.). (2006, 2002, 1997, 1992). *The strengths perspective in social work practice*. New York: Allyn and Bacon/Longman.

Snyder, C. R. & Lopez, S. J. (2007). *Positive psychology: The scientific and practical explorations of human strengths*. Thousand Oaks, CA: Sage Publications

Weick, A., Rapp, C. A., Sullivan, W. P., & Kisthardt, W. E. (1989). A strengths perspective for social work practice. *Social Work, 89*, 350–354.

CHAPTER SEVEN

THE STRENGTHS PERSPECTIVE IN CRIMINAL JUSTICE

MICHAEL D. CLARK

PRELIMINARY QUESTIONS

This chapter will introduce the application of the strengths perspective to the field of criminal justice. As the development of a background is important for any sketch, four preliminary questions are asked to establish a backdrop:

1. *Why does criminal justice focus almost exclusively on problems, failure, and flaws when it is an offender's strengths, resources, and aspirations that propel law-abiding behavior?*

   Problems are important and certainly call for our attention, but criminal justice departments who have adopted the strengths perspective understand that *problems do not include directions on how to get us past the trouble.* Problems may get the ball rolling and start the process, but that is not the same as saying problems will finish the job. Change always comes from a person's place of power and strength. Criminal justice certainly knows this on some level, yet systemically the methods and practices to elicit, amplify, and utilize strengths are not in place.

2. *Why does our field occupy itself with punishment when a host of new meta-analytic research has proven that the exclusive use of punishment—in the absence of treatment— increases criminal behavior?*

   The persistent nature of the problem arises in the very efforts to solve it. The attempted solution has become the problem. Even though these meta-analyses (Gendreau et al., 2002; Gendreau, Little, & Goggin, 1996; Gibbs, 1986; Taxman, 1999) are very clear that pure punishment makes things worse, the field of criminal justice has found it difficult to transition away from harsh and heavy-handed tactics to more motivational interventions (Walters, Clark, Gingerich, & Meltzer, 2007). Criminal justice seems like a massive naval vessel trying to alter its course. It doesn't "turn on a dime," thus, leaving any change of directions to be a slow and cumbersome process.

Treating offenders as subhuman entities that need punishment to change has been not only tolerated, but in some instances applauded. A good summation is offered by Viets et al. (2002), "There is no reason to believe that offenders respond to fundamentally different principles of learning, thinking, and motivation than the rest of humankind. Confrontational approaches . . . become a self-fulfilling prophecy, engendering evasiveness and resentment while doing nothing to decrease the likelihood of repeat offenses" (p. 27). With our criminal justice departments geared toward punishment and slow to change, then hear again the words of Oliver Hazard Perry: "We have met the enemy, and they are ours."

3. *Why do we construct solutions solely from our point of view, when we are not the ones being asked to change?*
   If officers don't listen to those they supervise, they may fall prey to establishing court plans that are more for the officer than they are for the probationer. Consider that effectiveness rates for working with offenders have not improved since the 1960s (Clark, 2007). During this five-decade span, all punishment and offender treatment has had one frame of reference—it has occurred from the criminal justice professional's point of view. Telling offenders *why and how*—why they should change and how to go about these alterations has not brought the intended results. Can criminal justice change perspectives to one that may possibly offer more productivity—the offender's point of view? With little or no formal training to help them understand human motivation, criminal justice staff continue to predominantly advise, castigate, and coerce. Without knowledge of the mechanics of human behavior change, conditions and efforts so critical to assist change are ignored or left to wither. Burnett (2004) points out that it has now been about forty years since Matza's (1969) influential call for criminologists to adopt a method of "appreciation" in which the aim is to comprehend and to illuminate the subject's view and to interpret the world as it appears to him or her. It was almost fifteen years ago that Berg (1994) suggested, "Stay close to the client's definition of the problem and possible solutions, since it is he or she who will be asked to do the necessary changing" (p. 36). Could this be the decade that we finally turn to this sensibility?

4. *When receiving probation services, probationers only spend an average of one-third of one percent (.03 percent) of their lifetime with their probation officer* (Farrell, 2002). *So, if probationers end up changing, where does it come from?*
   It is a stretch to think large lifestyle changes are enacted because of what criminal justice staff do. The far more convincing notion is that the bulk of change comes from what offenders do. Stephen Farrell (2002), a noted criminologist in Great Britain, states, ". . . continued concentration upon 'what the officer/probation services does' inevitably misses a huge number of other factors which are at play when people desist or persist." (p. 175). Even newly minted criminologists would concede that most change is self-change, whether it occurs via contact with the criminal justice field, from participation in treatment, or through self-determination. Will criminal justice ever begin an earnest investigation into the other 99.7 percent of a defendant's life to find what intrinsic reasons for change may exist—and what indigenous resources await to power those changes?

A BASELINE

The field of criminal justice has developed over time to deal with crime and justice. It's a huge complex that consumes billions of dollars annually and affects millions of citizens and their families. Consider these recent figures:

■ More than 7 million men and women are currently under some form of criminal justice supervision in the United States (U.S. Department of Justice, 2006).
■ Among nations, the United States has one of the world's highest rates for incarcerated citizens, ranking with the most oppressive societies (Walters et al., 2007).
■ The rate of U. S. adult residents placed under correctional supervision nearly tripled between 1980 and 2005 (USDOJ, 2006).

When one reviews these figures, the oft-heard labels of "crisis" and "epidemic" regarding the state of this field seem wholly justified. Why is our criminal justice system an entity that cannot seem to stabilize? Worse yet, why is this a system that seems to be in a state of perpetual growth? There are several reasons for a field that seems to have all the earmarks of a "growth industry":

■ Major social problems scorch opportunities and resources. Poverty, inadequate healthcare, and the paucity of gainful employment at a living wage continue in the absence of public policies and social programs to address these significant problems. Desolation and despair abound and the lack of prospects (social capital) becomes a root cause for a good portion of illegal activity.
■ A second reason is a philosophical orientation toward offenders that creates a self-fulfilling prophecy. A lack of compassion and a penchant to label offenders as unsavory, dangerous, and disreputable only serves to perpetuate a climate of fear towards this group—and a reason to distance and separate them from the rest of society. There is a mindset that if ever a group were to deserve the label of "others"—reprehensible, undeserving, and beyond help—then offenders represent this class. Offenders are a group in our society whom it is generally acceptable, even laudable, to abuse and disparage because "these people" need or deserve it. We justify this treatment believing it is good for them and for society. We collectively imagine that degradation and contempt, even beyond measured punishment, somehow makes them better, and makes us a safer and a more just society. Enter a world where one act can make you deviant, but a thousand good acts may not bring redemption.
■ A third reason is a willingness to rely solely on the use of punishment as a means of addressing drug addiction and crime. The public erroneously believes in the effectiveness of punishment for reducing crime and making our streets safer. A domino effect is created where punishment does not bring the results, which issues a call for more of what's not working. Politicians fall prey to the public's cry, believing they must be seen as the toughest on crime in order to be elected to office. All of this prompts

the enactment of new laws that call for harsher punishment and longer sentences. This situation twists into a never-ending pretzel of futility.

As bleak as this all sounds, *I do not wish to share in the pessimism that nothing is good and nothing seems to get better!* Over my career, I have seen too many advances and improvements in the field of criminal justice to indulge in cynicism and gloom. It is the premise of this chapter that many of the advancements underway in the field of criminal/juvenile justice are being propelled by a strengths perspective, whether the actions are unwitting or intentional.

A PHRASE FOREVER LINKED: "CRIME AND PUNISHMENT"

Crime. Punishment. To become aware of how culturally linked the two issues have become—and to understand how truly ineffective they are in tandem—is to begin to appreciate the central benefit for the application of a strengths approach to this field. Delivering punishment via the criminal justice system in the United States is a truly complex social act. Hollin (2002) notes that the key point to focus on with respect to the administration of punishment are the *outcomes to be achieved.*

- If the criminal justice field seeks *retribution*—that is, to answer crime with painful responses and impose sanctions for the criminal behavior—then the punitive measures ladled out (arguably) achieve that outcome.
- If the criminal justice field seeks *incapacitation* for public safety—that is, to lock someone up behind bars and thereby prevent them from committing any more crimes—then inflicting a loss of freedom (e.g., punishment) will achieve that outcome as well.
- However, if the criminal justice field seeks to *change behavior*—that is, to supplement prosocial behavior to override and eliminate antisocial criminal behavior, then the achievement of this outcome is highly uncertain. (pp. 245–246).

Using punishment to change behavior is the foundation to deterrence theory. However, Hollin (2002) continues by citing that punishment has not proven effective for either general or specific deterrence. For *general deterrence,* or the notion that punishing criminals will deter other members of society from committing crimes, the returns on punishment for deterring the actions of others have been poor. It is also doubtful that punishment lends itself to *specific deterrence,* or the notion that it deters the specific person and motivates long-term behavior change at the individual level. Rather, new meta-analyses notes that punishment, in the absence of any treatment, *increases* criminal behavior (Walters et al., 2007). Hollin (2002) concludes that on either level (society or individual) "punishment demonstrably fails to motivate offenders to change" and wonders what the criminal justice field will turn to as alternative methods for changing behavior (p. 246).

THE TWO Cs OF PROBATION HISTORY—CONTROL AND COMPLIANCE

At its most elemental level, the field of criminal justice—as an extension of our government—is charged with public safety and preserving order. To "speak the language" and be considered a true member in the world of criminal justice, one must understand the levels of success that loom for the average correctional professional.

The first level can be determined in how one answers the question: *Is it strengths based to handcuff a citizen and lock him or her up in a detention center?*

If you answered, "yes—under certain circumstances," you've attained the critical first level for understanding how strengths-based practice is implemented within this field. When someone is out of control and is harming others, placing self and those around them in physical jeopardy, then appropriate authorities taking control is certainly warranted. Restraint is necessary to stabilize and bring into control those who have lost all control.

It is at the next level—compliance—where further differences begin to emerge between those that think they understand the application of a strengths approach and those who truly do. Compliance is conceptualized as a waystation, an incremental stop on the journey to behavior change. We can always use the court's authority to have probationers parrot back to us what we want to hear, but deference is not change. Conformity is not transformation.

In the face of frustration, staff will often take the stance of "We didn't come find you (offender), you found your way to us (court, probation department) through your illegal behavior, now it's your task to take our direction and cooperate." Although seemingly correct, this a posture that creates resistance. With confrontation initiated, this stance will inevitably have to rely on coercion and heavy-handed methods to achieve cooperation. Human motivation is much more complicated than establishing what is the "right" or "wrong" thing to do—and it is created out of a host of cultural, gender-based and community-specific resources and dynamics. Gaining compliance to ensure stability following an out-of-control situation is imperative, and demanding obedience is important for crisis situations. However, a strengths-based doctrine does not believe obedience is a lofty goal—even dogs can be taught to obey.

Compliance, while part of a continuum of control, cannot rest as a final goal. Behavior change is always in ascendancy with strengths-based practice. In community corrections, it is important to be able to appreciate how internal and external forces work together to facilitate positive behavior. Because we work with a mandated population, change might begin because of external pressure (e.g., conditions of probation), but later can be continued for internal reasons (e.g., probationer sees personal benefits). The process would ideally take the form of the incremental stages, "I have to change, I need to change, I want to change." Officers can choose to use strategies that move change to the "inside" or just as easily allow compliance to remain pressure-driven and superficial. It is important for those who seek to increase a defendant's readiness to change to understand where change comes from.

ADDING ONE MORE: THE 3 Cs OF STRENGTHS PERSPECTIVE —CONTROL, COMPLIANCE, *AND CHANGE*

Raising motivation levels and increasing an offender's readiness to change requires a certain "climate"—a helpful attitude and a supportive approach that one would take with an offender. This climate becomes grist for developing a helping relationship—and it is imperative that this relationship occur between agent and probationer if enduring change is to occur. This chapter continues to sketch a criminal justice field that begins to form an atmosphere for assisting behavior change. I will examine this type of climate across the criminal justice field (the macro perspective), within probation departments (the mezzo perspective), and into the individual pairing of any officer and offender (the micro perspective).

Across the Criminal Justice Field (macro): What Business Are We In?

Duncan, Miller, and Sparks (2004), promoting outcome-informed efforts, recall a landmark article by Theodore Levitt, a Harvard business professor. Levitt (1975) recounted the rise of the railroad industry throughout much of the 1800s and into the next century. The railroad industry vaulted to tremendous success as it laid track from city to city, crisscrossing and connecting our continent. Millions of dollars were pocketed by those laying the track and building this nation's rail infrastructure. The pace of life quickened and demand rose for speedy travel.

However, as the first baby boomers began to leave their nests in the 1960s, the railroads were in trouble—actually in serious decline. Why? Railroad executives would answer that it was due to the need for speedier transportation and faster communication that was being filled in other ways (i.e., cars, trucking industry, telecommunications). That reasoning made no sense to Levitt. To this business professor it begged a question. Duncan, Miller, and Sparks (2004) note the irony:

> The railroad industry, Levitt (1975) argued, was not in trouble "because the need was being filled by others . . . but because it was not filled by the railroads themselves." Why did the industry not diversify when it had the chance? Because, as it turns out, railroad executives had come to believe they were in the *train* rather than the transportation business. (pp. 81–82)

Due to this limiting conception, trucking and airfreight industries prospered while locomotive engines fell into disrepair, parked on rusted track in the back of neglected railroad yards. The railroad industry had come to believe it was in the railroad business instead of the transportation business. It would seem that probation, as a criminal justice entity, is much like the railroad industry of our past century—it has come to believe that it is in probation business rather than the behavior change business. Our field seems primarily concerned with the process of probation—ensuring adequate supervision, compliance to probation orders, and the completion of mounds of attendant paperwork. Process takes center stage rather than a principal focus on strategies and techniques that will encourage positive behavior change (outcomes).

The problem lies in the mindset that pervades the probation field that allows outcomes to take a back seat to process. Consider a recent lament by a deputy director who manages a fairly large community corrections division. Engaged in a discussion regarding the "business of probation" during a recent training session, he offered his state's probation officer of the year award as an example. This annual contest awards much more than a certificate or a new wristwatch—the prize is a week-long vacation in the Caribbean! As can be imagined, staff keep a constant eye on their efforts and work hard to win the prize. However, this deputy director noted the field is so process oriented that whatever agent might win this trip would do so because of timely paperwork completion, more face-to-face meetings than required, comprehensive report writing, and punctual court appearances. Yet if outcomes were considered, this same officer, enjoying the sun and waves from a relaxing beach-side cabaña, might be embarrassed to know his or her caseload detailed a 30 percent absconding rate or a 60 percent recidivism rate. Sadly, this situation is not one of a kind. Another state's officer of the year award is even easier to determine; it is awarded to the staff member who has the highest rate for collection of court fees. Process is king. The business of probation occupies the limelight.

For those who might bristle at this implication, a quick inventory is telling: If your department requires new-agent training, how much of that orientation curriculum involves motivational enhancement training or strategies/techniques to encourage positive behavior change? Consider any continuing education training recently conducted by your department. More often than not, training titles would have included phrases such as, "Managing the . . . ," "Supervising the . . . ," "Officer Safety," "Computer Training," "Risk Assessment," or the ubiquitous phrase, "How to Deal with the . . . (sex offender, dually diagnosed, hostile client, etc.)" This is not to imply these training topics are unimportant, but rather to point out the sheer absence of any tactical curiosity regarding positive behavior change. Whether training topics or journal articles, both appear pertinent to probation services—not behavior change. The business of probation proliferates. Managing trumps motivating. Supervision obscures relationships. Intimidation overshadows encouragement. Compliance remains in ascendancy. Whither change?

Looking to our past may help us to understand the present, allowing us to examine why we find ourselves in this current state. It would seem we were born into a correctional world that had always known tension between the ideals of punishment and treatment. Our field seems unable to extricate itself from a seemingly hypnotic hold of a "tough-as-nails" approach. To try and understand how the probation field became mesmerized is to appreciate two swings of the crime control pendulum that have occurred over the last fifty years. Psychological and sociological theories of criminal behavior gained prominence in the 1940s and helped the principle of rehabilitation of offenders (offender treatment) to flourish throughout the 1950s and 1960s (Gendreau & Ross, 1987). However, evidence to support the treatment paradigm did not keep pace by tracking outcomes and building supportive evidence, so the pendulum swing of correctional policy started to move back to the punishment and "just desserts" approach. Rehabilitation lost favor by the late 1970s and began to recede during the 1980s.

One swing followed another as the ideal of punishment lost ground. Clive Hollin (2001) notes, "If the 1980s saw the fall of the rehabilitation ideal, then the early 1990s witnessed a spectacular resurrection. . . . (This) resurrection of treatment can be directly traced to the impact of a string of meta-analytic studies of the effects of offender treatment published towards the end of the 1980s and into the 1990s" (p. 10). The predominance of punishment had not demonstrated effectiveness, and in many instances, was shown to increase recidivism. With the advent of the 1990s, supervision and treatment enjoyed more certainty of success (Andrews & Bonta, 2003; Bernfield et al., 2001).

How, then, is probation staff to be responsive to motivational issues and work to enhance offender readiness to change, when a good portion of our criminal justice culture (macro) remains stuck in an adversarial "get-tough" atmosphere? Anthropology may offer an explanation. Steven Pinker, in his 1997 landmark book, *How the Mind Works,* notes there are parts of our current human brain and body that once served a survival purpose in our primordial cave-dwelling past—yet today these same body parts no longer serve any real function. These anthropological remnants become an appropriate analogy for the "tough-as-nails" stance that many embrace within our probation field. What worked for the sole emphasis on retribution continues only as an obstacle for employing strengths and assisting change (starting positive behavior).

A Second Pendulum Swing?   We've witnessed the pendulum swing between the punishment and treatment camps in our field, yet could there actually be two pendulums? This author (Clark, 2006) has proposed earlier there are two, one that is research based and another that is practice based. The research pendulum swings in the foreground, set in motion by criminologists who suggest what course of action will reduce crime. However, I have noted there is a second pendulum, with a swing moving in the background, moving much slower and shadowing the first. This pendulum swing involves the atmosphere and attitudes of those who work within the probation field. The strengths perspective assists the practice pendulum, which is created by—but not always in sync with—the research pendulum. To understand this second pendulum is to understand that our field seems shackled by a lag-effect, out-of-date attitudes held by many in the field who seek not only compliance from offenders but dominance and primacy over them as well. This hold-over from the "just desserts"/punishment era remains alive, suppressing behavior change as it limits an offender's involvement to passive and submissive roles. The brain is dead, but the body continues.

Within Probation Departments (mezzo): The Obstacle of the "Either/Or"

What about this recent pendulum swing has brought our field back to a focus on treatment? What is this business of behavior change? How does change occur? And more importantly to our field, how can department policy and a probation officer's efforts increase an offender's readiness to change? These questions can guide departments toward a fundamental change in both attitude and objectives.

Change is a process that often takes time. It can occur by sudden insight or dramatic shifts (i.e., epiphanies, "wake up calls"), but the vast majority of change occurs slowly and incrementally. The stages of change theory (Prochaska & DiClemente, 1983) has even mapped out these incremental steps, lending support to the idea that change is a process rather than a point-in-time event. When working with probationers new to our system (or those returning) who may pose harm to themselves or others, initial objectives must begin with offender stabilization. Those who are out of control must be brought into control; hence compliance becomes an all-important first step in offender supervision. If this were not true, we would be neglecting our primary mission of social control at the community's peril.

It's time to expose a form of "either/or" conceptualization by probation staff that ends up as a stumbling block for improved outcomes. This block is analogous to brewing tea. To enjoy a cup of tea, it's not hot water *or* tea leaves; rather, it's hot water *and* tea leaves, the key combination that allows the brew to be served. However, there are those who would strip this sensibility from our own field of probation. Their concrete thinking would have us believe in a limiting contrast; that we either secure compliance or increase the readiness to change, that one either imposes sanctions or establishes a helping relationship. This contrast is so pervasive it is seldom noticed or examined. The strengths perspective contends that objectives of control and motivation can exist side by side. This "both/and" inclusiveness will be sketched out later in this chapter.

Those who show little respect to offenders and adopt an adversarial style are only successful in imposing (once again) another type of unproductive either/or contrast: Either one is tough or soft. A tough, unyielding approach could be characterized as "holding the line." Those who take a tough approach justify their harsh attitudes and abrasive conduct toward offenders believing this hardened stance is the only true option. To do otherwise would constitute a soft approach, which is merely "wanting to be liked" or "trying to be friends." While heavy-handed advocates may not achieve acceptable levels of success with their adversarial approach, they feel a relief that (at least) they will never be accused of acting indulgent or pandering to the offender. It has long been a reaction in our field to blame the offender when change does not occur (Clark, 1995). Rather than examine our own efforts, a lack of improvement is explained away as more evidence of the intractable nature of probationers.

Why is a tough approach tolerated in our field? How can it be purged? Our field needs to dissuade the "us vs. them" mindset as it becomes a hindrance to all—hampering the officer/probationer relationship, department objectives, offender improvement, and ultimately the safety of our communities. Space prohibits a review of the multitude of studies (Hubble, Duncan, & Miller, 1999; Miller & Rollnick, 2002) that find a confrontational counseling style limits effectiveness. One such review (Miller, Benefield, & Tonnigan, 1993) is telling. This study found that a directive-confrontational counselor style produced twice the resistance, and only half as many "positive" client behaviors as did a supportive, client-centered approach. The researchers concluded that the more the staff confronted, the more the clients drank at twelve-month follow-up. Problems are compounded as a confrontational style not only pushes success away, but can make matters worse.

It would seem that those who swagger and take delight in adopting a "tough" approach do so without knowledge of this large body of research regarding counselor style. It is at this juncture that many probation staff claim, "We're not counselors!—our job is to enforce the orders of the court." This claim only serves to disappoint and underscore that our field remains fixated on the business of probation—not the business of behavior change.

This brings to mind staff who do not adopt this abrasive style but must work around those who do. These staff witness the insensitive attitudes and disrespectful treatment of offenders and become reactive to it. However, much like a crowd that shrinks back in a bully's presence, these same department colleagues and supervisors fall silent and fail to challenge this callous conduct. It is understandable why many are reluctant to confront. The defense used by the tough crowd is as insidious as it is absolute. "Tough-as-nails" staff again evoke an either/or contrast. They contend that to challenge their insensitive behavior could only come from someone who was "soft"—and staff thought to be soft lack authority and substance. This incredulous mindset shields them from criticism and any subsequent self-evaluation, shielded because anyone who might call their behavior into question would be thought to lack credibility for the sole reason that they disfavor heavy-handed ways! The criticism, or the person who might raise it, would be dismissed—a priori—as lacking integrity.

I am reminded of a probation supervisor who tried to confront a staff member who was known for intimidation tactics and would brag in back office chatter about his ill treatment of probationers. When the supervisor tried to contend that his use of intimidation was both unethical and ineffective, the officer confounded the interchange by a numbing use of the either/or contrast. The officer retorted, "So, what you're saying is that I should molly-coddle them (probationers)?" "No," the supervisor answered, "But you can't use the stick all the time. There are times to use the carrot as well." The officer retorted sarcastically, "So, I'm supposed to be their friend, right?" "No," again replied the supervisor, "But I speak of basic respect." "Respect?" cried the officer, "Respect these people after what they've done?" "Look," the supervisor pleaded, "it's just not effective to constantly go after them." The officer rejoined with a rhetorical question, "So, you're telling me that hugging them is more effective?" After several go-rounds, the exasperated supervisor finally stated, "I guess what I'm trying to say is that you just need to be a little more 'touchy-feely' with those you supervise." The probation officer finished the exchange with the mocking statement, "That's right! When I touch them, I want them to feel it!" Frustrated by the close-mindedness, the supervisor withdrew.

With overwhelming research in hand that a confrontational style inhibits outcomes, it would seem that allowing the voice of those who say the world is flat to coexist with those who know it to be round brings assurance and honor to no one. Our field cannot rise to become change-focused if a confrontational style is tolerated as an acceptable way of "doing business." A heavy-handed approach is a backwards style that becomes an obstacle for the field in toto.

A clarification is necessary. When a strengths perspective is adopted, confrontation is still present but in a vastly different form. Confrontation changes to become an effort to have probationers confront themselves. Two motivational experts, William Miller and Stephen Rollnick (1991), note that the goal of helping with those locked into self-defeating behaviors is to create a "self-confrontation" that prompts mandated clients to "see and accept an uncomfortable reality" (p. 13). This awareness, of coming face-to-face with a disquieting image of oneself, is often a prerequisite for intentional change. However, one would not try to impose this awareness by forcing it upon someone through a confrontational style. To do so often makes matters worse. Multiple research studies (Rollnick, Mason, & Butler, 1999, Tomlin & Richardson, 2004) repeatedly demonstrate that a harsh, coercive style often prompts a "paradoxical response"—the more one is directive and presses, the more the other backs away. Rather than evoking change, it causes an offender to become more entrenched in the problem, arguing and defending his or her current negative behavior. Probation agents are familiar with this "backing away." It can take either active or passive forms, gearing up with the strong emotionality of arguing and tense opposition, or alternately, by shutting down through the absence of emotions, as with passive-aggressive silence or a "Who cares?" dismissal.

How probation officers can help an offender to see and examine his or her situation clearly and change accordingly—all while avoiding the active or passive forms of this paradoxical response? Criminal justice staff need to find the "middle ground."

Finding the Middle Ground

To understand and further behavior change is to understand the interpersonal climate between officer and probationer that encourages change. A strengths approach steers clear of both the hard and soft approach. The "hard" approach is overly directive and places offenders in passive, recipient roles. A "soft" approach correspondingly places the officer in a role that is too passive. A soft approach is also vulnerable to a condition characterized as "professional dangerousness" (Turnell & Edwards, 1999), where an officer, in attempting to keep a hard-won relationship at all costs, refuses to bring violations to the court's attention when he or she should ("I won't tell this time—but don't do it again"). Here the officer has swung too far to the opposite extreme and is not directive enough. The hope and belief that the officer can build an alliance and work together with an offender to make things better is not the same as ignoring violations. Believing that offenders are worth doing business *with* is not at all the same thing as adopting the easiest way of doing business with them.

It would seem neither side wins this debate as both approaches reduce offender outcomes—each for a different reason. An emerging strength-based approach finds middle ground by those who understand the "both/and" inclusion. With a strengths perspective utilized by probation staff, officers are taught to cooperate with the probationer, not the criminal behavior. Probation officers can examine how to impose sanctions and build helpful relationships, and with training, agents can build the skills to supervise for compliance and increase the defendant's readiness for change.

This is not new to our field. Start your own single-subject research by asking any probation supervisor to offer a frank (but discreet) evaluation of the department staff they supervise. Many supervisors can easily walk down their department hallways—and with candor—point to agents who have the abilities to build helpful alliances with offenders without compromising probation orders. These staff seem to understand that compliance and behavior change are not mutually exclusive efforts. What are the traits and skills that make these agents so different? With an eye to effective relationships that are so essential for encouraging change, why are not more probation departments hiring with these inclusive (therapeutic) abilities as criteria for employment?

As noted, there is an abundance of research citing how a confrontational approach repels those we work with and becomes an obstacle for change. Probation departments must speed up this practice pendulum swing by finding their voice, labeling the "tough" approach for what it is—an obstacle. Departments must become empowered to establish a climate that will both ensure compliance and foster hoped-for behavior change.

Into the Individual Pairing of Officer and Probationer (micro): A Helpful Mix

I am unrepentantly optimistic as movements are occurring both outside our field and within our own ranks—all to help the second pendulum swing of officer attitudes to keep pace. There are efforts underway that sketch a helpful mix for how to hold the line with offenders, while at the same time encouraging positive behavior change in probation work (Clark, 1997; Mann et al., 2002).

A further contribution involves a critical look at the power attributed to a probation agent and how that power is used. I have argued elsewhere (Clark, 2001) and repeat my contention that a therapeutic relationship in probation work can be established through (1) perspective, (2) role-taking by the officer, and (3) skillful negotiations with the probationer.

Perspective.   To become versed in assisting change, probation staff must adopt a "lens" or a way of viewing the offender that is consistent with the strengths perspective (Clark, 1997, 1998). The strengths perspective in the justice field is first and foremost a belief in the offenders' ability to change. Although it would be naïve and disingenuous to deny the reality of the harm inflicted by those we work with, Saleebey (1992) cautions:

> If there are genuinely evil people, beyond grace and hope, it is best not to make that assumption about any individual first . . . even if we are to work with someone whose actions are beyond our capacity to understand and accept, we must ask ourselves if they have useful skills and behaviors, even motivations and aspirations that can be tapped in the service of change and to a less destructive way of life. (p. 238)

This strengths perspective embraces the science of "getting up." For the previous forty years, criminal justice has focused on the science and classification of "falling down" as evidenced by our sole focus on deficits, disorders, and failures. The strengths perspective pays attentions to what strengths, resources, and assets probationers might turn to as they attempt to manage and overcome their troubles.

Role-Taking.   There is great power attached to a court. When used appropriately, it can help to change the trajectory of someone's life, bringing health and improvements that radiate throughout a family (and across the larger community). But when this power is abused or misapplied, the trauma and pain that result can continue long after court documents yellow with age. Who wields this power that holds such potential for benefit or harm? A helpful motivational perspective answers, "Not the officer!" The locus of power is actually centered in the judicial bench rather than in any individual officer. To bring this power home to roost with the officer is not only incorrect but can limit or stifle the very relationship that becomes the conveyor of positive behavior change. Take, for example, a short passage included in a chapter entitled "Ethical Considerations," found within the latest edition of Miller and Rollnick's text on motivational interviewing (2002):

> . . . consider a counselor who works with offenders on parole and probation and who has the power at any time to revoke that status and order incarceration (p. 166).

Although this excerpt speaks to the power of "counselors" who work with offenders, it could be argued that the power attributed to the supervising probation officer would be even greater. However, accurately stated, no officer is truly vested with the power to jail an offender, apply new consequences, or to increase consequences by personal decision or whim. This is not a case of "splitting hairs" with a play on words. An agent must petition the court. The court then works to substantiate the alleged violations of probation in a formal hearing, and it is the court that determines guilt or innocence and imposes additional sanctions where appropriate.

There is no intent to disparage those who may not fully understand the judicial process, only to point out how pervasive this misperception has become across our culture. The statement that the probation officer ". . . has the power at any time to revoke that status and order incarceration . . ." demonstrates something akin to an unfounded "urban legend" that gains credibility only through the endless retelling. Legend becomes fact. This mistaken attribution of power is not only limiting for the motivational-inclined officer, but an incorrect understanding of probation jurisprudence.

The strengths model does not gloss over personal abuses of power, or even systemic bias that prompts disrespectful treatment of defendants. Officers can (and do) illegitimately grasp at this power base ("I'll lock you up!") or consistently intimidate as a personal style, heaping abuse dissolutely on probationers. However, abuses of power are not specific to probation agents and can occur within any helping endeavor. Abuses may well crop up with greater frequency in the criminal justice field, yet I would assert that this becomes an ex post facto argument for the greater expansion, rather than preclusion, of a strengths perspective within the ranks of criminal justice.

Misperceptions are understandable and easy to overlook when proffered from outside the criminal justice field, but far more troublesome when furthered by criminologists within the field. Consider this short treatise from Mills (1980):

> The distinguishing feature of corrections that differentiates it from other helping professions is the large amount of socially sanctioned authority, both actual and delegated, carried by the corrections official. . . . The officer must learn to become comfortable with his authority, and to use it with restraint in the service of the officer and client's objectives. The reaction of some inexperienced officers is to banish the "big stick," and go hide it in the judge's chambers or in the warden's office. Such officers seem to believe that social casework and counseling can proceed in corrections in the same basis as in an outpatient clinic, that their "good guy in the white hat" image is somehow tarnished by the possession of so much power over their clients. Officers who conduct investigations and counseling while denying their own authority are usually perceived as being weak, and are subject to easy manipulation by their clients. (p. 46)

With all due respect, a strengths-based orientation would suggest that officers do exactly what Mills cautions against! A strengths approach, as utilized within the field of probation, is determined not to personally assume the "big stick." It furthers an officer's ability to influence change when he or she places the "stick" with the judge, the supervisor, or even to use "agency policy" as a convenient catch-all. This becomes not a "weakness" as purported by Mills, but rather a strength. When using a strengths approach with mandated clients, I am mindful of the distinction of "power versus force": greater power to increase readiness to change and improve outcomes can be harnessed with the use of strengths perspective, by establishing fit with a probationer ("Are we together on this?"), than with use of adversarial force from the "me vs. you" nexus of dominance. I believe the ability to create and maintain a therapeutic relationship—so essential to the work of assisting behavior change—can only be realized by placing the "big stick" with others.

Skillful Negotiation.   Nowhere is the adage "wearing two hats" more appropriate than with a probation officer in the field of criminal justice. It begins with an honest explanation of the duality of an officer's roles, certainly to supervise and report compliance to probation orders but also to act as a helper and lend assistance; should compliance become an issue, the officer negotiates "How do we (you, significant others, and myself) keep them (the judge, the court, agency policy) off your back?" In training, I find that staff new to the strengths perspective have a hard time negotiating these dual roles. Concrete thinking of either/or tends to dominate. "I either supervise or seek compliance (applying sanctions for failure to comply) or I practice a strengths perspective and try to motivate and establish a therapeutic alliance." It's not "tea leaves or water," it's a good-enough blend that creates the brew. Helping staff to adopt a "both/and" conception is central to the business of behavior change.

Our field's ambivalence regarding intimidation and heavy confrontation must be systemically addressed. There is a tiresome practice of privately judging this behavior as reprehensible—yet publicly we say nothing. If behavior change is truly paramount, then intimidation and heavy-handed treatment is inappropriate and must be openly denounced across our field and within our departments. Only then will we stop the false dichotomy of "tough/soft" that continues to drain our field of its effectiveness. Only then will probation departments be populated with staff that can enforce orders and increase the readiness to change. Only then will a true decision be made as to whether we're in the business of probation or whether we're in the business of behavior change.

THE BUSINESS OF BEHAVIOR CHANGE

Historically, motivation has been viewed as something that resides within the offender. Probation officers hope for enough motivation to make some progress but often end up frustrated when they find very little. Regardless of amount, motivation has usually been thought to be a characteristic of offenders—it's theirs to give ("cooperative," "workable") or theirs to withhold ("resistant," "poor attitude"). Within this model, the probation officer becomes an enforcer of a legal contract, but not necessarily an active participant in the behavior change of the offender. Here is a common description of an officer's role:

> The probationer, in consultation with his lawyer, negotiates for probation supervision (and conditions) in lieu of jail time. In our initial meeting, and throughout our work together, I tell the probationer what is expected of him and make it clear what the penalties will be should he fail to comply. We have regular meetings to verify that he is making progress on his conditions, and I answer any questions he might have. If he breaks the law or shows poor progress

on his conditions, I see to it that appropriate sanctions are assessed. Throughout the process, the probationer is well aware of the behavior that might send him to jail, and if he ends up there, it's his own behavior that gets him there.

Reflected in this statement is an officer who is essentially cut out of the change process, except as an observer. The strengths perspective in criminal justice champions the idea that we don't have to wait for the offender to "get motivated"—motivation is interactive. There may be quite a lot we can do to raise motivation, even during brief interactions.

Understanding Motivation

How we understand motivation will directly affect what we do (or don't do) to increase it. Understanding motivation involves five important issues.

1. *Motivation is changeable.* Motivation is not a fixed trait like height or eye color; it can be increased or decreased. Although there will always be some factors that are out of our control, there may be quite a lot we can do to raise motivation.

2. *Motivation predicts action.* Motivation predicts how likely an offender will begin an action and carry through with it. Motivation to change is not a guarantee of action, but it does predict the likelihood that a client will change. Because of this, motivation is fundamental to behavior change.

3. *Motivation is behavior-specific.* To say an offender is "unmotivated" in a global sense (as a personality description) is to misunderstand how motivation works. For example, some offenders may not be motivated to "stop drinking" but may feel the need to work on their anger. They may be reluctant to comply with a certain condition of their probation, yet have a strong desire to "get off probation."

4. *Motivation is interactive.* Motivation changes because of relationships between people. Exchanges between the officer and probationer have the potential to increase or decrease the offender's perceived importance and confidence for change. The questions and statements that an officer chooses can influence what an offender talks and thinks about, and subsequently how he or she behaves.

5. *Motivation can be affected by both internal and external factors, but internally motivated change usually lasts longer.* Consider two offenders who agree to complete a substance abuse evaluation. One agrees to the evaluation to avoid jail, while the other agrees because he or she is concerned that his or her drug use is causing family problems. Both may be compliant, but the second is more likely to make changes that lower the probability that he or she will engage in future criminal behavior. Research repeatedly finds that internally motivated change is far more enduring over time (Deci & Ryan, 1985; Viets et al., 2002).

Given the right situation, most probation officers would strive to help offenders toward behavior change, but few are equipped with the right tools. Simple notions of what things "should" motivate offenders are often insufficient. Change, when it happens, seems to be the result of a combination of factors—a sort of motivational "alignment"—rather than increased levels of just one factor.

The findings regarding motivation suggest at least four conclusions:

1. In probation services, the interaction between a probation officer and offender can have a large impact on a probationer's motivation. The way a probation officer interacts with an offender can raise or lower motivation.

2. Often, the things that we assume would be motivating to an offender simply are not. Thus, motivation is a process of finding out what things are most important to a particular individual, as well as what plan will work best for attaining them.

3. Not all moments are created equally. There seem to be "teachable" windows where people are more receptive to feedback from their environment and more interested in trying out new behaviors. Looking for where the momentum is, rather than where it is not, seems to be a sensible first step.

4. A desire to achieve an outcome (importance), belief that it can be achieved (confidence), and a belief that the new behavior is freely chosen (autonomy), seem to be the optimal conditions for change.

The Strengths Perspective—Embracing a Helpful Style

No two offenders are alike—they enter our probation departments with a complex array of different experiences, traits, values, and personality styles. So if offenders come to a probation department, each with their individual characteristics, what conclusion could be reached if one heard mainly arguing and resistance talk coming from any one probation office or cubicle? It would stand to reason that it is not the offenders who are responsible for the negative responses, but rather the officers' approach. Probation officer style can be a major determining factor whether the offender comes down on the side of resistance, or alternately, increases his or her readiness to change during probation meetings. An officer's "style" is simply the way he or she relates to probationers. As noted earlier, one style can be tough as nails and coercive, while another style can be more encouraging and motivational.

Consider this example of officer style. In departments where intake and supervision are separated, supervising POs report that the ease or difficulty of their first meeting with a new probationer is heavily influenced by what happened during the intake interview. An officer from a small probation department gave this description:

> For the initial appointment, I can predict what kind of attitude the offender will show up with depending on which of the two intake officers this person met with. If I see one name, I know the person will be reluctant to come in and I'll spend a portion of my time trying to undo all of the damage that has been done. If I see the other name, not only do I know the client will show, I know I will have a hard time living up to the positive image that this person created of a probation officer. It's like night and day—actually, more like heaven and hell!

Accurate *and* Balanced

There is a great difference between accurate information gathered and reported on a probationer and information reported in a balanced fashion. While no probation department would knowingly allow inaccurate information to be presented, many allow unbalanced information—as common practice. Consider a scenario by placing yourself in the hypothetical position of a mandated client. You have run afoul of the law. You have admitted guilt for a crime and now are in between the hearing where you admit guilt and the subsequent hearing where you will be sentenced. You are required by the court to keep an appointment to meet with a supervising officer who will draw up a plan to report to the court as to how to resolve your situation—how you are to be sentenced. You are fortunate enough to be assigned a male officer who seems fair and concerned about your case. As you first meet and take a seat in his office, he describes his role and begins to gather information about "who" you are (background information in general) and "what" you have done (law-breaking behavior in specific). During the interview, the officer seems efficient and attentive. As you discuss your failures and your successes, you feel relieved and somewhat hopeful that this just may turn out "okay." The interview concludes and your next "appointment" is actually your sentencing hearing.

When you arrive for this scheduled court appearance, your officer (or your attorney) hands you a copy of this investigation report that has been filed about you, your life, and what the court should "do" with you. As you take a minute to read this report, you're shocked to find that the only information that has been recorded within lists all of your failures and flaws. Very few, if any, of your strengths, past successes, skills, talents, or resources are listed. You're quickly called into the courtroom and once your hearing is underway, should you find your voice to object to the unbalanced nature of this report, you may well be in for a surprise. In all probability, the officer would respond to your objection by claiming the report is "accurate" and that he "stands by" the information presented. Further, he defends that he can easily confirm that "all information reported is correct." There is a high probability that your objection would be dismissed.

This supposed scenario is actually repeated on a daily basis across the criminal justice field. The greatest problem with *accurate yet unbalanced* reporting is that only half of this court defendant has been brought forward. The strengths perspective would caution that the most important half, the half that represents the greatest advantage for building solutions, is left ignored and more importantly, unused. Attorneys and the legal profession are not trained to appreciate a balanced view. Seligman (2002) reports, "Pessimism is seen as a plus among lawyers, because seeing troubles as pervasive and permanent is a component of what the law profession deems prudence. A prudent perspective enables a good lawyer to see every conceivable snare and catastrophe that might occur in any transaction" (p. 178). Unfortunately, a trait that makes a good lawyer does not translate into allowing balanced reporting.

For those familiar with sentencing reports, the bias toward an exclusive focus on the defendant's failures and flaws is easy to spot. Once jurisdiction has been established and the court process moves disposing (sentencing) of a case, a troubling scenario can arise. Officers who have moved to a strengths approach find obstacles. In attempting to bring a balanced view of the defendant into the courtroom, they can end up belittled. In giving equal voice to a defendant's successes as well as his or her failures, to speak of potential or possibilities as well as pathologies, the balanced perspective can be dismissed by attorneys who believe the officer has become "too close" to the defendant and is thought to have "lost perspective" due to this closeness. All in one disapproving criticism, the advantage of a balanced report is reframed as a negative and the balance—so necessary for best decisions—is jettisoned. Content is now confounded.

POTENTIAL TROUBLE SPOTS: ENFORCING PROBATION ORDERS AND DELIVERING SANCTIONS WITHOUT LEAVING A STRENGTH-BASED STYLE

One of the things that makes probation officers unique is their conspicuously dual role. We help the probationer to plan, but dispense sanctions if he fails; we ask for honesty, but also report to the court. Indeed, it is understandable why some officers have a hard time navigating this dual role. The tendency is to move to one side—to become too harsh or too friendly—when a more middle-of-the-road approach is called for. In reality, probation officers are more like consultants, in that we manage the relationship between court and probationer. This is not as far-fetched as some would believe. In truth, we neither make decisions for the probationer nor for the court. If we treat the position from the perspective of a consultant, we can avoid some of the pitfalls inherent in this dual role. Adopting this middle-of the-road stance makes us not only an effective advocate for the court, but also allows us greater power to influence the actions of the probationer. The strengths perspective can make change more likely, but it is by no means a magic bullet. When violations occur, there are several strategies for keeping a motivational edge.

1. *Explain your dual roles (become the "go-between").* A strengths perspective encourages officers to be honest with offenders about all aspects of their probation, including conditions, incentives, and sanctions. Officers should fully explain up front to the probationer about their dual role—yet do so as someone who represents "both sides." For instance:

> I want to make you aware that I have a couple of roles here. One of them is to be the court's representative and to report on your progress on the conditions that the court has set. At the same time, I act as a representative for you, to help keep the court off your back and manage these conditions, while possibly making some other positive steps along the way. I'll act as a "go-between"—that is, between you and the court, but ultimately you're the one who makes the choices. How does that sound? Is there anything I need to know before proceeding?

2. *Address Behavior with an "Even Keel" Attitude.* Adopting a new approach like the strengths perspective is clearly a process. Even after an initial training, there is a common pitfall for many officers when compliance problems occur. At some point, if a probationer remains ambivalent (e.g., lack of progress), they believe it makes sense to move out of a motivational style and switch over to more coercive and demanding strategies. Staff who initially found the benefits of motivational work will justify heavy-handed tactics—perceiving them to be a natural response to resistance, even remarking that difficult offenders seem to be "asking for it." A critical idea is missed—there is a difference between enforcing sanctions based on lack of progress and switching styles to a more heavy-handed approach. One can enforce court orders and assess sanctions as appropriate, without leaving motivational strategies behind.

Force, for all its bluster, can often make a situation worse. This is especially true when addressing violations. Offenders may already be on the defensive about their progress, and an agitated officer can make the offender's attitude worse. For this reason, we suggest that officers address violations with an "even keel" attitude, addressing the behavior, dispensing the appropriate sanction, but not getting agitated or taking the violation personally.

Motivationally inclined officers offer their support—and their regrets—to the probationer who might be considering a violation of probation orders:

PO: We've talked about this before. In another two weeks, you will be in violation of this court order. We have also talked about how it is up to you. You can certainly ignore this order, but sanctions will be assessed.

Probationer: "Darn right I can ignore it—this is so stupid!"

PO: "It seems unfair that you're required to complete this condition. It feels to you like it might be a waste of your time."

Probationer: "Yeah. I can't believe I have to do this!"

PO: "It's important that I tell you that my (supervisor, judge, responsibilities, policy, position) will demand that I assess a consequence if it's not completed before the next two weeks."

Probationer: "You don't have to report this."

PO: "Unfortunately, that's part of my job. I have to follow orders here. So, this will be something I'll have to do."

Probationer: "You mean you can't just let it go?"

PO: "No, I don't have a choice. But—you have a choice, even if I don't. Is there anything we can do to help you avoid these consequences before the end of the month (next meeting, court deadline)?"

Probationer: "I'll think about it, it just seems unfair."

A confrontational approach is always an option, but at this point simply recognizing the offender's reluctance, and fairly informing him or her about what is likely to happen, improves the likelihood that a decision for compliance will eventually overtake the emotions of the moment.

In this example, the officer refuses to leave the middle, neither defending the court's order, nor siding with the offender to stop the sanction. When it comes to the specific sanction, the officer defers to the court, and re-emphasizes a collaborative relationship: "How do we (you, significant others, and myself) keep them (the judge, the court, agency policy) off your back?" Finally, the officer emphasizes the offender's personal responsibility. Offenders don't have to complete their conditions; they always have the option of taking the sanction.

The strengths perspective steers clear of both the hard and soft approaches. The hard approach is overly directive and defends the court's authority ("You better do this!," "Drop the attitude, you're the one who broke the law," "Don't blame the court"). Less examined is the soft approach. This approach leaves the officer defending the probationer ("I won't tell this time—but don't do it again," "Do you know what the court would do if I brought this to its attention?"). A positive alliance is not the same as ignoring violations to keep a good relationship at any cost ("You better get it together or I'll have to do something"), nor is it the same as allowing the situation to become personal and attempting to "out-tough" the offender ("I'll lock you up!"). Both approaches miss the mark because they prevent the officer from occupying the middle ground.

A motivational approach is about finding the middle ground as a consultant who works with both sides (the court and the offender). Officers can work in partnership with the offender, while still being true to their court roles. Officers can respect personal choice, but not always approve of the offender's behavior. By their skills and strategies, agents can supervise for compliance and, at the same time, increase readiness for change.

REJOINDERS FROM THE STRENGTHS PERSPECTIVE

In an effort to move from problem talk to solution talk, answers are advanced from the strengths perspective to the four troublesome questions that opened this chapter.

1. *Why does criminal justice focus almost exclusively on problems, failure, and flaws when it is an offender's strengths, resources, and aspirations that propel law-abiding behavior?*

    Response: Exceptions are found in a growing number of departments who have begun to practice from a strengths perspective (Clark, 2007). It is true that problems do not include directions on how to get us past the trouble and that change always comes from someone's place of power and strength. To increase mediocre outcomes, the field of criminal justice will need to learn how to elicit, amplify, and reinforce a probationer's strengths. Further, these methods will need to become both *customary and expected.*

    There is no need to reinvent the wheel. Criminal justice can turn to the field of forensic social work and the strengths perspective as we import this new body of knowledge. Strengths assessments (assessments that are both accurate and balanced) have been developed and are readily available. Organizational procedures and practice methods that increase cooperation, motivation, and a probationer's readiness to change are in use and can be imported by the interested officer or department manager.

2. *Why does our field occupy itself with punishment when a host of new meta-analytic research has proven that the exclusive use of punishment—in the absence of treatment—* ***increases*** *criminal behavior?*

    Response: A good share of the mediocre outcomes that criminal justice suffers from can be traced to the field's reliance on punishment to change behavior. In tandem to this has been allowing mere compliance to the court's authority to be positioned as a "good enough" goal. I suggest that it is only through the strengths perspective that we can move off this "freeway to failure." The strengths approach does not endorse "coddling" or "rewarding" offenders for their misbehavior—however, we are emphatic in our call to relinquish interventions that makes this situation worse. This chapter has made the call for criminal justice to move beyond compliance and strive for positive behavior change.

    A demanding task is to first change a department's culture if the true "business" of behavior change is to take root. However, the old adage is applicable here: "The master's tools will never be allowed to dismantle the master's house." Probation departments must overcome several decades of a "get-tough" mindset. Departments will find it difficult to change the practice efforts of their staff without first adopting a strengths climate within their policy and procedures. The seasoned administrator knows the effort required here—this will not happen by calling a special staff meeting to make a declaration ("change by announcement"). Assistance is available by turning to a considerable body of knowledge and skills that has been assembled by the strengths approach.

3. *Why do we construct solutions solely from our point of view, when we are not the ones being asked to change?*

> *Response:* We've spent decades spinning and constructing interventions from our point of view (e.g., "This is what offenders need"). Mary McMurran (2002) suggests, "A different and potentially more useful perspective is to look at motivation to change from an offender's point of view" (p. 5). Criminal justice departments reap a windfall for changing their philosophy of intervention. When probation departments import the strengths perspective, they can access interventions that are borne from a collaborative exercise, calling the field toward a shared view of what drives a person's motivation. A key point is that intrinsic motivation, or internal reasons that fuel the impetus to change, are engaged by elicitation (pulling it out) rather than installation (pushing it in). The strengths perspective could well be construed as a "science" of utilizing an offender's perspective. As applied to criminal justice, McMurran (2002) continues, "Whether in compulsory or voluntary treatment, it seems that the most reliable way to influence behavior change is through an empathic, empowering approach" (p. 8). Interesting that both of McMurran's suggestions noted in this response represent indirect references to the strengths perspective.

When someone commits a crime and enters the criminal justice system, two questions beg to be asked, "How did you get into this mess?" and "How can you get out of it?" It would seem that over 100 years ago, the field of criminal justice decided that the first question was the important one. Consequently, much of the history of working with probationers has shown an interest in causation and the differing ways to answer this first question. In the last decade, a growing number of strengths-based practitioners have begun to focus solely on the second question. They care much more about initiating behavior change (action) than ascribing causation. As the field of criminal justice attempts to move beyond compliance to increase a defendant's readiness to change, a piercing question is posed that juxtaposes outcomes with solutions: *"Do you want to be right or do you want to be successful?"* You don't need to incorporate the probationer's perceptions, nor establish any collaborative relationship to be "right" in how the problem is viewed or how interventions are plotted. However, if one wants to be successful with mandated populations, then the probationer's views and a collaborative relationship are a must.

4. *When receiving probation services, probationers only spend an average of one-third of one percent (.03 percent) of their lifetime with their probation officer. So, if probationers end up changing, where does it come from?*

> *Response:* One of the most comprehensive studies to date on the outcomes of probation services was completed by Farrell (2002) in the United Kingdom. His project, "Tracking Progress on Probation," studied both the efforts of the officers and the outcomes of the probationers. Two important differences in this study: (A) The line of inquiry was not to examine punishment or treatment in the traditional sense, but "obstacles" to healthy lifestyles and how these obstacles were,

or were not, overcome; and, (B) rather than the common line of inquiry or "official view," this study sought out and included the views and perceptions of both the officer *and the probationer.* The results of this study point the way to the strengths perspective:

> The elements which this study has most frequently found to be of most help in assisting probationers to overcome obstacles and avoid further offending have not come from officers, etc., but from the probationers themselves (their motivation) and from changes in the nature of the social contexts in which they lived. (p. 213)

This outcome points to the larger context of a probationer's life and places the theatre of change where it belongs; on the probationer and all that surrounds him or her. Once again, criminal justice does not need to reinvent the wheel but can import policies and procedures that account for the person-in-context (person-in-the-environment). This has long been the venue of social work in general and the strengths approach in specific.

CONCLUSION: TAKING CRIMINAL JUSTICE "BACK TO THE FUTURE"

Forensic social work and the strengths perspective are not new to criminal justice. The strengths movement in criminal justice may seem to be a contradiction of terms, yet historical roots can be found in this field. Although criminal justice has not rallied to strengths work to the extent of other disciplines, it can lay claim to being one of the first to try it. A historical view of probation by Lindner (1994) indicates that police officers were the first discipline in the late 1800s to work with probation clients. Police were quickly replaced by social workers who were favored because they brought a more positive focus to supervision. So, too, with juvenile justice. Early youth pioneers developed strengths-based models for adolescent work. Jane Addams, who was heralded for founding the modern juvenile court system in this country, promoted the principles of the strength perspective. However, the juvenile court system would never embody the youth development principles Addams promoted.

This chapter closes with thoughts of importing this past into future endeavors of the justice field. What might happen if we hired and trained correctional staff for their abilities to assist behavior change? What if large numbers of correctional staff were trained in seeking balanced assessments, increasing resources and intrinsic motivation, and viewing offenders in a more respectful way? How would it affect outcomes if all stakeholders in crime were invited into a process of resolution and offenders were generally seen as preparing for change (like those entering treatment), rather than sub-human cons? What if we assumed that the central purpose of the criminal justice field is not to enact vengeance, but to assist the readiness to change?

I believe this can occur as I have seen happening in the here-and-now within probation departments that are in the process of adopting a strengths orientation. Is it so surprising that profound changes can happen, in professionals and in systems, in relatively short periods to time? Perhaps, just perhaps, over the next two decades we will look back on today's criminal justice practices as archaic and ask in disbelief, "If we were trying to change criminal behavior to make us all safer, how could this coercive mindset and heavy-handed practices ever have occurred?"

DISCUSSION QUESTIONS/EXERCISES

1. Why does the field of criminal justice seem so preoccupied with punishment and incarceration? Who benefits from such a perspective?

2. Why do you think that the United States incarcerates many more people, often for longer periods of time, than any other Western nation?

3. A major conundrum in the field is that people seem to think that it is either punishment or treatment. But it can be both. How would that look?

4. If you worked in the criminal justice system, say as a probation or parole officer, how would you begin to incorporate a strengths approach in your practice?

5. Talk to a probation officer and present your view of a strengths approach. Ask what his/her view of it is in the juvenile justice system.

REFERENCES

Andrews, D. A. & Bonta, J. (2003). *The psychology of criminal conduct* (3rd ed.). Cincinnati: Anderson Publishing Co.

Berg, I. K. (1994). *Family based services: A solution-focused approach.* New York: W.W. Norton.

Bernfield, G. A., Farrington, D. P., & Leschied, A. W. (2001). *Offender rehabilitation in practice: Implementing and evaluating effective programs.* New York: John Wiley and Sons.

Burnett, R. (2004). To reoffend or not to reoffend? The ambivalence of convicted property offenders. In S. Maruna & R. Immarigeon (Eds.), *After crime and punishment: Pathways to offender reintegration.* Portland, OR: William Publishing.

Clark, M. D. (1995, Spring). The problem with problem solving: A critical review. *Journal for Juvenile Justice and Detention Services, 10*(1), 30–35.

Clark, M. D. (1997, April). Strength based practice: A new paradigm. *Corrections Today,* 201–202.

Clark, M. D. (1998, June). Strength-based practice: The ABC's of working with adolescents who don't want to work with you. *Federal Probation, 62*(1), 46–53.

Clark, M. D. (2001, June). Influencing positive behavior change: Increasing the therapeutic approach of juvenile courts. *Federal Probation, 65*(1), 18–27.

Clark, M. D. (2006). Entering the business of behavior change: Motivational interviewing for probation staff. *Perspectives, 30*(1), 38–45.

Clark, M. D. (2007, June). *Increasing motivation through responsivity: A keystone to offender behavior change.* Keynote address presented at the 32nd Annual Training Institute of the American Probation & Parole Association , Philadelphia, Pennsylvania.

Deci, E. L. & Ryan, R. M. (1985). *Intrinsic motivation and self-determination in human behavior.* New York: Plenum.

Duncan, B., Miller, S., & Sparks, J. (2004). *The heroic client: A revolutionary way to improve effectiveness through client-directed, outcome-informed therapy.* San Francisco: Jossey-Bass.

Farrell, Stephen. (2002). *Rethinking what works with offenders: Probation, social context and desistance from crime.* Portland, OR: William Publishing.

Gendreau, P., Goggin, C., Cullen, F., & Paparozzi, M. (2002). The common-sense revolution and correctional policy. In J. McGuire (Ed.), *Offender rehabilitation and treatment: Effective programmes and policies to reduce re-offending* (pp. 359–386). Chester, UK: John Wiley and Sons.

Gendreau, P., Little, H., & Goggin, C. (1996). A meta-analysis of the predictors of adult offender rehabilitation: What works. *Criminology, 34*(4), 575–608.

Gendreau, P. & Ross, R. R. (1987, September). Revivification of rehabilitation: Evidence from the 1980s. *Justice Quarterly,* 349–407.

Gibbs, J. P. (1986). Deterrence theory and research. In G.B. Melton (Ed.), *The law as behavioral instrument: Nebraska Symposium on Motivation* (vol. 33, pp. 87–130). Lincoln: University of Nebraska Press.

Hollin, C. R. (2001). To treat or not to treat? An historical perspective. In C. Hollin (Ed.), *Handbook of offender assessment and treatment* (pp. 3–15). Chester, UK: John Wiley and Sons.

Holin, C. R. (2002). Does punishment motivate offenders to change? In M. McMurran (Ed.), *Motivating offenders to change: A guide to enhancing engagement in therapy* (pp. 57–73). New York: John Wiley and Sons.

Hubble, M., Duncan, B., & Miller, S. (1999). *The heart and soul of change: What works in therapy.* Washington, DC: American Psychological Association.

Levitt, T. (1975, September-October) Marketing myopia. *Harvard Business Review, 19*–31.

Lindner, C. (1994). The police contribution to the development of probation: An historical account. *Journal of Offender Rehabilitation, 20,* 61–84.

Mann, R. E., Ginsburg, J. I.D., & Weekes, J. R. (2002). Motivational interviewing with offenders. In M. McMurran (Ed.), *Motivating offenders to change: A guide to enhancing engagement in therapy* (pp. 87–102). West Sussex, UK: John Wiley and Sons.

Matza, D. (1969). *Becoming deviant.* Englewood Cliffs, NJ: Prentice Hall.

McMurran, M. (2002). Motivation to change: Selection criterion or treatment need? In M. McMurran (Ed.), *Motivating offenders to change: A guide to enhancing engagement in therapy.* New York: John Wiley & Sons.

Miller, W. R., Benefield, R. G., & Tonnigan, J.S. (1993). Enhancing motivation for change in problem drinking: A controlled comparison of two therapist styles. *Journal of Consulting and Clinical Psychology,* 455–461.

Miller, W. R. & Rollnick, S. (1991). *Motivational interviewing: Preparing people for change.* New York: Guilford Press.

Miller, W. R. & Rollnick, S. (2002). *Motivational interviewing: Preparing people for change (2nd ed.).* New York: Guilford Press.

Mills, R. (1980). *Offender assessment: A casebook in corrections.* Cincinnati: Anderson Publishing,

Pinker, S. (1997). *How the mind works.* New York: Norton.

Prochaska, J. O. & DiClemente, C. C. (1983). Stages and processes of self-change in smoking: Toward an integrative model of change. *Journal of Consulting and Clinical Psychology,* 390–395.

Rollnick, S., Mason, P., & Butler, C. (1999). *Health behavior change: A guide for practitioners.* New York: Churchill-Livingstone.

Saleebey, D. (Ed.). (1992). *The strengths perspective in social work practice.* New York: Longman.

Seligman, M. E. P. (2002). *Authentic happiness: Using the new positive psychology to realize your potential for lasting fulfillment.* New York: Free Press.

Taxman, F. S. (1999). Unraveling "what works" for offenders in substance abuse treatment. *National Drug Court Institute Review,* 2(2), 93–134.

Tomlin, K. M. & Richardson, H. (2004). *Motivational interviewing & stages of change: Integrating best practices for substance abuse professionals.* City Center, MN: Hazelden.

Turnell, A. & Edwards, S. (1999). *Signs of safety: A solution and safety oriented approach to child protection casework.* New York: W.W. Norton.

U. S. Department of Justice, Office of Justice Programs, Bureau of Justice Statistics. (2006). *Probation and parole in the United States, 2006.* Retrieved January 30, 2008, from www.ojp.usdoj.gov/bjs/abstract/ppus06.htm

Viets, V. L., Walker, D. D., & Miller, W. R. (2002). What is motivation to change? A scientific analysis. In M. McMurran (Ed.), *Motivating offenders to change: A guide to enhancing engagement in therapy* (pp. 57–73). New York: John Wiley and Sons.

Walters, S. T., Clark, M. D., Gingerich, R., & Meltzer, M. (2007, June). Motivating offenders to change: A guide for probation & parole officers. *Practice Monograph, National Institute of Corrections* (NIC). U.S. Department of Justice. (NIC accession number 022253).

CHAPTER EIGHT

IMPLEMENTATION OF BRIEF STRENGTHS-BASED CASE MANAGEMENT

An Evidence-Based Intervention for Improving Linkage with Care

RICHARD C. RAPP

D. TIMOTHY LANE

Since 1990, the Center for Interventions, Treatment, and Addictions Research (CITAR) at Wright State University's Boonshoft School of Medicine has conducted clinical trials of case management's role in helping persons who have substance abuse problems. The goals of the studies were to determine whether a strengths-based approach to case management would facilitate substance abusers' linkage with and retention in treatment and improve their functioning in critical life domains (Rapp, Siegal, Li, & Saha, 1998; Siegal, Li, & Rapp, 2002; Siegal et al., 1995). The adaptation of strengths-based case management (SBCM) to substance abuse grew from seminal work at the University of Kansas School of Social Welfare in supporting persons who had persistent challenges with mental health problems (Rapp & Chamberlain, 1985). The use of strengths-based case management services has also spread to work with older adults (Chapin, 2001; Fast & Chapin, 2002). In most of these applications, SBCM has been structured as a long-term intervention of many months and in some cases, years.

During the last seven years CITAR researchers have had the opportunity to test the effectiveness of a *brief* approach to strengths-based case management in two settings. The National Institute on Drug Abuse–funded *Reducing Barriers to Drug Treatment Services Study (DA 015690)* tested the ability of brief SBCM to improve substance abusers' linkage with treatment following assessment at a centralized intake unit. The *ARTAS Linkage to Care Demonstration Project* was funded by the Centers for Disease Control and Prevention to test a similar intervention's ability to improve linkage with medical services among persons who were recently diagnosed with HIV. Brief SBCM (B-SBCM) has been measured by number of sessions, usually five, and weeks, usually eight to twelve. This chapter will discuss our B-SBCM experiences with two groups: persons who have substance abuse problems and persons who have recently been diagnosed with HIV. Many of the issues surrounding the implementation of SBCM as a brief intervention are similar across the two groups and the healthcare systems that provide services to them.

This chapter will cover two areas that are relevant to a trial of a brief model of SBCM. First, we will highlight the evidence base for case management as it applies to improving the linkage with services for substance abusers and persons who are HIV positive. Second, we will discuss issues surrounding the implementation of B-SBCM to improve the linkage in both substance abuse and HIV care settings.

STRENGTHS-BASED CASE MANAGEMENT: AN EVIDENCE-BASED LINKAGE INTERVENTION

Linkage with Substance Abuse Treatment

Case management, including strengths-based case management, has been associated both descriptively and empirically with improving treatment for substance abusers. Case management is explicitly recognized by The National Institute on Drug Abuse (NIDA) as a crucial component in the treatment of addictions (National Institute on Drug Abuse, 1999) and is consistent with several principles of effective practice (Simpson, 2002). NIDA also recognizes case management as an important component in at least two efficacious interventions: counseling for cocaine addiction and cognitive-behavioral therapy (Carroll, 1998; Daley, Mercer, & Carpenter, 1999).

The most compelling evidence of case management's evidence-based status comes from studies of its role in improving linkage with treatment. A meta-analysis of studies reporting on case management's impact on linkage found a mean effect size of .42 and a range of .08 to .89 (Hesse, Vanderplasschen, Rapp, Broekaert, & Fridell, 2007). The strongest effect was observed in a study of veterans and aftercare treatment conducted by Rapp and colleagues at the Center for Interventions, Treatment, and Addictions Research (Rapp et al., 1998; Siegal et al., 2002). Effect size was increased by the use of manuals to guide the intervention (.56 vs. .21) and by using strengths-based or assertive community treatment models when compared to generalist case management (.70 and .74 vs. .20).

Strengths-based case management (SBCM) has been consistent in improving linkage with treatment in a variety of settings. SBCM is based on the same generalist functions as most models (such as monitoring and advocating), but includes three critical elements: an emphasis on strengths, teaching goal-setting methods to clients, and establishing a strong working alliance (Rapp, 2006; Siegal et al., 1995). Linkage rates have been increased among a general population of substance abusers (Vaughan-Sarrazin, Hall, & Rick, 2000), opioid dependent drug users entering agonist treatment programs (Strathdee et al., 2006), and crack cocaine users entering aftercare treatment (Rapp et al., 1998; Siegal et al., 2002).

The most recently completed trial of SBCM involved a brief model of case management provided to substance abusers within 60 days following assessment at a centralized intake unit (Rapp et al., 2006). Clients met with case managers for up to five sessions to identify and resolve tangible barriers that interfered with treatment linkage. Results of the trial demonstrated that brief SBCM was effective in improving linkage, compared to a standard of care condition 55.0 vs. 38.7 percent (p < .01). Brief SBCM also improved linkage more than a one-session motivational intervention (55.0 vs. 44.7 percent, p < .05). Brief SBCM was particularly effective in improving linkage with outpatient treatment (52.3 vs. 28.7 percent, p < .01).

Linkage with HIV and AIDS Care

Although case management has received widespread attention in HIV and AIDS care, there are relatively few empirical studies of case management's role in improving healthcare utilization or quality of life. Fewer still have assessed the primary goal of case management—that is, helping persons who are HIV-infected or who have AIDS to link with services that meet their needs. The relationship between case management and improved linkage with services appears to be complex.

Medical care directly related to the treatment of HIV/AIDS is perhaps the most important service that persons with HIV/AIDS can access. Case management has been associated with increased medical care received by injection drug users with HIV (McCoy, Metsch, Chitwood, & Miles, 2001). A study of over 2,000 HIV-infected persons receiving Ryan White CARE case management found an inconsistent effect on healthcare outcomes (Katz et al., 2001). Having had contact with a case manager in the preceding six months predicted improved utilization of 2- and 3-drug antiretroviral regimens and treatment with protease inhibitors. Adherence to Highly Aggressive Antiretroviral Treatment (HAART) is a consistent predictor of better, long-term health (Murphy et al., 2001; Vittinghoff et al., 1999). Case management was not associated with utilization of ambulatory care, emergency department visits, or hospitalization. Although not addressed in the study, it is possible that the case management–associated use of pharmacologic treatment mediated the need for emergency-oriented medical care. It is difficult to attribute the exact role that case management played, since no description of the case management intervention was provided.

In Missouri, healthcare administrators provided case management services in an effort to reduce the number of inpatient days utilized by HIV/AIDS clients (Twyman & Libbus, 1994). The rationale for doing so was the expectation that case managers actively supported clients in the community, improving health status and overall stability, and reducing their need for hospitalization. Results showed that case-managed clients utilized as many days of inpatient hospitalization as the non-case management group. Because of their close relationship to clients and their willingness to advocate on their behalf, it may be that case managers actually facilitated hospitalization. Non-case managed clients may not have had an advocate to promote hospitalization.

Patients receiving case management consistently report that unmet needs decreased because of their relationship with a case manager. In an evaluation of the Robert Wood Johnson Foundation's AIDS Health Services Program, having a case manager was positively related to having service needs met (Fleishman, Mor, & Piette, 1991). Participation in interactive case management resulted in a reduction in the number of unmet service needs (Thompson et al., 1998). In all these studies the implication was that case managers facilitated successful contact with wide-ranging social and health care services.

Findings from a Centers for Disease Control and Prevention (CDC) clinical trial demonstrated a significant improvement in linkage with medical care due to Brief SBCM (Gardner et al., 2005). Based on these results, a ten site study was commissioned to determine the efficacy of B-SBCM as implemented by community care providers outside the bounds of a tightly controlled clinical trial. The implementation study also produced a significant improvement in linkage rates (Craw et al., in press). As a result of findings in both studies, B-SBCM was designated as an effective practice by the CDC (Gardner, personal communication, December 18, 2007). Efforts are currently underway to prepare and disseminate materials that will be used by CDC regional implementation experts.

IMPLEMENTING SBCM IN SUBSTANCE ABUSE TREATMENT AND HIV CARE SETTINGS

Transferring an evidence-based intervention (EBI) from research trial to community practice can be difficult and is often unsuccessful. An extensive body of literature has examined technology transfer, dissemination, adoption, implementation, and related issues. It is beyond the scope of this chapter to treat these matters in any depth. We will focus instead on the specific instance of implementation of brief strengths-based case management (B-SBCM) in substance abuse treatment and HIV care settings, from the perspective of both clients and care providers.

A brief explanation of terms will help clarify the discussion. The term *care provider* refers globally to substance abuse treatment and HIV care. When necessary, specific reference will be made to one provider or another. Rather than differentiate substance abuse counselor in one setting from nurse in another, the term *practitioner* is used to describe professionals who deliver services to clients. *Case managers* will identify a special class of provider, professionals who deliver B-SBCM to clients. *Administrators* are staff members who make decisions in both settings. *Implementation* is a term used to describe the overall process of moving EBIs from trial to practice. When capitalized, Implementation will signify the Implementation Phase of an established implementation model.

Clients

Movement of an EBI from clinical trial to practice is almost always discussed from the perspective of treatment programs. Little attention has been paid to the impact that the transfer has on clients. CITAR researchers have focused on client responses to new applications of strengths-based case management, hoping to identify how clients perceive the intervention and its essential features.

A guiding principle of strengths-based case management is that clients are to be in control of setting goals and deciding on the methods for achieving those goals (Rapp, 2006; Rapp, Kelliher, Fisher, & Hall, 1994). Although case managers provide support and information to clients and can teach a process for goal setting, ultimately all decisions are those of the client. In each of the clinical trials of B-SBCM conducted by CITAR, there were concerns about implementing a brief intervention with clients who have extensive and long-standing problems, including the problem of choosing effective alternatives to drug abuse or high-risk health behaviors. B-SBCM holds that clients can be and should be responsible for their own behaviors, including decisions about linking to substance abuse treatment or accessing HIV-related medical care. By promoting the client-driven process, resistance is reduced and clients can begin to develop a sense of their own self-efficacy in making positive changes.

In both projects, the overarching goal of case management and service providers was predefined for patients: to improve linkage with substance abuse treatment or HIV-related healthcare. While both goals seem to be desirable, not all clients will immediately agree. Any number of barriers, both internal and external, client and system based, may lead clients to resist recommendations to seek services. Experienced strengths-based care providers were concerned that having a goal already in place would be at odds with the client driven nature of SBCM and would provoke resistance.

Additional client challenges were anticipated because of the time-limited nature of B-SBCM. Case managers who had previously used long-term case management were skeptical that they could establish a productive working relationship with clients and help them link with care in only five sessions. Case managers were concerned that clients, who were accustomed to long-term services, would not see five sessions as helpful.

Initial concerns about the negative effects of B-SBCM on clients were not borne out. Qualitative interviews with clients and case managers indicated that dealing directly with the pre-established program goal helped to preserve the client-driven nature of SBCM and minimized resistance. This was accomplished by clearly describing for clients the overall goal of linkage with services. Case managers explained their view that following through could be beneficial to the client. In ARTAS, reasons included slowing the progression of the disease, improving quality of life, and helping clients qualify for additional social services. In the Reducing Barriers Project, treatment follow-through could lead to an alleviation of problems associated with substance abuse and a reduction in barriers to care. Case managers emphasized that it was the client's choice whether to follow through with the goal and, if so, when. In both instances, case managers made it clear that they would work with clients on objectives and strategies that the client identified as important—even if the objectives were not directly related to medical care or substance abuse treatment.

Some additional explanation may help clarify this apparent deviation from the program goals. Even when clients were ambiguous about the overall program goal of linkage, they were given the freedom to identify other objectives, so long as the objectives did not interfere with linkage. In almost every instance, these client-identified objectives eventually turned toward linking with care or reducing barriers to care. For example, a 45-year-old self-described drug addict was not initially committed to attending the drug treatment program to which he had been referred. His main concern was finding employment. As he and his case manager developed strategies for improving his employment options, they inevitably encountered the barrier of employee drug testing. This led the client to investigate and resolve his ambiguity about drug treatment. He eventually identified linkage to care as one of his primary objectives. In cases such as this, establishing an effective relationship and respecting client choice almost always resulted in the client's adopting the overall goal of linkage to care.

In regard to the time-limited nature of the intervention, the overall impact appeared to be positive rather than negative. Anecdotally, both case managers and clients indicated that the limited amount of time available to them increased their efficiency in setting and accomplishing goals. Again, the driving principles of SBCM seemed to lead to this result—when the case manager demonstrated a desire to focus on strengths, supported client decision making, and developed a productive working relationship, clients were much more likely to view the program as having real value—value that they wanted to use while case management services were available.

CITAR trainers emphasized that case managers should follow through with the established curriculum and consistently use the three critical elements of B-SBCM: focus on strengths, client-driven goal setting, and emphasis on relationship. These critical elements are the components of an intervention that have been linked to successful outcomes. Although these actions do not guarantee success, they have consistently been viewed positively by clients and have led to improved linkage rates.

Program

The challenges and potential solutions surrounding implementation of EBIs such as SBCM can be framed by a model developed at the Institute for Behavioral Research at Texas Christian University (Simpson, 2002; Simpson & Flynn, 2007; Simpson, Joe, & Rowan-Szal, 2007). The Program Change Model describes the four phases that programs experience as they learn about a new intervention (exposure), decide to try the intervention (adoption), start to use it (implementation), and, if an intervention is found to be useful and compatible with the mission and resources of a program, incorporate it (routine practice). Progress through each stage is influenced by staff and organizational characteristics found in four domains: motivation for change, resources, staff attributes, and organizational climate (Simpson, 2002). Fixed program characteristics have also been associated with intervention adoption (Knudsen, Ducharme, & Roman, 2007; Rubenstein, Mittman, Yano, & Mulrow, 2000). The Program Change Model serves as a useful construct to describe the implementation of B-SBCM in both substance abuse treatment and HIV care settings.

Two changes were made in the way the Program Change Model describes the phases of implementation. Rather than *adoption*, the concept of *adaptation* seems to be more descriptive of the phase during which programs decide to implement the intervention. Guydish makes the point that ". . . even in the context of rigorous effectiveness research, experimental interventions *will be adapted* [emphasis added] to local conditions" (Guydish, Tajima, Manser, & Jessup, 2007) (p. 186). In the stress between adaptation of an EBI and maintainence of contextual influences that are deemed important, the tendency will be for contextual influences to be more powerful than the opportunity to implement an EBI (Racine, 2006).

The Program Change Model uses *Routine Practice* to describe the phase when programs deliver EBI services to clients on an ongoing basis. This term seems to refer to only one component of continued use of an EBI, i.e., providing services to clients. Continued use is more complex than that and includes integrating, or *incorporating*, the EBI into all facets of a provider's services.

Exposure Phase

Healthcare professionals are exposed to EBIs such as SBCM through several dissemination methods, including hearing about the interventions from other professionals, reading about them in a trade journal, or having their use mandated by state or local regulatory or funding entities. In the beginning of both B-SBCM studies it was apparent that some program administrators and clinical practitioners knew of strengths-based case management. They had learned about strengths-based practice through passive dissemination strategies such as one-time training sessions and manuals, dissemination methods that have shown little or no effect on improving the implementation of interventions in any segment of healthcare (Davis, Thomson, Oxman, & Haynes, 1995; Fixsen, Naoom, Blase, Friedman, & Wallace, 2005; Lomas, 1991). Both manuals and workshop training are static; they can provide information about an EBI, but are not responsive to the dynamic contextual issues present in healthcare settings.

Another form of exposure takes place when administrators and practitioners have provided or observed case management. Previous experience provided administrators and practitioners with some understanding of case management, although that understanding was not always useful in training potential case managers. An example of this occurred in HIV care where new case managers had worked previously as Ryan White case managers. The Ryan White Comprehensive AIDS Resources Emergency (McKleroy et al., 2006) Act of 1990 institutionalized case management in the continuum of HIV/AIDS resources in order to provide community-based care to people with AIDS (Benjamin, 1988; McKinney, 1998). Ryan White case management is usually characterized as long-term, caseload heavy, and out of necessity emphasizing a brokerage approach of case management. Alternately, SBCM was to be brief, was intended to link clients with Ryan White case managers, and was very assertive in following up with clients and advocating for their receipt of services.

Most administrators, case managers, or their supervisors had formal training in delivering case management services. Although most staff were able to broadly intuit what strengths-based case management meant, few had formal training in SBCM. The exception was a comprehensive HIV/AIDS services provider where several staff members had graduated from a school of social welfare where the curriculum was based on strengths principles. Some case managers identified themselves as using a strengths-based approach although they had not received formal training.

Potential case managers' initial exposure to B-SBCM occurred in several steps that emphasized the (1) theoretical and practical basis of B-SBCM, (2) critical elements of SBCM, (3) evidence supporting B-SBCM's effectiveness, (4) barriers to implementing B-SBCM, and (5) adaptations of B-SBCM that are permissible without diminishing its effectiveness.

Training was conducted in three phases. Preparation and Introductory Training consisted of two days of intense training that described the origins of B-SBCM and provided both case managers and their supervisors the opportunity to practice essential skills. The second phase consisted of a Preceptorship where case managers and their supervisors traveled to a site where B-SBCM was being used and had the opportunity to watch the intervention being used. Last, Ongoing Support took place when CITAR trainers traveled to each provider's site to observe the intervention.

Preparation and Introductory Training.   Several weeks prior to the initial training, a brief survey was sent to each prospective trainee, both case managers and their supervisors. All providers were required to send a supervisor to the training. This mandate was enforced in the hope that it would increase providers' interest in using B-SBCM, lead to supervision that was based on strengths principles, and increase incorporation of SBCM into a provider's ongoing services. The survey was used to gather information about the specific characteristics of the locations in which B-SBCM was to be implemented and trainees would find helpful during training. This information helped direct the training by providing CITAR trainers a view of the population in need, community resources that were available, and an appreciation of any special problems or concerns that existed in the case manager's community. Fine tuning the curriculum and training manual ensured that the training time was used most effectively.

Case managers received a draft version of one of two implementation manuals. Substance abuse treatment sites received *Treatment Linkage Case Management: Improving Linkage for Persons Referred to Substance Abuse Treatment*; HIV providers received *ARTAS Linkage Case Management: Improving Entry to Medical Care Among Persons Recently Diagnosed with HIV*. Both manuals contained information about the core principles of strengths-based case management and its critical elements: emphasizing client strengths, client-directed goal planning, and developing a strong relationship with clients. The manuals also contained a session-by-session curriculum that was specific to each of the two target populations. Although manuals have limited value in ensuring implementation of an EBI, they and other passive strategies can be useful in increasing knowledge about an intervention (Fixsen et al., 2005)

Case managers and their supervisors then attended two days of training that used both didactic and experiential learning methods. Training focused on providing practitioners with the knowledge and skills necessary to adhere to the protocols of B-SBCM. Training provided case managers with an understanding of the internal and external boundaries of the approach, how to avoid using techniques that were not part of the approach, and how to modify existing skills and strategies to affect it. In addition to providing information and skills, trainers sought to build enthusiasm for SBCM.

The first day of actual training included didactic presentations focusing on case management, the evolution of strengths-based approaches, and the process by which these interventions lead to desired outcomes. Techniques for implementing B-SBCM were presented, as were research findings from previous studies of long-term SBCM. Research findings were presented in formats that were understandable by trainees with minimal statistical skills and that were applicable to diverse practice settings. Each session during the day was followed by a period when trainees could ask questions and share comments about what they had heard.

The second day began with a review of the first day's activities and led to discussions about effectively applying the basic components of SBCM in substance abuse treatment and HIV healthcare settings. Most of the day consisted of experiential activities such as role plays, videotaping, and critiquing performance to make the training event effective. Experiential, rather than didactic training, provided a more thorough understanding of the intervention than could have been accomplished with didactic training (Farmer et al., 2007; Martin, Herie, Turner, & Cunningham, 1998). By actually using the intervention, providers gained initial skills and were able to identify contextual influences present in their own organizations that could effect implementation, either positively or negatively. One trainer was responsible for recording the process of the training and documenting important issues that were raised during the two days of training. This process material was used to modify the draft versions of the two implementation manuals.

Preceptorship.   Within approximately two months after the introductory training, case managers from each provider participated in a two-day, structured preceptorship with experienced case managers who were already using a brief model of SBCM. Case managers identified the preceptorship as one of the most helpful components of the training experience.

The preceptorship began with a half-day discussion period where trainees asked questions of both senior CITAR staff and experienced case managers. At least one day was devoted to trainees accompanying experienced case managers as they met with clients. Debriefings were held to allow the trainees to validate their observations and address any questions or concerns. Clients provided written consent before participating in any preceptorship activities.

Case managers also observed a focus group of clients who had participated in the SBCM program. This allowed trainees to hear about strengths-based case managers from the individuals who participated in the intervention. Following completion of the focus group, case managers had the opportunity to ask questions of clients.

Adaptation Phase

The Adaptation Phase is a critical point in the overall implementation process—the point at which treatment providers make an initial decision whether or not to use an evidence-based intervention such as SBCM. Adaptive elements are changes in an intervention that need to be made before it can be implemented. Adaptive elements are necessitated by the barriers and system characteristics surrounding an intervention (Johnsen et al., 1999). Adaptive elements, primarily structural in nature, can include length and number of sessions (dosage), ability to meet clients in diverse settings, providing transportation, funding, staffing levels, and caseload. Adapting some aspects of an intervention has been viewed as critical to its implementation, and necessary to provide clinical value given local circumstances, social needs and cultural identity (Blakely et al., 1987; Hohmann & Shear, 2002).

There are different views about how much an intervention can be changed before it is no longer the same intervention. Some researchers are definitive in their view that accepting the presence of adaptive elements when implementing an EBI destroys its effectiveness (Drake et al., 2001; Szulanski & Winters, 2002). An alternative view is that EBIs may be changed in some respects without altering the critical elements of an intervention. Critical elements are behaviors or techniques that predict successful clinical outcomes. There are seldom precise criteria that specify what must be retained and what can be adapted. What some program developers or care providers see as extraneous, others may see as a critical element.

During the two-day introductory training and the preceptorship, case managers and their supervisors identified influences in their organization they believed could negatively influence implementation of B-SBCM. Most commonly, barriers included lack of time to meet with clients, territoriality on the part of other organizations, and case managers having multiple duties that could conflict with the strengths perspective. A further examination of barriers was conducted with senior administrative staff at each provider organization. They confirmed the observations of practitioners.

An optimal approach for addressing barriers and approaching adaptation in an organized way would have been to use a structured implementation method to guide adaptation and implementation. Unfortunately, this was not a planned part of either B-SBCM study. Still, providers did attempt to address barriers. Every barrier, and the potential interaction of barriers, was considered and discussions were held as to how they could be addressed most efficiently. In some instances noncritical aspects of the intervention were altered, and in other instances changes were made to contextual factors. Some barriers—coordinating the role of case managers with other practitioners—were resolved fairly easily; case managers also had good organizational support in using the critical elements. Some barriers—lack of a written memorandum of understanding between agencies, territoriality—were more intractable. The final metric in all of these actions was whether critical elements were affected.

A frequent example of the need to view adaptation creatively was the issue of case managers transporting clients to needed services. In both trials of B-SBCM case managers were able to transport clients to needed services. Clients have identified transportation as an important part of what strengths-based case managers provide (Brun & Rapp, 2001; Strathdee et al., 2006). Beyond its immediate value of getting a client to a treatment appointment, case managers believed that the informal time spent in the car facilitated relationship building and encouraged clients to discuss topics in a casual setting. Although providing transportation is not a critical element of B-SBCM, it is a valuable aspect of the intervention. Despite its value, some service providers have a prohibition against transporting clients, and many funders do not view travel time as a reimbursable activity. Alternative methods for facilitating clients' transportation needs were identified. Some providers allowed case managers to transport clients; in other settings case managers met clients at agencies or rode public transportation with them. Some providers had a fund they could use to pay for clients' transportation to important services. Relationship building could be facilitated in other ways, including meeting in informal settings such as libraries and churches. Ultimately, treatment programs may seek changes in local or even state policies to make transportation possible.

Implementation Phase

The Implementation Phase begins when a provider decides to use an EBI and practitioners actually provide the intervention to clients. The final decision to use an EBI should occur after providers believe they have identified all of the barriers that could negatively impact actual service delivery. One of the most important tasks present in the Implementation Phase is that of maintaining fidelity to an EBI. Fidelity is adherence to the structure and techniques of an EBI (Mowbray, Holter, Teague, & Bybee, 2003). While fidelity may be assessed for every component of an EBI, at a minimum, fidelity to the critical elements should be maintained. Critical elements are the strategies and actions that are the predictors of desirable clinical outcomes. If fidelity is not maintained, then something other than the planned EBI is being implemented. Whatever the clinical outcomes, they cannot be attributable to the EBI.

Numerous studies have linked levels of fidelity with better clinical outcomes (Mowbray et al., 2003; Orwin, 2000). When fidelity is poor, problems accrue to all parts of the client–practitioner–researcher triad. Clients receive services that are not evidence-based and therefore not the best practice available. Treatment providers also experience a negative consequence in that they may dismiss the EBI as ineffective and discontinue its use. Skepticism about the value of investing scarce resources in future attempts to use EBIs may result. Efforts to evaluate the effectiveness of the intervention become difficult, if not impossible, when practitioners do not actually deliver the intervention as intended. The implications of poor fidelity to researchers have been discussed in great detail (Bond, Evans, Salyers, Williams, & Kim, 2000; Orwin, 2000).

The challenges of maintaining fidelity to a psychosocial intervention can be appreciated in the context of B-SBCM. The five core functions of case management—assessment, planning, linking, monitoring, and advocacy—must be used to help clients link with services. A strengths perspective requires that these functions be carried out while emphasizing client strengths, client-directed goal planning, and development of an effective working alliance between case manager and clients (Redko, Rapp, Elms, Snyder, & Carlson, 2007; Saleebey, 2006). The systematic application of these critical elements is what distinguishes SBCM from other models of case management.

Further, B-SBCM is session- and time-limited, composed of up to five contacts per client, delivered over a set period of time established by the implementing agency, usually 60 to 90 days. Contacts are not confined to any particular length and may take several hours each. Each description of the client contact contains specific instructions for case managers. Case managers may also provide direct services such as transportation and attending meetings with physicians or social services agencies.

Pilot Testing.   Pilot testing is one of the two essential strategies for maintaining good fidelity to B-SBCM. It occurs at the juncture of the Adaptation and Implementation Phases. Pilot testing consists of implementing the EBI under real-world conditions, with the expectation that lessons will be learned and further adaptations will be called for. Pilot testing will frequently reveal barriers and unique situations that neither administrators nor practitioners had considered. As important, the pilot period affords an opportunity for administrators and supervisors to observe actual delivery of services by practitioners. There are no absolute requirements for the length of a pilot period or the number of clients involved. The best recommendation for how to conduct a pilot test is to try it under diverse conditions, including with clients who may present special challenges. A pilot period will generally help identify many of the causes of poor fidelity: poor training and organizational preparation, tendency to resort to well-known methods when stressed, organizational and staff characteristics that interfere with continued use of the EBI, and contextual influences outside of the program (e.g., funding withdrawn) (Aarons, 2004; Lehman, Greener, & Simpson, 2002).

Supervision.   In addition to pilot testing, effective supervision is critical to the successful implementation of B-SBCM. At its most fundamental, the goal of supervision is to support and assist case managers as they encourage clients to link with treatment. To promote that goal, supervisors should help case managers maintain a high level of fidelity to the critical elements of B-SBCM and to other adaptations that have been made to the intervention. Supervision provides other benefits that either directly or indirectly aid fidelity adherence. They include providing a fresh, creative perspective on challenges that the case manager is having with clients, and supporting case managers while they work with a very challenging population and settings where a deficit model frequently prevails.

Close supervision should take place routinely, not just as a response to a difficult case or troubled employee. Regular strengths-focused case staffing accomplishes several desirable goals. The quality of services to clients is improved. The exchange of ideas results in creative solutions that address challenging client situations. Use of a strengths-based format to staff cases reinforces the critical elements of SBCM. In particular, supervisors should help case managers learn and practice techniques to involve clients more fully in their own goal setting. Regular staffing also provides a way for supervisors to anticipate potentially troubling situations between clients and case manager.

Incorporation Phase

Routine practice, or alternately, incorporation, is the long-term integration of an EBI into providers' usual and customary services. There are no evidence-based criteria for demonstrating what steps facilitate integration. Several actions on the part of providers do seem to warrant future research. At a minimum, incorporation would consist of practitioners providing the intervention to clients with a high degree of fidelity. Additional criteria seem to determine the sustainability of the intervention over time. Examples of these additional features include (1) developing a manual that contains a detailed description of the intervention and how it is applied to clients; (2) submitting the intervention, in writing, for approval by providers' governing boards; (3) listing references to the intervention in all provider materials; (4) training administrative and support staff in their role in ensuring the success of B-SBCM; (5) ensuring that a high percentage of eligible clients actually receive the intervention; and (6) arranging for booster sessions of intervention training.

The primary goal of the two B-SBCM studies was to establish the effectiveness of B-SBCM in improving linkage with services. The study design did not directly support plans for long-term incorporation of the interventions. The providers involved in the trials were eager to find ways to sustain the brief interventions. Sustainability was considered at two levels: obtaining financial support to continue the intervention and clinical support for the case managers. CITAR trainers revisited sites approximately eight months after their implementation of B-SBCM. During the visits, trainers observed case managers with clients and discussed the most important steps that providers could take to maintain B-SBCM. Trainers felt that the single most important task for promoting sustainability was continued clinical supervision. This was borne out in by case manager and supervisor responses in follow-up interviews.

CONCLUSION

This chapter presented empirical evidence on the effectiveness of a brief model of strengths-based case management in improving linkage with care. The same beneficial results occurred whether clients were seeking to enter substance abuse treatment or medical care associated with being HIV positive. These are particularly important findings for strengths-based case management as it suggests that emphasizing client strengths and allowing clients broad discretion in making their own decisions can be effective in helping them achieve important clinical outcomes.

These findings combine with earlier studies, not presented here, to suggest several consistent benefits of SBCM, whether brief or long-term. Positive outcomes accrue to clients who receive strengths-based case management, particularly in the areas of drug use, employment, and criminal justice involvement (Rapp et al., 1998; Siegal et al., 2002; Siegal, Rapp, Li, Saha, & Kirk, 1997). The relationship between strengths-based case management and at least two of the positive outcomes—drug use and criminal justice involvement—seem to be accounted for by the ability of case managers to keep clients involved in services following primary treatment.

In order for either brief or long-term SBCM to be effective, it must be implemented in provider agencies, and implemented in such a way that the process does not strip away the qualities that make it effective. The experience of staff at CITAR has been that B-SBCM can be adapted to diverse practice settings without losing the effect of the critical elements.

DISCUSSION QUESTIONS/EXERCISES

1. Discuss with co-workers or colleagues the barriers you would face in attempting to implement a brief model of strengths-based case management in your agency. As a group, rank order the top five barriers with "1" being the most difficult to resolve and "5" being the easiest to resolve. For each barrier discuss: (a) the adaptations that could be made to brief strengths-based case management to facilitate its implementation, without diminishing its critical elements; and (b) the changes in your organization that could be made to improve implementation.

2. How does brief SBCM differ from SBCM? Point out at least three key differences.

3. Explain how evidence-based practices differ from those that are not. How critical are these differences?

4. In this study, what were the reactions of clients to the change to a brief form of SBCM? Do you think these can be generalized to other populations? Why or why not?

REFERENCES

Aarons, G. A. (2004). Mental health provider attitudes toward adoption of evidence-based practice: The Evidence-Based Practice Attitude Scale (EBPAS). *Mental Health Services Research, 6*, 61–74.

Benjamin, A. E. (1988). Long-term care and AIDS: Perspectives from experience with the elderly. *Millbank Quarterly, 66*(3), 415–443.

Blakely, C. H., Mayer, J. P., Gottschalk, R. G., Schmitt, N., Davidson, W. S., Roitman, D. B., et al. (1987). The fidelity-adaptation debate: Implications for the implementation of public sector social programs. *American Journal of Community Psychology, 15*, 253–268.

Bond, G. R., Evans, L., Salyers, M. P., Williams, J., & Kim, H. W. (2000). Measurement of fidelity in psychiatric rehabilitation. *Mental Health Services Research, 2*(2), 75–87.

Brun, C. & Rapp, R. C. (2001). Strengths-based management: Individuals' perspectives on strengths and the case manager relationship. *Social Work, 46*, 278–288.

Carroll, K. M. (1998). *A cognitive-behavioral approach: Treating cocaine addiction*. Rockville, MD: National Institute on Drug Abuse. (NIH Publication Number 98–4308).

Chapin, R. (2001). Building on the strengths of older women. In K. J. Peterson & A. Lieberman (Eds.), *Building on women's strengths: An agenda for the 21st century* (revised ed.). Binghamton, NY: Haworth Press.

Craw, J. A., Gardner, L. I., Marks, G., Rapp, R. C., Bosshart, J., Duffus, W. A., et al. (in press). Brief strengths-based case management promotes entry into HIV medical care: Results of the Antiretroviral Treatment Access Study-II (ARTAS-II). *Journal of Acquired Immune Deficiency Syndromes (JAIDS)*.

Daley, D. C., Mercer, D. E., & Carpenter, G. (1999). *Counseling for cocaine addiction: The collaborative cocaine treatment study model*. Rockville, MD: National Institute on Drug Abuse. (NIH Publication Number 99–4380).

Davis, D. A., Thomson, M. A., Oxman, A. D., & Haynes, R. B. (1995). Changing physician performance: A systematic review of the effect of continuing medical education strategies. *Journal of the American Medical Association, 274,* 700–705 [Abstract].

Drake, R., Goldman, H., Leff, H., Lehman, A., Dixon, L., Mueser, K., et al. (2001). Implementing evidence-based practices in routine mental health service settings. *Psychiatric Services, 52,* 179–182.

Farmer, A. P., Legare, F., McAuley, L. M., Thomas, R., Harvey, E. L., McGowan, J., et al. (2007). Printed educational materials: Effects on professional practice and health care outcomes (Protocol). *Cochrane Database of Systematic Reviews, 2003*(3).

Fast, B. & Chapin, R. (2002). The strengths model with older adults: Critical practice components. In D. Saleebey (Ed.), *The strengths perspective in social work practice.* White Plains, NY: Longman.

Fixsen, D. L., Naoom, S. F., Blase, K. A., Friedman, R. M., & Wallace, F. (2005). *Implementation research: A synthesis of the literature* (No. FMHI Publication \#231). Tampa, FL: University of South Florida, Louis de la Parte Florida Mental Health Institute, The National Implementation Research Network.

Fleishman, J. A., Mor, V., & Piette, J. (1991, October). AIDS case management: The client's perspective. *Health Services Research, 26,* 447–470.

Gardner, L., Metsch, L. R., Anderson-Mahoney, P., Loughlin, A. M., Del Rio, C., Strathdee, S., et al. (2005). Efficacy of a brief case management intervention to link recently diagnosed HIV-infected persons to care. *AIDS, 19,* 423–431.

Guydish, J., Tajima, B., Manser, S. T., & Jessup, M. (2007). Strategies to encourage adoption in multisite clinical trials. *Journal of Substance Abuse Treatment, 32,* 177–188.

Hesse, M., Vanderplasschen, W., Rapp, R. C., Broekaert, E., & Fridell, M. (2007). Case management for persons with substance use disorders. *Cochrane Database of Systematic Reviews 2007, Issue 4.* Art. No.: CD006265. DOI:10.1002/14651858.CD006265.pub2.

Hohmann, A. A. & Shear, M. K. (2002). Community-based intervention research: Coping with the "noise" of real life in study design. *American Journal of Psychiatry, 159*(2), 201–207.

Johnsen, M., Samberg, L., Calsyn, R., Blasinsky, M., Landow, W., & Goldman, H. (1999). Case management models for persons who are homeless and mentally ill: The ACCESS demonstration project. *Community Mental Health Journal, 35,* 325–346.

Katz, M. H., Cunningham, W. E., Fleishman, J. A., Andersen, R. M., Kellogg, T., Bozzette, S. A., et al. (2001). Effect of case management on unmet needs and utilization of medical care and medications among HIV-infected persons. *Annals of Internal Medicine, 135,* 557–565.

Knudsen, H. K., Ducharme, L. J., & Roman, P. M. (2007). Research participation and turnover intention: An exploratory anaylsis of substance abuse counselors. *Journal of Substance Abuse Treatment, 33*(2), 211–217.

Lehman, W. E. K., Greener, J. M., & Simpson, D. D. (2002). Assessing organizational readiness for change. *Journal of Substance Abuse Treatment, 22,* 197–209.

Lomas, J. (1991). Words without action? The production, dissemination, and impact of consensus recommendations. *Annual Review of Public Health, 12,* 41–65.

Martin, G. W., Herie, M. A., Turner, B. J., & Cunningham, J. A. (1998). A social marketing model for disseminating research-based treatments to addictions treatment providers. *Addiction, 93*(11), 1703–1715.

McCoy, C. B., Metsch, L. R., Chitwood, D. D., & Miles, C. (2001). Drug use and barriers to use of health care services. *Substance Use and Misuse, 36*(6&7), 789–806.

McKinney, M. M. (1998). Service needs and networks of rural women with HIV/AIDS. *AIDS Patient Care and STDs, 12*(6), 471–480.

McKleroy, V. S., Gallbraith, J. S., Cummings, B., Jones, P., Harshbarger, C., Collins, C., et al. (2006). Adapting evidence-based behavioral interventions for new settings and target populations. *AIDS Education and Prevention, 18*(Supplement A), 59–73.

Mowbray, C. T., Holter, M. C., Teague, G. B., & Bybee, D. (2003). Fidelity criteria: Development, measurement, and validation. *American Journal of Evaluation, 24*(3), 315–340.

Murphy, E. L., Collier, A. C., Kalish, L. A., Assmann, S. F., Para, M. F., Flanigan, T. P., et al. (2001). Highly active antirctroviral therapy decreases mortality and morbidity in patients with advanced HIV disease. *Annals of Internal Medicine, 135,* 17–26.

National Institute on Drug Abuse. (1999). *Principles of drug addiction treatment: A research-based guide.* Retrieved NIH publication number 99–4180, from www.drugabuse.gov/PODAT/PODATIndex.html

Orwin, R. G. (2000). Methodological challenges in study design and implementation. Assessing program fidelity in substance abuse health services research. *Addiction, 95*(Supplement 3), S309–S327.

Racine, D. P. (2006). Reliable effectiveness: A theory on sustaining and replicating worthwhile innovations. *Administration and Policy in Mental Health and Services Research, 33*, 356–387.

Rapp, C. A. & Chamberlain, R. (1985). Case management services for the chronically mentally ill. *Social Work, 30*(5), 417–422.

Rapp, R. C. (2006). Strengths-based case management: Enhancing treatment for persons with substance abuse problems. In D. Saleebey (Ed.), *The strengths perspective in social work practice* (4th ed.). Boston: Allyn and Bacon.

Rapp, R. C., Kelliher, C. W., Fisher, J. H., & Hall, J. (1994). Strengths-based case management. A role in addressing denial in substance abuse treatment. *Journal of Case Management, 3*(4), 139–144.

Rapp, R. C., Siegal, H. A., Li, L., & Saha, P. (1998). Predicting postprimary treatment services and drug use outcome: A multivariate analysis. *American Journal of Drug and Alcohol Abuse, 24*(4), 603–615.

Rapp, R. C., Xu, J., Carr, C. A., Lane, D. T., Wang, J., & Carlson, R. G. (2006). Treatment barriers identified by substance abusers assessed at a centralized intake unit. *Journal of Substance Abuse Treatment, 30*(3), 227–235.

Redko, C., Rapp, R. C., Elms, C., Snyder, M., & Carlson, R. G. (2007). Understanding the working alliance between persons with substance abuse problems and strengths-based case managers. *Journal of Psychoactive Drugs, 39*(3), 241–250.

Rubenstein, L. V., Mittman, B. S., Yano, E. M., & Mulrow, C. D. (2000). From understanding health care provider behavior to improving health care: The QUERI framework for quality improvement. *Medical Care, 38*(6), Supplement I: I129–I141.

Saleebey, D. (2006). *The strengths perspective in social work practice* (4th ed.). Boston: Allyn and Bacon.

Siegal, H. A., Li, L., & Rapp, R. C. (2002). Case management as a therapeutic enhancement: Impact on post-treatment criminality. *Journal of Addictive Diseases, 21*(4), 37–46.

Siegal, H. A., Rapp, R. C., Kelliher, C. W., Fisher, J. H., Wagner, J. H., & Cole, P. A. (1995). The strengths perspective of case management: A promising inpatient substance abuse treatment enhancement. *Journal of Psychoactive Drugs, 27*(1), 67–72.

Siegal, H. A., Rapp, R. C., Li, L., Saha, P., & Kirk, K. (1997). The role of case management in retaining clients in substance abuse treatment: An exploratory analysis. *Journal of Drug Issues, 27*(4), 821–831.

Simpson, D. D. (2002). A conceptual framework for transferring research to practice. *Journal of Substance Abuse Treatment, 22*, 171–182.

Simpson, D. D. & Flynn, P. M. (2007). Moving innovations into treatment: A stage-based approach to program change. *Journal of Substance Abuse Treatment, 33*(2), 111–120.

Simpson, D. D., Joe, G. W., & Rowan-Szal, G. A. (2007). Linking the elements of change: Program and client responses to innovation. *Journal of Substance Abuse Treatment, 33*(2), 201–209.

Strathdee, S. A., Ricketts, E. P., Huettner, S., Cornelius, L., Bishai, D., Havens, J. R., et al. (2006). Facilitating entry into drug treatment among injection drug users referred from a needle exchange program: Results from a community-based behavioral intervention trial. *Drug and Alcohol Dependence, 83*(3), 225–232.

Szulanski, G. & Winters, S. (2002). Getting it right the second time. *Harvard Business Review, 80*, 62–69.

Thompson, A. S., Blankenship, K. M., Selwyn, P. A., Khoshnood, K., Lopez, M., Balacos, K., et al. (1998). Evaluation of an innovative program to address the health and social service needs of drug-using women with or at risk for HIV infection. *Journal of Community Health, 23*(6), 419–440.

Twyman, D. M. & Libbus, M. K. (1994). Case-management of AIDS clients as a predictor of total inpatient hospital days. *Public Health Nursing, 11*(6), 406–411.

Vaughan-Sarrazin, M. S., Hall, J. A., & Rick, G. S. (2000). Impact of case management on use of health service by rural clients in substance abuse treatment. *Journal of Drug Issues, 30*(2), 435–463.

Vittinghoff, E., Scheer, S., O'Malley, P., Colfax, G., Holmberg, S. D., & Buchbinder, S. P. (1999). Combination antiretroviral therapy and recent declines in AIDS incidence and mortality. *The Journal of Infectious Diseases, 179*, 717–720.

. . . . .

CHAPTER NINE

THE STRENGTHS MODEL WITH OLDER ADULTS
Critical Practice Components

HOLLY NELSON-BECKER

ROSEMARY CHAPIN

BECKY FAST

ROSA

Rosa Garcia and her husband Leonardo have always been leaders in the Mexican American community where they raised their four children. Rosa became a citizen when she married Leonardo. His family immigrated to Kansas City, Missouri, before he was born. Their home was one where new immigrants to this country often gathered for help in understanding how to survive the day in their new country. Her four children had all gone to college on her income as a maid and the factory wages of her husband Leonardo. When they graduated, the children gradually moved away from home as they became more and more successful in their careers. Only Carmen, the youngest child, lived nearby. However, she worked at the local elementary school and she had to spend what little free time she had caring for her own small children and her disabled mother-in-law who lived with the family. Rosa always told the children when they phoned or arrived on rare visits home that she was doing well. They believed her because they wanted to believe it was true.

Rosa's husband Leonardo died suddenly of a heart attack a month before his 78th birthday. Eighty years-old, Mrs. Garcia was becoming increasingly frail. Although she had been very active in the Catholic Church, many Sundays now she just did not feel strong enough to attend Mass. She misses this important source of spiritual support. Also, she no longer can carry a sack of groceries home, even though the grocery store is only two blocks away. As a result her diet is now very poor. Her eyesight is not sharp and when she tripped over a rug in her house, she was not able to get up until a neighbor had stopped by the next day and helped. The neighbor notified Carmen, who rushed over. Rosa's injuries did not require hospitalization. However, Carmen was now fearful that her mother was no longer safe by herself and so she was ready to help her mother sell the house and move into a nearby nursing care facility.

On the advice of the neighbor who had found her, Carmen contacted a social worker at Casa Central, an Area Agency on Aging (AAA) affiliated agency, who was able to meet her at her mother's house. The social worker was licensed as a geriatric care manager. She talked to Rosa and learned that her independence was something Rosa valued above all else. With the social worker's help, Rosa was able to discuss her concerns with Carmen. The social worker was able to present several options for supports so Mrs. Garcia could choose what she wanted and could continue to live in her own home. The social worker agreed to Mrs. Garcia's request to continue checking back with her during her transition to service use. Mrs. Garcia observed that the social worker had listened to her and advocated for her with her daughter. She invited the social worker to continue in a case management role.

Rosa has entered into the complex web of long-term care services. Luckily, she has a social worker who uses a strengths-based practice model and is skilled at developing rapport. When such an approach is absent, many older adults like Rosa will not even consider looking at service options. The strengths model of case management is designed for people like Rosa who will require different types of help and levels of intensity in caring and service provision as their health improves or deteriorates. Respect for the dignity and uniqueness of individuals like Rosa is operationalized through the model's practice principles and methods. Furthermore, social workers using the strengths model are alert to the additional barriers to service access that Mexican American women may face. Workers operating from a strengths approach are interested in building on the strengths that have helped older adults overcome previous difficult times in their lives.

This chapter describes how the strengths model of case management is implemented in the long-term care of older adults, specifically in the provision of home and community-based services. The application of the strengths model of case management with seniors living at home in the community is beginning to be a focus of theory and research as social workers and others seek to reformulate constructs about aging (Ronch & Goldfield, 2003).

The first section of this chapter presents the conceptual framework that guides and directs the helping efforts with older adults. The next section delineates the critical practice components of a strengths-based case management approach in long-term care, especially practice methods designed to support older adult autonomy, and meet resource-oriented needs while promoting cost effectiveness and efficiency. The significance of developing expertise with an aging immigrant population is discussed, along with the value of incorporating a spiritual assessment component and the need to integrate policy components in case management practice. Finally, the potential of the strengths model in changing long-term care environments is explored.

CONCEPTUAL FRAMEWORK FOR PRACTICE

Strengths-based case management for older adults is derived from the basic principles and functions of the strengths model developed in the 1980s for persons with severe and persistent mental illness living in the community (Perkins & Tice, 1995; Rapp, 1992; Ronch & Goldfield, 2003; Sullivan & Fisher, 1994). In addition, the strengths approach links to concepts of successful aging (Rowe & Kahn, 1998) and selective optimization with compensation (Baltes, 1993), well known in the literature on aging. Rowe and Kahn indicated that low risk of disease, high mental and physical functioning, and active engagement with life were important in successful living. However, many older adults can apply that strict definition to any situation, even one of diminished physical or mental capacity, through the choices they make. Consonant with this, selective optimization with compensation is a cognitive behavioral approach that acknowledges older adults may need to adapt to changing biological conditions (Baltes, 1993). However, they can still select activities that are important to them and enjoy their participation by creatively compensating for what they may no longer be able to accomplish. Another more moderated view of successful aging than Rowe and Kahn's designation identified five key factors—independence, participation, dignity, care, and fulfillment—that lead to a sense of well-being in later life (Galambos & Rosen, 1999).

Furthermore, aging well is another term that is now used in the literature as both a goal and a process. It is defined by Kahana and Kahana (1996) as a holistic approach by which older adults are able to adapt self and the environment to respond proactively to the challenges of aging. Aging well becomes possible when older adults are able to minimize some of the negative effects of losses that are often associated with aging –such as loss of loved ones, employment, and some physical or mental ability—and maximize the benefits that can accompany a long life, such as a wide network of family and friends, the wisdom developed through years of facing and overcoming obstacles, and accumulated material and socioemotional assets. The focus on the social environment and social networks in defining what it means to age well is also supported by the ecological perspective, which recognizes the influence of interactions and relationship among the older adult, other individuals, and the older adult's social and physical environments. The concept of environmental press suggests that older adults do best when they have the opportunity to participate to the maximum of their ability: If they are given too little to do, they lose skill over time, but if given more than they are able to successfully accomplish, they can become frustrated and lose motivation. The strengths perspective builds on the strengths and resources of older adults and their communities to help older adults achieve the goals that are meaningful to them.

Case management has been a part of social work practice since its inception (Johnson & Rubin, 1983). Like all social work practice, strengths-based case management for older adults rests on a foundation of values, knowledge, and skills. But there are several distinguishing features emanating from the values and philosophy of the model that set it apart from other long-term care case management practice approaches. These distinctive features include a shift from traditional models of helping based on medical necessity to a strengths-based model that addresses the whole person in his or her environment.

Five key principles of the strengths perspective with older adults are the following:

- All individuals have strengths at every stage of life and under all conditions.
- All experiences, even negative or unexpected ones, may present opportunities for growth.
- Traditional diagnosis and assessment in direct practice often make assumptions that limit rather than expand capacity.
- Collaboration with an older adult client can motivate him or her to achieve his or her aspirations. Older adults may have important aspirations yet to accomplish.
- Any environment has resources to be uncovered or co-constructed.
- A civil society engages in care for all of its members.

In the strengths framework, discovering, developing, and building on the person's internal and external resources is a focal point. In contrast to many other long-term care case management models, the strengths-based helping process emphasizes consumer participation and decision making.

Medical and rehabilitation models typically emphasize professional diagnosis and treatment of the symptomatology to eradicate or ameliorate the "problem." Authority for and control over decisions lies in the hands of the professional. The unspoken premise is that persons in need of assistance lack knowledge or insight about the identified physical or mental health problem and certainly about how it might be resolved. Professional expertise is needed to assess and treat the troublesome condition (Freidson, 1988).

In contrast, the primary purpose of strengths case management is to recognize the inherent abilities that a person has developed over a lifetime of active effort. The aim of this approach is to help older persons maintain as much control over their lives as possible: to capitalize on what they can do and to compensate for what they cannot do. The goal of strengths case management is to stabilize the older person's routine within the acceptable bounds determined by the individual, often despite advancing disability. Assessment and planning strategies are woven from the social, spiritual, psychological, and physical needs and strengths of an older person. For example, in a medical model case management system, a patient with a broken hip might be hospitalized, have the hip treated, and then be released. The medical needs may have been well met, but matters such as transportation, housing modifications, financial assistance, social isolation, and some physical limitations might never be considered. For most older adults, well-being is more than a medical matter. What is equally significant is the ability to engage in reciprocal interactions, contribute and feel useful, prevent or cope with social isolation, and develop an acceptable routine of daily life despite the disease or illness (Smith & Eggleston, 1989). Even if an individual suffers from a serious chronic condition, where these other needs are addressed, he/she may experience a sense of heightened well-being.

The assumption underlying the medicalization of aging services is that older people, and especially those with chronic disabilities, require the involvement of medical professionals to protect them from further injury and debilitation. In advanced age, chronic rather than acute illnesses are, for the most part, the major medical problems. The leading chronic conditions among older people include heart disease, cancer, stroke, diabetes, chronic obstructive pulmonary disease, as well as asthma and osteoporosis (CDC, 2004). However, these conditions merely annoy some older people who are able to lead relatively normal lives despite aches, pains, and minor physical limitations. Others are significantly limited in their ability to carry out both necessary and preferred daily activities, such as cooking, housework, yard work, and leaving the house to socialize. Of course, many older people also are periodically afflicted with acute illnesses (that is, conditions lasting less than three months).

The stress inherent in providing and receiving emotional support and getting instrumental help with household tasks and personal care are the most pressing challenges during later life transitions for older adults and their families. Decreased functional abilities—the degree of independence in functioning a person possesses in the face of illness—may overwhelm an individual's coping response. He or she may need help with activities of daily living (ADLs) such as bathing, dressing, grooming, eating, toileting, walking, and transferring.

Instrumental activities of daily living (IADLs) such as shopping, preparing meals, managing money and medications, doing homework, and using a telephone or transportation are other important needs. Despite functional deficits, older people demonstrate remarkable resiliency. They often possess an underutilized or untapped capacity for growth and change even in the context of difficult life challenges. Like younger persons with disabilities, some older adults need only minimal assistance to arrange and manage supports and resources so that they can remain in the community and lead the life they choose.

The conceptual framework for the strengths model of case management with older adults places self-determination as the central value; that value directs the focus to personal goal achievement. Consumer power is the preferred balance in the fulcrum of the case management relationship. The older adult as well as the community must be viewed as possessing valuable inherent resources and strengths. Thus, the case managers' task is to help older adults identify and achieve access to both formal and informal resources in order to reach the outcomes they desire. Table 9.1 presents key elements of the strengths model and delineates differences from traditional medical/rehabilitative models of helping.

The purpose of strengths-based case management is to assist older adults in identifying, securing, and sustaining external and internal resources that are needed for customary interdependent (as opposed to independent or dependent) community living (Chapin, Nelson-Becker & Macmillan, 2006; Kisthardt & Rapp, 1991). Strengths-based case management allows older persons to determine for themselves where they want to live and demands belief in their capacity to choose and to handle the consequences of their choices. Such attitudes affirm the dignity and worth of older adults in spite of prevalent myths and stereotypes that clearly represent bias and prejudice against elders. This is a revisionist view of aging.

Despite the strong preference of older adults to remain in their homes as long as possible, family and professional relationships can strongly affect the older adult's sense of self and the type of long-term care he or she decides on. A significant step in this direction is to establish a foundation of genuine dialogue and collaboration supporting community choices (Kivnick & Murray, 2001; Perkins & Tice, 1995). Assisting older persons with identification of the problems at hand while facilitating their participation in finding solutions helps them stay in community-based housing as long as possible. An overarching goal of strengths-based case management, anchored in the value base of client self-determination, is to facilitate consumer involvement and choice. Providing older people with options and including them in decision making about possible institutional placement increases the likelihood of satisfaction with the choices made. When the older consumer remains active in making medical and social decisions, both the consumer and the providers achieve greater satisfaction.

Asking for additional help can be extremely difficult for an older person. Motenko and Greenberg assert that "the ability to acknowledge the need for help and ask for help is evidence of mature dependence, a crucial transition in late life" (1995, p. 387). These authors suggest that older persons are better able to accept increased dependence if they are given authority to make decisions about the nature of the help needed and how it should be provided. Simply stated, being in charge is essential to personal pride and life satisfaction, particularly for older adults who have been operating independently throughout their lives (Langer, 1989). The more older persons feel in control of their lives by solving their own problems, the less the likelihood of unnecessary dependency and learned helplessness.

TABLE 9.1   The Strengths Conceptual Model Contrasted with Traditional Medical/Rehabilitative Models of Helping

FACTOR	STRENGTHS MODEL	MEDICAL/REHABILITATIVE MODELS
Value Base: *General* *Philosophical*	Older adults have ongoing potential to grow, heal, learn. Older adults possess ability to identify needs and wants. Older adults have inherent and unique individual strengths as well as environmental strengths/resources.	Medical community has best standpoint to identify problem. Older adult must comply with prescribed treatments as determined by clinical trials and medical expertise.
Value Base: *Cultural*	Client is a consumer. Ideographic—older adults have ability and authority to determine their best solutions.	Client is a patient—passive recipient of services. Nomothetic and paternalistic—society must take care of older adults who face decreasing physical ability.
Knowledge *Base*	Case manager brings knowledge of resources and understanding of human capacity for change to client relationship.	Medical community is the custodian and gatekeeper of biological and health knowledge.
Knowledge *Base:* *Problem* *Resolution*	Consumer has decision-making capacity. Client knowledge and natural community resources used first. Other resources sought as needed.	Problem resolution dependent upon professional expertise and ability to synthesize vast quantities of information.
Skill Base: *General*	Professional develops rapport and trust. Professional collaborates with client. Professional combines own resources and environmental resources to help achieve client-identified goals.	Professional assesses nature of person's problem, provides diagnosis, and treatment.
Skill Base: *Case* *Management*	Case manager coaches, supports, and encourages. Case manager replaces self when possible with natural helpers. Case manager rejuvenates and creates natural helping networks. Case manager provides services within daily routines.	Professional contact limited to assessment, planning, evaluating functions. Identified problems are managed medically. Patient is taught skills as needed to overcome deficits.

In the strengths model, social workers identify consumer abilities and create or find situations to use those abilities in the achievement of personal goals. Lasting change, we believe, can happen only when you collaborate with an individual's aspirations, percep-tions, and strengths. Most consumers are competent and able to participate in the plan-ning and delivery processes. Doing so brings renewed self-confidence and independence precipitated by moving with the elder in the direction he or she chooses and in situations and contexts where the person feels capable and willing. If consumers are acknowledged as experts in defining their needs, the role of the social worker must change to reflect a greater appreciation of that consumer expertise.

Helping individuals like Rosa Garcia manage their own inevitable aging process and the physical and emotional losses involved assists them to be better equipped to make sound decisions regarding what type of help they desire. When considering the needs of older persons and their families, risk and security must be carefully balanced. The conflict between the two becomes even clearer for older adults who are more severely disabled.

Table 9.2 presents a continuum of possible behaviors available to case managers for facilitating higher or lower levels of participation and involvement by the consumer. This table is intended to provide guidance to social workers attempting to foster the participation of frail or disabled older adults who are competent in decisions about their care needs. The continuum ranges from absolute authority (having the locus of control with the case manager) to a self-directed care approach (shifting the control to an informed consumer). The midpoint indicates shared responsibility by both parties for

TABLE 9.2   Continuum of Decision Making

ABSOLUTE AUTHORITY	IMPOSING	JOINT ACTION	LIMITED CONSTRAINTS	SELF-DIRECTED CARE
The case manager pressures the consumer to accept the problems or solutions without input or participation in the decision. The person's understanding of the issues are solicited but the case manager retains absolute authority over decisions.	The case manager defines the problem and selects the solutions that are the most promising. Consumer preferences are taken into consideration.	Together, both parties brainstorm a possible range of solutions. The case manager and consumer are both responsible for identifying consumer strengths and resources for implementing the plan of care. Decisions are not made unless both individuals agree on them.	The consumer offers preferences about the type, role, and the level of service provision. Information and counseling is given by the case manager to assist the consumer in making informed decisions. The consumer retains the final decision within limits defined by the case manager.	Consumer choices are supported through being allowed to choose the mix, frequency, duration, and timing of formal/informal service provision within organizational boundaries. In this system, the case manager becomes a consultant to and resource for consumers to help make viable arrangements.
CASE MANAGER DIRECTED DECISION MAKING		COLLABORATIVE DECISION MAKING		CONSUMER DIRECTED DECISION MAKING

managing the multiple effects of the consumer's disabilities and illnesses, and for individualizing the consumer's resources.

The goal of strengths-based case management is to encourage more active consumer participation in long-term care decisions. The case manager begins where the consumer is and moves with him or her on the continuum to the highest possible level of participation. The aim is to expand consumer confidence in making crucial decisions such as when to seek care and what options to select, and to move toward consumer-directed decision making. Rosa Garcia, introduced in the first case vignette, had never taken care of the finances, the car, or fixing the house before her husband died. She was at a loss initially about how to handle what she saw as traditionally male duties that her husband always had performed. In those arenas, she first wanted family to make more of the decisions. However, she wanted to retain the responsibilities that she had during her marriage. In time, she felt more confident about managing her late husband's duties and subsequently wanted less direction from her family and case manager.

At the self-directed end of the continuum (see Table 9.2) consumers determine what services they need. However, self-directed care does not preclude the case manager from developing a supportive structure that enables individuals with disabilities to take responsibility for planning their own lives with the assistance of family, friends, and community members.

One difficulty lies with the minority of older persons whose judgment is so impaired that increased responsibility for care decisions poses a danger to self and others. Questions inevitably arise about whether the person should participate in decision making and at what level. Frail or disabled older adults have the right to be involved in decisions about their long-term care. Even consumers with cognitive or psychiatric disabilities should be afforded as many choices as possible. The challenge is to be thoroughly aware of their rights and the *real* limitations of their physical and mental conditions, perhaps assessed by a neuropsychological examination to determine decisional capacity. Given patience and time, a relationship can be established even with a very frail older person who fades in and out cognitively. His or her fears can be identified, concerns expressed, trust established, and actions taken in which the older adult is a willing partner to the maximum of his or her potential and capacity. Strengths-based case managers strive to understand how their relationship supports or limits the autonomy of older individuals.

CRITICAL PRACTICE COMPONENTS OF EFFECTIVE CASE MANAGEMENT

The purpose of strengths-based case management is to assist older adults in identifying, securing and sustaining external and internal resources that are needed for customary interdependent (as opposed to independent or dependent) community living (Chapin et al., 2006; Kisthardt & Rapp, 1991). Strengths-based case managers strive to understand how their relationship supports or limits the autonomy of older individuals. Specifically, the strengths model's potential to increase case management effectiveness with older adults occurs through the following practice methods: (1) personalized assessment and planning, (2) assertive outreach to natural community resources and services, (3) emergency crisis planning, and (4) ongoing collaboration and caregiving adjustments.

Personalized Assessment and Planning

Assessment from a strengths perspective is holistic, rather than determining the criteria an older adult might meet in diagnosis. Consumer knowledge and motivation rather than professional expertise are the basis of the assessment and planning process (Pray, 1992). A standard functional assessment does not generate a complete picture of the older person's strengths, coping strategies, motivations, and potential for change (Kivnick, 1993). Eligibility for long-term care services based on functional limitations prompts social workers to view their consumers in terms of ADL and IADL typologies. In fact, so much emphasis is placed on functional limitations that an older person's quality of life is often reduced to *nothing more* than a list of ADLs and IADLs. Vulnerable older adults soon realize that in order to receive help, they too must describe themselves in those terms. In Rosa Garcia's case, an initial focus on the deficits in her ADLs could have reinforced a suspicion that the social worker intended to find her incapable of remaining at home. Careful attention to her desires during the initial relationship building created an environment where functional limitations as well as capacities could be acknowledged and used in the care planning process.

Strengths-based assessment and planning focuses on the optimization of the older person's strengths and resources. Applied helping strategies are implemented to support the individual's sense of control and capacity to function at home. This is accomplished through identifying supports and resources that take the person's limitations into consideration but also counterbalance them with discovery of strengths and activities that might fit with the individual's desires and interests (Sullivan & Fisher, 1994). Most social workers are indeed committed to acknowledging the consumers' strengths. However, the majority of assessment and care planning tools provide little space or incentive for recording what the older person desires, is doing, has done, and can do to maintain his or her independence. This omission hinders even the best intentions. This omission is significant. Rarely, if ever, are consumer strengths seen as integral to the planning process so that services are provided and activities structured to maximize and promote existing or potential strengths. Subsequently, social workers may fail to get to know the older person in a holistic way, whereas an appreciation of the whole person almost always creates a positive interaction. When this kind of relationship is developed, the case manager is better able to assist the consumer in developing an individualized plan of action.

Given system barriers such as large caseloads and organizational policies, the strengths assessment and planning process with senior adults should, at minimum, cover these items:

1. Exploring commonalties: shared values, experiences, interests.
2. Learning how the person has coped with difficulties in the past.
3. Focusing on the strengths within the person and his or her environment.
4. Visioning together what kind of life the consumer wants.

Basic questions to ask include:

- Who is important to you in your life? (Social support)
- What do you do during a normal day? (Normal activities)
- What makes life worth living for you? (Life satisfaction—meaning, spiritual foundation, if any)

- What has worked well for you in the past? (Coping skill inventory)
- What is going well for you right now? (Present-oriented strengths)
- If things could be different, what would you wish for? (Visioning)

The strengths assessment process is not meant to replace existing standardized assessments for conferring and allocating benefits. However, it is unjust to suppose that the whole picture of a person is captured in diagnostic, functional, or psychotherapeutic assessments. Only through creating *life* plans rather than care plans will an older person be able to live meaningfully in the community. The above focal points and questions can serve as guides for gathering the information needed to develop such plans. An actual strengths assessment and personal plan can be seen in Fast and Chapin (2000, pp. 39–56).

Assertive Outreach to Natural Community Resources and Services

The strengths perspective on case management practice offers an alternative conception to resource acquisition. Before using formal paid services, the case manager is expected to determine first that naturally occurring, environmental, and community resources are not available. Natural helpers include a collective of supporters to be developed and sustained such as neighbors, apartment managers, grocery store clerks, church or youth groups, adult children, and others with whom the older client comes into contact on a daily or weekly basis. The presence of naturally occurring resources is a strength of all communities and an available resource in all communities when actively pursued (Sullivan, 1997).

The strengths model advocates employing natural helpers and resources whenever possible. From the perspective of older adults, such help may be more acceptable because it is often based on friendship or a perception of mutual need, is easily accessible, lacks stigma, and is usually much cheaper. However, other older adults would rather not encumber their existing social network. In fact, when older adults are asked to help identify their helping networks, they will often say that no one is around who can help them. The avoidance of acknowledging dependency, combined with pride, may prevent older people from recognizing or voicing their level of reliance on others. Therefore, it is imperative for strengths-oriented case managers to identify and support these helpers without undermining the older individual's self-esteem and dignity. Assistance from family, friends, employers, and colleagues often is not recognized by the older adult as help because it is extended in a subtle manner. This help is given by informal social helpers as they interact with the individual during the normal rhythms of the day. These social network members may notice that their older friend is having some difficulty with walking, eating, or shopping and, without being asked, help the person with these tasks.

Social supports take on increased significance as older adults become more frail. One of the losses experienced by this population is the shrinkage of the informal support system. Many consumers no longer have a full social support system that can help them. One of the critical functions of the social worker is to help secure and sustain connections to informal resources. The social worker's goal is to facilitate a more adequate fit between the individual's desires and the resources in his or her environment. This includes the social worker's help to recognize and map out what assets are already being used to some degree and to include other community capacities that have not yet been mobilized.

Acquisition of natural community resources is predicated on the belief that includ-ing consumers in the decision about who or what entity can provide the service that will further promote acceptance of the help received. The challenge for most social workers is locating and expanding a natural support system for consumers. In Rosa's situation, many of her friends and acquaintances, except for her children, were equally frail. The social worker needs to be informed about the naturally occurring resources in the wider com-munity, as well as in the consumer's personal network. It is important to generate as many potential resources as possible with consumers and their primary caregivers. Older per-sons may withhold existing support network information out of a desire to maintain the appearance of independence.

A useful strategy for case managers to identify natural helpers is to accompany the older person through a typical day in order to learn what help is given, by whom, and how often (Lustbader & Hooyman, 1994). By accompanying the person to the doctor, hair-dresser's, etc., and by listening to the conversations, more often than not, a social worker will discover that the older person has more social contact than the social worker realized. Or, the case manager might discover a different interactive style outside the home than that seen at home.

In developing the service mix, caregiver burden is acknowledged. Support networks of family and friends should not feel overtaxed. Assertively working to relieve primary caregiver burden is basic to developing a workable care plan. Ongoing dialogue, assessment of perceived burden, and role adjustment must occur with informal caregivers when they are providing some of the major components of care. One of the chief problems with nat-ural helpers is finding ways to limit their involvement because they are within easy reach on a potentially unlimited basis. Many who could help would rather not get involved because they fear being overwhelmed by the needs that may eventually occur. Occasion-ally, some older people alienate those who could help by complaining about the help or by expecting too much help.

Despite the emotional bonds linking older adults with their families, friends, and other established caregivers, these individuals often lack the expertise to provide comprehensive long-term care. Further, a previous history of caregiver abuse or neglect in a given situation could necessitate agency assistance to care for and protect the vulnerable adult from infor-mal assistance. However, formal providers, while often equipped with the necessary tech-nical skills, cannot fully satisfy affective needs or deliver the kind of idiosyncratic care that reflects a lifetime of shared values and experiences.

Balancing expensive formal care with less-expensive informal resources can help con-trol costs while ensuring necessary assistance is provided in ways acceptable to the older adult. In Rosa's case, the social worker discovered that a man who rented Rosa's garage to store an antique car had a daughter in high school. With Rosa's agreement, the social worker hired the girl to shop for groceries. Rosa prepared a list that the girl's father picked up when he drove by on his way to work (he also usually dropped in to see how Rosa was doing on these occasions). When the social worker explored with Rosa what her experiences as a Mexican American woman had been in seeking formal service, Rosa indicated that she was hesitant to try to negotiate a formal care system primarily staffed by European Americans. Her preference was to rely on friends or relatives to help her obtain services. The high school girl and her father were recognized both as a source of help and as trusted friends who could aid Rosa in her efforts to gain access to other resources.

Undoubtedly, there will never be enough paid formal services to meet the needs of a growing frail older adult population. However, focusing primarily on the deficits in the social environment only further restricts imagination and the number of helping resources realized.

Emergency Crisis Planning

Most older adults come to the attention of a social worker at a time of crisis. Crisis frequently occurs as the result of an acute care hospitalization. This experience leaves frail older adults in a weakened state suffering from depression, anxiety, or a sense of failure if the admission was caused by a fall, medication mismanagement, or lapses in personal care. During these instances, when the person's resilience is low, they are most ready to yield to professional and caregiver choices and goals. Advocating for the person's wishes and increasing older adult involvement in the decision-making process increases the likelihood that alternatives to institutional care will be chosen if available. High care costs often result because the case manager has not had time to deal with the problem before it becomes a crisis or because services are simply allocated to the consumer without trying to fully assess and resolve the situation. Kulys (1983) found that older adults typically do not plan for a health-related crisis. This potential for unwanted institutionalization precipitated by unexpected crises can be mitigated by planning ahead for crisis services.

In the strengths model, an emergency plan is discussed and negotiated with the consumer and the primary caregivers before a health crisis develops. This plan is rehearsed and reviewed. Specific behaviors may be performed to ensure that they can be followed in an emergency. A monitoring device or alert may be worn. A recent innovation in care planning is that many communities now collect old cell phones that may still be used to call 9-1-1. Redistribution to frail older adults may mean that they have the device in their pocket or nearby to call for help.

An established emergency plan takes into consideration that most frail older adults will probably need time-limited, acute-care crisis services at some point. However, at a large number of crisis junctures, either low- or high-cost rapid response mechanisms can be selected, depending on how knowledgeable the consumer and caregivers are about the existing resources and their accessibility. When a structured plan for dealing with crises involving natural and formal resources is not in place, then high-cost services become the simplest and most readily available option. On a broader community level, the lessons from Hurricane Katrina which struck New Orleans in 2005 suggest the need for greater involvement by case managers in macro planning. There was no city or state plan for evacuating vulnerable older adults, particularly those residing under institutional care in the aftermath of the storm. Because of the intense pressure on evacuating other groups of medically needy individuals such as those in hospitals, there were few resources available for nursing care facilities. As a result, a number of older adults in nursing homes died (Urban Institute Report, 2006). Those institutions faring better had parent corporations who provided limited resources. Nonetheless, the need for advance planning, clear methods of communication, rapid deployment of resources, and better coordination was apparent. A strengths approach focuses on anticipating key crisis points and speaking with caregivers about handling emergent situations as strategies for effective case management under critical conditions.

Ongoing Collaboration and Caregiving Adjustments

In the strengths perspective, monitoring is a continuous process that begins when care goals are established. The social worker frequently contacts and collaborates not only with the older person, but also with her or his family members, friendly visitors, senior citizen groups, nurses, and other support networks. The social worker's role goes far beyond that of "appointments secretary" to that of leader, trainer, and supervisor of a cadre of paid and unpaid helpers.

Skilled and effective case management presupposes that securing resources provides minimal benefits unless they are sustained and individualized to meet consumer preferences. Even after the older adult has gained access to desired services and resources, a lot of effort may need to be expended to sustain aging in place. The challenge of strengths-based case management is to resolve or at least reduce the interpersonal conflicts within the personal support networks that inevitably arise. Relationship-driven collaboration recognizes the value of each person's input and the benefits of making the helping experience mutually advantageous for everyone. The goal of continuous contact is to strengthen the consumer's self-care capacities and the caregivers' ability to help through the transfer of knowledge and skills by social and medical service providers, all coordinated by the case manager.

For example, an older consumer with hearing difficulty may become extremely frustrated when the taxi driver, whom he calls for rides to the grocery store, leaves after momentarily honking the horn. Facilitation of the resource use frequently involves educating the helper. Attention to building partnerships with resource providers, whether volunteer or paid, is very important. Tailoring the help to meet the needs of the consumer should be done in a nonthreatening way, not only for the sake of the present consumer but for all future consumers who may use that resource.

Ongoing contacts with the consumer and their helpers enable the case manager to influence cost effectiveness through increasing, decreasing, or terminating any or all services expeditiously. Applebaum and Austin (1990) assert that rapid response to consumer changes can have a dramatic impact on service costs. The overutilization of services typically results from not adjusting prescribed amounts of delivered services to the current situation as it unfolds. Reduction in case management costs as well as paid services can be expected in the strengths model because efforts are reduced and shifted to more frail and needy individuals as other consumers regain increased levels of self-sufficiency.

IMMIGRATION AND STRENGTHS-BASED CASE MANAGEMENT

Increasingly large numbers of older adults in the United States will have been born overseas and will have immigrated here to be with their families (Federal Interagency Forum, 2006). Declining attention to health because of perceived barriers in the use of formal healthcare, combined with language limitations, may lead to engagement with case management services at a higher level of intensity. There will be an increased need for case managers with the cultural competency and sensitivity to ask older adults how they see their needs rather than making assumptions that may not have cross-cultural validity. In addition, case managers operating out of a strengths approach will seek to understand how these older adults have typically interacted with the healthcare system in their countries of origin as well as what particular stigma mental illnesses such as depression may carry. Case managers may want to develop connections with cultural informants, such as medical anthropologists, who can teach them how best to assist this new group of aging adults, many of whom they may be unable to communicate with directly.

Urban areas may attract large numbers of older adults with a common ethnic heritage. This means a potential ready social support system will be available in the geographic regions that case managers have access to. Cultural change models in long-term care indicate that no longer should all older adults be served from a standard U.S. menu but, rather, than ethnic palates will dictate new offerings and dishes. Familiar customs and cultural celebrations can be encouraged in senior centers and other places where older adults congregate. Case managers operating from a strengths approach will move creatively to support these types of endeavors and other innovations.

INTEGRATION OF SPIRITUAL ASSESSMENT
AND INTERVENTION IN SOCIAL WORK PRACTICE
WITH OLDER ADULTS

Incorporation of religious and spiritual assessment routinely, and spiritual intervention where requested by older adult clients, can help to support and enrich older adult coping capacity and empowerment. This is particularly the case in the current cohorts, which came of age in a generation of strong religious connections (Ai, 2000; Koenig, 1994; Pargament, 1997). Initially a social worker could ask preliminary questions to determine what provides the older adult with a sense of meaning and purpose and whether religion and/or spirituality are valued to any extent. A framework for preliminary questions is suggested in Nelson-Becker, Nakashima, and Canda (2006).

Spiritually sensitive practice as detailed in Canda and Furman (1999), promotes attention to those aspects of life that provide value. While spiritual dimensions may be interwoven in problem-focused narratives that bring older adult clients to seek case management and other kinds of social work help, these dimensions also may form a context that lies beyond satisfaction of immediate concrete needs or development of long-term goals. Older adults typically value the importance of religion and spirituality in their lives, with 58 percent reporting that religion is very important, the highest rating on a four-point scale in a Gallup poll (PRCC, 2001).

Although value is often appraised positively, religion too may hold the bitterness of social disapprobation (Spilka, 1986) where an older adult may have experienced lack of acceptance or where rigid interpretations of sacred texts may have been the source of personal guilt or shame. Beliefs about religion and spirituality are shaped by individual attributes, by life experience and personal problem-solving history, and by the larger societal context in which one matures. To ignore this dimension that has critical importance to many older adults, especially to members of marginalized cultural groups for whom religious centers became a source of social and historical connection as well as a spiritual resource, is to disregard a potential resource for healing and managing ongoing challenges in the aging experience.

Many older adults rely on their faith to sustain them as they seek to build competence in new areas. "If you don't want to take [the lesson] over, do all you can not to fail the lesson of the day. I believe in this. God didn't send me here unequipped. I came fully equipped for whatever demand the world makes of me," reported one older African American woman (Nelson-Becker, 2004, p. 166). Others rely on nature-based spirituality to find a larger context to understand and work through immediate problems. "What I see out my window [Lake Michigan] gives me a sense of eternity and my place in it," commented one older Holocaust survivor (Nelson-Becker, 2003, p. 95). Rosa Garcia, as is common with many Hispanic older women, found support within the religious community.

Personal religious traditions and rituals should be explored as part of a strengths-based assessment focusing on whether religion or spirituality should be engaged to build on personal strengths. Practical philosophies emerge out of a long trajectory of life experience and often contain religious and spiritual aspects. They develop largely because they work; they are effective in meeting a need or purpose. Openness to listening to spiritual and religious narratives, both in assessment and as one form of intervention, offer a resource that until recently, many social workers (who tend as a group to be less religious than their older clients) were hesitant to address. If assessment determines that religion is important to the older adult and she or he wants to discuss it, further expansion of religion as a resource may be explored by questions in eleven separate domains. These include, among others; affiliations, belief, behavior, emotion, values, spiritual well-being, and intrinsic and extrinsic spiritual focus definitions. Multiple questions for each focus can be found in Nelson-Becker et al. (2006). Typically, not every domain would be addressed during a session. Instead, a strengths-based case manager would explore domains that a client chose to consider that might offer potential for greater understanding and participation in life. Often, merely creating the space for religious and spiritual conversations can offer great benefit for older adults struggling with spiritual questions and seeking validation and meaning during times of new challenge.

INTEGRATION OF POLICY APPLICATIONS IN SOCIAL WORK PRACTICE WITH OLDER ADULTS

Social workers are expected to engage in policy practice on behalf of clients. Policy practice focuses on trying to change policies that disadvantage our clients in legislative, agency, or community settings. Policy practice approaches infused with the strengths perspective guide us to make sure the voices of our clients are heeded by policy makers at all levels (Chapin, 2007). As social workers, we are listening posts—transmitters and interpreters of information—and can help make the challenges, strengths, and goals of our clients known to policymakers who may have little direct contact with the people we—and they—serve.

Living to be 65, 75, or even 100 is a testament to the strengths of older adults. Longer lives mean many people will have more years to contribute to their communities and families and ours. However, they will need our support in pressing for the development of the policy and program infrastructure necessary to make it possible for our society to reap the benefits of increasing life expectancy. The strengths perspective can be used as a philosophical base in guiding case managers to focus on the empowerment of older adults, thus adding weight to their own intrinsic and external assets and resources.

The focus on empowerment is critical for both the older men and women who are our clients. For example, Rosa Garcia has been a respected community for many years. As she returns to the community center and to her church, the case manager can help support her and her friends and family in their efforts to make certain that policies to ensure equitable treatment of Mexican Americans are developed and enforced. Young adults can be encouraged to see the effects on themselves and the entire community when older adults are without needed resource, and then to join with older adults to try and advocate for more effective and responsive policies. Ideas for citizens and professionals becoming more proficient in policy practice are available from a variety of sources (see, for example, Jansson, 2003; Schneifer & Lester, 2001, and Chapin, 2007).

Policymakers also need to understand the structural barriers that our clients, particularly people of color, face in achieving their goal of remaining in the community. One powerful barrier is the continuing lack of culturally competent health care providers. Another is the personal history of racial discrimination that older clients have experienced with many societal institutions. Claims for benefits and services to overcome these metalevel barriers are formulated based on the right to equal access to resources for citizens regardless of gender, race/ethnicity, age, or disability. One valuable role of the social worker is to win attention for older client perspectives. Another important role is that of helping to produce more equitable policies as a collaborator with older adult activists.

The strengths perspective is premised on social work values of self-determination and social justice. Social policies and programs should build on individual and community strengths and resources and remove structural barriers that disadvantage our clients. Effective policies can lead to empowerment, choice, and opportunity for our clients in keeping with the strengths perspective. Access to needed healthcare and opportunities for social integration are particularly important areas for policy advocacy if we are to adequately serve the increasingly diverse elder population. Development of policy practice skills is critical to full incorporation of the strengths perspective into case management with older adults.

UTILITY OF THE STRENGTHS MODEL IN THE CHANGING LONG-TERM CARE ENVIRONMENT

Traditionally, aging has been viewed as synonymous with disease, and a medical framework of care has been implemented to try to cure the problems associated with growing older. Traditional medical/rehabilitative models of helping remain prominent in most community-based, long-term care case management systems. As pressure to control healthcare costs mount, treatment decisions will be closely monitored to conserve clinical and fiscal resources. Many of these plans have been attacked for reducing consumer involvement and authority to direct the course of their help. Older adults have been expected to be passive recipients of care. However, in the changing medical marketplace, there are incentives for providers to reduce the overutilization of services, which, in turn, increases the need for older adults to take responsibility for ensuring that their healthcare needs are met. This change means that the traditional roles of a passive patient and doctor as the sole decision maker are being revised. Case management that focuses on both consumer empowerment and cost consciousness is clearly needed.

Since its inception, case management has been viewed as a potentially significant mechanism for coordinating services and controlling costs to prevent premature institutionalization. In an era of limited resources, private and public payers are demanding accountability for client outcomes and cost (Quinn, 1992). Effectiveness of a case management approach has been frequently evaluated according to its ability to reduce unnecessary institutionalization. However, much less effort has been made to define and measure effectiveness of case management from a standpoint of facilitating consumer involvement and empowerment and its subsequent impact on client outcomes and cost.

The need to first articulate and then to evaluate the effectiveness of strengths-based goals, planning processes, and tasks is imperative if fiscal control becomes the driving force behind case management. Home and community-based care have historically been embedded in the medical model delivery system where critical social, emotional, spiritual, and supportive service needs are often overlooked. The challenge for case management and home-based care becomes one of providing quality services that are acceptable to clients and effective in maintaining functioning while keeping a cost-conscious stance (Kane & Kane, 1987). Likewise, research demonstrating the efficacy of discrete case management models is still limited.

More needs to be learned about the effectiveness of case management models. Particular attention needs to be focused on the varying goals, tasks, processes, case management roles, and impact upon the lives of older persons. Long-term care case managers operating strictly from a functional or broker perspective of service provision, as was the case in the Channeling Demonstration Projects, may not employ the strengths model's emphasis on mutual decision making and reciprocity and the active pursuit and empowerment of natural helpers (Rose, 1992). They also may fail to carry out a case management process that establishes a trusting relationship and a purposeful counseling approach for dealing with the emotional stresses accompanying illness and loss of functions (Amerman, Eiserberg, & Weisman, 1985). The model of case management employed influences cost effectiveness.

Evidence from Medicaid long-term care case managers trained in the use of the strengths model indicates that older adults who participate in strengths-based case management have increased levels of informal support, a more sustainable balance of formal and informal services, and fewer transitions between home and healthcare facilities (Fast, Chapin, & Rapp, 1994). In other areas research is also beginning to find evidence for the value of reinforcing strengths-based approaches for older adults in the community (Isaacowitz, Vaillant, & Seligman, 2003), in the field of care management (Bartelstone, 2003), in clinical work with older adults who are survivors of trauma (Cook, 2002), and in work with older adults who misuse alcohol (Perkins & Tice, 1999). Case management effectiveness from a strengths approach is embedded in its ability to meet case management's dual mission in long-term care—maximizing client control, dignity, and choice while containing cost.

CONCLUSION

This chapter has explored the essential practice components of the strengths model of case management with older adults in need of long-term care. This model of case management supports self-determination, maximizes consumer choice and interdependence, and can potentially help contain long-term care costs. Increasingly, larger numbers of our older adult population will be first-generation immigrants. This will necessitate flexibility in our systems of long-term care as we adapt and incorporate new types of strengths-based resources and strategies. The importance of self-determination and consumer choice in creating an affordable home and community-based long-term care system should not be overlooked.

Spiritual assessment and possible inclusion of spiritual and/or religious resources constitute an important element of practice, especially with its implications for positive health outcomes. Articulation, implementation, and evaluation of the strengths model of long-term care case management with older adults can help professionals focus on the capacities rather than on the frailty of older adults. Spirituality, in its call to find avenues of meaning and purpose in the aging journey, is one such capacity.

Furthermore, awareness of the value inherent in empowerment of all individuals and the social work imperative to empower older adults through engagement in policy formulation and change, can immeasurably enrich ongoing societal transformation as we become a society that engages the resources of older adults themselves to meet future challenges. May we be successful in that task.

DISCUSSION QUESTIONS/EXERCISES

1. How is a vision of aging successfully and productively supported by the strengths model?

2. What are some effective strategies for helping older consumers believe in their own abilities, try out new behaviors, and set and accomplish personal goals?

3. In what ways can case managers involve frail, older consumers in the assessment and planning process?

4. How can case managers help enhance the empowerment of older citizens? What kind of practical steps could they take?

5. In what ways can religion and spirituality serve as both resources and/or barriers for older adults?

6. What kinds of contributions can older adults make to their communities?

7. How can social workers encourage older adults to become involved in influencing policy at the community, agency, and policy levels?

8. Which of your older relatives have aged successfully? Why do you think so? What relatives have not done so well? How are they different?

REFERENCES

Ai, A. (2000). Spiritual well-being, population aging, and a need for improving practice with the elderly: A psychosocial account. *Social Thought, 19*(3), 1–21.

Amerman, E., Eiserberg, D., & Weisman, R. (1985). Case management and counseling: A service dilemma. In C. Austin et al. (Eds.), *Experience from the natural long-term care channeling demonstration.* Seattle, WA: Institute on Aging, University of Washington.

Applebaum, R. & Austin, C. (1990). *Long-term care case management: Design and evaluation.* New York: Springer.

Baltes, P. B. (1993). The aging mind: Potential and limits. *The Gerontologist, 33*(5), 580–594.

Bartelstone, R. S. (2003). Care management: A strengths-based approach to mental wellness with older adults. In J. L. Ronch & J. A. Goldfield (Eds.), *Mental wellness in aging: Strengths-based approaches* (pp. 85–111). Baltimore, MD: Health Professions Press.

Browne, C. V. (1995). Empowerment in social work practice with older women. *Social Work, 40,* 358–364.

Canda, E. R. & Furman, L. D. (1999). *Spiritual diversity in social work practice.* New York: Free Press.

Centers for Disease Control (CDC). (2004). *Chronic disease overview.* Retrieved June 16, 2004 from www .cdc.gov/nccdphp/overview.htm

Chapin, R., Nelson-Becker, H. & Macmillan, K. (2006). Strengths based and solution focused approaches to practice with older adults. In B. Berkman & S. D' Ambruso (Eds.), *The Oxford handbook of social work in health and aging.* New York: Oxford University Press.

Cook, J. M. (2002). Traumatic exposure and PTSD in older adults: Introduction to the special issue. *Journal of Clinical Geropsychology, 8*(3), 149–152.

Chapin, R. (2007). *Social policy for effective practice: A strengths approach.* Boston: McGraw-Hill.

Fast, B. & Chapin, R. (2000). *Strengths case management in long term care.* Baltimore: Health Professions Press.

Fast, B. Chapin, R., & Rapp, C. (1994). *A model for strengths-based case management with older adults: Curriculum and training program.* Unpublished manuscript, The University of Kansas at Lawrence.

Federal Interagency Forum on Age Related Statistics. (2006). *Older Americans update 2006.* Retrieved October 14, 2007, from www.agingstats.net/main_site/default.aspx

Freidson, E. (1988). *Profession of medicine.* Chicago: University of Chicago Press.

Galambos, C., & Rosen, A. (1999). The aging are coming and they are us. *Health and Social Work, 24*(1), 73–77.

Isaacowitz, D. M., Vaillant, G. E., & Seligman, M. E. (2003). Strengths and satisfaction across the adult lifespan. *International Journal of Aging and Human Development, 47*(2), 181–201.

Jansson, B. (2003). *Becoming an effective policy advocate* (4th ed.). Pacific Grove, CA: Thomson/Brooks Cole.

Johnson, P. J. & Rubin, A. (1983). Case management in mental health: A social work domain? *Social Work, 28,* 49–55.

Kahana, E. & Kahana, B. (1996). Conceptual and empirical advances in understanding aging well through proactive adaptation. In V. Bengston (Ed.), *Adulthood and aging: Research on continuities and discontinuities* (pp. 18–41). New York: Springer.

Kane, R. A. & Kane, R. L. (1987). *Long-term care: Principles, programs, and policies.* New York: Springer.

Kisthardt, W. & Rapp, C. A. (1991). Bridging the gap between principles and practice: Implementing a strengths perspective in case management. In S. M. Rose (Ed.), *Social work practice and case management.* White Plains, NY: Longman.

Kivnick, H. Q. (1993, Winter/Spring). Everyday mental health: A guide to assessing life strengths. *Generations,* 13–20.

Kivnick, H. Q. & Murray, S. V. (2001). Life strengths interview guide: Assessing elder clients' strengths. *Journal of Gerontological Social Work, 34*(4), 7–32.

Koenig, H. G. (1994). *Aging and God: Spiritual pathways to mental health in midlife and later years.* New York: Haworth Press.

Kulys, R. (1983). Future crisis and the very old: Implications for discharge planning. *Health & Social Work, 8,* 182–195.

Langer, E. J. (1989). *Mindfulness.* Cambridge, MA: Perseus Books.

Lustbader, W. & Hooyman, N. (1994). *Taking care of aging family members.* New York: Free Press

Motenko, A. K. & Greenberg, S. (1995). Reframing dependence in old age: A positive transition for families. *Social Work, 40*(3), 382–389.

Nelson-Becker, H. (2003). Practical philosophies: Interpretations of religion and spirituality by African-American and Jewish elders. *Journal of Religious Gerontology, 14*(2/3), 85–99.

Nelson-Becker, H. (2004). Meeting life challenges: A hierarchy of coping styles in African-American and Jewish-American older adults. *Journal of Human Behavior in the Social Environment, 166.*

Nelson-Becker, H., Nakashima, M., & Canda, E. R. (2006). Spirituality in professional helping interventions. In B. Berkman & S. D' Ambruso (Eds.), *Oxford handbook of social work in health care and aging* (pp. 797–807). Boston: Oxford University Press.

Nelson-Becker, H., Nakashima, M., & Canda, E. R. (2007). Spiritual assessment in aging: A framework for clinicians. *Journal of Gerontological Social Work, 48* (3/4), 331–347.

Pargament, K. I. (1997). *The psychology of religion and coping.* New York: Guilford Press.

Perkins, K. & Tice, C. (1995). A strengths perspective in practice: Older people and mental health challenges. *Journal of Gerontological Social Work, 23*(3/4), 83–97.

Perkins, K. & Tice, C. (1999). Family treatment of older adults who misuse alcohol: A strengths perspective. *Journal of Gerontological Social Work, 31*(3–4), 169–185.

Pray, J. E. (1992). Maximizing the patient's uniqueness and strengths: A challenge for home health care. *Social Work in Health Care, 17*(3), 71–79.

Princeton Religious Research Center (PRCC). (2001, March). Index of leading religious indicators remains at high level. *Emerging Trends, 23*(3).

Quinn, J. (1992). Case management: As diverse as its clients. *Journal of Case Management, 1*(2), 38.

Rapp, C. A. (1992). The strengths perspective of case management with persons suffering from severe mental illness. In D. Saleebey (Ed.), *The strengths perspective in social work practice.* White Plains, NY: Longman.

Ronch, J. L. & Goldfield, J. A. (Eds.). (2003). *Mental wellness in aging: Strengths-based approaches.* Baltimore, MD: Health Professions Press.

Rose, S. M. (1992). *Case management social work practice.* White Plains, NY: Longman.

Rowe, J. W. & Kahn, R. L. (1998). *Successful aging.* New York: Pantheon Press.

Schneider, R. & Lester, L. (2001). *Social work advocates.* Belmont, CA: Brooks/Cole.

Smith, V. & Eggleston, R. (1989). Long-term care: The medical model versus the social model. *Public Welfare, 47*, 27–29.

Spilka, B. (1986). Spiritual issues: Do they belong in psychological practice? Yes-but! *Psychotherapy in Private Practice, 4*(4), 93–100.

Sullivan, W. P. (1997). On strengths, niches, and recovery from serious mental illness. In D. Saleebey (Ed.), *The strengths perspective in social work practice* (2nd ed.). New York: Longman.

Sullivan, W. P. & Fisher, B. J. (1994). Intervening for success: Strengths-based case management and successful aging. *Journal of Gerontological Social Work, 22*(1/2), 61–74.

Urban Institute. (2006). *After Katrina.* Retrieved December 1, 2007, from www.urban.org/uploadedPDF/411348_katrinahospitals.pdf

CHAPTER TEN

ASSESSING STRENGTHS

Identifying Acts of Resistance to Violence and Oppression

KIM M. ANDERSON

CHARLES D. COWGER

CAROL A. SNIVELY

The proposition that strengths are central to helping relationships continues to gain popularity (Blundo, 2001; Greene, Lee & Hoffpair, 2005; Oko, 2006) and sophistication, especially in regard to practice with diverse, vulnerable, and oppressed populations. Developments in strengths-based practice have included a repositioning of power and authority within helping relationships to encourage ownership in the expression of personal and shared narratives and in decisions of how to seek and receive help. While earlier descriptions of strengths-based assessments have explored issues of power and authority through a discussion of the political nature of the assessment process (Cowger, 1998; Cowger, Anderson, & Snively, 2006; Cowger & Snively, 2002), few guidelines were provided to assist the social worker in sharing this political context with the individual or group seeking assistance. A gap between theory and practice was created by a lack of clear recommendations about how to shift the power and control within the assessment process. This gap can be a challenging one for practitioners to bridge, especially those who work within deficit-based systems of care, encounter high demands for work productivity, and are rewarded for using deficit-based classification systems (e.g., reimbursement for services rendered). In this chapter, the authors draw on Kim Anderson's (2001; 2006; Anderson & Danis, 2006) work with individuals experiencing oppressive social circumstances to expand our previous discussions on promoting empowerment during the assessment process. This chapter addresses how findings from Anderson's resiliency research can inform strengths-based assessment strategies and help social workers resist a common tendency to revert to problem description during the assessment process. Examples of strengths-based assessment questions are provided that uncover individuals' acts of resistance in the face of violence and oppression.

ASSESSMENT AS POLITICAL ACTIVITY

The primary purpose of social work is to assist people in their relationships with one another and with social institutions in order to promote social and economic justice (Council on Social Work Education, 1994). Practice, thus, focuses on developing more positive and promising transactions between people and their environments and ending oppressive social transactions. However, taking seriously the element of promoting social and economic justice in those transactions may not result in conventional models of practice. Indeed, practice that is guided by social and economic justice requires methods that explicitly deal with power and power relationships.

Assessment that focuses on deficits presents obstacles to the exercise of personal and social power and reinforces those social structures that generate and regulate the unequal power relationships, victimizing vulnerable individuals, families, groups, and communities. Goroff (1983) persuasively argues that social work practice is a political activity and that the attribution of individual deficiencies as the cause of human problems is a politically conservative process that "supports the status quo" (p. 134).

Deficit-based assessments target the help seeker as "the problem" because the context of oppression is stripped. Much of professional practice as it is currently conducted shifts the focus of attention from oppressive social systems to individual deficits (Dietz, 2000). The helper addresses the behaviors and feelings presented. Often the person seeking help is not able to see how behaviors, feelings, and circumstances were generated as reactions to oppression. Because of this block, the helper only hears the part of the story where the individual, family, or community is in crisis and does not hear how the circumstances were created for the crisis to occur. For example, from a deficit perspective, the person who is unemployed, the family who is homeless, or the residents who live in a declining community are "the problem." Social work interventions that focus on what is wrong with the help seeker—for example, why he or she is not working—reinforce the powerlessness the help seeker is already experiencing because he or she does not have a job, a home, or a safe community in which to live. At the same time such an intervention lets economic and social structures that do not provide employment or housing opportunities "off the hook" and reinforces social structures that generate unequal power. To assume that the cause of personal pain and social problems is individual deficiency "has the political consequences of not focusing on the social structure (the body politic) but on the individual. Most, if not all, of the pain we experience is the result of the way we have organized ourselves and how we create and allocate life-surviving resources" (Goroff, 1983, p. 134). Here Goroff is referring to our social not our personal organization as the root of individual problems.

Personal pain is political. Social work practice is political. Diagnostic and assessment metaphors and taxonomies that stress individual deficiencies and sickness reinforce the political status quo in a manner that is incongruent with the promotion of social and economic justice. Practice centered on pathology is reminiscent of "blaming the victim" (Ryan, 1976). Practice based on metaphors of client strengths and empowerment is also political in that its thrust is the development of client power and the more equitable distribution of societal resources—those resources that underlie the development of personal resources. Yet, Larry Davis (2001, p. 6) warns us that both resiliency research and a strengths perspective can have negative political implications, too. The focus on resiliency and strengths, he argues, is "a focus on individual explanations for problems primarily caused by societal shortcomings" and may be used "against the very populations we are attempting to assist." This emphasis in turn may inadvertently serve to direct attention away from issues of social injustice and inequality.

Specifically in regard to assessment, there is a growing body of social work practice literature that reflects a strengths perspective in regard to individual, family, and community assessment and helps to repoliticize social work practice with an emphasis on oppressive social relations (Cohen, 1999; Delgado & Barton, 1998; DeJong & Miller, 1995; Early & GlenMaye, 2000; McQuaide & Ehrenreich, 1997; Poole, 1997; Russo, 1999; Solomon, 1976). Notable examples of the application of strengths-based theory to practice and research provide a framework for understanding the experiences of minority families (Billingsley, 1968, 1992; Boyd-Franklin & Bry, 2000; McAdoo & McAdoo, 1985) and research that focuses on adolescents as competent citizens (Finn & Checkoway, 1998). Emerging concepts from resiliency research, such as Anderson's (2001; 2006; Anderson & Danis, 2006) "resistance to oppression," can also help social workers bridge the gap between strengths-based theory and practice and further politicize and develop the assessment process.

RESILIENCY? OR JUST A NEW SPIN ON OLD PROBLEMS?

Strengths-based practice and resiliency literature are interconnected and similar in many ways. Both emphasize assets and resources of the person(s) seeking help rather than symptomatology and problems (Saleebey, 1997; Wolin & Wolin, 1993). Both recognize that people's ability to live well in the present depends on their ability to recognize and uncover their strengths (Barnard, 1994; Saleebey, 1997). In addition, both understand that people are doing the best that they can with the resources available to them (Saleebey, 1997; Wolin & Wolin, 1993). Finally, both recognize that people may lose sight of their strengths and abilities because their trauma and pain are too great, and the practitioner's role is to assist in uncovering their submerged areas of resilience (Barnard, 1994; Saleebey, 1997). Despite these similarities, strengths and traditional notions of resilience differ regarding environmental context. In this regard, resiliency literature has been criticized for simply "repackaging" a deficit-based perspective to appear as if it is strengths oriented.

Resiliency literature has emerged over the years from studies in developmental psychopathology that focused on the "adverse" conditions placing children at risk for developing adult pathologies (Byrd, 1994) and the ways in which youth avoid problems despite exposure to adverse conditions. To this end, risk and protective factors have been identified within individual, family, and community domains (Safyer, Griffin, Colan, Alexander-Brydie, & Rome, 1998). Experiences and conditions are categorized as risk factors because their presence deprives youth of important developmental experiences, relationships, and opportunities, making them vulnerable to participation in antisocial activities or ill health (Bowen & Chapman, 1996; Safyer et al., 1998). Some of these adverse conditions studied included poverty (Werner & Smith, 1992), parental mental illness (Beardslee & Podorefsky, 1988), inner-city living (Luthar, 1993), and child abuse and neglect (Farber & Egeland, 1987).

Other experiences and conditions are considered protective in that they encourage healthy development and/or mediate the direct effects of the declined community or dysfunctional family system on adolescent health and well-being (Safyer et al., 1998). For example, the presence of supportive adults can decrease the likelihood of adolescents participating in antisocial behavior by increasing adolescents' exposure to protective factors (Stiffman et al., 1999) and minimizing exposure to risk factors. Both risk and protective factors are thought to have a cumulative effect, or "pile-up . . . as the number of developmental assets increase, risk behavior patterns decrease and thriving behaviors (e.g., school success, affirmation of diversity, prosocial behavior) increase" (Public/Private Venture, 2000, p. 133). Uncovering the attributes that help youth to thrive and resist the negative effects of stress induced by violence, community disorder, and other negative social conditions is often the focus of resiliency research (Anderson, 2001).

While it is helpful to isolate and name which aspects of the environment have a positive or negative influence on youth outcomes, there is disagreement regarding how to think about and name these environmental factors. Some scholars argue that the terms "risk" and "protective factors" imply that the youth is completely malleable by her or his environment and minimizes the youth's capacity to effect change (Medoff & Skylar, 1994). Categorizing experiences and conditions as either inducing problems or saving the youth from problems perpetuates the idea of youth as victims, not competent individuals who can make good choices for themselves, their families, and their communities (Finn & Checkoway, 1998). In contrast, a strengths perspective focuses on competencies, assets of the individual and the environment, as well as the individual's prosocial behavior, e.g., the ways in which the youth has sought to better his or her environment (Snively, 2002).

In addition, associating the term "at risk" with persons who are of minority status and disenfranchised creates a new label for old stigmas. "In many ways, the wholesale labeling of children of single mothers and inner city children generally, as 'at risk' has become a stigmatizing code word for 'illegitimate'—which also means contrary to law, rules and logic" (Medoff & Skylar, 1994, p. 206). A true strength-based framework avoids this repackaging of old deficit-based concepts. Terminology that emphasizes assets, such as healthy or positive youth development, competency, capacity, etc., is preferred over older victim terminology. While early conceptualizations of resiliency played an important role in shifting perspectives about problem definition, the language of "risk" and "protective" factors has inadvertently reproduced the deficit helping model.

THE RESISTANCE TO OPPRESSION FACTOR

While the resiliency literature has much in common with the strengths perspective and is informative for the social work practitioner, it is particularly limited with its narrow focus on individual circumstances and its exclusion of oppressive social circumstances (Anderson, 2001). The recognition and understanding of oppression and abuse and their relationship to resilience are crucial factors to address while making a holistic assessment. Behaviors are often forged in resistance to subjugation that consequently promotes one's survival and perseverance (Anderson, 2006). Individuals typically are resistant to their oppression and use a variety of mental and behavioral strategies to prevent, withstand, stop, or oppose their subjugation and its consequences (Wade, 1997; Wineman, 2003). Helping people to see how they have actively resisted their oppression is important because they often may view their responses as passive and blame themselves for the social problems they have experienced. The helper can acknowledge and affirm strategies of resistance as they are illuminated throughout the assessment process. These resilient capacities are often submerged beneath pain and discomfort and are difficult to access if those engaged in the helping relationship are not equipped to view these protective strategies as strengths (Anderson, 2006).

For example, consider the social problem of incest where the child is dominated by her or his perpetrator and learns that her or his emotional and physical survival depends on her or his acquiescence (Blume, 1990). In the professional literature, incest is often presented as devoid of a context that adequately addresses power relations. Consequently, the effects of oppression, particularly subordination, are often not taken into account in clinical work with incest survivors (Anderson, 2001). Instead, the helper focuses on the pathological symptoms presented by the survivor in response to the oppressive experience of incest. Therefore, if a child who is being sexually victimized stops eating, it is viewed as an eating disorder stemming from depression rather than resistance to oppression (Dietz, 2000; Herman, 1992). This perspective is in sharp contrast to how the same behaviors are interpreted for a different group such as prisoners of war whose hunger strikes are viewed as acts of defiance and signs of resistance to their captors' subjugation. Both the children and prisoners are refusing to eat in response to violence; however, societal response to the refusal to eat could not be more different. A prisoner of war who engages in a hunger strike would be regarded as a hero, but the child would be regarded as ill. In response, the helper would typically focus the assessment on the child's eating behavior instead of acknowledging the child's power in drawing attention to her- or himself through a creative manner, discovering the reasoning for the hunger strike and educating the child about her or his rights. This focus on sexual victimization as an "individual problem" obscures the societal context of sexual violence toward children and limits how the helper would proceed in the assessment process.

GUIDELINES FOR STRENGTHS ASSESSMENT

These guidelines for strengths assessment are presented with the understanding that assessment is a process as well as a product. Assessment as process is helping people define their situations (that is, clarify the reasons they have sought assistance) and assisting them in evaluating and giving meaning to those factors that affect their situations. The assessment as a product is an agreement, in many cases a written agreement, between the worker and the person seeking help as to the nature of the problem situation (descriptive) and the meaning ascribed to those factors influencing the problem situation (analytic and interpretative).

A deep source of meaning can be acquired from the stories of individuals that may be used to guide the assessment process, particularly from those who have endured oppression. "The self-narrative is an individual's account of the relationships among self-relevant events across time" (Laird, 1989, p. 430). Composing a narrative reflects efforts to cope with adversity through developing a sense of coherence, continuity, and meaning (Laird, 1989). Individuals' identities are shaped by the sense they make of their own life stories. Providing an opportunity to share their life stories validates help seekers' wisdom and experiences and, at the same time, assists them in developing a deeper understanding of the many dimensions to their life circumstances. Therefore, social work practitioners can be supportive by encouraging an open expression of the details and implications of help seekers' resistance to oppression.

The following guidelines are based on the notion that the knowledge guiding the assessment process is based on a socially constructed reality (Berger & Luckmann, 1966). Also, the assessment should recognize that there are multiple constructions of reality for each person's situation (Rodwell, 1987) and that problem situations are interactive, multicausal, and ever-changing. In addition, they address important aspects in creating a safe environment for people to tell their stories of violation and oppression.

1. **Document the story.** The assessment process allows help seekers' ideas, thoughts, and memories to be expressed in their own words, reflects personal and social values, repositions help seekers as experts of their own situations, and places the burden on the helper to gain an understanding regarding the meaning of the situation of those who seek help. Professional and social sciences nomenclature is incongruent with an assessment approach based on mutual participation of the social worker and the person seeking help. Goldstein (1990) convincingly stated, "We are the inheritors of a professional language composed of value-laden metaphors and idioms. The language has far more to do with philosophic assumptions about the human state, ideologies of professionalism, and, not least, the politics of practice than they do [sic] with objective rationality" (p. 268). Assessment as a product should be written in simple English and in such a way as to be self-explanatory to all involved. Whenever possible, use direct quotes to name and describe the problem and solutions.

2. **Support and validate the story.** Individuals know the depth and reality of what they have experienced in their life journeys. If the social worker demonstrates respect for that ownership, the story will be more fully shared. Individuals/families/groups and communities seeking help need to have their expertise regarding their situations validated. They need to ascribe meaning to their experiences as a way of regaining control and feeling competent. Central to a strengths perspective is a deeply held belief that people ultimately are trustworthy. To prejudge an individual as being untrustworthy is contrary to the social work–mandated values of respecting and recognizing one's dignity, and prejudgment may lead to a self-fulfilling prophecy. When social workers are involved in cases where the physical welfare of the individual is at risk, such as child protection or domestic violence, the protection of victims of abuse may supersede this guideline.

3. **Honor self-determination.** Professional judgments or assumptions may well be the most detrimental exercises perpetrated on people seeking help. Instead, think of persons seeking help as experts of their own situations or stories. They should not feel "forced" into having to perform for professionals who may have preconceived ideas of what and how healing should take place. Assist in the discovery of their own points of view, choices, and vision. This "letting go" by social work practitioners may be difficult if they feel people seeking help are incompetent because their victimization has left them too "damaged." If they are perceived as pathological, then the strength and courage in one's process of surviving and healing is obscured. Help seekers need to have control over what information they contribute as well as control of the direction

of the treatment process. Their control is essential because they are being asked to give something so personal of themselves—their life stories.

4. **Give preeminence to the story.** The help seeking person's knowledge and lived experiences need to be of central importance in guiding the assessment process. His or her view of the situation, the meaning he or she ascribes to the situation, and his or her feelings or emotions related to that situation are the central focus for assessment. Assessment content on the intrapersonal, developmental, cognitive, mental, and biophysical dynamics of the person are important only as it enlightens the situation presented by the individual. It should be used only as a way to identify strengths that can be brought to bear on the presenting situation or to recognize obstacles to achieving individual and group objectives. The use of social sciences behavior taxonomies representing the realities of the social scientists should not be used as something to apply to, thrust on, or label a person.

5. **Discover what is needed.** There are two aspects of the helping contract. These include: "What is wanted and expected from service?" and "What does the person want to change?" This latter want involves the person's goals and is concerned with what one perceives to be a successful resolution to the problem situation.

6. **Move the assessment toward strengths.** The stories of persons seeking help provide numerous examples of strengths as they use their struggles with overcoming their adversity as a catalyst for growth and change. Practicing from a strengths perspective means believing that the strengths and resources to resolve a difficult situation lie within the individual's interpersonal skills, motivation, emotional strengths, and ability to think clearly. A person's external strengths come from family networks, significant others, voluntary organizations, community groups, and public institutions that support and provide opportunities for help seekers to act on their own behalf and institutional services that have the potential to provide resources. Discovering these strengths is central to assessment.

7. **Discover uniqueness.** The importance of uniqueness and individualization is well articulated by Meyer (1976): "When a family, group or a community is individualized, it is known through its uniqueness, despite all that it holds in common with other like groups" (p. 176). Although every person is in certain respects "like all other men [sic], like some other men, and like no other men" (Kluckholm, Murray, & Schneider, 1953, p. 53), foundation content in human behavior and social environment taught in schools of social work focuses on the first two of these, which are based on normative behavior assumptions. Assessment that focuses on one's strengths must be individualized to understand the unique situation each person is experiencing. Normative perspectives of behavior are only useful insofar as they can enrich the understanding of this uniqueness. Pray's (1991) writings on assessment emphasize individual uniqueness as an important element of Schön's (1983) reflective model of practice and are particularly insightful in establishing the importance of individual and group uniqueness in assessment.

8. **Reach a mutual agreement on the assessment.** Social workers can minimize the power imbalance inherent in the helping relationship by stressing the importance of the individual's understandings and wants. The worker's role is to inquire, listen, and assist the person in discovering, clarifying, and articulating. The help seeker gives direction to the content of the assessment. The person must feel ownership of the

process and the product and can do so only if assessment is open and shared. Rodwell (1987) articulated this well when she stated that the "major stakeholders must agree with the content" (p. 241). All assessment in written form should be written with the person(s) seeking help.

9. **Avoid blame and blaming.** Assessment and blame often get confused and convoluted. Blame is the first cousin of deficit models of practice. Causal thinking represents only one of many possible perspectives of the problem situation and can easily lead to blaming. Concentrating on blame or allowing it to get a firm foothold in the process is done at the expense of moving toward a resolution to the problem. Generally, blaming leads nowhere, and, if relegated to the person seeking help, it may encourage low self-esteem. If assigned to others, it may encourage learned helplessness or deter motivation to address the problem situation and perpetuate oppressive dynamics.

10. **Assess; but do not get caught up in labels.** Diagnosis is incongruent with a strengths perspective as it is understood in the context of pathology, deviance, and deficits and is based on social constructions of reality that define human problem situations in a like manner. While diagnosis is associated with a medical model of labeling that assumes unpopular and unacceptable behavior as a symptom of an underlying pathological condition, it is often required to access services. It has been argued that labeling "accompanied by reinforcement of identified behavior is a sufficient condition for chronic mental illness" (Taber, Herbert, Mark, & Nealey, 1969, p. 354). A diagnosis should not be viewed as the central feature of help seekers' identities or life experiences or the only outcome of an assessment.

ASSESSMENT PROCESS

Our assessment process reflects the two-stage process first suggested by Mary Richmond (1917). She proposed that the social worker first study the facts of the situation and then diagnose the nature of the problem. Correspondingly, the first component is a process of clarifying why the person has sought assistance and how the situation would look if satisfactorily changed. The second component involves evaluating and giving meaning to those factors, which impinge on the presenting situation.

Component 1: Defining the "Problem" Situation

Individuals, families, groups, and communities who seek assistance often do so in response to a "problem" situation or experience. The word *situation* or *experience* has a particularly important meaning because it affirms that problems always exist in an environmental context and are often related to oppressive circumstances. Problem situations have a life of their own and are generated by combinations of unpredicted contingencies, incongruities, and systems' disequilibrium. Understanding problem situations in this way allows the worker and help seeker the freedom to capitalize on personal and environmental strengths to resolve the problem. Consider again the child who stops eating to draw attention to her or his abusive home environment. He or she may continue to starve her or himself as a means to draw attention even after being removed from the abusive home life. The tendency in this situation is for the social worker to focus on eating patterns instead of illuminating how the child's control over eating was a form of resistance to the abuse. In this manner the helping relationship is organized around changing individual eating behaviors rather than changing the unhealthy living situations that created the need for such coping strategies, encouraging the help seeker to further resist abuse in her or his life, and/or helping others to do the same.

Defining the problem situation or experience is an important first step in the helping process because it guides how the helping process will proceed. To anchor the problem definition within a strengths perspective, it is particularly important at the beginning of the assessment to acknowledge that the person seeking help is in charge of telling his or her story. The social worker can help facilitate this process in so far as the person's understanding of the problem situation/presenting issue is honored and not displaced by the social worker's perspective.

The role of the social worker, then, is to draw out the story from the person seeking assistance. In situations where the help seeker consists of more than one person (e.g., a family, group, or community), multiple definitions of the problem will exist based on the various members' understanding of the situation. In these cases, it is the role of the social worker to find the common ground in their narratives.

Questions for the Assessment Process: Beyond "What Are Your Strengths?"

Helping professionals need to listen and not avoid individuals' stories of suffering to uncover acts of protection, defiance, survival, and transcendence. A central component to the social work process, then, becomes the practitioner's ability to uncover strengths and to make them accessible in a useful way. Since individuals often internalize shame and blame about their victimization experiences, providing a view of themselves as resourceful gives credit to their ability to persevere despite insurmountable odds. Consequently, they may view themselves differently, particularly their strengths, by recognizing how they actively responded to adversity in the past and may now channel their survival strategies into confronting present struggles.

Domination and brutality inundate our society, at both the personal and institutional levels (Wineman, 2003). Yet, standing alongside the entire range of debilitating effects of oppression, most individuals display a stunning capacity for survival and perseverance. Consequently, individuals' responses to oppression may serve as a catalyst in the mobilization of individual recovery and societal transformation. The assessment process may facilitate an individual's realization of his or her strengths, worth, and resiliency through assisting the help seeker to uncover actual acts of resistance and develop them into a story of personal agency (Wood & Roche, 2001). In doing so, assumptions that individuals are complicit in their own victimization are challenged as personal truths are unsilenced and one's heroism is underscored. Consequently, as help seekers' acts of individual and collective resistance are uncovered, their identities and realities are reconstructed, orienting them more toward strengths-based life stories rather than problem-saturated ones. Once individuals realize that they can formulate their life stories any way they choose, they can then find ways to change the meaning of the past, to alter its grasp on the present, and to mark out a different life course (Gasker, 2001; Harvey, Mischler, Koenen, & Harney, 2001).

The following questions may be used to assist the help seeker who has experienced family violence, for example, to share his or her story and uncover experiences of and responses to oppression, including his or her counter-acts of rebellion, which in turn may further activate self-concepts of courage, survival, and resiliency. Consequently, during the assessment process, help seekers are asked about how they responded to the violence rather than how they were affected by it:

1. What signs/cues in your abuser* alerted you to danger?
2. Did you ever challenge the name-calling or reasoning of your abuser?
   - Such as, did you sense that something was not right about the violence even though your abuser made excuses for it?
   - Did you try to avoid or divert the violence toward yourself? Toward other family members?
3. Did you ever purposely not do something your abuser demanded of you?
   - Such as, were there ways you defied being isolated?
4. Did you ever defy your abuser in a way that surprised you?
   - Such as, did you ever physically or verbally challenge the abuser?
   - Did you ever tell someone about the violence?
5. In what ways did you try to make the relationship nonviolent?
   - Such as, did you try and talk your abuser out of the violence?
   - Did you avoid him or topics in an attempt to divert the violence?
   - Did you try to be different (e.g., nonviolent) from how your abuser acted?
6. What ways did you protect yourself and other family members from the abuser?
   - Such as, did you make plans to escape the violence?
   - Did you seek out help from family members, friends, or professionals?

Component 2: Framework for Assessment

The second assessment component involves giving meaning to those factors that influence the problem situation and linking the problem. The model proposed here revolves around two axes. The first axis is an environmental factors versus help seeker factors continuum, and the second is a strengths versus obstacles continuum (see Figure 10.1).

When the axes in Figure 10.1 are enclosed, each of the four quadrants that result represents important content for assessment. Because assessment instruments themselves have tended to focus on help seeker's deficits, they are less likely, then, to tap into clients' resilience, particularly acts of resistance, because " . . . we can only see and know that which our paradigms allow us to see and know" (Barnard, 1994, p. 137). To counterbalance this deficit-focus, previous versions of this chapter emphasized personal/interpersonal strengths within the assessment process. Exemplars were provided for each of the following factors: cognition (e.g., reasoning is easy to follow), emotion (e.g., has a range of emotions), motivation (e.g., willing to accept responsibility for problems), coping (e.g., is well-organized) and interpersonal relationships (e.g., has friends) (Cowger et al., 2006;

---

*The prior questions use the term "abuser" to acknowledge the person responsible for committing the violence; however, the help seeker's terminology should take precedence in the assessment process, which, instead, may include a relationship quality such as a partner, parent, or caretaker rather than "abuser."

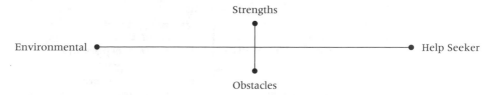

FIGURE 10.1   Assessment axes.

Cowger & Snively, 2002). These exemplars of help seeker strengths were not intended to include all assessment content and knowledge that a social worker must use in practice. Important topics such as assessing specific obstacles to empowerment, assessing power relationships, and assessing the relationship between personal empowerment and social empowerment were not considered. Although preceding discussions (Cowger, 1998; Cowger et al., 2006; Cowger & Snively, 2002) recognized how the social environment shapes people's lives, the assessment process mainly addressed personal and interpersonal dimensions rather than social and political ones.

The momentum for the current strengths assessment adaptation includes Anderson's findings (2001; 2006; Anderson & Danis, 2006) regarding the connection between acts of resistance to oppression and its promotion of resiliency for individuals experiencing family violence. Anderson (2001) broadens the traditional definition of resiliency (i.e., competency despite enduring adversity) to include individuals' survival strengths that develop as a means to protect themselves from oppression. These findings inform us that resistance to powerlessness includes acts of courage, determination, and resourcefulness that are often not legitimized by professionals or institutions because the assessment process often neglects to consider the wider social and political context influencing individual adversity. The personal is political; therefore, personal suffering is political too (Wineman, 2003); yet, during the assessment process there is often little emphasis on the causes of human suffering from a social and political perspective. Naming and challenging oppression when it emerges from the narrative in social work practice would involve helping individuals come to terms with oppressive experiences, to examine the effects of oppression, and to uncover ways that oppression was resisted. Practitioners, then, during the assessment process would need to merge an understanding of individual issues with an awareness of power relations that are embedded in the larger social environment. Therefore, the uniqueness of each situation is acknowledged *and* the political context is illuminated so that the person seeking help can recognize the ways he or she has already fought against oppressive experiences and will begin thinking about how to achieve a socially just result for her- or himself and others.

In the following discussion regarding the content within a strengths assessment (see Figure 10.2), data is recorded in all four quadrants to assist workers and help seekers in considering those strengths and resilient capacities to be uncovered when addressing the dynamics of oppression and abuse. Workers may use the information to (1) stimulate thinking about strengths and their importance in the practice process, (2) assist in identifying strengths that otherwise would not be thought of, (3) assist in identifying and selecting positive and supportive content to be shared with help seekers, (4) provide a foundation for a case plan that is based on help seeker competency and capability rather than inadequacy, and (5) bolster worker confidence

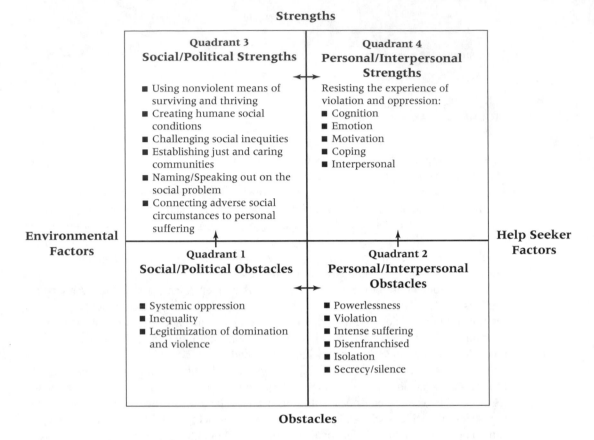

FIGURE 10.2   Framework for assessment.

and belief in the person seeking help. The role of the social worker, therefore, is to nourish, encourage, assist, enable, support, stimulate, and unleash the strengths within people; to illuminate the strengths available to people in their own environments; and to promote equity and justice at all levels of society. Promoting empowerment, then, means not only that human beings possess the strengths and potential to resolve their own difficult life situations, but also that they increase their strength and contribute to the well being of society by doing so.

Quadrant 1: Social/Political Obstacles: Systemic Oppression, Inequality, and Domination   Acquiring assessment information for Quadrant 1, regarding social and political obstacles, illustrates how oppressive social circumstances may degrade personal experience and cause wide-ranging harm for individuals and families. Social and political content is included (as opposed to solely focusing on personal/interpersonal factors) to provide an assessment context for social inequities and unequal power relations. Oppression, the systemic abuse of power, renders people subjectively powerless as in the case with individuals subjected to family violence (Wade, 1997). Help seekers may not specifically use the terms "oppression"; instead, they may capture their experiences of domination through terms such as torment, torture, abuse, terrify, defile, threaten, coerce, force, intimidate, pressure, and instill fear. In most cases the lasting, major damage caused by violence is emotional and psychological—essentially, the devastation of the human spirit. In the moment of violence, the victim's survival task is to maintain some semblance of normalcy, coherence, integrity, control, meaning, value, and equilibrium. Yet, this must be done in the face of an overpowering assault (i.e., oppression, domination, and violence) which threatens to annihilate victims psychologically and in some cases physically as well (Herman, 1997; Wineman, 2003). At the core of victimization is that you are acted upon against your will (Herman, 1997; Wineman 2003). In turn, powerlessness—the experience of being without options—is the hallmark of traumatic experience.

Quadrant 2: Personal/Interpersonal Obstacles: Consequences of Oppression   Obtaining information for Quadrant 2, concerning personal and interpersonal obstacles, shows how oppression is a social toxin that literally makes people sick through the mechanism of trauma, therefore, causing massive personal suffering. Social injustices such as family violence, racism, economic brutality, and homophobia all routinely violate individual, group, and community integrity, and in the face of overwhelming personal and institutional forces, people are repeatedly rendered powerless (Wineman, 2003). Experienced with differing frequency and with varying severity, the harms caused by violence and oppression diminish and debilitate countless lives. Common psychological/interpersonal obstacles related to trauma include intense suffering, having no voice, isolation, and a sense of powerlessness. Help seekers may cope with these obstacles through substance abuse, self-injury, depression, suicide, violence against others, chronic fear, shame, anxiety, eating disorders, dysfunctional relationships, physical illness, and psychotic episodes (Herman, 1997; Wineman, 2003). Because many social workers understand institutional and social problems at a discrete micro level and, consequently, locate the source of problems exclusively within the individual, help seekers' traumatic reactions are often perceived as some disorder or deficit that then creates negative expectations about their potential to address the stressors in their lives (Dietz, 2000). Among helpers and seekers of assistance there is a general lack of understanding for how problematic behavior is originally produced within an oppressive context often as a coping strategy or method of survival. Consequently, it is important to cultivate ways to assist help seekers with the expression of suffering and to connect such expressions to an analysis of systemic oppression (Wineman, 2003).

Quadrant 3: Social/Political Strengths: Promoting Empowerment   Attaining information for Quadrant 3, regarding social and political strengths, illustrates how personal and social empowerment is synergistic. Individually and collectively, vulnerable individuals and groups have responded to oppressive conditions through acts of constructive resistance, including mobilizing effective social change movements to overcome social problems such as poverty, family violence, racism, and homophobia. By fortifying opportunities to achieve success for self and others, those who are gaining personal and social power help to create a more socially just environment in which to live. Social empowerment acknowledges that individual behavior and identity is "bound up with that of others through social involvement" (Falck, 1988, p. 30). Empowerment is experienced through interaction with others, a process of gaining power within and through social relationships. Persons, groups, or communities who are socially empowered have the resources and opportunity to play an important role in shaping the environment (e.g., challenging social inequities, creating humane social conditions, and raising awareness of social problems), and therefore they positively influence many lives including their own.

An individual's method of resisting oppression may serve not only as a vehicle in individual recovery but in societal transformation as well. Wineman (2003) powerfully addresses the connection between personal healing and the political process:

> Individual recoveries are not enough by themselves to change the structures of oppression, but they are indispensable to social change when they are linked to political consciousness and activism. We need to make as many of these kinds of links as we can, which means finding as many ways as we can to tap our unbearable pain and use it to expand the boundaries of what we had imagined to be possible, personally and politically. (p. 274)

Each time oppressed individuals resolve never to harm anyone the way they have been mistreated, they are using constructive resistance in the service of genuine social change. The effects of oppression may never disappear completely; however, focusing on strategies of resistance can promote individual and collective resilience and recovery.

Quadrant 4: Personal/Interpersonal Strengths: Acts of Resistance in the Face of Oppression   Exploring oppression and its consequences in Quadrants 1 and 2 assists in understanding why and how personal strategies of resistance (i.e., Quadrant 4) develop, because wherever you find oppression, you find people trying to defend and protect themselves (Wade, 1997; Wineman, 2003). At the moment when violence takes place, individuals are always figuring out how best to survive and thrive in regard to extraordinary social circumstances. Individuals are not idle or silent regarding their victimization. They typically are resistant to their oppressor's domination and use a variety of mental and behavioral strategies to prevent, withstand, stop, or oppose their subjugation. Individuals' acts of resistance, therefore, may serve as the catalyst for survival and perseverance and for the subsequent development of strategies that promote resilience and recovery. As individuals come to understand the injurious actions perpetrated on them, they may, for example, resolve to be different from their oppressors and, therefore, choose to end a cycle of harming self and others rather than perpetuating it.

Engaging help seekers in a conversation regarding the details and implications of their resistance may assist them to experience themselves as stronger, more insightful, and more capable of responding to the difficulties in their current lives (Wade, 1997). Focused listening enables social workers to detect opposition to oppression within help seeker's terminology, including words such as resist, take back, stand up to, confront, oppose, challenge, win, defy, fight, battle, protect, defend, rebel, question, contest, object, go up against, disagree, and argue. Identifying and building on the positive aspects of the self that had their origins in the resistance of their oppressive experiences then becomes the central focus in treatment. Unfortunately, in social work practice, resistance is often defined as a refusal to comply with the advice of professionals or the prescribed process of treatment (Anderson, 2001). Or, the term "resistance" is viewed negatively as used in psychoanalysis as a psychological defense against threatening material in the unconscious mind. Historically, in other words, "resistance" has pathology-oriented meanings rather than self-preserving ones. Instead, resistance may be looked at as an indicator of health and is "health inducing" (Wade, 1997).

Exemplars of Personal and Interpersonal Strengths (Quadrant 4)   In order to acknowledge, affirm, and extend help seekers' acts of resistance, social work practitioners have to be knowledgeable of them. Morris (1997) argues that professional clinical literature has been far too silent on clients' power of resistance, resilience, and their capacity to change and heal themselves after oppressive experiences. To address this gap during the assessment process, Quadrant 4, which addresses personal and interpersonal strengths, has been modified from previous strengths assessment discussions (Cowger et al., 2006; Cowger & Snively, 2002; Hwang & Cowger, 1998) to include the influence of oppressive social circumstances. This addition addresses social and political dimensions, particularly the "resistance to oppression" factor as identified previously in the chapter to assist social workers who are seeking to practice in empowering ways. Although these added exemplars are drawn from Anderson's research in the area of family violence, they may be transferred to other experiences of oppression (refer to Table 10.1).

TABLE 10.1   Assessment of Help Seeker Strengths (Quadrant 4 of Assessment Axes)

STRENGTHS ASSESSMENT (PRIOR PERSONAL/INTERPERSONAL STRENGTH EXEMPLARS)	STRENGTHS ASSESSMENT (ADDED PERSONAL/INTERPERSONAL STRENGTH EXEMPLARS: THE "RESISTANCE TO OPPRESSION" FACTOR)
Cognition: ■ Sees the world as most other people see in own culture. ■ Has an understanding of right and wrong, from own cultural, ethical perspective. ■ Is insightful as to how one's own behavior affects others and how others affect him- or herself. ■ Is open to different ways of thinking about things. ■ Reasoning is easy to follow. ■ Considers and weighs alternatives in problem solving.	Cognition: ■ Is conscious of acting differently from the oppressor. ■ Understands that one's problems are related and interactive with other people and other institutions. ■ Understands that some behaviors and feelings are related to previous oppressive life experiences. ■ Understands that one can take charge of one's life and bring about changes. ■ Believes facing adversity can make one stronger. ■ Believes his or her life can be different than present situation.
Emotion: ■ Is in touch with feelings and is able to express them. ■ Expresses love and concern for intimate others. ■ Demonstrates a degree of self-control. ■ Can handle stressful situations reasonably well. ■ Is positive about life; has hope. ■ Has a range of emotions. ■ Emotions are congruent with situations.	Emotion: ■ Has capacity to channel anger into defending or advocacy for others. ■ Committed to overcoming feelings of helplessness, powerlessness, and lack of control. ■ Shows compassion for others rather than hatred and malice. ■ Breaks one's silence regarding victimization to "release" overwhelming and threatening emotions.

(continued)

TABLE 10.1 *(continued)*

STRENGTHS ASSESSMENT (PRIOR PERSONAL/INTERPERSONAL STRENGTH EXEMPLARS)	STRENGTHS ASSESSMENT (ADDED PERSONAL/INTERPERSONAL STRENGTH EXEMPLARS: THE "RESISTANCE TO OPPRESSION" FACTOR)
Motivation: ■ When having problematic situations, doesn't hide from, avoid, or deny them. ■ Willing to seek help and share problem situation with others he or she can trust. ■ Willing to accept responsibility for his or her part or role in problem situations. ■ Wants to improve current and future situations and is committed to improve his or her situation.	Motivation: ■ Wants to move beyond coping/surviving to empowerment. ■ Wants to prevent or stop the violence. ■ Wants to take action in a purposeful way to improve one's situation. ■ Wants to overcome the consequences of violence and oppression. ■ Wants to transcend from isolation to making connections with others. ■ Wants to influence his or her choices. ■ Has a strong desire to heal. ■ Committed to opposing maltreatment in whatever form. ■ Wants to maintain a positive life force.
Coping: ■ Persistent in handling family crises. ■ Is well organized. ■ Follows through on decisions. ■ Is resourceful and creative with limited resources. ■ Attempts to pay debts despite financial difficulty. ■ Prepares for and handles new situations well. ■ Has dealt successfully with related problems in the past.	Coping: ■ Ready to identify and fight injustices within the family, community, and broader society. ■ Chooses not to act like an oppressor: hateful, racist, and abusive. ■ Seeks physical and mental escapes from the violence. ■ Develops safety plans for protection of self and others. ■ Stands up for self rather than submitting to injustice. ■ Refuses to comply with the oppressor. ■ Tries to divert oppressor's access to self and others.
Interpersonal: ■ Has friends that provide a supportive network. ■ Seeks to understand friends, family members, and others. ■ Makes sacrifices for friends, family members, and others. ■ Performs social roles appropriately (e.g., parental, spouse, son or daughter, community). ■ Is outgoing and friendly.	Interpersonal: ■ Committed to breaking interpersonal cycles of harm and dysfunction. ■ Holds him- or herself and others accountable. ■ Confronts harm done by others such as bullying in schools or sexual harassment in the workplace. ■ Heals through connecting with others who face adversity. ■ Is available as a resource for others who are facing oppression.

TABLE 10.1   *(continued)*

STRENGTHS ASSESSMENT (PRIOR PERSONAL/INTERPERSONAL STRENGTH EXEMPLARS)	STRENGTHS ASSESSMENT (ADDED PERSONAL/INTERPERSONAL STRENGTH EXEMPLARS: THE "RESISTANCE TO OPPRESSION" FACTOR)
Interpersonal: ■ Is truthful. ■ Is cooperative and flexible in relating to family and friends. ■ Is self-confident in relationships with others. ■ Shows warm acceptance of others. ■ Can accept loving and caring feelings from others. ■ Has sense of propriety, good manners. ■ Is a good listener. ■ Expresses self spontaneously. ■ Is patient. ■ Has realistic expectations in relationships with others. ■ Has a sense of humor. ■ Has sense of satisfaction in role performance with others. ■ Has ability to maintain own personal boundaries in relationships with others. ■ Demonstrates comfort in sexual role/identity. ■ Demonstrates ability to forgive. ■ Is generous with time and money. ■ Is verbally fluent. ■ Is ambitious and industrious. ■ Is resourceful.	Interpersonal: ■ Seeks out role models who reflect self-confidence and control over their own lives while being loving and caring toward others. ■ Builds close and secure relationships that one turns to in times of adversity.

CONCLUSION

Inherent in these assessment guidelines is the recognition that to focus on help seeker strengths and to practice with the intent of help seeker empowerment is to practice with an explicit power consciousness. Whatever else social work practice is, it is always political, because it always encompasses power and power relationships.

In summary, social work literature has emphasized philosophy and theory that presents a strengths perspective, but continues to lack well-developed practice directives, guidelines, and know-how for incorporating this perspective into practice. Assessment based on a strengths perspective places environmental and personal strengths in a prominent position. Problem situations are understood as coping responses to oppressive experiences. Thus the context of oppression needs to be understood before the helping relationship can focus on strengths. Guidelines for soliciting help seekers' narratives and assessing their strengths have been presented in an attempt to bridge the gap between theory and practice.

DISCUSSION QUESTIONS/EXERCISES

1. Choose a client (individual, family, or community) that you are working with and, using the model in Figure 10.2, Framework for Assessment, fill in the quadrants as best you can. For instance, if you are working with a client who self-harms through cutting, would you put this information under Quadrant 2 as a personal/interpersonal obstacle or under Quadrant 4 as a personal/interpersonal strength (i.e., act of resistance)? Or under both? What additional assessment information do you need from a social and political context (i.e., Quadrants 1, 3) to make this determination?

2. Discuss how you might use assessment to help clients understand the connection between their individual problems (i.e., Quadrant 2) and societal ones (Quadrant 1). For example, if you are working with a client who has experienced childhood sexual abuse, in Quadrant 1 you might note the frequency of child sexual abuse by citing national incidence rates. Consequently, you might address that childhood sexual abuse occurs in epidemic proportions and, thus, is a social problem affecting millions of people, including the client her- or himself. In addition, you might explore the causes of child sexual abuse on a macro level and then discuss how these might relate to the client's situation.

3. Discuss how facilitating clients' stories of protest may promote empowerment during the assessment process. For example, how might the resistance to oppression information in Table 10.1, Assessment of Help Seeker Strengths, be used to raise the help seeker's awareness of her or his story of protest, thereby honoring his or her strengths, resilience, and agency in the face of violence? Such as, a domestic violence survivor may blame her- or himself for not preventing or stopping the violence because in order to survive she or he may have accommodated her or his batterer's demands. To counteract the client's view of shame and blame, you might go through the information in Table 10.1 with her or him to highlight a person's remarkable capacity for survival and perseverance in the face of intimate violence.

4. Discuss how you might adapt the model in Figure 10.2, Framework for Assessment, to varying clients and situations. For instance, if you have a gay youth struggling with self-acceptance, he or she could use music to address the four quadrants of the assessment. In Quadrant 1 the youth might select music that addresses society's lack of tolerance for homosexuality while also doing this for Quadrant 2 regarding obstacles to acceptance on both a personal and interpersonal level. This process could also be replicated in Quadrants 3 and 4 where music is selected that encompasses resistance to oppression (e.g., homophobia) on both a macro and micro level.

REFERENCES

Anderson, K. M. (2001). Recovery: Resistance and resilience in female incest survivors. Doctoral dissertation. University of Kansas, *Dissertation Abstracts, 62* (09), 3185A.

Anderson, K. M. (2006). Surviving incest: The art of resistance. *Families in Society, 83*(3), 409–116.

Anderson, K. M. & Danis, F. (2006). Adult daughters of battered women: Resistance and resilience in the face of danger. *Affilia, 21*(4), 419–432.

Barnard, C. (1994). Resiliency: A shift in our perception? *The American Journal of Family Therapy, 22*(2), 135–144.

Beardslee, W. R. & Podorefsky, D. (1988). Resilient adolescents whose parents have serious affective and other psychiatric disorders: Importance of self-understanding and relationships. *American Journal of Psychiatry, 145*(1), 63–69.

Berger, P. L. & Luckmann, T. A. (1966). *The social construction of reality.* Garden City, NY: Doubleday.

Billingsley, A. (1968). *Black families in White America.* Englewood Cliffs, NJ: Prentice-Hall.

Billingsley, A. (1992). *Climbing Jacob's ladder: The enduring legacy of African American families.* New York: Simon & Schuster.

Blume, S. E. (1990). *Secret survivors: Uncovering incest and its aftereffects in women.* New York: Ballantine Books.

Blundo, R. (2001). Learning strengths-based practice: Challenging our personal and professional frames. *Families in Society, 82*(3), 296–304.

Bowen, G. L., & Chapman, M. V. (1996). Poverty, neighborhood danger, social support, and the individual adaptation among at-risk youth in urban areas. *Journal of Family Issues, 17*(5), 641–665.

Boyd-Franklin, N. & Bry, B. H. (2000). *Reaching out in family therapy.* New York: Guilford Press.

Byrd, R. (1994). Assessing resilience in victims of childhood maltreatment. Doctoral dissertation. Pepperdine University, *Dissertation Abstracts International, 55*(03), 1177B. (UMI No. 9417679).

Cohen, B. Z. (1999). Intervention and supervision in strengths-based social work practice. *Families in Society, 80*(5), 460–466.

Council on Social Work Education. (1994). Curriculum policy statement for master's degree program. In *Handbook of accreditation standards and procedures.* Washington, DC: Author.

Cowger, C. D. (1998). Clientism and clientification: Impediments to strengths based social work practice. *Journal of Sociology and Social Welfare, 25*(1), 24–36.

Cowger, C., Anderson, K. M., & Snively, C. (2006). Assessing strengths: The political context of individual, family, and community empowerment. In D. Saleebey (Ed.), *The strengths perspective in social work practice* (4th ed., pp. 93–113). Boston: Allyn & Bacon.

Cowger, C. D. & Snively, C. A. (2002). Accessing client strengths: Individual, family and community empowerment. In D. Saleebey (Ed.), *The strengths perspective in social work practice* (3rd ed., pp. 106–123). Boston: Allyn & Bacon.

Davis, L. E. (2001). The problem of race: A renewed focus. The Carl A. Scott Memorial Lecture conducted at the annual program meeting of the Council on Social Work Education, Dallas, TX.

De Jong, P. & Miller, S. D. (1995). How to interview for client strengths. *Social Work, 40*(6), 729–736.

Delgado, M. & Barton, K. (1998). Murals in Latino communities: Social indicators of community strengths. *Social Work, 43*(4), 346–356.

Dietz, C. (2000). Responding to oppression and abuse: A feminist challenge to clinical social work. *Affilia, 15*(3), 369–389.

Early, T. J. & GlenMaye, L. F. (2000). Valuing families: Social work practice with families from a strengths perspective. *Social Work, 45*(2), 118–130.

Falck, H. S. (1988). *Social work: The membership perspective.* New York: Springer.

Farber, E. & Egeland, B. (1987). Invulnerability among abused and neglected children. In E. J. Anthony & B. J. Cohler (Eds.), *The invulnerable child* (pp. 253–288). New York: Guilford Press.

Finn, J. L. & Checkoway, B. (1998). Young people as competent community builders: A challenge to social work. *Social Work, 43*(4), 335–344.

Gasker, J. (2001). 'I didn't understand the damage it did': Narrative factors influencing the selection of sexual abuse as epiphany. *Journal of Poetry Therapy, 14*(3), 119–133.

Goldstein, H. (1990). Strength or pathology: Ethical and rhetorical contrasts in approaches to practice. *Families in Society, 71*(5), 267–275.

Goroff, N. N. (1983). Social work within a political and social context: The triumph of the therapeutic. In S. Ables & P. Ables (Eds.), *Social work with groups: Proceedings of 1978 symposium* (pp. 133–145). Louisville, KY: Committee for the Advancement of Social Work with Groups.

Greene, G. J., Lee, M. Y., & Hoffpair, S. (2005). The languages of empowerment and strengths in clinical social work: A constructivist perspective. *Families in Society, 86*(2), 267–325.

Harvey, M. R., Mischler, E. G., Koenen, K., & Harney, P. (2001). In the aftermath of sexual abuse: Making and remaking meaning in narratives of trauma and recovery. *Narrative Inquiry, 10*(2), 291–311.

Herman, J. (1992). *Trauma and recovery.* New York: Basic Books.

Hwang, S. C. & Cowger, C. D. (1998). Utilizing strengths in assessment. *Families in Society, 79*(1), 25–31.

Kluckholm, C., Murray, H. A., & Schneider, D. M. (Eds.). (1953). *Personality in nature, society, and culture.* New York: Alfred A. Knopf.

Laird, J. (1989). Women and stories: Restorying women's self-constructions. In M. Goldrick, C. M. Anderson, & F. Walsh (Eds.), *Women in Families* (pp. 427–450). New York: W. W. Norton & Company, Inc.

Luthar, S. (1993). Annotation: Methodological and conceptual issues in research on childhood resilience. *Journal of Child Psychiatry, 34*(4), 441–443.

McAdoo, H. P. & McAdoo, J. L. (Eds.). (1985). *Black children: Social, educational and parental environments.* Beverly Hills, CA: Sage.

McQuaide, S. & Ehrenreich, J. H. (1997). Assessing client's strengths. *Families in Society, 78*(2), 201–212.

Medoff, P. & Sklar, H. (1994). *Streets of hope: The fall and rise of an urban neighborhood.* Boston: South End Press.

Meyer, C. H. (1976). *Social work practice* (2nd ed.). New York: Free Press.

Morris, C. (1997). Mental health matter: Toward a non-medicalized approach to psychotherapy with women. *Women & Therapy, 29*(3), 63–77.

Oko, J. (2006). Evaluating alternative approaches to social work: A critical review of the strengths literature. *Families in Society, 87*(4), 601–611.

Poole, D. (1997). Building community capacity to promote social and public health: Challenges for universities. *Health and Social Work, 22*(3), 163–170.

Pray, J. E. (1991). Respecting the uniqueness of the individual: Social work practice within a reflective model. *Social Work, 36,* 80–85.

Public/Private Venture. (2000, Fall). The science foundations of youth development. In N. Jaffe (Ed.), *Youth development: Issues, challenges, and directions* (pp. 18–64). Philadelphia: K. Pittman, M. Irby, & T. Ferber.

Richmond, M. (1917). *Social diagnosis.* New York: Russell Sage Foundation.

Rodwell, M. K. (1987). Naturalistic inquiry: An alternative model for social work assessment. *Social Service Review, 61*(2), 231–246.

Russo, R. J. (1999, January-February). Applying a strengths-based practice approach in working with people with developmental disabilities and their families. *Families in Society, 80,* 25–33.

Ryan, W. (1976). *Blaming the victim.* New York: Vintage Books.

Safyer, A. W., Griffin, M. L., Colan, N. B., Alexander-Brydie, E., & Rome, J. Z. (1998). Methodological issues when developing prevention programs for low-income, urban adolescents. *Journal of Social Service Research, 23*(3/4), 23–46.

Saleebey, D. (1997). The strengths approach to practice. In D. Saleebey (Ed.), *The strengths perspective in social work practice* (pp. 49–57). New York: Longman.

Schön, D. A. (1983). *The reflective practitioner: How professionals think in action.* New York: Basic Books.

Solomon, B. (1976). *Black empowerment: Social work in oppressed communities.* New York: Columbia University Press.

Stiffman, A. R., Hadley-Ives, E., Elze, D., Johnson, S., & Dore, P. (1999). Impact of environment on adolescent mental health and behavior: Structural equation modeling. *American Journal of Orthopsychiatry, 69*(1), 73–86.

Taber, M., Herbert, C. Q., Mark, M., & Nealey, V. (1969). Disease ideology and mental health research. *Social Problems, 16,* 349–357.

Wade, A. (1997). Small acts of living: Everyday resistance to violence and other forms of oppression. *Contemporary Family Therapy: An International Journal, 19*(1), 23–39.

Werner, E. & Smith, R. (1992). *Overcoming the odds: High risk children from birth to adulthood.* Ithaca, NY: Cornell University Press.

Wineman, S. (2003). *Power-under: Trauma and nonviolent social change.* Cambridge, MA: Author.

Wolin, S. J. & Wolin, S. (1993). *The resilient self.* New York: Villard Books.

Wood, G. G. & Roche, S. E. (2001). Representing selves, reconstructing lives: Feminist group work with women survivors of male violence. *Social Work with Groups, 23*(4), 5–23.

CHAPTER ELEVEN

A SHIFT IN THINKING

Influencing Social Workers' Beliefs About Individual and Family Resilience in an Effort to Enhance Well-Being and Success for All

BONNIE BENARD

SARA L. TRUEBRIDGE

> *The world we have created is a product of our thinking; it cannot be changed without changing our thinking. If we want to change the world, we have to change our thinking.*
> —Albert Einstein (1879–1955)

One of the recurring messages in resilience research posits the relationship that beliefs have with resilience: Resilience begins with what one believes (e.g., Benard, 2004; Werner & Smith, 1992; Yero, 2002). In this chapter, we suggest that a positive and sustainable reform and transformation in human services that deserves more attention focused on the role that beliefs have in social work—specifically beliefs about individual and family resilience. Our experience and work in the fields of social work and education suggest that practitioners, administrators, and policymakers who understand the theory of resilience and authentically believe that all individuals and families have the capacity for resilience can promote and enhance the possibility for positive and healthy individual and family outcomes. In accordance with this thinking, and with the support of literature and research in social work, we contend that all stakeholders interested in increasing the successful outcomes of individuals and families can benefit by developing a deeper understanding of individual and family resilience and an enhanced awareness regarding the role that one's beliefs have in shaping such a concept. We suggest that within the field of social services, well-designed preservice training programs and professional development opportunities are two concrete ways to attain such understanding and awareness.

Practitioners and administrators in human services are continually striving to identify ways in which they can enhance their clients' well-being and life success. Concurrently, limited resources propel policymakers to seek and identify tools, strategies, and programs that may cost-effectively address social welfare concerns. The assumption that frequently underlies these efforts is that "quicker is better." This often leads to decisions and policies that result in structural and systemic changes that they hope will enhance the efficient and effective use of resources and delivery of services.

Unfortunately, authentic and deep change may not occur. All systems and structures are driven by people, and unless the beliefs of the individuals who work within such systems and structures are adequately, appropriately, and regularly addressed, such systems and structural changes may be well-intentioned but not sufficient or capable of creating and sustaining positive changes. We contend that one of the first things that individuals engaged in any human service profession, where they are providing services and supports to other individuals, need to understand is how their beliefs can influence their practice and affect others. This is especially relevant in the fields of social work and education. Our work as researchers and our experiences as practitioners supports our conviction that well-designed and implemented preservice and professional development programs in social work have the ability to influence social workers' beliefs about individual and family resilience in an effort to enhance positive outcomes for all.

RESILIENCE: THE FOUNDATION
OF A STRENGTHS-BASED PRACTICE

Resilience research in social work focuses on healthy development and successful outcomes especially for individuals and families facing difficult life challenges in their homes, schools, and communities. The construct of resilience is complex and elicits much discussion in the research community regarding how it is defined and how it is measured. For our purposes in this chapter, we define resilience simply as the ability to successfully adapt in the face of adversity. Resilience research posits that resilience is a capacity that all individuals have and supports the premise that social work practitioners who possess an understanding of individual and family resilience and the belief that resilience is a process that can be tapped within each individual and family can engage in a practice that can make a positive and powerful contribution in the lives of others.

The strengths-based perspective in social work practice is grounded in resilience research (Benard, 2004). "At the heart of the strength based perspective is a belief in the basic goodness of humankind, a faith that individuals, however downtrodden or debilitated, can discover strengths in themselves that they never knew existed" (von Wormer, 1998). Literature consistently supports the positive influence and impact that the strengths-based perspective has in the field of social work (Saleebey, 2002). Understandably, it is not always easy to adhere to a strengths-based perspective and practice when the policies of social service agencies have historically embraced a treatment/problem and deficit orientation.

As we engage in our work, we do so with the intent of supporting and influencing an attitude and philosophical shift—a shift to alter all relationships, beliefs, and opportunities so that they focus on human capacities and gifts rather than on challenges and problems. Research in the area of resilience exists. Research in the area of beliefs exists. A theoretical assumption about the relationship between beliefs and resilience exists: Resilience begins with beliefs (Benard, 1993; Benard & Marshall, 1997). Although this theoretical assumption exists, additional policies and practices in human services supporting this relationship are needed.

It is important to note that we approach our work being aware and respecting the power of semantics and recognizing the philosophical and important discussions regarding the appropriate and preferred use of words used in the practice of social work. It is with such understanding that we use some terms interchangeably. For instance, throughout this chapter the terms social work, human services, and social services are used to refer to the delivery of agency services supporting the well-being of all individuals and society at large. Individuals, families, and clients are used to refer to the people accessing services. The terms practitioners, social workers, human service providers are used to refer to the people who provide services.

OUR CONCEPTUAL FRAMEWORK

This chapter is grounded in the conceptual framework illustrated in Figure 11.1. The hourglass figure (Truebridge & Benard, 2007) is comprised of two inverted triangles. Benard and Marshall (1997) developed the top triangle, which reflects the theory of resilience. The bottom triangle was developed by Truebridge (2007a), which reflects the relationship between beliefs and resilience. This section of the chapter unpacks the components of our conceptual framework. We will begin by focusing on the top triangle and discussing the components of the triangle moving from the bottom to the top.

A. Beliefs

Resilience begins with what one believes. Beliefs are socially constructed judgments and evaluations that we make. Yero (2002) refers to beliefs "as judgments and evaluations that we make about ourselves, about others, and about the world around us. Beliefs are *generalizations* about things such as causality or the meaning of specific *actions*" (p. 21). Research on practitioner beliefs in the fields of education and social work focuses on understanding how beliefs affect and influence practices and outcomes. Research has shown social workers' beliefs and perceptions about such issues as domestic violence (Danis, 2003), poverty (van Wormer, 1998; Weiss, 2006) and foster care (Beeman & Boisen, 1999; Peters, 2005) can negatively or positively affect their decisions for interventions and practices that ultimately affect client outcomes. This is very powerful, especially since a practitioner's beliefs and perceptions about a particular client or family can be developed without regard to prior knowledge about, or experience with, that client or family. Compounding this, it has been hypothesized that a client's self-efficacy, the perception and belief of his or her own abilities and capacity for learning and change, can positively or negatively be affected by a social worker's perceptions and beliefs (Ryan, Merighi, Healy, & Renouf, 2004). As Walsh writes, "Resilience-based therapy inspires people to believe in their own possibilities for regeneration to facilitate healing and healthy growth" (1998, p. 77). This requires a practitioner who believes in his or her client's resilience and who mirrors this belief back to the client.

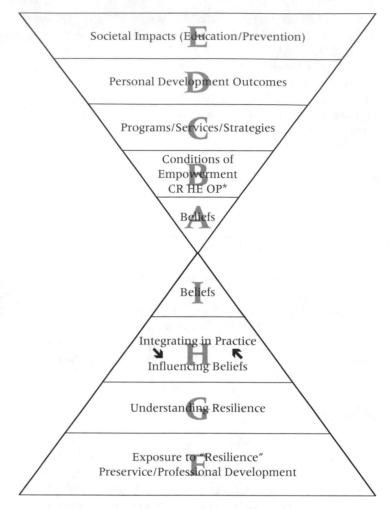

FIGURE 11.1   The conceptual framework of our work.
*CR- caring relationships, HE- high expectations, OP- opportunities for participation

Norgaard (2005) discusses how preconceived attributions and beliefs can undermine the work of individuals employed in providing services to others.

> The problem that can arise from the use of these preconceived attributions is that they may leave an individual less open to change or consideration of other perspectives. Once this occurs, a risk of becoming locked into outdated belief systems that become self-perpetuating through their repeated application to events in the environment develops. (p. 2)

Practitioner attributes, attitudes, and beliefs about clients can differ based upon such things as a client's race/ethnicity, size, social class, and gender. As an example, Keating and Robertson (2004) in their study of black communities and the mental health system quoted mental health professionals who talked about how they feared the physical size of their clients especially in relation to violent outbreaks (p. 444). In discussing the findings of their study, Keating and Robertson (2004) recognize the work of Barnes and Bowl (2001) and Spector (2001) and state that "staff are rightly concerned about violence, but it would appear that racial biases in perceptions of dangerousness influence patient management" (p. 445).

With respect to the relationship that beliefs have with resilience, Benard posits in her theory that the process of promoting resilience and being able to consistently provide and promote the three protective factors (caring relationships, high expectations, opportunities for participation and contribution) in any environment (home, school, or community), begins by believing that all individuals have the capacity for resilience.

> Practitioners with a "resilience prospective" believe that all people have a resilient nature. Moving to a resiliency approach requires a personal transformation of vision . . . the lens through which we see our world. To make systemic changes . . . depends on changing hearts and minds. (Benard, 1993)

The following list, supported by resilience research, provides examples of positive beliefs about individual and family resilience that social service providers should authentically embrace:

- All people have the capacity for resilience.
- Most individuals do make it despite exposure to severe risk.
- One person can make a difference in the life of another person.
- Coming from a risk environment does not determine individual or family outcomes.
- Challenging life experiences and events can be opportunities for growth, development, and change.
- There's nothing wrong with you that what's right with you can't fix.
- Bad behavior does not equate with being a bad person.
- As a practitioner, it is *how* you do *what* you do that counts.
- To help others you need to help yourself.
- Resilience begins with what one believes.

B. Conditions of Empowerment

All individuals have basic human needs that include, but are not limited to, needs for safety, love, belonging, power, accomplishment, and meaning. Research continues to support the findings that environmental conditions play a role in whether these needs are met. Benard (1991, 2004) identifies three elements known as protective factors that, when present, contribute to creating environments that not only meet these needs, but also foster resilience in individuals and families. As stated before, the three protective factors are as follows: (1) providing caring relationships, (2) maintaining high expectations, and (3) providing opportunities for meaningful participation and contribution. When these protective factors are present in an environment, such as a family, school, or community, the environment becomes one that is optimal for fostering individual and family resilience—one that mitigates and buffers the negative effect that trauma, adversity, and/or stress may have on an individual and/or family and engages the individual's or family's protective adaptation systems. When practitioners believe in the resilience of their clients, they naturally convey the attributes of a caring relationship, especially empathic listening and patience. The practitioner also communicates high expectation messages to clients, messages that clients have everything they need within themselves to succeed, that their strengths will help them address their challenges, that they can mend stronger where they are broken, and so on. Similarly, a resilient belief system on the part of the practitioner, which sees clients as a resource, will engage them as active participants in problem solving and will look for opportunities for clients to be resources to others.

C. Programs/Services/Strategies

When the practitioner has created the supportive and empowering climate for growth and success, then attention can be placed on what programs, services, and strategies will best support and sustain these protective factors. Approaches such as mentoring, meaningful work or artistic expression and service to others stand out as research-based strategies that reinforce the protective factors or conditions of empowerment.

D. Personal Developmental Outcomes

What results from this model of resilience practice is the development and emergence of individuals' personal resilience and strengths, such as social competence, ability to problem solve, autonomy, and sense of purpose and future (Benard, 1991, 2004). In a family situation, the individual strengths become collective, contributing to family health and well-being.

E. Societal Impacts

The flow of the theory continues: Individual client strengths and positive development outcomes contribute to a reduction in societal health risk behaviors such as child abuse, alcohol and other substance abuse, mental illness, and an increase in successful outcomes such as high school graduation, employment, positive parenting, and citizenship.

A PROCESS TO INFLUENCE BELIEFS

Benard's work in resilience consistently affirms that resilience begins with what one believes. Truebridge (2007a), in her work, builds upon the work by Benard (2004) and attempts to contribute empirical findings specifically to support the claim that the theory of resilience begins with beliefs and that providing human service practitioners and administrators with opportunities to understand the theory of resilience and to reflect upon their own beliefs, especially how they pertain to individual and family resilience, is a positive step in the field of social work. The following discussion deconstructs the bottom triangle in Figure 11.1 beginning from the bottom and progressing to the top.

F. Exposure to the Concept of Resilience

Affecting practitioners' and administrators' belief systems about individual and family resilience through well designed and supported preservice or professional development programs are two concrete ways to transfer resilience research into social work practice. There are already preservice programs and professional development training programs in the field of social services that make resilience the core concept of their program (Protective Services Training Institute of Texas, 2004a, 2004b; Truebridge, 2007b). Well-designed and implemented human services preservice and professional development programs should provide participants with a working understanding and awareness of resilience in themselves and in the individuals and families that they work with. We spend some time in this section to provide some background and pertinent information about resilience. All or part of this can serve as information that would be beneficial to impart in a preservice or professional development program.

Resilience.   Resilience research emerged about forty years ago as researchers began asking the question: Why do some children who are threatened by exposure to high risk environments successfully adapt while others do not? The study of resilience has expanded from an early focus on the individual to a broader, more inclusive focus that situates risk not in children, but rather in a variety of socioeconomic systems, institutions, and harmful public and social policies. This section begins by providing insight into the history of resilience. It then continues by identifying the definition of resilience that is currently embraced by most researchers followed by discussions about the emergence of resilience in other disciplines and the complexity of resilience as a construct.

History. There has been a dramatic shift in the study of resilience in the fields of human services, education, human development, prevention, and intervention. It is a shift from viewing the world and individuals through traditional problem-based, deficit, pathological models to positive, protective, and preventive models. The shift comes from an increasing body of research in neuroscience, psychology, social work, and education that recognizes resilience not only internally in clients but also externally in families, communities, and wider social environments. The vast body of resilience research has provided the foundation for many popular movements, such as asset development, positive youth development, strengths-based practice, and positive psychology.

Although resilience is now widely understood as a process, it hasn't always been clearly defined as such. Early resilience studies focused on the personal qualities of resilient children. As a result, resilience was seen by many to be a trait. Luthar, Cicchetti, and Becker (2000) discuss the negative repercussions that can result from this interpretation. "To say that resilience is a trait is in essence to say that some individuals simply do not 'have what it takes' to overcome adversity" (p. 546). This perspective was not embraced, nor universally demonstrated, in resilience research.

As the study of resilience grew in the 1980s and 1990s, so did the complexities. Two additional features of resilience spawned new questions. One was the "locus" of resilience. The other was the issue of time. Goldstein and Brooks (2005) note that rather than identifying the work in resilience as a search for factual phenomena, Rutter (1987) identified the work in resilience as a search "for the developmental and situational mechanisms involved in protective processes" (pp. 2–3). Resilience moved beyond the scope of just recognizing personal traits that contributed to the protective process and included the interaction of environmental or contextual factors external to the individual—family, school, community, and other external systems. Benard (1991, 2004) was able to identify and categorize three important environmental processes that buffer risk and foster resilience: (1) forming caring relationships, (2) maintaining positive and high expectations, and (3) providing opportunities for meaningful participation and contribution. These protective processes or protective factors contribute to the development of individual strengths. Benard's (1991) identification of individual personal strengths that buffer risk and foster resilience include social competence, problem solving and metacognition, a sense of autonomy and identity, and a sense of purpose and belief in a bright future.

Time became a second feature that generated new questions in resilience research. Findings recognized that resilience is an adaptive process that can fluctuate depending upon one's changing life circumstances. Resilience is neither linear nor permanent. In the 1990s and early 2000s the discussion of development and perspective was added to those of context and time. With reference to the Rochester Resilience Project (Wyman, Cowen, Work, & Kerley, 1993), Wright and Masten (2005, p. 27) note that it continued to raise questions about resilience not only in terms of context-specific adaptation but also in terms of development by recognizing resilience as a process that promoted children's mastery of normative developmental tasks. Perspective became another area of focus in resilience research. How an individual perceives an experience was shown to play an important role in individual variability with resilience (Ungar, 2004).

Although there now is agreement in the field that resilience is a process rather than a trait, literature still gets misinterpreted. This is often the result of the inconsistent use of terminology in the field such as *risk, vulnerability, protective mechanisms, protective processes*, and *protective factors*. Because resiliency and resilient were often misinterpreted to refer to traits, Luthar et al. (2000) note that "Masten (1994) recommended that the term resilience be used exclusively when referring to the maintenance of positive adjustment under challenging life conditions" (p. 546).

A complex definition. Luthar et al. (2000) refer to resilience as "a *dynamic process encompassing positive adaptation within the context of significant adversity*" (p. 543). Research has provided discussions that articulate the complexities of this definition. One major complexity presents itself because of the two components that are embedded within the definition of resilience.

The definition of resilience is comprised of two separate constructs: significant adversity and positive adaptation. As a result, resilience as a construct—its definition, application, and assessment—is complicated because of having to define, operationalize, and assess the two additional constructs of positive adaptation and significant adversity. Positive adaptation has been operationalized in a variety of ways, including the identification of successfully manifesting specific social competences, stage-salient developmental tasks and/or school-based or life-stage markers. Further discrepancies and complications to the study of resilience exist because positive adaptation begs the question, "Does that mean *better than expected* outcomes or positive outcomes in spite of adversity?"

Significant adversity, or risk, has often been operationalized by identifying individuals' exposure to high-risk environments and then quantifying the statistical probabilities of maladjustment. Some high-risk environments identified include ones where poverty, violence, substance abuse/addiction, and/or parental depression are prevalent. More studies are beginning to appear in literature (Levine, 2006) that recognize affluent communities as high-risk environments as well. Adding to the complexity of significant adversity, resilience research finds that significant adversity is not always easily defined by the identification of one high-risk variable. A number of resilience studies have focused on how multiple and cumulative high-risk environmental factors affect outcomes (Gutman, Sameroff, & Cole, 2003; Rutter, 1979; Sameroff, Gutman, & Peck, 2003). It is evident that the multitude of ways to identify and categorize positive adaptation and significant adversity continue to complicate the study of resilience.

As inquiry into resilience has increased, so too have the variations in the use and definition of the term *resilience.* Ungar (2004) defines resilience as "the outcome from negotiations between individuals and their environments for the resources to define themselves as healthy amidst conditions collectively viewed as adverse" (p. 342). Ungar argues that most definitions of resilience situate themselves in an ecological paradigm that do not and cannot adequately accommodate the breadth and depth of differentiation that individuals have as they construct meaning out of experiences. Ungar's work (2004) also provides a level of analysis and depth illuminating the influence that politics has on the study of resilience. Ungar (2004) also points out the political implications associated with how resilience is defined. "Each localized discourse that defines a group's concept of resilience is privileged, more or less depending on the power of those who articulate it" (p. 345). There have been a number of discussions that illustrate the disservice that is done to the field of resilience when the identification of socially normative and appropriate behaviors are upheld as the litmus test of resilience. Kaplan (1999) adds insightful discourse to this issue as he discusses the interplay between resilience, normative judgment, and subjectivity. What may be considered a manifestation of resilience to one population may be undesirable to another. Take the example of a teen who chooses to be in a gang. By most normative social standards, this behavior would be labeled as being undesirable, if not blatantly deviant. Embracing a different perspective and using a "resilience lens" yields an alternative explanation of why a youth may join a gang. What if the teen was to feel vulnerable and targeted for some unconscionable consequence because he was NOT in a gang. In this case, the teen may suggest that he or she became a part of a gang in order to stay alive on the streets. Was that individual demonstrating resilience? Ungar (2004) posits that it would be conceptually wrong for one definition and understanding of resilience to stand alone.

Since the construct of resilience has emerged in a number of disciplines, just as Reinhartz (1992) suggests with respect to feminist research and perspectives, a transdisciplinary approach can lead to cumulative research which can enhance the understanding of a construct. Although a universal definition of resilience continues to be contested in the research community, a review of the literature clearly identifies much about resilience that the research community does agree upon. Furthermore, much of what the resilience research community does agree upon can be embraced by stakeholders in human services in their efforts to enhance individual and family success for all.

G. Understanding Resilience

Although practitioners and administrators can develop an understanding of resilience, understanding a concept doesn't always mean that it gets seamlessly transferred into practice nor does it mean that it automatically influences one's belief system. We are cognizant that in keeping with this research, simply dispensing information on resilience and belief research through a preservice or professional development program is not sufficient. Some people, even when they hold a belief that contradicts what they have been taught about best practices in preservice education or professional development programs, continue to engage in practices that are more aligned to their long-held original beliefs. Disseminating information about the relationship between resilience and beliefs may not be enough for social workers to change their current practice.

H. Influencing Beliefs and Integrating Resilience into Practice

The ability to influence beliefs is difficult and daunting. However, because social workers' belief systems can influence and orient their practice, the development of quality social workers often resides in the ability to challenge their beliefs. Although the definition of beliefs may semantically differ across the disciplines, one commonality that often does emerge is the claim that beliefs are constructed and inferred. "Belief is based on evaluation and judgment; knowledge is based on objective fact" (Pajares, 1992, p. 313). Research supports the claim that the longer one has held onto a belief, the harder it is to change that belief. Some of these beliefs and subsequent practices were recognized as not always being warranted and, in turn, not leading to optimal client outcomes.

A review of the literature and research on social workers' beliefs supports the claim that preservice education and professional development can influence practitioners' beliefs and practices in a number of ways. Research has demonstrated that well-crafted staff development programs can influence social workers' understandings, beliefs, and attitudes about domestic violence, kinship foster care, and poverty.

Although beliefs that transfer into practices can be influenced through well-designed preservice and professional development programs, as Guskey (1986) contends, some practitioners find that their practices precede their beliefs. Thus, practitioners in social work who embrace an intuitive theory of individual and family resilience, who without being prompted or taught, may engage in a practice where high expectations are held, caring relationships are fostered, and opportunities for contribution and engagement are provided and encouraged, experience positive client outcomes that in turn will influence the social worker's beliefs.

> Expertise is facilitated by knowledge, context-related knowledge through examples and experience of practice. . . . Through building up a repertoire or index of practice, the practitioner is able to "home in on" a case, to see where it is similar to previous cases and to initiate a set of procedures for action. The development of expertise, then, requires integration of conceptual, procedural, strategic and personal knowledge and cannot be facilitated by a general heuristic skill learned out of its context. (Macauley & Cree, 1999, p. 191)

Such "expert" social workers, even without the formal knowledge of resilience theory, continue to intuitively instill it in their practice because they witness how their practice promotes and sustains positive client success—especially for clients and families who come from high-risk environments. Thus, the relationship between developing caring relationships, maintaining high expectations, and providing opportunities for engagement becomes part of that practitioner's craft, his or her knowledge and beliefs—knowledge and beliefs about best social work practices that are accumulated and reinforced from continued experiences (e.g., Guskey, 1986; Macauley & Cree, 1999). This is reflected by the arrows that point in both directions in Figure 11.1.

I. Beliefs

The goal of the preservice and professional development program in social services is to have participants embrace the belief that all individuals and families have the capacity for resilience. Practitioners who have this belief are equipped with some of the most important tools of social work that will successfully support them as they support others—empathy, compassion, hope, optimism, and self-efficacy, their knowledge that they can make a difference.

PRESERVICE AND PROFESSIONAL DEVELOPMENT

As we said, providing preservice and professional development does not always easily transfer into practice. However, well-designed and implemented preservice and professional development programs enhance the prospects that good research about "best practices" will actually transfer into a practitioner's practice. Preservice and/or professional development programs provide opportunities to support practitioners in their exploration and capacity of being their own agents of change as a catalyst to activate, enhance, and support their clients' belief in the powers and capabilities that they themselves possess in being *their own* agents of change.

Macauley and Cree (1999) discuss professional development programs in the context of social work as opportunities to engage in the transfer of learning—a complicated process that they basically define as "prior learning affecting new learning or performance" (p. 183). Yet, to be effective, the composition, quality, and implementation of a preservice or professional development program focusing on the concept of resilience is imperative.

In the next major section, we offer an example of a format that could be used for a preservice or professional development course. Regardless of the format that one ultimately chooses to work from, we offer a brief list of some of the most critical elements that should be incorporated into any program.

Reflective Practices

Thoughtful and deliberate staff development and preservice programs that introduce, discuss, and explore the concepts of resilience and beliefs benefit from having participants engage in activities and exercises that encourage and elicit reflective thinking (Postle, Edwards, Moon, Rumsey, & Thomas, 2002; Schon, 1991). By becoming more self-aware and reflective, one is able to examine deeply held beliefs, attitudes, and dispositions and begin to recognize how these beliefs, attitudes, and dispositions may influence not only their practice but also the outcomes for clients.

Having individuals engage in reflective practices and providing them with opportunities to challenge their beliefs, particularly about clients' resilience, can be incorporated into social service preservice and professional development programs in a variety of ways. One way is by having participants maintain reflective journals, which are a valuable tool for the storage and transference of knowledge (e.g., Barth, 2004; Hiebert, Gallimore, & Stigler, 2002; MacLean & Mohr, 1999). The journal is a written tool with a narrative structure (Cochran-Smith, 2000; Connelly & Clandinin, 1986; Maxell, 2005). Using the tool of a journal, participants reflect by reconstructing their experiences.

Participants can be asked to maintain a written journal throughout the duration of the professional development program that provides opportunities for contemplation of their experiences. Some entries in the journal can be at the discretion of the participants while other entries can be guided by a question or a topic such as: When you look back upon your life, think about an experience where you felt someone believed something about you that wasn't true.

Guided imagery activities that ask participants to visualize times in their lives when they experienced relationships, messages, or experiences that were transformational for them is another reflective practice that can be embedded in social work professional development. In this process, practitioners essentially generate their own protective factors, which, of course, align with resilience research. Challenging them to put into their practice what mattered to them in their lives is a powerful and effective change strategy.

Group Discussions and Professional Learning Communities

Sustaining a personal belief in resilience is far more probable if one is part of a supportive professional learning community. Opening yourself up to your inner beliefs is not easy. Many of us are critical enough about ourselves that we do not need to provide fodder for others to be able to criticize us. Thus a critical component in any learning environment is to create a community with a climate of mutual trust, safety, and respect. One way to do this is by taking some time as a group to collectively establish some group norms and values. These can be posted and/or discussed at the outset of any course or program with the understanding that everyone has agreed to be respectful of them. Although every group will have its own unique norms, many groups will find that they have similar areas or topics that they address. The following brief list offers three broad areas that are usually reflected as a group develops norms:

1. *Participation.* All participants are equal and each person's voice and opinion count.
2. *Communication.* People will speak and listen respectfully to one another without interrupting; there are no "put-downs." Members of the group will refrain from having any side conversations.
3. *Interaction.* Everyone will contribute equally. Members of the group will be respectful of beginning and ending on time.

One final comment about group norms: It is important to note that these are group norms—not ground rules. Group norms are developed together as a group whereas ground rules usually imply that they are coming from a top-down structure. Norms help to facilitate effective, efficient, productive, and respectful group dynamics. Rules are restrictive. Group norms should be revisited and revised and are unique to each group. Ground rules are seen as final, permanent, and perceived as if "one size fits all."

Real-Life Experiences

Although practitioners can be equipped with appropriate theories and beliefs, they still face difficulties in implementation because the context, complexities, and pressures of real life often get in the way. Thus, preservice and professional development programs in social services may benefit by incorporating opportunities for real-life and interactive experiences into their programs. Although preservice and professional development programs are important venues to learn about resilience, it is just as important to recognize and remember that informal opportunities for social workers to meet with their peers and discuss their real-life cases and experiences are just as valuable, and at times can even have more impact on the transfer of knowledge from one practitioner to another (Smith, Cohen-Callow, Dia, Bliss, Gantt, Cornelius, & Harrington, 2006). Videos and DVDs illustrating best practices in resilience are also effective learning tools.

A powerful practice for bringing real-life experiences into professional development and for facilitating change in beliefs is to conduct a client "fishbowl" process in which practitioners hear what clients actually think and feel about their services. This process has two requirements: (1) a set of agreements that all will honor and respect and (2) an appreciative inquiry approach in which clients agree to reframe their complaints and issues as suggestions and recommendations for change.

The sharing of real-life stories that illustrate the resilience process is also a powerful tool for effecting belief change. It only takes one person who rises above the trauma, adversity, and challenge that practitioners see in their clients' lives every day to show that resilience is indeed possible. Who are we to say who has it and who does not?

Research

In terms of the sharing of resilience research, some individuals prefer to have more research than others. Research should be made available, understandable, and accessible in a format that transmits knowledge in a manner that conveys an appreciation and respect for practitioners' time and workload.

Parallel Process

Resilience literature supports the finding that personal resilience, professional resilience, and client resilience are intertwined (Protective Services Training Institute of Texas, 2004a; 2004b). Furthermore, the resilience of an agency or department depends on the attitudes, beliefs, and dispositions of individuals working throughout the agency and/or department. In social work, the ability to embrace a resilience perspective needs to be supported through a parallel process that provides professional development growth opportunities on all levels—not just for practitioners but also for managers, supervisors, directors, and all staff (Reingold & Liu, 2007; Sandifort, 2004).

Cultural Context

Different cultures embrace different perspectives and values often embedded in such activities as traditions, child-rearing, boundaries, and achievement. Thus, it is imperative that all individuals working in human services develop an understanding and appreciation of resilience within a cultural context. As stated in the document prepared by the Protective Services Training Institute of Texas (2004b):

> Professionals involved in resilience work are more likely to be successful when their interventions respect and draw from the individual's cultural identity and culture values, rather than imposing solutions based on the dominant culture. For example, a group intervention—reflecting a cultural value of group harmony and interdependence—may be more effective than one-on-one work. (p. 24)

That said, the only way to truly know if you are being culturally sensitive is to check out your assumptions with the individuals you are serving. It is all too easy to assume, for example, that all African Americans have a cultural value of group harmony. There is individual variation within all cultures. If you really listen to your clients, they will tell you how to help them.

POSSIBLE FORMAT FOR A PROFESSIONAL DEVELOPMENT PROGRAM ON RESILIENCE

The format that we offer follows the process identified in our conceptual framework. The professional development course activities can include, but not be limited to, videos, small and large group discussions, client listening circles, personal reflection, and reflective journal writing. The professional development program for practicing social workers should be designed to accommodate the schedules and needs of practitioners. The structure and time frame for designing and implementing the professional development program should continually be evaluated with regard to the efficiency and effectiveness of the preservice or professional development program.

This is an example of a professional development program format that has been used to bring the concept and practice of resilience to practitioners in the fields of social services and education. Modifications and adaptations are always necessary so that each program is inclusive and respectful of the unique features of everyone involved—the service providers, service recipients, and agency.

This particular program was developed around the theme "You Matter!" Its theme reflects the message that every person in human services and education has the power to make a difference in the lives of others. This particular program is implemented as a series with three 2-hour modules. The duration between sessions should be determined so participants are able to adequately practice and reflect upon some of the strategies presented. The following information* provides you with brief overview of each module.

*Adapted from a professional development series developed by Benard, Burgoa, and Truebridge, 2007.

Module 1

Participants learn the major messages and contributions of resilience and research, the personal strengths associated with resilience and how to use strength-based approaches in their work with clients. Activities can include:

- Emphasizing the power of words and the need to reframe "deficit" language into strengths-based language, i.e., hyperactive vs. energetic; distractible vs. curious; explosive vs. passionate.
- Making connections with their own resilience by reflecting on personal stories that demonstrate their internal personal strengths.
- *Homework:* Practice using strengths-based language in your work and personal life.

Module 2

Participants learn how the protective factors of caring relationships, high expectations, and opportunities for participation meet the needs of individuals and families. Activities can include:

- Engaging in a guided imagery exercise to explore and identify the effect that caring relationships, high expectations, and opportunities to participate had on their personal lives.
- Reviewing the resilience conceptual framework.
- Watching a video of best practices in action and identifying when there are real-life examples of caring relationships, high expectations, and opportunities to participate.
- *Homework:* Engage in a self-reflection activity and identify times at work when you fostered caring relationships, high expectations, and opportunities to participate among the individuals and families you work with.

Module 3

Participants engage in personal reflection and dialogue about their practices and attitudes in providing and conveying the three protective factors to their clients. Participants learn the significance of collegial support in supporting resilience practices.
Activities can include:

- Engaging in role plays using strengths-based communication and reframing, especially with difficult situations that might occur with clients or with colleagues.
- Dialoguing about how resilience begins with our beliefs—that resilience starts with us and the beliefs we have in our hearts about not only the individuals and families that we work with, but also our own resilience.
- Identifying what you need from your colleagues to support your own resilience beliefs.
- Publicly committing to one strengths-based practice to support your client's resilience and one to support your colleagues.

CONCLUSION

Individuals working in human services need ongoing opportunities to acknowledge and explore the immense influence, responsibility, and privilege that they have as practitioners to affect the lives of others. It is imperative to provide opportunities for social work practitioners in preservice and professional development venues to understand and genuinely believe that individual and family resilience is a capacity and process that not only can be tapped within every individual and family but also supported in every setting.

To reiterate, research supports the importance of studying beliefs in the context of social work because beliefs influence the behaviors of practitioners, which in turn influence the behaviors and success of their clients (e.g., Ryan, Merighi, et al., 2004). Discussions about social work reform and transformation cannot be limited to discussions about *best practices* as reflected in competencies, techniques, and programs. Such best practices are only as good as the practitioners who are able to implement them with *their* best practices and beliefs, thus creating climates conducive to positive individual and family outcomes. As Walsh (1997) states, "When there's improvement, it usually isn't that the services *per se* were different, it's about a change in the person who delivered the service and the way they delivered it" (p. 7).

Social work reform focusing solely on spending more money to alter services, programs, and curriculum may be misdirected. When making changes in human services, we often are compelled to look at the parts that are believed to be in need of improvement. Perhaps it is time that we reframe the needs in social services. Reframing allows service providers, service recipients, and policymakers the opportunity to gain new perspectives, which in turn allows them to explore new territory by seeing situations and solutions through a different lens. Affecting practitioners' and administrators' belief systems about individual and family resilience through well-designed and supported preservice and/or professional development programs communicates an important message—a message that applies to all fields of work where individuals are in relationships with other individuals—it's not *what* you do . . . it's *how* you do it. With this perspective, practitioners, administrators, and policymakers may more readily embrace and advocate for a "theory of change" in social services where the change agent resides not *with the programs* incorporated in the system but rather *within the individuals* involved with the system.

DISCUSSION QUESTIONS/EXERCISES

1. In your agency, what plans or programs are in place to (a) teach the basics of resilience theory and research and (b) enhance the resilient capacities and assets of workers and staff? If there are none or few, what would you do as a student, worker, or supervisor to bring them to the agency or unit?

2. In your educational and work history, have there been times when the work environment was more or less resilience promoting? What were the differences between those times and, if appropriate, the environments?

3. With a colleague make plans to employ one of the modules that Benard and Truebridge outline in an in-service training. Now amend it to be appropriate for a cultural or ethnic group employed at your agency.

REFERENCES

Barnes, M. & Bowl, R. (2001). *Taking over the asylum.* London: Palgrave-Macmillan.

Barth, R. S. (2004). *Learning by heart.* San Francisco: Jossey-Bass.

Beeman, S. & Boisen, L. (1999). Child welfare professionals' attitudes toward kinship foster care. *Child Welfare, 78,* 315–334.

Benard, B. (1991). *Fostering resiliency in kids: Protective factors in the family, school and community.* Portland, OR: Western Center for Drug-Free Schools and Communities.

Benard, B. (1993, March). Resiliency requires changing hearts and minds. In *Western Center News, 6.* Western Regional Center for Drug-Free Schools and Communities Far West Laboratory for Educational R & D.

Benard, B. (2004). *Resiliency: What we have learned.* San Francisco, CA: WestEd.

Benard, B., Burgoa, C., & Truebridge, S. L. (2007). *You matter! The power of after school program staff to make a difference in the lives of children and youth.* Training and materials prepared in accordance with a California Department of Education grant awarded to WestEd.

Benard, B. & Marshall, K. (1997, Spring). A framework for practice: Tapping innate resilience. *Research/Practice,* 9–15. Minneapolis: University of Minnesota, Center for Applied Research and Educational Improvement.

Cochran-Smith, M. (2000). Blind vision: Unlearning racism in teacher education. *Harvard Educational Review, 70,* 157–190.

Connelly, F. M. & Clandinin, J. (1986). On narrative methods, personal philosophy, and narrative unities in the study of teaching. *Journal of Research in Science Teaching, 23,* 293–320.

Danis, F. S. (2003). Social work responses to domestic violence: Encouraging news from a new look. *Affilia, 18,* 177–191.

Goldstein, S. & Brooks, R. (Eds.). (2005). *Handbook of resilience in children.* New York: Kluwer Academic/Plenum Publishers.

Guskey, T. R. (1986). Staff development and the process of teacher change. *Educational Researcher, 15,* 5–12.

Gutman, L. M., Sameroff, A. J., & Cole, R., (2003). Academic growth curve trajectories from 1st grade to 12th grade: Effects of multiple social risk factors and preschool child factors. *Developmental Psychology, 39,* 777–790.

Hiebert, J., Gallimore, R., & Stigler, J.W. (2002). A knowledge base for the teaching profession: What would it look like and how can we get one? *Educational Researcher, 31,* 3–15.

Kaplan, H. (1999). Toward an understanding of resilience: A critical review of definitions and models. In M. D. Glantz & J. L. Johnson (Eds.), *Resilience and development: Positive life adaptations* (pp. 17–83). New York: Kluwer Academic/Plenum Publishers.

Keating, F. & Robertson, D. (2004). Fear, black people and mental illness: A vicious circle? *Health and Social Care in the Community, 12,* 439–447.

Levine, M. (2006). *The price of privilege.* New York: Harper Collins Publishers.

Luthar, S. S., Cicchetti, D., & Becker, B. (2000). The construct of resilience: A critical evaluation and guidelines for future research. *Child Development, 71,* 543–562.

Macauley, C. & Cree, V. E. (1999). Transfer of learning: Concept and process. *Social Work Education, 18,* 183–194

MacLean, M. S. & Mohr, M. M. (1999). *Teacher-researchers at work.* Berkeley, CA: National Writing Project.

Masten, A. (1994). Resilience in individual development: Successful adaptation despite risk and adversity. In M. C. Wang & E. W. Gordon (Eds.), *Educational resilience in inner-city America: Challenges and prospects* (pp. 3–25). Hillsdale, NJ: Erlbaum.

Maxwell, J. A. (2005). *Qualitative research design: An interactive approach* (2nd ed.). Thousand Oaks, CA: Sage Publications.

Norgaard, J. M. (2005, February) *The measurement of attribution of battering: A review of the literature.* Downloaded December, 23, 2007, from www.ceu-hours.com/courses/battering.html

Pajares, F. (1992). Teachers' beliefs and educational research: Cleaning up a messy construct. *Review of Educational Research, 62,* 307–332.

Peters, J. (2005). True ambivalence: Child welfare workers' thoughts, feelings, and beliefs about kinship foster care. *Children and Youth Services Review, 27,* 595–614.

Postle, K., Edwards, C., Moon, R., Rumsey, H., & Thomas, T. (2002). Continuing professional development after qualification—partnerships, pitfalls and potential. *Social Work Education, 21,* 157–169.

Protective Services Training Institute of Texas. (2004a). Fostering personal, client and family resilience: Part 1: Resilience, the resilient child, and the resilient professional [printed version of online training module]. *Protection Connection, 11* (3). Austin, TX: Author. Funding provided by Texas Department of Family and Protective Services.

Protective Services Training Institute of Texas. (2004b). Fostering personal, client and family resilience: Part 2: Resilience in DFPS clients [printed version of online training module]. *Protection Connection, 11* (4). Austin, TX: Author. Funding provided by Texas Department of Family and Protective Services.

Raths, J. & McAninch, A. C. (2003). Teacher beliefs and classroom performance: The impact of teacher education. *Advances in Teacher Education.* (Vol. 6). Greenwich, CT: Information Age Publishing, 23–42.

Reingold, D. & Liu, H. (2007). *Do poverty attitudes of social service agency directors influence organizational behavior?* Paper funded by grants from The Joyce Foundation, Indiana's Family and Social Service Administration, and the Indiana Township Association. Retrieved January 4, 2008, from www.pmranet.org/conferences/AZU2007/ArizonaPapers/Reingold_Liu.pdf

Reinhartz, S. (1992). *Feminist methods in social research.* New York: Oxford University Press.

Rutter, M. (1979). Protective factors in children's responses to stress and disadvantaged. In M.W. Kent & J. E. Rolf (Eds.), *Primary prevention of psychopathology: Social competence in children* (pp. 49–74). Oxford, UK: Blackwell.

Rutter, M. (1987). Psychosocial resilience and protective mechanisms. *American Journal of Orthopsychiatry, 57,* 316–331.

Ryan, M., Merighi, J. R., Healy, B., & Renouf, N. (2004). Belief, optimism and caring: Findings from a cross-national study of expertise in mental health social work. *Qualitative Social Work, 3,* 411–429.

Saleebey, D. (Ed.). (2002). *The strengths perspective in social work practice* (3rd ed.). Boston: Allyn & Bacon.

Sameroff, A. J., Gutman, L., & Peck, S. C. (2003). Adaptation among youth facing multiple risks: Prospective research findings. In S.S. Luthar (Ed.), *Resilience and vulnerability: Adaptation in the context of childhood adversities* (pp. 364–391). New York: Cambridge University Press.

Sandfort, J. (2004). Why is human services integration so difficult to achieve? *Focus, 23,* 35–38.

Schon, D. A. (Ed.). (1991). *The reflective turn: Case studies in and on educational practice.* New York: Teachers College Press.

Smith, C. A., Cohen-Callow, A., Dia, D. A., Bliss, D. L., Gantt, A., Cornelius, L. J., & Harrington, D. (2006). Staying current in a changing profession: Evaluating perceived change resulting from continuing professional education. *Journal of Social Work Education, 42,* 465–482.

Spector, R. (2001). Is there a racial bias in clinicians' perceptions of the dangerousness of psychiatric patients? A review of the literature. *Journal of Mental Health, 10,* 5–15.

Truebridge, S. L. (2007a). *Logic model illustrating how preservice and professional development programs influence practitioners beliefs about resilience.* Unpublished document.

Truebridge, S. L, (2007b). *Resilience: A strengths-based approach to transforming lives.* Presentation to the Family and Children and Family Services Division of the San Francisco Department of Human Services.

Truebridge, S. L. & Benard, B. (2007). *A conceptual framework for resilience that translates theory into practice.* Unpublished document.

Ungar, M. (2004). A constructionist discourse on resilience: Multiple contexts, multiple realities among at-risk children and youth. *Youth & Society, 35,* 341–365.

van Wormer, K. (1998). *Social work, corrections, and the strengths approach.* A paper presented at the Canadian Association of Social Workers National Social Work Conference, June 20–24, Edmonton, Alberta, Canada.

Walsh, F. (1998). *Strengthening family resilience.* New York: Guilford Press.

Walsh, J. (1997). The eye of the storm: Ten years on the front lines of new futures. *An Interview with Otis Johnson and Don Crary.* Baltimore, MD: Annie E. Casey Foundation.

Weiss, I. (2006). Factors associated with interest in working with the poor. *Families in Society: The Journal of Contemporary Social Services, 87,* 385–394.

Werner, E. & Smith, R., (1992). *Overcoming the odds: High-risk children from birth to adulthood.* Ithaca, NY: Cornell University Press.

Wright, M. O. & Masten, A. S. (2005). Resilience processes in development: Fostering positive adaptation in context of adversity. In S. Goldstein & R. Brooks (Eds.), *Handbook of resilience in children.* New York: Kluwer Academic/Plenum Publishers.

Wyman, P.A., Cowen, E.L., Work, W.C., & Kerley, J. H. (1993). The role of children's future expectations in self-system functioning and adjustment to life stress: A prospective study of urban at-risk children. *Development and Psychopathology, 5,* 649–661.

Yero, J. L. (2002). *Teaching in mind: How teacher thinking shapes education.* Hamilton, MT: Mindflight Publishing.

CHAPTER TWELVE

HONORING PHILOSOPHICAL TRADITIONS

The Strengths Model and the Social Environment

W. PATRICK SULLIVAN

CHARLES A. RAPP

It has been nearly twenty years since the original statement on the strengths perspective appeared in the journal *Social Work*. Far from being warmly received, the article was originally rejected and finally appeared in the section "Briefly Stated" only due to ample amounts of persuasion and persistence shown by lead author Ann Weick. Since that time the strengths model has been implemented in a diverse array of practice arenas and has been the centerpiece of many books and articles. As would be expected, over time the original concepts inherent to the model have been modified or "reinvented" sometimes for the better, sometimes for the worse. It is our contention that one of the key principles of the strengths perspective, the pivotal role of the social environment in human and social development, is routinely abandoned in new iterations of the model and often ignored entirely in direct practice. This potential omission is of concern as a focus on the healthy and generative functions of the social environment and the importance of tapping such resources in the service of consumer goals has been historically viewed as a fundamental principle of the model and reflects important philosophical assumptions about human and social development.

To highlight the key role of the environment in human and social development is likely viewed by many social workers as self-evident. After all, as Saleebey (2004) notes, social work has "long claimed its niche as the space where traffic between the environment and individuals, families, and groups occurs" (p. 7). Accordingly, any reasonable model of human behavior must account for the influence of extraindividual forces on development. The reciprocal relationship between people and the environment, however construed, is a fundamental precept in social work and most professions concerned with the health and well-being of people. Yet, while general systems theory and ecological models may provide excellent templates for understanding human development and behavior, it is decidedly more difficult to use this knowledge to effect desired change (Thyer & Meyers, 1998; Wakefield, 1996).

Human development and growth is a transactional process that occurs within a social context. In the best of all circumstances young children are reared in environments where the meeting of basic needs is a guarantee, and families can secure the additional resources and supports necessary for a child to thrive. Successful adults are also adept in the art of acquiring and accessing resources central to improving their overall quality of life. However, each day social workers encounter individuals and families where this transactional process, this intersection if you will, is compromised. A wide range of converging forces seemingly conspire to restrict access to life-enhancing resources for those individuals. Kretzmann and McKnight (1993) poignantly refer to "strangers," those marginalized citizens who may be labeled, oppressed, segregated, or simply ignored. Sometimes the challenges people face *do* restrict their ability to interact effectively with the outside world. At the other end of the spectrum are cases where social resources are unjustly withheld from those facing unique challenges, the result of impulses as wide-ranging as fear and the desire to protect.

To deny access to genuine interaction and participation in community life, as well as the enriching resources the social environment can offer, thwarts both human and social development. In such cases individuals are sequestered in a world demarcated by physical and emotional barriers, both real and experienced, and have limited access to the tools necessary to escape their current predicaments. While we seem to be comfortable labeling and rejecting others who are different or require assistance, the net impact is a loss to society as a whole. As Kretzmann and McKnight (1993) have illustrated, the contributions of these very people, those viewed by some stakeholders as too damaged or too impaired to play a worthwhile role in the realization of the collective good, really do have talents and abilities that can be tapped to enhance community capacity.

In a similar vein, many of us have been trained to view the social environment with a jaundiced eye—yes, crime, drug abuse, domestic violence, and blight can be easily recognized. In some settings it is particularly difficult, and more time consuming to take another glance, to take an inventory of those aspects of the proximal social environment that promote growth, create opportunities, and offer basic building blocks for individuals and entire communities to reach their goals. Nonetheless, to be a successful strengths-based practitioner it is as important to complete an inventory of community assets as it is to engage in the strengths discovery process with individuals and families.

The strengths perspective offers a way to address, in a new and bold fashion, the range of social issues and problems that currently vex us. In spite of our best efforts to date, many of the most pressing problems faced by individuals, families, and the larger society appear to be intractable, and this alone should implore us to strike out in new directions. This paper reaffirms a basic premise of the strengths model—that important gains are made in direct practice, community capacity, and public policy when efforts are extended to match and develop the inherent strengths of people *and* the social environment.

BASIC ASSUMPTIONS

The strengths perspective emerged from a series of case management pilot projects developed at the University of Kansas in the early 1980s, all focused on people facing serious and persistent mental illnesses. Clearly what made these projects unique was the focus on consumer strengths, an unheard of proposition within the context of traditional mental healthcare at that point in history. In these early moments the term strengths model had not yet been coined, indeed the name given to describe this effort was the Resource-Acquisition model—a designation that underscored the proposed centrality of community resources in the process of recovery from mental illness.

The Resource-Acquisition model was predicated on two key assumptions that had guided innovative work in the field of child welfare. The first assumption asserts that behavior is a function, at least in part, of the resources available to people (Davidson & Rapp, 1976). While this may strike some as a peculiar notion, Saleebey (2002) observes:

> We often look inward or to the family to explain and understand behavior, but the immedi-ate context—interpersonal, built, physical—is a powerful influence on how we feel, think, and act. So the environment—be it school, neighborhood, playground, and its people and structures—can be a powerful force in helping people to turn around their lives. (p. 230)

The second assumption, one that clearly links individual practice to social advocacy, is that our society values equal access to social resources (Davidson & Rapp, 1976). Here it is recognized that some families involved with the child welfare system, people facing seri-ous mental illnesses, and others who can be deemed "strangers" often have difficulty access-ing resources that should be available to them, and as a result professionals are often called upon to abet their efforts to obtain those social goods vital to their well-being.

Case management services cast in such terms had a familiar ring to veteran social workers regardless if they had served as front-line caseworkers or in community organiza-tion roles. Here was an approach that honored time-worn principles that evolved into more modern systems or ecological models of practice. However, in spite of the apparent simi-larities between existing practice theory and "good old-fashioned casework," it became apparent that an unbending focus on personal and environmental strengths required new methods and new tools to be sure, but also a new way of viewing problems and solutions.

The person-in-environment perspective, germane to social work practice, recognizes the interdependence of people with the world around them. In daily life, contact with the environment nurtures, supports, protects, entertains, confuses, and may threaten us. Accord-ingly, in direct practice it is essential for social workers to evaluate the impress of family, work, and the community at large on individual behavior and functioning. Yet, in conducting this assessment process there tends to be an overemphasis on the deficits or toxic elements in the social environment. While there are undoubtedly gaps and noxious elements present in the world around us, such a negative view of the social environment is not without its conse-quences. Kretzmann and McKnight (1993) have noted that the common analysis of com-munity problems, often denoted as a needs assessment, can have an iatrogenic impact on community residents. While it cannot be disputed that neighborhoods and communities often face real concerns and real troubles, Kretzmann and McKnight (1993) remind us that this is only part of the total picture. The danger comes when residents begin to incorporate this neg-ative view of their world, and draw inferences about themselves as a result:

> Once accepted as the whole truth about troubled neighborhoods, the "needs" map deter-mines how problems are to be addressed, through deficiency-oriented policies and programs. Public, private and non-profit human services programs, often supported by university research and foundation funding, translate the programs into local activities that teach people

the nature and extent of their problems, and the value of services as the answer to their problems. As a result, many lower income urban neighborhoods are now environments of service where behaviors are affected because residents come to believe that their well-being depends on being a client. They begin to see themselves as people with special needs that can only be met by outsiders. (p. 2)

By narrowing the focus to problems, threats, and gaps in the social environment, our view of helping resources and the people we serve, as illustrated above, becomes unnecessarily constricted. The strengths model of social work practice offers an alternative conception of the people we often refer to as clients and their social environment. This perspective promotes matching the inherent strengths of individuals with naturally occurring resources in the social environment. Such naturally occurring resources are a source of strength in all social environments and available in all social environments. Recognizing, recruiting, and using these strengths can help maximize the potential of our clients and our community.

What is proposed here is a decidedly reciprocal process. Far too often the consumers social workers serve are viewed as burdens on the community—and it follows that when resources are made available to them this is viewed as a gift or charity. It is argued here that true social development occurs when those we serve are viewed as community assets, not as liabilities. Indeed, recognizing the talents of those pushed to the margins is a vital first-step in the enhancement of community capacity.

> Each community boasts a unique combination of assets upon which to build its future. A thorough map of those assets would begin with an inventory of the gifts, skills, and capacities of the community's residents. Household by household, building by building, block by block, the capacity mapmakers will discover a vast and often surprising array of individual talents and productive skills, few of which are being mobilized for community-building purposes. This basic truth about the "giftedness" of every individual is particularly important to apply to people who find themselves marginalized by communities. It is essential to recognize the capacities, for example, of those who have been labeled mentally handicapped or disabled, or those who are marginalized because they are too old, or too young, or too poor. In a community whose assets are being fully recognized and mobilized, these people will be part of the action, not as clients or recipients of aid, but as full contributors to the community-building process. (Kretzmann & McKnight, 1993, p. 6)

ENVIRONMENT DEFINED

It is important to begin by considering the term *environment,* a concept that proves to be more elusive than it would appear. For some, the term quickly conjures up images of nature and the increasing concerns about the degradation and depletion of the earth's resources. For others, the built environment, particularly the condition of inner cities comes quickly to mind. Historically, social policies such as urban renewal were launched on an assumption that environmental conditions contributed to the pathological behavior of individuals and major social problems such as crime. In the area of mental health care, by illustration, there have been periods in the past and even today where environmental conditions have been seen to cause or provoke a person's vulnerability for the expression of mental illness (Faris & Dunham, 1939; Torrey & Yolken, 1998). Furthermore, the potential power of environmental manipulation in treatment has influenced the physical design of psychiatric hospitals, and alterations in the treatment process inside the walls as reflected in past innovations such as the introduction of therapeutic communities and ward government.

Environment is defined in *Webster's New World Dictionary* (1979) as "all the conditions, circumstances, etc. surrounding, and affecting the development of, an organism." This definition indicates that environment cannot be understood monolithically, that in reality all people function in a wide range of "environments" each day. Saleebey (2004) argues that "there is a sense of the environment that social work has, to a significant degree ignored—that is, the immediate, proximal, often small environment where people play out much of their lives" (p. 7). Consider those individuals considered socially adept. As a society we tend to admire people who can operate comfortably and with facility in a host of settings—from a rural bar to a boardroom of a Fortune 500 company. Some seem to have an almost innate knack to prosper socially, but it is more likely that they honed this skill through exposure and experience.

The developmental process described here is one that many people have experienced at various points in their life—and it is equally likely that most of us could find ourselves in social contexts for which we lack preparation. To illustrate, few of us have attended a state dinner, or visited the Pope or the Queen of England—hence, we would need instruction on proper protocols. However, despite the novelty of a given task, past experience and confidence can be drawn upon to navigate unfamiliar terrain. As we will explore later, many who seek social work services face isolation and social impoverishment, while others approach new situations with great anxiety and fear. Some may lack the basic experience that helps build the fund of knowledge that can be called upon to deal with novel situations and as a result a negative feedback cycle loop ensues that erodes a person's confidence, reinforces the disinclination to accept new challenges, and provides ammunition for others to shun them. In the final analysis people caught in this vicious cycle can slip into the world of "strangers" representing a personal and social loss.

The Social Niche

One useful framework that can be used to explore the transactional nature of human development is the concept of the social niche as devised by Taylor (1997). Taylor (1997), much like Thyer and Myers (1998), argues that the ecological metaphors present in social work provide an important framework for thought and possibilities for action. Ecological models, Taylor (1997) observes, "draw attention to person-environment transactions . . . and it emphasizes [sic] holistic thinking and interactive process" (p. 217). Human beings are social creatures, and as such the niche they occupy is a function of complex forces that go well beyond those needed for mere survival. Taylor's (1997) construct of "social niche" reflects this distinction and underscores the reality that humans

> need social support, help in the construction of social norms and social skills, aid in setting socially meaningful goals, group feedback to establish and maintain consensus on social reality, and reciprocal ties of mutual aid. The variety and need for such social and intangible resources is uniquely human. (p. 219)

If these social inputs are necessary for all humans to grow and develop, they are critically important to many people who commonly use social work services. Consider those who face serious and persistent mental illness. Tragically, basic opportunities are lacking in the lives of many that face such daunting challenges. Social support networks shrink with each hospitalization, leaving the individual and family to survive by their wits. Social rejection is omnipresent despite sustained efforts to enlighten the populace about the realities of mental illness. As a result, many are relegated to special environments, notable in their differentiation from the world in which most adults reside, segregated spatially and emotionally from others. They suffer, in Taylor's (1997) words, from niche entrapment, becoming totally defined by their social category, in highly stigmatized environments with others of "their kind," and afforded few opportunities to obtain the feedback, skills, or opportunities to escape.

Figure 12.1 provides a theoretical representation of the factors that impact the nature of the social niche one occupies. While few people use the term niche in daily life, there are indications that we do think about our relationship with the surrounding environment with some regularity. For example, a job may be considered a "good fit," or a relationship gone astray is often deemed to be a poor "match." Similarly when we immediately feel comfortable in new surroundings it is deemed to "feel like home" or we simply note that we "feel at ease." Good fits or matches require fewer emotional or physical adjustments, and when we land in an ideal setting or situation we tend to perform at our best, enjoy greater confidence,

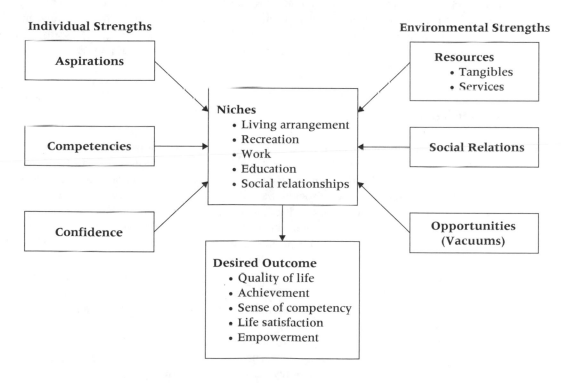

FIGURE 12.1   Factors impacting the nature of niches.

and feel protected and supported. When those blessed with resources and opportunities believe that key elements of their life are less than ideal they may, in everyday parlance, decide to "make a change." A new job may be secured, a better home purchased, or the search may for a new mate initiated. Returning to Figure 12.1, the aspirations, competencies, and confidence of the individual (strengths) are aligned with environmental strengths such as social supports, opportunities, and tangible and service resources within the individual's various niches to promote the desired outcomes—a better quality of life and a higher level of achievement, for example.

Contrast this with the experience of many people who seek or are directed to seek social work services. In the worst scenario we find people who are homeless or living in settings that increase their chances of being victimized and exploited. Other consumers, like those who are violated physically and emotionally, may live in constant fear and even when helped they may be placed in unfamiliar surroundings that are frightening or isolating. The ability to make seemingly rational decisions and to plan for the future is compromised when faced with dire poverty. In the face of these troubling situations many consumers cannot "make a change." Not only are the resources needed to facilitate escape from entrapping niches lacking, but often others (e.g., professionals, families) assume they are helping by making choices for them. The desire of consumers to "feel at home" is not a criterion for placement in a congregate living facility, nor is "a good match" the primary concern in the assignment of a roommate. It is suggested here that there are endemic aspects of the helping enterprise that impede recovery. Certainly, there are pragmatic considerations, primarily economic, that shape the structure and process of helping. However, there are also opportunities to forge new partnerships with the consumer and community that may prove to be both clinically and economically efficacious.

IN SEARCH OF THE PERFECT NICHE

As noted above, among those "strangers" striving to gain a foothold in community life are people challenged by mental illnesses. Their road to recovery and full community participation and citizenship is at best circuitous, and many suffer from niche entrapment. Once, physical segregation from mainstream society was viewed as a treatment norm, but in time fiscal constraints, philosophical shifts, and legal decisions, affirming individual rights and due process, have reduced the reliance on inpatient psychiatric care. However, while community-based care has become the standard in the mental health service world, it has been noted that "individuals with psychiatric disabilities living outside the hospital may be described as in the community, but not of it" (Ware, Hopper, Tugenberg, Dickey, & Fisher, 2007, p. 469).

Community integration is more than a matter of *where* one lives, works, and plays. It also involves less tangible but real dimensions like the sense of belonging, and the perception and experience of being valued and embraced. Indeed, social exclusion may now be more common that physical seclusion, but in both cases the impact on people is insidious. Social exclusion has overt and covert dimensions, and one task of social work, through individual practice, social policy, and/or advocacy, is to challenge the barriers that keep various "strangers" from exercising their rights as citizens and to aid them in the quest to realize their personal goals. Ware and associates (2007) define social integration "as a process, unfolding over time, through which individuals who have been psychiatrically disabled increasingly develop and exercise their capacities for connectedness and citizenship" (p. 471).

In mental health, as in other similar fields, it is important to draw a distinction between impairment and disability (Burchardt, 2004; Race, Boxall, & Carson, 2005). Burchardt (2004) considers impairment to be "a condition of the body or mind," while disability "is the loss or limitation of opportunities to take part in the life of the community on an equal level with others" (p. 736). When focusing on impairments, various therapeutic and rehabilitative interventions are used to treat or compensate for the identified malady. In contrast, disability, as construed above, can be viewed as a matter of social justice and, hence, elements of the physical environment, values, attitudes, social mores, and public policies come into play.

When considering mental illness, if the challenge of social integration is viewed as the consequence of individual impairment, then standard interventions, such as psychotherapy or its variants and medication, will be preferred interventions. If it is believed that the forces of exclusion and discrimination are the main culprits, social action and advocacy should follow (Ware et al., 2007).

Effective practice is buttressed when public policy and public attitudes are aligned and affirm the right and desirability of creating opportunities for all people to contribute to community life and well-being. Yet, creating opportunities for disenfranchised people and, in the process, slowly changing attitudes and values is a drama played out each day, person by person. As opposed to a forced choice between impairment or disability, the search for the perfect niche is a strength-based approach that rests on the recognition and exploitation of individual capabilities and environmental opportunities.

In the real world of practice there is much to overcome. Erdner, Magnusson, and Nystrom (2005) argue that the persistent and negative attitudes held by others foster a sense of alienation among individuals with mental illnesses. Always an outsider, the person becomes estranged from others and often leads a lonely life. Additionally, the negative image of self by others can be accepted, and through his or her own action or paralysis, one unwittingly contributes to the alienation.

As a social process, stigma is widely viewed as a powerful force that leads to discrimination and the constricting of opportunities and rights. Grajerud and Severinsson (2006) suggest that the experience of stigma increases the sense of living on the margins of society. Not only does this increase anxiety, but it is related to "the feeling that one is not needed, lacking the ability to be gainfully employed, not feeling involved in contributing to society, low income and that contact with others only occurs via health professionals" (pp. 290–291).

While public education campaigns and protests have occasional successes, contact between people and the party being discriminated against has shown the most consistent positive effects (Corrigan et al., 2001; Deforges et al., 1991; Holmes et al., 1999; Link & Cullen, 1986) and that the changes seem to be maintained over time (Corrigan, Markowitz, Watson, Rowan, & Kubiak, 2003). This means that service delivery approaches that emphasize access to naturally occurring resources may very well have an effect on reducing stigma. For example, supported employment that arranges competitive jobs and normal wages is not only more effective at achieving employment goals than sheltered work progress but may be "stigma-busting" as well. This may be true for supported housing vs. group homes, mainstream classroom education vs. segregated special education classes, and where opportunities exist for fun and recreation outside of mental health sponsored and chaperoned activities.

The relationship between mental health and social support has been well documented. Lin, Ye, and Ensel (1999) argue that different layers of structure, from the neighborhood to interpersonal ties, create the "bases on which certain support functions (e.g., instrumental and expressive support) may be elicited" (p. 344). They contend that participation and involvement in community life contributes to the sense of belongingness, when ties and networks are formed as a result of this interaction, bonding relationships are formed, and finally the close, intimate, and intense ties that may follow constitute binding relationships.

The recovery journey may be a slow and arduous one and ultimately is an individual *and* social process. Social integration for those facing mental illnesses and others on the margin is a lofty goal, nevertheless, consistent with the strengths perspective; big goals are accomplished via the smallest of steps. Grajerud and Severinsson (2006) suggest "to be an active participant in a social situation, for example, in a club or working environment, leads to a sense of belonging and promotes group solidarity, cultural harmony, the opportunity to participate in new groups, and to experience mutual support where everyone helps each other" (p. 289). The impact of a simple activity like serving as a volunteer or returning to school can have a range of positive effects on the life of an individual. Berkman, Glass, Brissette, and Seeman (2000) posit:

> Participation and engagement result from the enactment of potential ties in real life activity. . . . through opportunities for engagement, social networks define and reinforce meaningful social roles . . . which provide a sense of belonging and attachment. Those roles that provide each individual with a coherent and consistent sense of identity are only possible because of the network context which provides the theatre in which role performances take place. (p. 849)

The importance of opportunities, to draw from a bedrock principle of the strengths perspective, equal access to resources, cannot be minimized. In considering the struggle to make social integration and citizenship become a reality, Ware and associates (2007) draw from the capabilities framework devised by Nobel Prize–winning economist Amartya Sen. Capability is operationally defined as a

> Degree of human agency—what people can actually do and be in everyday life. What people can do and be is in turn contingent on having competencies and opportunities. Opportunities are provided by social environments. To ensure capability, social circumstances must offer opportunities for individual competency to be developed and exercised . . . individual development is contingent of supportive social environments, and . . . core concepts of competency and opportunity in delineating the process through which social integration develops. (p. 470)

If it is agreed that recovery and social integration provide the foundation for an inspiring mission for mental health services, the challenge is to breathe life into this effort. There are three approaches to helping, or three levels of setting where clients served by social workers commonly receive services to improve their lives (see Figure 12.2). The first level

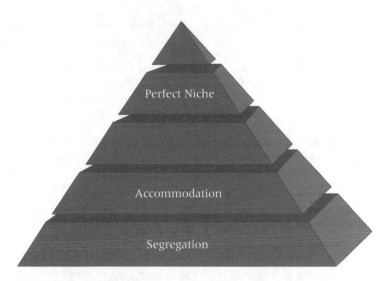

FIGURE 12.2   Three Levels of Service/Setting

contains settings that are segregated, usually by the problem, status, or affliction being confronted by the client. This would include total institutions like nursing homes, psychiatric hospitals, and residential treatment facilities, but also includes sheltered workshops, group homes, day treatment, special education classes, etc.

The second level focuses on attempts to alter natural community resources and settings to accommodate the particular needs and desires of clients. Examples could include using a teacher's aide in mainstream classes to help a disabled student; simplifying the flow of work so a person with a developmental disability can perform a particular job, and apartment programs that have on-site staff available for support. In general, the process is one of identifying a desirable resource/setting and making changes (sometime quite small) in that environment so that it "works" for the client.

The third level, perfect niches, are those in which you do not change the individual or the environment. It is where "the requirements and needs of the setting are perfectly matched with the desires, talents, and even idiosyncrasies of the person" (Rapp & Goscha, 2006, p. 168), or where these idiosyncrasies are irrelevant. Consider the following case examples drawn from real-life examples in the practice of strengths-based case management.

Jack, a middle-aged man diagnosed with schizophrenia, had been receiving services at the mental health center for many years. He had been committed to a state psychiatric hospital on several occasions, but in recent years, when in crisis he was admitted to the local general hospital for short-term care. Jack had tried to live independently, but at the moment was a resident in the center's apartment program. He often expressed a desire to work, and when pressed, he commonly noted that his goal was to be a banker. For years his dream had been dismissed as unrealistic and delusional. Luckily, a newly assigned case manager took Jack seriously and began to explore this option. In conversation, Jack recognized that he would need to pay greater attention to his personal appearance. The case manager accompanied Jack to the local Goodwill store and helped him select a relatively inexpensive suit.

Drawing from a small pool of funds at her disposal, the case manager purchased the suit. With some trepidation, but with the support of the case manager, Jack approached a local bank and inquired about any possibilities for volunteer work. To the surprise of many, the bank offered Jack a chance to perform an important job, but one that often was overlooked and avoided by staff. Several times a week Jack would put on his new suit, walk to the bank and deposit all the available change in the sorter that created rolls of coins. The bank was so pleased with Jack's performance that they turned this into a paid position.

Another case example highlights how an astute case management team worked with a person to recast what most viewed as an annoying idiosyncrasy into a marketable skill.

Jillian had been coming to the center so long that her tenure exceeded all but the most senior staff member. She could be best described as doing "okay." It had been years since her last hospitalization, but her life consisted of hours sitting in the clubhouse and occasional participation in programs offered in the partial hospital program. Nonetheless, she was familiar to all for her familiar refrain, "Hello, how you doing?" It was something she might ask of the same person five times in a day, or once again after having passed him or her in the hall just seconds before. Some found the trait amusing, most ignored her, while some, particularly other program participants, were annoyed. At a team meeting, a case manager asked, in rhetorical fashion, what might be the cause of this behavior. Another team member, intrigued by the question decided to explore it further. Meeting with Jillian he began to understand just how lonely she was, how before her first episode that she loved to be around people and was the type that could easily strike up conversations with complete strangers. Prompted by an idea he asked, "How would you like the chance to meet more people?" With a spark rarely, if ever, seen, Jillian looked up and said, "I would love to." Working together the case manager and Jillian hit on an idea. Her natural inclinations all pointed to the possibility that she could serve as a formal greeter. The center has had success in employment opportunities at a nearby upscale hotel, and management was more than willing to give Jillian a trial run at this role. The job came complete with a hotel uniform, and before her first day, Jillian attended training on the expectations and requirements of the job. It was a perfect fit. With guidance, some of the problematic aspects of her interpersonal style were smoothed over, and soon she had worked into a full-time job. Soon her involvement with the mental health center was reduced to medication checkups and occasional support services.

In many respects the case examples offered above represent the end product of a great investment in time and energy on the part of both parties. In the following section, various aspects of the process of strengths-based practice are placed under the microscope.

NICHE ENRICHMENT AND DEVELOPMENT: MOBILIZING PERSONAL AND ENVIRONMENTAL STRENGTHS; A CLOSER LOOK

At the beginning of this chapter it was noted that interest in the strengths model has exploded, and this is particularly so in the area of clinical or therapeutic services. In the realm of direct practice there has been a great deal of work in such areas as designing assessment and interviewing tools, employing methods that enhance client motivation and interest in change, and in the process of goal and case planning that would be consistent with a strengths model.

Returning to Figure 12.1, these efforts have largely focused on the left side of the equation—those attributes, attitudes, and behaviors on the part of individuals that can contribute to "niche" enrichment and personal development. It would stand to reason that competent professionals would be interested in discerning those attitudes and actions that can enhance the important work of consumers. In the immediate sections to follow some attention will be devoted to these concerns. However, to be true to the strengths model, attention must also be devoted to the right side of Figure 12.1, and here the attention shifts to methods and models concerned with the identification and acquisition of social resources consumers need to accomplish goals that they deem important to their life. Again examples from mental health practice will be used for illustration.

Professional-Consumer Relationships

We will begin this exploration with a discussion of one basic environmental interchange, but one vitally important to consumers—the helping relationship. When people are involved in professional services, it is usually a difficult time in their life. Being under care reflects a sentiment held by self or others that, at the present, it is impossible for the individual to carry forth of his or her own volition. For many people the period is marked by one of the most profound of human emotions— despair. Despair is the feeling of being cast adrift in a world filled with the darkest of emotions and left without means of escape. A ubiquitous element in the recovery matrix is hope—a feeling at the polar opposite of despair. As an emotional state, hope reflects a bedrock belief in a better future and the inherent promise that cherished goals can be realized. First-person accounts of the process of recovery confirm that hope is an indispensable ingredient for success:

> When one lives without hope, (when one has given up), the willingness to "do" is paralyzed as well (Deegan, 1988, p. 13).
> Hope is crucial to recovery, for our despair disables us more than our disease ever could (Leete, 1993, p. 122).
> My mood changed—I was happy and hopeful once again (Fergeson, 1992, p. 29).
> I find myself being a role model for other clients and am only a bit uncomfortable with this. For the first time, I begin to feel real hope (Grimmer, 1992, p. 28).
> Success will never be realized if it cannot be imagined (Leete, 1993, p. 126).

Ideally, an encounter between a professional and a consumer should be hope provoking. So many consumers have faced a constant string of disappointments and have been dissuaded from goals that they have held dear. How might hope be reactivated? An exhaustive discussion of interpersonal practice will not be attempted—instead, a few basic themes will be introduced with the prospect that this short discussion will stimulate further inquiry into this essential phase of helping.

Virtually all methods of assessment in the helping professions focus on exploring the contours and textures of a person's problems, deficits, maladies, and pathology (Cowger, 1997). This process, in which client's have to recall their inadequacies, is far from hope-inducing and, worse still, can actually increase the sense of despair. In recent years, specialized assessments tools, geared to capture the competencies, goals, and dreams of consumers (Cowger, 1997; McQuaide & Ehrenreich, 1997; Rapp & Goscha, 2006). have been developed to support strengths-based practice. Without question these assessments direct the attention of consumers (and practitioners) to different aspects of the consumer's life. It gives the consumer a chance to reveal what has gone well in his or her life, what he or she enjoys, and what he or she still hopes to do. Much of the magic that can happen rests on the nature of the interaction between the client and professional, not the quality of the tool that is used.

Strengths assessments, or the process of strengths discovery, is an ongoing and fluid process that evolves as the relationship develops, more is learned, and comfort increases. The data that is gleaned is different from that generated from more traditional assessment processes—it involves an inventory of current and former activities, interests, goals, dreams, friends, favorite haunts and people, spiritual interests—all designed to paint a picture and tell a story—it is expansive, not reductionist.

Facilitating Purpose

While hope may be the core ingredient to the helping process, the next step is perhaps the most crucial—translating this renewed optimism into action. Accordingly, a critical task for those in helping roles is to help facilitate the sense of purpose in the lives of consumers.

For those facing the most stringent of challenges, the intrinsic desire to attack each day has been vanquished. Consider this bleak portrait of mental illness: "I have nothing to live for, no drive but to just exist. . . . Sometimes I sleep 12 to 14 hours because there's nothing else to do. No zest" (Stanley, 1992, p. 25). This respondent's observation is shared by many struggling through mental illnesses and other difficult life challenges, but the steps taken by many of these individuals to start on the road back are particularly instructive.

> And so I took my dreams off the back burner and claimed them as my personal goals, understanding, writing and doing something to help others who were afflicted. Doing so was neither grandiose or magnanimous. It was survival (Keil, 1992, p. 6).
>
> One short term goal was to further myself educationally, and I took buses to get to college (Reilly, 1992, p. 20).
>
> You can live through any kind of a situation, if you find a reason for living through it. We survivors were daily living through impossible situations precisely by finding reasons for living (Fergeson, 1992, p. 30).
>
> With Mark's death, I was snapped into a new awareness that resulted in my not only caring about others, but having a cause worth fighting for (Risser, 1992, p. 39).

Human services vary widely in the degree to which they facilitate or suppress purpose. In many environs, our programs and interventions are directed toward survival and maintenance. People are asked to adopt "clienthood" as their primary role, or passively accept the recommendations of experts. Other programs create environments rich with opportunities for clients to contribute and feel that there is purpose in what they do. Any review of the success of support groups, consumer-directed programs, or vibrant community development activities underscores the importance of creating opportunities for people to serve in important and meaningful roles—oftentimes focused on helping others. In some situations, people are pressed into service because there are more important roles to be filled than people to fill them. Barker (1960) referred to such settings as undermanned, while more recently Rappaport,

Reischl, and Zimmerman (1992) have used the gender-neutral term *underpopulated*. Not surprisingly, good community developers are wise to harness the talents of residents and move them quickly to positions with significant responsibility and leadership functions.

Returning to Figure 12.1, a key force in niche enrichment comes from the expansion of individual talents and skills. Historically, the prime vehicles to help consumers in this life domain have been structured training programs or in treatment settings, skill-building exercises, and groups. It is certain that these efforts have been helpful to many. On the downside, teaching people skills in a laboratory is similar to teaching history as a series of facts and dates without proper context. Education, strictly speaking, works better when there are chances to practice in real life. Here, people often must stretch, that is, assume unaccustomed responsibilities that force them to learn additional skills. In daily life, people often speak of "growing with the job." Such risk taking helps people gain a sense of mastery and prepares them to consider future challenges that will aid in their personal development.

This method of self-enrichment, and by extension, niche enlargement is only possible if people are afforded real opportunities and real-life settings. The deficit perspective, in contrast, rests on the identification of the real or perceived inabilities of people. Once identified and labeled, these individual deficits can become insurmountable barriers to people's prospering, especially when coupled with an inflexible and inhospitable social milieu. Consider the central role of work—long noted as a key step in the recovery from mental illness. Traditional vocational programming found in many health programs, captured by the phrase "food, filth, and folding," does not mitigate this issue. For work to significantly contribute to recovery, it must provide a connection to mainstream cultural activities and symbols. Traditional work programs, such as in-house services or enclaves, *may* be important steps toward recovery but do so by building confidence and skills and by providing structure and modeling opportunities. The argument here is that this should not routinely be considered an end or desired state.

In the field of mental health, increased attention is being paid to mobilizing environmental strengths and a growing empirical base supporting it. Five social interventions have been designated as evidence-based practices for adults with psychiatric disabilities: assertive community treatment (ACT), family psychoeducation (FPE), supported employment (SE), integrated dual diagnosis treatment (IDDT), and illness management and recovery (IMR). Each of these practices views the environment as a resource:

> FPE provides a forum and a structure whereby families and others can enhance their ability to provide support by increasing their understanding and by employing a problem-solving orientation. ACT prescribes that team members work with landlords, employees, teachers, coaches, and families so that they are able to support consumers as they create the type of life in the community that they desire. SE focuses on assisting consumers in the process of obtaining and keeping regular competitive jobs in the community. Many of the practices, such as job development, job accommodations, and follow-along supports, are directed to work with employers. IDDT prescribes work with consumers' social networks and families as necessary to help consumers modify their behavior. IMR encourages family members or friends to help the consumer pursue his or her goals and creates environmental cues to remember to take medications (e.g., notes strategically placed, audio cues from alarm clocks, or pairing the timing of taking medication with other daily routines such as brushing teeth). (Rapp & Goscha, 2006, p. 208)

THE MATCH GAME: ALIGNING INDIVIDUAL
AND ENVIRONMENTAL STRENGTHS

Fostering a sense of hope and facilitating purpose are key ingredients in any successful professional helping relationship and should be desired outcomes at all phases of the process of care. It is vitally important that the early phases of helping, notably the assessment process, stimulate this response in individuals and families. Faithfully executed, any strengths discovery process should meet this standard, and there are several models of strengths-based assessment to choose from (see Cowger, 1997; Graybeal, 2001; McQuaide & Ehrenreich, 1997; Rapp & Goscha, 2006).

Rapp and Goscha (2006) have noted some key differences between strengths assessments and what might be tabbed the traditional or dominant model of assessment. One key difference is found in the end product. Where traditional assessments may help narrow down the specifics of a client's problem or malady—or even lead to a diagnosis—the strengths assessment is designed first and foremost to discover the client's wants, desires, dreams, and goals and does so from an ethnographic perspective. Hence, it is the consumer or family or community, not the professional who drives the process. Furthermore, the assessment considers a wide range of life domains, including work, leisure, social supports, health, and spirituality, and explores past and current aspirations, as well as those specific to each area. The intent is to use this assessment, which is viewed as an ongoing process, to decipher a range of possible life goals that can be the focus of the helping relationship.

Intriguingly, the *process* of strengths discovery may be more valuable than the initial document that is generated. The ability of the practitioner to tease out the dreams, desires, and wishes of consumers is indispensable to success. From here the consumer/professional team explores past activities and interests in key life domains and begins an initial inventory of community resources that are essential for consumers to realize their goals and dreams.

As a dynamic tool, the strengths assessment should aid the delineation of consumer goals in key life domains (work, housing, health, leisure, etc.). These goals should be tailored to the specific needs of the clients ranging in degree of difficulty and level of specificity. At times additional supports are needed, like job coaches or mentors, but these services are still geared to augment consumer strengths and reflect an appreciation of the innate ability of all consumers to work.

Thus, by simple modifications in the environment, a context is created for the individual to experience success. So, at each successive step, beginning at the level of the one-to-one relationship, involvement with social agencies, to the first steps back into community, supports, feedback, and experience interact with the drive and will of consumers to succeed.

For those well versed in strengths-based helping, the material above is familiar. For social workers, the humanistic aspect of strengths-based practice had immediate appeal. Shifting focus from the flawed to the healthy aspects of individuals and families also seemed to ring true with practice wisdom. However, truly operationalizing the key values of the strengths perspective is far more difficult than meets the eye for, as Blundo (2001) has observed, staying true to the model requires "a real shift in orientation or basic viewpoint rather than merely adding a component" (p. 302). In terms of assessment, a component has been added when a section on client strengths has been appended to the end of a traditional assessment form but little else changes, or when a practitioner devotes some attention to the goals and dreams of consumers but steadfastly believes that no progress can be made on such goals until the focal problem has been eradicated or reduced. This is traditional practice cloaked in strength's language. The pull to attend to problems and deficits is omnipresent, and for many it is believed that more proactive work cannot proceed until such issues are dealt with. The strengths assessment represents an ongoing effort to build from a different base and constantly searches for clues that can be used to tie a consumer's aspirations and goals to an environmental resource that can move the person toward greater health and satisfaction and to expand the avenues of available support that can be called upon in times of need.

There is little question that there are many facets of clinical social work practice that have been enhanced by the current interest in the strengths perspective. Nonetheless, the strengths model is also compromised, as a reviewing of the keystone assumptions would indicate, when practice focuses solely on the soul and psyche of the individual and ignores the resources and opportunities available in the social environment. Far too often, social workers hold a narrow view of the range of resources available to people served—and in nearly any social agency anywhere in the United States and likely around the globe, most lament the lack of such resources. The problem is that most practitioners, even those versed in the strengths model, engage in a deficits-based match game. Here the perceived problem or challenge a consumer faces is matched with the specialized resources designed to offset the identified condition. In simple terms, a client in need is routinely and automatically matched with a social service in spite of the reality that the demand for such services routinely outstrips the availability of these services. Some individuals clearly need these specialized services while others do not, but in essence social workers always face a log jam, one that can paralyze them and those they serve. Is there a way out?

The match game, played by strengths rules, is a far different process—one that may be more difficult and time consuming, but one that hopefully leads to better long-term results. First, the strengths assessment, as noted above, should lead to a distinct and unique set of consumer goals, and to help realize these goals it is often necessary to access a wide range of normally occurring community resources. These resources are not specialized and designed to serve clients but rather are the whole host of community offerings available to all citizens. Furthermore, these community resources may not be a business or an organization at all but a person or a park, a family, or an Internet chat group. When resources are so conceived, a world of possibilities is revealed—a world that expands well beyond a tattered and dog-eared resource book that rarely has time to rest on the bookshelf of a harried social worker. Helping clients gain access to community resources usually occurs on a case-by-case basis and that alone is why it is far easier to follow predictable routes and use tailor-made services. It is for this reason that the strengths discovery process should be broadened beyond the individual and family and must include an inventory of the possible resources in the immediate social environment with an emphasis on those that seem directly relevant to the clients' goals.

Mapping Community Assets

Kretzmann and McKnight's (1993) model of community development, particularly the method of identifying and mapping community assets, provides an important template for practitioners and programs who strive to assess strengths in the social environment. This process focuses on three key levels: the gifts of individuals, citizen's associations, and local institutions. As noted above, a central premise of this model is that those often overlooked—youth, older adults, and labeled people—should be viewed as assets to a community, not liabilities. Indeed, any strengths assessment should be designed to capture those abilities and interests that both serve individuals well in their future endeavors and may prove to be a benefit to the community as well. Any strengths and assets inventory should include not only formal organizations and groups, but churches, various clubs, athletic programs, and cultural groups should not be ignored. Finally, local institutions, business, schools, and other education programs, as well as other social service programs located within the community must also be identified.

A review of the central tenets of assets-based community development mirrors, in a larger frame, guiding principles of strengths-based practice. First, community development "starts with what is present in the community, the capacities of its residents and workers, the associational and institutional base of the area—not what is absent or what is problematic, or what the community needs" (Kretzmann & McKnight, 1993, p. 9). Second, the model is "internally focused," seeking solutions to problems first at the local level. Finally, the model is "relationship driven" and an important thrust of the work is to "build and rebuild the relationships between and among local residents, local associations and local institutions" (Kretzmann & McKnight, 1993, p. 9).

The parallel between assets-based development and strengths-based practice underscores why these apparently disparate activities should be tightly coupled. Unfortunately, given the narrow manner in which some individual challenges are understood, the relevance of any community level intervention is routinely overlooked. For example, it is undoubtedly true that serious and persistent mental illnesses are conditions impacted greatly by mysteries of the brain and body that we have yet to uncover. However, the process of recovery from these same illnesses cannot be left to science alone as the solutions to the real-world problems people face as a result of illness—areas such as friendship, love, and meaningful work—are directly tied to the world around them.

CONCLUSION

Resource acquisition and advocacy have always been central themes in the strengths perspective. From the beginning these activities have been highlighted as important to bringing the model alive. For many of us, taking advantage of the opportunities that surround us are second nature—sadly, for others, the process is painfully difficult.

There are several key questions and activities that can guide the resource acquisition effort in a manner that addresses both individual and community need (Rapp & Goscha, 2006). It is important to note that the process of matching consumer goals with resources is often a creative effort. Locating such resources is critical given the reality that most specialized helping resources are scarce, expensive, and in the final analysis may not forward the goals and dreams of consumers as adequately as those outside the human service world.

The first step is to consider what formal and informal resources exist to help a consumer meet a stated goal. A simple goal, such as learning to cook nutritious meals, could involve an in-house program, a community education course, formal university training, or finding a retired person in the community who would be willing to help. Some of these possible solutions will never be known if there hasn't been an effort to explore a wide range of nontraditional sources for the help people need.

Second, it is crucial to consider how accessing a resource may benefit others, including those not affiliated with the program. Drawing from the example above, it may be that some older adults would enjoy the companionship of others, and offering assistance to a consumer who is learning to cook may also help fulfill their desire to continue to make a worthwhile contribution to the community. In this case the ability to cook is a talent or gift—one that could be shared with others. In this process the consumer is linked to the larger community, not a specialized world saturated with other clients and professionals. In specialized work programs for those with mental illness, notably supported employment, organizations often benefit by securing a cadre of eager, reliable, and committed workers, and as a result, it is a win-win situation for all parties concerned (Anthony & Blanch, 1988).

Hopefully, other stakeholders will begin to view marginalized citizens and the organizations that support them as true community assets. Getting to this point will likely take some time given the wide range of clientele social workers serve. Given this reality, it is wise to assume that barriers will be encountered as consumers attempt to gain access to the resources they need. Here relationships must be established and maintained, staff must be seen as dependable and trustworthy, and necessary supports must be available to clients to help ensure their success. When working with consumers who are likely to raise community anxiety, it is important to ascertain who the true gatekeepers to community resources are and to work to develop a relationship with these same individuals, maintain the lines of communication, and seize every opportunity to recognize and reward those who have gone the extra mile accommodating the clients you serve. There are times when those we serve will be discriminated against on the basis of their challenge, and here a range of more active advocacy efforts, including invoking legal standards may be necessary (Rapp & Goscha, 2006).

The quest is twofold. First, social workers accept that their primary responsibility is to the consumer. With this in mind, social agencies must endeavor to put consumers center stage and ensure that programs and policies are designed for the benefit of those they serve, not simply for their convenience. Here, consumer input is gathered on all fronts and this data is used to alter the day-by-day operations of the agency.

Social workers and human service agencies also have a responsibility to the communities that host them and an obligation to help shape those environments where people live, learn, work, and play, in a fashion that supports individual and collective welfare. Individual and social development is inextricably intertwined and when both are advanced individuals and communities prosper.

Community capacity has been defined as:

> the interaction of human capital, organizational resources, and social capital existing within a given community that can be leveraged to solve collective problems and improve or maintain the well-being of that community. It may operate through informal social processes and/or organized efforts by individuals, organizations, and social networks that exist among them and between them and the larger systems of which the community is a part. (Chaskin, Brown, Venkatesh, & Vidal, 2001, p. 7)

In essence, one of the impossible missions that social workers have accepted is to ensure that no one is ever left behind. At times, it seems like an isolated fight, one that is contested in a world of indifference. This work suggests that one fruitful strategy is to change the rules of engagement by linking the best of strengths-based practice with cutting-edge models in community development with a single goal in mind—to enhance the capacity of individuals and society by recognizing and tapping the talents and gifts of marginalized citizens and to nourish the generative tendencies in the social environment. In the end, each of us strives for the perfect niche.

DISCUSSION QUESTIONS/EXERCISES

1. What does it mean to say that human development is a transactional process that occurs within a social context?

2. How would you describe a social niche?

3. What is the nature of the relationship between individuals and environments in the strengths perspective?

4. Part of a strengths approach to service is facilitating purpose in the lives of consumers. What does that mean? Can you give an example?

5. What is the perfect niche?

REFERENCES

Anthony, W. & Blanch, A. (1988). Supported employment for persons who are psychiatrically disabled: An historical and conceptual perspective. *Psychosocial Rehabilitation Journal, 11*(2), 5–23.

Barker, R. G. (1960). Ecology and motivation. In M. R. Jones (Ed.), *Nebraska Symposium on Motivation.* Lincoln, NB: University of Nebraska Press.

Berkman, L., Glass, T., Brissette, I., & Seeman, T. (2000). From social integration to health: Durkheim in the new millennium. *Social Science & Medicine, 51*, 843–857.

Blundo, R. (2001). Learning strengths-based practice: Challenging our personal and professional frames. *Families in Society, 82*(3), 296–304.

Burchardt, T. (2004). Capabilities and disabilities: The capabilities framework and the social model of disability. *Disability and Society, 19*(7), 735–751.

Chaskin, R., Brown, P., Venkatesh, S., & Vidal, A. (2001). *Building community capacity.* New York: Aldine De Gruyter.

Corrigan, P. W., Markowitz, F. E., Watson, A. C., Rowan, D., & Kubiak, M.A. (2003). An attribution model of public discrimination towards persons with mental illness. *Journal of Health and Social Behavior, 44*, 162–179.

Corrigan, P. W., River, L., Lundin, R.K., Penn, D. L., Uphoff-Wasowski, K., & Campoin, J. (2001). Three strategies for changing attributions about severe mental illness. *Schizophrenia Bulletin, 27*, 187–195.

Cowger, C. (1997). Assessing client strengths: Assessing for client empowerment. In D. Saleebey (Ed.), *The strengths perspective in social work practice* (2nd ed., pp. 59–73). New York: Longman.

Davidson, W. S. & Rapp, C. (1976). Child advocacy in the justice system. *Social Work, 21*(3), 225–232.

Deegan, P. E. (1988). Recovery: The lived experience of rehabilitation. *Psychosocial Rehabilitation Journal, 11*, 11–19.

Desforges, D. M., Lord, C. G., Ramsey, S. L., Mason, J. A., Van Lueewen, M. D., & West, S. C. (1991). Effects of structured cooperative contact on changing negative attitudes toward stigmatized social groups. *Journal of Personality and Social Psychology, 60*, 531–544.

Erdner, A., Magnusson, A., & Nystrom, M. (2005). Social and existential alienation experienced by people with long term mental illness. *Scandinavian Journal of Caring Sciences, 19*, 373–380.

Faris, R. & Dunham, H. W. (1939). *Mental disorders in urban areas.* Chicago: University of Chicago Press.

Fergesen, D. (1992). In the company of heroes. *The Journal, 3*, 29.

Grajerud, A. & Severinsson, E. (2006). The struggle for social integration in the community—the experience of people with mental problems. *Journal of Psychiatric & Mental Health Nursing, 13*, 288–293.

Graybeal, C. (2001). Strengths-based social work assessment: Transforming the dominant paradigm. *Families in Society, 82*(3), 233–242.

Grimmer, D. (1992). The invisible illness. *The Journal, 3*, 27–28.

Holmes, E. P., Corrigan, P. W., Williams, P., Canar, J., & Kubiak, M. (1999). Changing public attitudes about schizophrenia. *Schizophrenia Bulletin, 25*, 447–456.

Keil, J. (1992). The mountain of my mental illness. *The Journal, 3*, 5–6.

Kretzmann, J. & McKnight, J. (1993). *Building communities from the inside out: A path towards finding and mobilizing community assets.* Evanston, IL: Center for Urban Affairs and Policy Research. Neighborhood Innovations Network. Northwestern University.

Leete, E. (1993). The interpersonal environment: A consumer's personal recollection. In A. B. Hatfield & H. P. Lefley (Eds.), *Surviving mental illness* (pp. 114–128). New York: Guilford Press.

Lin, N., Ye, X., & Ensel, W. (1999). Social support and depressed mood: A structural analysis. *Journal of Health and Social Behavior, 40*, 344–359.

McQuaide, S. & Ehrenreich, J. H. (1997). Assessing client strengths. *Families in Society, 78*(2), 201–212.

Race, D., Boxall, K., & Carson, I. (2005). Towards a dialogue for practice: Reconciling social role valorization and the social model of disability. *Disability & Society, 20*(5), 507–521.

Rapp, C. A. & Goscha, R. J. (2006). *The strengths model: Case management with people with psychiatric disabilities* (2nd ed.). New York: Oxford University Press.

Rappaport, J., Reischl, T., & Zimmerman, M. (1992). Mutual help mechanisms in the empowerment of former mental patients. In D. Saleebey (Ed.), *The strengths perspective in social work practice* (pp. 84–97). New York: Longman.

Reilly, S. (1992). Breaking loose. *The Journal, 3*, 20.

Risser, P. A. (1992). An empowering journey. *The Journal, 3*, 38–39.

Roach, J. (1993). Clinical case management with severely mentally ill adults. In M. Harris & H. Bergman (Eds.), *Case management for mentally ill patients* (pp.17–40). Langhorne, PA: Harwood Academic Publishers.

Saleebey, D. (2002). Community development, group empowerment, and individual resilience. In D. Saleebey (Ed.), *The strengths perspective in social work practice* (3rd ed., pp. 228–246). New York: Longman.

Saleebey, D. (2004). "The power of place": Another look at the environment. *Families in Society, 85*(1), 7–16.

Stanley, R. (1992). Welcome to reality—Not a facsimile. *The Journal, 3*, 25–26.

Taylor, J. (1997). Niches and practice: Extending the ecological perspective. In D. Saleebey (Ed.), *The strengths perspective in social work practice* (2nd ed., pp. 217–227). New York: Longman.

Thyer, B. & Myers, L. (1998). Social learning theory: An empirically-based approach to understanding human behavior in the social environment. *Journal of Human Behavior in the Social Environment, 1*(1), 23–32.

Torrey, E. F. & Yolken, R. (1998). Is household crowding a risk factor for schizophrenia and bipolar disorder? *Schizophrenia Bulletin, 24*(3), 321–324.

Wakefield, J. (1996). Does social work need the eco-systems perspective? Part 1. Is the perspective clinically useful? *Social Service Review, 70*(1), 1–32.

Ware, N., Hopper, K., Tugenberg, T., Dickey, B., & Fisher, D. (2007). Connectedness and citizenship: Redefining social integration. *Psychiatric Services, 58*(4), 469–474.

Webster's New World Dictionary (second college edition). Buralnik, D. B. (Ed.). (1979). New York: World Publishing.

CHAPTER THIRTEEN

EXPLORING THE TRUE NATURE OF INTERNAL RESILIENCE

A View from the Inside Out

JACK PRANSKY

DIANE P. McMILLEN

There can be no greater strength than the strength that exists automatically and naturally within each and every human being.

—Jack Pransky

The significance of this statement cannot be underestimated. It has profound implications for how those operating in the fields of social work, human services, and prevention approach their work from a strengths-based perspective. It has profound implications for how we work with individuals, families, communities, and organizations, and for outcomes.

Readers of this book already know the advantages of working from a strengths-based rather than a deficit-based approach. We, the authors of this chapter, suggest it is equally important to further look at where we believe people's strengths truly come from and how those strengths become manifest. We can look in two different directions: We can see people's strengths coming to them either from the outside in or emerging from the inside out. This chapter offers what it means to see and work from an inside out perspective.

STRENGTHS FROM THE OUTSIDE IN

From a traditional, outside in perspective, strengths are built, taught, or given to people. People are provided the information needed to make informed decisions. Skills are built to ensure these are healthy, responsible decisions. Supports are provided to help people gain the strength to actually make and follow through with those decisions. Healthy environments are constructed to ensure people are nurtured in ways so that they feel capable and important and have the power to affect what happens to them in life. Community members are helped to organize to solve their common problems (Pransky, 2001/1991). These are all very worthy pursuits and a great leap from focusing on overcoming risk factors. Yet the outside in strengths-building approach may also carry with it, inadvertently, the very subtle message that people lack something that they need to gain from outside themselves. For example, if we say people need life skills to make it in an untidy, dangerous world, are we assuming, subtly, that they presently lack something that we must provide for them to make them okay? Or, if children grow up in an unhealthy environment, are we saying, subtly, that they won't make it unless that environment improves or they find a supportive mentor who can guide them out of their plight? At the very least this is food for thought.

STRENGTHS FROM THE INSIDE OUT

Looking at strengths from the inside out is very different from the above norm. Here we begin with the premise that everyone at their core, at their essence, within their soul, is pure "health," pure love, and has pure peace of mind and pure wisdom. In other words, at their essence *people already are everything they are looking for.* Everyone has the strength or natural capacity innately, built into the very fabric of their being, to rise above unhealthy circumstances and transcend their problems. Many people, of course, do not exactly walk around looking like they operate from this state of "health." What if the only reason for this is because they use their very own thinking, inadvertently, to obscure their own essence, to cover it up, so it appears hidden (Pransky, 2003)? Yet, when their minds calm down or their heads clear, their mental health and wisdom become unveiled. When people realize this is who they truly are inside, and it is only hidden from view because of their own thoughts, their typical thinking tends to relinquish its grip, and this natural capacity, with all its built-in traits, automatically and naturally rises to the surface. It is much like letting go of a beach ball under water —because it is buoyant, the real work is holding it down.

We assert that what people already have inside them is their greatest strength. People are capable of realizing this and what gets in the way of this understanding. When they do, they are freed from the prison of their own minds, and their well-being and wisdom appear and begin to guide them through life. With this realization, an individual's strength gets illuminated and seems to magnify. It begins to affect others around him or her. It then ripples out to affect communities and organizations. When practitioners in the fields of social work and human services, prevention and resiliency, come to understand what it truly means to see from the perspective of and work from the inside out there is limitless potential. When this occurs, the possibility of individual, community, and societal change moves to far deeper level.

This chapter will introduce readers to this exciting new understanding and approach to helping. We hope readers will see how everyone has the potential for well-being and wisdom and to live in a world of possibility.

HOW THIS NEW UNDERSTANDING EMERGED

The precipitating event in the evolution of this understanding in the fields of prevention and human services occurred in the autumn of 1987 when Dr. Roger Mills walked into the Modello Housing Project for the first time. This was a community beset with all the problems associated with poverty and racism. He arrived with great hope, buoyed from having had deep personal insights about his own life after being exposed to the philosophy of Sydney Banks (1998), who had a spontaneous epiphany of extraordinary proportions that had completely changed his life and the lives of others around him. Having been trained as a community psychologist, Mills wanted to translate what he learned from Banks into a completely new, inside out approach to community change (which later became known as "health realization," "innate health," a "principle-based understanding," or "The Three Principles"). Most of the people who sincerely wanted to create change in this inhospitable housing project near Miami, Florida, considered his approach crazy. They said his ideas would never work. They said he was approaching the task backwards. "Dr. Mills," they argued, "with all due respect, what does self-esteem or people's thoughts have to do with the fact that their roofs are falling in, that they're dodging bullets on the way home, that their kids are involved with drugs, that their old man is beating on them and sleeping with their daughter? All these terrible things are going on in their lives. What does this have to do with 'thought,' or anything you're talking about?'" (Pransky, 1998, p. 29).

These objections seem right, of course, but only on the surface. Both Modello and a neighboring low-income housing project called Homestead Gardens in Dade County, Florida, were replete with substance abuse, drug gangs, shootings, domestic violence, child abuse, addiction, welfare dependency, school failure, truancy, and more. Here police officers would not enter unless they were "three deep." Yet, something remarkable happened in these communities: Dramatic changes occurred in the residents' lives, in their families, and in the community—changes of a magnitude most of us only dream is possible. In the three years after Mills introduced his approach, for the 150 families and 650 youth served by the program, household use of or selling drugs dropped from 65 percent to less than 20 percent; the overall endemic crime rate decreased by 70 to 80 percent; the teen pregnancy rate dropped from 50+ percent to 10 percent; school dropout rates dropped from 60 percent to 10 percent; endemic child abuse and neglect decreased by 70+ percent; households on public assistance went from 65 percent to negligible; and the parent unemployment rate dropped from 85 percent to 35 percent (Pransky, Mills, Sedgeman, & Blevens, 1997).

Modello: A Story of Hope for the Inner-City and Beyond (Pransky, 1998) chronicled in detail how lives were affected. For example, Thelma was a severe alcoholic being violently abused by her crack-addicted boyfriend who, in turn, abused her kids. She ended up stopping her alcohol dependency without going into treatment, halted her physical abuse and her children's abuse, and completely turned her life around. Ruby was a crack addict and violent woman who, through gaining this understanding, came to see enough worth in herself to go into treatment, and she experienced a 180 degree turnaround in her life. Miss Cicely was an extremely withdrawn mother of some of the project's main drug dealers and of a daughter so severely addicted to crack that her weight had dropped to 80 pounds and she was prostituting herself to support her habit. Yet, through Cicely's new insights, she helped her daughter break her addiction, and then Cicely became president of the project's residents council. Lisa was suicidal, with no self-confidence, continually being put down by her partner, welfare-dependent, yet through her insights ended up rising above it all, getting her GED, then securing a good job in which she flourished. Lenny was a teenage drug dealer whose life turned around to such an extent that with his gang he began a "crime watch" to keep out all drug dealers, graduated from high school (he had been failing and truant), and went on to college. These are but a few examples of the profound individual, family, and neighborhood changes that took place there. To see such powerful and positive changes in communities where little hope existed would lead most of us to be genuinely curious about what happened, to really question what intervention could have sparked such a turnaround in individual, family, and community life.

Replication

As Health Realization/Three Principles projects spread into other communities, equally impressive findings were reported. For example, one year after introducing this approach into the Coliseum Gardens housing project in Oakland, California, which was once known as "the murder capital," the murder rate plummeted to zero, and there had not been another homicide in seven subsequent years. In addition, violent crimes were reduced by 45 percent, drug assaults with firearms were reduced by 38 percent, and gang warfare and ethnic clashes between Cambodian and African American youth ceased (Pransky et al., 1997). Such results subsequently led to broad application in a number of other settings.

The National Resilience Resource Center (NRRC) at the University of Minnesota applies this understanding in its work with school, community, and organizational leaders. By tapping the natural innate health or resilience of youth, families, communities, and the school system at North Junior High in St. Cloud, Minnesota, from school year 1997–1998 to school year 1998–1999 suspensions were 70 percent lower, fights were reduced by 63.8 percent, and incidents of violence dropped 65.1 percent. In addition, a school improvement survey documented increases in faculty believing students respected each other (34 percent), students respected adults (44 percent), and 40 percent said they believed that positive interaction among students increased (Marshall, 2005).

Other promising results from this inside out approach have occurred in a variety of settings and populations, such as prisons, mental health centers, substance abuse treatment centers, and community revitalization programs. At a children's remedial reading clinic reading achievement doubled (Stewart, 1988). In a two-year special education program, 85 percent of the children made progress (Heath, Emiliano, & Usagawa, 1992). Other related results are presented later in this chapter.

PONDERING THESE RESULTS

The obvious questions are, "What happened?" "What exactly is this inside out, strengths based approach?" "How does it work?" "What made these people change in this way?"

In essence, all people affected as a result of this inside out approach changed because they had new insights about how their and all people's experience of life gets created. By "experience of life" we mean their perceptions, their resulting feelings, and what they see as "real" or "the way it is."

The question then becomes, "What did these people learn about how reality gets created that resulted in their seeing their own inherent strengths, acting on their innate health, living in health and well-being, and ultimately changing their communities?"

The Power of New Insight

Before discussing the specific understanding that changed people, let us stop for a moment and reflect on what could possibly make people's lives change from the depths of despair, from severe substance abuse, from domestic violence and other serious problems to well-being, peace of mind, less stress, and better relationships. Practically speaking, what do we mean when we say one's experience of life can change? Imagine what might happen within the mind of a resident of a low-income, inner-city housing project, or anyone for that matter, who goes from seeing herself and her circumstances in one way and then realizes something new and begins to see herself and her life in a completely different way. For example, imagine what it would be like for one's way of being in the world to change

from:	"I'm stuck in this place. I'm stuck with my lot in life."
to:	"I have the power within me to rise above my circumstances."
from:	"I'm completely worthless, so it doesn't matter what I do."
to:	"I'm a wonderful, fabulous person with a lot to offer."
from:	taking personally what other people do
to:	"It's just the way they see it. I don't have to take it personal."
from:	whatever is seen in a low mood is real and must be acted upon
to:	"I can't trust my thinking in my low moods; it's giving me faulty messages."
from:	blindly following one's thinking because it looks so real
to:	"I don't have to follow every thought that comes into my head."
from:	seeing limitations
to:	seeing hope and possibilities because anyone's thinking can change.
from:	"What other people do to me gets me messed up."
to:	"My own thinking about what other people do gets me messed up."
from:	"I'm going crazy and I don't know what to do."
to:	"When my mind is calm I have access to wisdom and common sense."
from:	"If my man is beating on me, at least I know that he loves me."
to:	"I'm worth more than that. I don't deserve to be treated that way."
from:	"I got raped when I was young, and now I'm damaged forever."
to:	"Sometimes bad shit happens, but I'm not going to let it ruin my life."
from:	"People are up to no good."
to:	"People are always doing their best, given the way they see things."

To be clear, we are not talking about cognitive reframing here. We are not talking about trying to help people reframe their thinking, or trying to think differently, or helping people to think more positively. In essence, we are talking about a shift in perspective from within that comes from a new insight that shifts people to a higher level of consciousness. We are talking about people seeing their lives from deeper wisdom or from a higher vantage point.

In the above examples these people had believed that the outside world caused them to feel badly; i.e., that their emotions were caused by the circumstances or situations or relations with other people in which they found themselves. Through new understanding they became free from their past ingrained ways of thinking. When this occurs, old thoughts, feelings, and behaviors fall like dominoes. As the old thinking falls away, in flows new thinking, and people develop a different way of seeing what happens to them, a new way of defining and imagining their lives and themselves.

The ability for people to change is innate; it is part of human nature. Internal change always happens through new insight. The people above changed because they had new insights. We would assert that new insight is the only way people change. The new understanding (introduced below) has been found to yield life-changing insights, if truly realized from within (Pransky, 2003). Our intent in describing this is to inspire readers to see and apply it in their personal and professional lives. The only prerequisite is an open, clear mind. The words themselves are not important because no words can accurately or adequately describe the nature of the inside world. What is important is the direction they point to.

THE "NEW" UNDERSTANDING: THE THREE PRINCIPLES

A movement in the consciousness of a number of people working in the fields of prevention, human services, and social work has gradually evolved from thinking we can "fix" problems with external remedies to recognizing that change must come from within. It is a perspective that views academic failure, violence, substance abuse, crime, and the myriad of other individual and community problems as symptoms of a deeper, root cause. Therefore, the inside out approach does not address symptoms or problems directly. Instead, it seeks to uncover people's innate health and natural well-being. Its intent is to move us beyond an outside in, external remedy approach directly to the internal source of well-being. At the heart of it the focus is not on *what* we think, but on *the fact that* we think; that every human being uses his or her power of thought to experience every event or circumstance in life. In this inside out understanding eliminating and preventing problems is the logical outcome of people uncovering their natural resilience or innate health. People who function in a calm state of mind and live in a state of health and well-being simply do not engage in problem behavior, at least in those moments.

This inside out understanding is based on three principles. It is important to note that we do not mean "principle" in the way it is most often used in this field, such as principles of effective programs or principles by which one can have a more healthy life. Here our definition of principle is more like its root definition, a universal law. What we mean by "principle" is *a force in the universe that always exists and is always at work, irrespective of people's awareness of it* (Pransky, 2003), something akin to the fact of gravity in the natural world. Before people knew about the principle of gravity, it was still working on them, holding them to the earth. The three principles referred to here are universal principles of how the mind works, or what is behind human mental functioning.

The three principles are *Universal Mind, Thought, and Consciousness*. As stated, the names are not important because they cannot fully describe these powers or gifts; it is what they point to that is critically important. By Universal Mind, we refer to the universal, formless energy or intelligence behind all life, the life force that is the source of all things. By Thought, we mean our power to create what we see of life. By Consciousness, we mean our power to experience what we have created of life and to be aware of what we are creating/experiencing.

Metaphorically, these principles are the operating manual that explains how we function psychologically. Marshall (2005) simply explains them using the terms *Knower*—every person has wisdom within, *Thinker*—we create our experience of life with our thinking, and *Noticer*—human beings have awareness, the ability to bring thoughts to life (p.135).

Taken together the three principles mean we can have no experience that is not created by our own thinking. We are capable of experiencing *only* what our thoughts create. It means that when we look out at the world and see what we call "reality," we are really only seeing "a reality"—our own "reality" that we have made up with our own thinking. Everyone's "reality" is different and is as fluid and changeable as our next thought.

> This does not mean that with our thinking we make up what happens out there in the world. It does mean that we make up what we *see* of whatever is "out there." The implications are enormous. When it looks as if we are stuck, we only *think* we are. When it looks like we have a problem, we only *think* we do. When we're in a bad mood and it looks as if we must take action right now, we only *think* we do. We can often see this with teenagers. They may be convinced that to be cool they have to smoke cigarettes or drink or join a gang. We know they don't really have to—it is only their thinking. We can often see this with sexual predators. They are convinced they must have the object of their sexual fantasies, no matter what. We know it is not really true—they only think it is. We can often see it with others. It is often more difficult to see it in ourselves. We are absolutely convinced that the way *we* see it is true or real. This is because Consciousness makes whatever we think look real—to us. (Pransky, 2003, pp.77–78)

ANOTHER STONE IN THE FOUNDATION

An outgrowth of these three principles and central to this understanding is the notion of innate health or people's natural resiliency. From this perspective innate resilience is two things: First, it is the ability of people to change their perspective, their thinking, and therefore change the quality of their lives; in other words, the ability for people to change is innate. Second, this health and wisdom arise from our spiritual essence and is, thus, our natural state. It contains the qualities of peace of mind, love, and wisdom. It emerges automatically as a whole package when our unhealthy thinking quiets down and our mind calms.

This may be what Emmy Werner (1996) meant when she said all people have within them a "self-righting mechanism." As a result of this the editors of *Resiliency in Action* (Henderson, Benard, Sharp-Light & Richardson, 1996) redefined resiliency as "an innate self-righting and transcending ability within all children, youth, adults, organizations, and communities" (p. 4). To date, despite the contributions of these esteemed researchers and practitioners, this definition still appears to be a minority view in the field at least in terms of practice, since most emphasis is placed on the external.

It would be wise to more seriously consider prevention and intervention practices that focus on this inherent self-righting mechanism. Werner made a prophetic statement when she said, "We need to look and see what [resiliency] researchers found in the first place. . . . It wasn't just that the children behavioral scientists studied were empty boxes into which someone poured 'resiliency'" (Werner, 1996, p. 19).

Resilience, then, as redefined here as our natural state, extant in all human beings. It only can be obscured by the use (or, misuse, shall we say) of our own power of thought. Our work is to simply help unveil or draw out what people already have within them. As Pransky (2003) states, *"We do not have to do anything to anyone to make them resilient; they already are!"* (p. 62). This means that something resides within the individual that in and of itself gives people their strength. We are all born with the innate ability to transform the way we experience life with our own thinking (Benard & Marshall, 1997). Instead of beginning with an incomplete person who becomes complete if he or she is in the right environment or learns the right skills or gains the right supports or gets the right information, we begin with a wholly complete person who has the innate capacity to realize his or her own internal health and strength and how it becomes obscured.

More Evidence

Evidence exists from outside this field in support of the inside out approach. With regard to posttraumatic stress disorder (PTSD), Bowman (1997) conducted a meta-analysis of 500-plus research studies. She found that after toxic events "only a minute fraction of people" developed PTSD. "Most people traverse these events with resilience after a period of initial distress, owing to combinations of personal factors that are significantly unacknowledged in the clinical literature concerning diagnosis and treatment" (p. 145). Bowman found "considerable evidence" from longitudinal studies that "happiness or the subjective experience of well-being is remarkably independent of significant life events, whether these events are positive or toxic in nature" (p. 110). She concluded that the stress response is internally generated. "Individuals structure the meaning of the event . . . and help shape the kind of emotional response the individual shows" (p. 76). Bowman asserts that "changes in the way an individual thinks about events and about their [sic] emotions and thoughts will be at the core of effective treatment" (p. 142).

With regard to health-related concerns such as use of contraceptives, alcohol abuse, and exercise, Bandura (1989) studied what made people be successful in these areas. In all cases he found "self-efficacy" to be the most consistent predictor of short- and long-term success. The crucial factor appeared to be whether people *believed* they could exercise control over potential threats to themselves. Bandura noted that self-efficacy affects thought patterns that may be self-aiding or self-hindering. Yet, as Pransky (2003) points out, self-efficacy itself is thought; people get to decide whether the thoughts they generate have power over them. In other words, the environment and all outside influences come to people via their own thought, and they *interpret* whether environmental factors are going to have power over them. Therein lies the essence of the flaw in the argument of those who suggest that the outside world—the environment, situations, events, other people—is *the* important influence on people's behavior.

When applied, additional research has recently emerged from within the field. Effects of a Health Realization initiative were examined at two Ramsey County, Minnesota, Juvenile Corrections programs initiated by the St. Paul Police Department. At Boys' Totem Town, 53 boys who had participated in the initiative, from two months to two years after discharge, showed a significant overall reduction compared with archived preinitiative data in self-reported use of substances. Specifically, tobacco use decreased by 19.6 percent, marijuana use by 81 percent, other illicit drug use by 80 percent, and alcohol use increased by 4.8 percent. At the St. Paul Juvenile Detention Center, among first-time detainees the recidivism rate was cut in half from two months to two years after discharge for those who completed the Health Realization program while there (38.2%; n = 110) compared with those who did not (77.8%; n = 45). In addition, the youth who completed the program reported that they had new perspective on life, got into trouble less, had less anger, had better relationships with their families, and decreased drug use. In conclusion, they stated,

> This initiative demonstrated that it is possible to teach youth in juvenile corrections how the quality of their thinking affects their behavior, and how to learn to recognize when their thinking isn't serving them. Youth of all ages and educational achievement were able to learn the basic principles of Health Realization, and were able to carry over what they learned into their home lives once they returned to their respective communities. These data are encouraging as to the ability to teach youth in juvenile corrections how to recognize the process of thinking, and how to self-right psychologically to the extent that it translates into behavioral change. (Singh, 2003, p. 14).

Sedgeman (2005) found that this training (called "Innate Health" at West Virginia University School of Medicine) significantly reduced stress among program participants. Banerjee, Howard, Mansheim, and Beattie (2007), in a randomized study at nine months post-admission at the Mariposa Lodge, found that substance use declined significantly among clients in both Health Realization and twelve-step treatments.

This type of training also translates into improved business practice (called "State of Mind [SOM]" training). Roy (2007) found that "increases in a workforce's productivity, efficiency, creativity, collaboration and resilience come as a complete package as the level of awareness of the role of Mind, Thought and Consciousness increases amongst a corporation's or group's constituents" (p.188). The results revolved around six main themes: (1) a cultural shift from "victim mentality" to a mindset of responsibility, (2) humility, (3) enhanced creativity, (4) greater trust and rapport, (5) improvements in employees' personal and professional lives, and (6) the belief that SOM improves business practice.

EVIDENCE OF EFFECTIVENESS FOR THE HEALTH OF THE HELPER

Health Realization/ The Three Principles has also shown significant, positive effects on the health of the helper. In 2005, Pransky and Carpenos conducted a seven-month, fourteen-session Health Realization Long-Term Professional Training (HRLTT) in Vermont (n = 20). Findings showed, on a 10-point Likert scale (10 = best) from preinitial Health Realization training (rated retrospectively), to postinitial training but before the start of HRLTT (which for participants ranged from one month to one year), to post HRLTT, the following mean score improvements occurred: well-being at work (from 6.5 to 7.9 to 8.5); well-being in the rest of life (5.6 → 7.5 → 9.0); stress at work (6.2 → 7.4 → 8.6); stress in rest of life (5.3 → 7.4 → 8.8); quality of relationships with "clients" (6.9 → 8.5 → 9.1); quality of relationships with coworkers and supervisors (7.1 → 8.4 → 9.0); effectiveness with clients (6.7 → 7.9 → 8.8). In addition, number of arguments/fights with their own kids per week decreased from 3.1 to 1.9 to 0.6 and arguments/fights with spouse/partner per month were reduced from 4.4 to 2.1 to 1.1. An independent statistical analysis of variance was conducted by Geber of Cornell University who found, "The average scores on the 3 responses to every question differed to such a degree that they were unlikely to be due to chance" (P = <.0001). She concluded that the training program was very effective in improving participants' responses to all questions (Pransky & Geber, 2005). A few participants' comments after the HRLTT are instructive:

> I was truly "lost in the woods" for most of my life prior to HR. I was confused, disoriented, scared, and felt hopeless about my life. There were times when I wanted to die. Since HR I have reconnected with my wisdom. . . . I am able to move through life joyfully. I experience lasting inner peace and contentment. . . . I am no longer lost in the woods, no longer confused, disoriented, scared, and without hope. I'm glad I'm alive. I am focused and live a happier, more carefree, and less stressful life. I am more productive at my job. My relationship with my husband and children is more relaxed and fun . . . —SB

> In the past, I have felt nervous about my decisions, a strong sense of uncertainty . . . , somehow deserving of bad things that have happened as a part of my life because I was not smart enough, not good enough, not able to trust myself, I was naïve, I acted in foolish ways, I was selfish, I was mean; therefore I deserved bad things. . . . A great sense of relief came over me that my innate health is with me through it all. I am a part of something bigger than my thoughts and experience. This . . . is empowering for me; to know that I made up ideas that were untrue and did not feel good—very punishing AND that I did not have to do that any more!! So, my *strength* has always been with me, I just forgot it was there. The sense of relief brings to me a feeling of *lightness*. . . . I do not have to carry these burdens of thought around with me any more . . . ; incredible. —AD

> Would it be too dramatic to open with a statement like "I'm convinced that our class has saved my emotional life"? [It] . . . will forever change how I perceive, experience, and live my life. I honestly feel that I have a newfound ownership of my life. The power of realizing that I have the ability to take conscious responsibility for maintaining a healthy approach to my life experience has, I'm pretty sure, been the catalyst that has transformed me. . . . I had lost all hope. . . . I feel I have truly made a transition from being an insecure, vulnerable avoider into a strong, hopeful, healthy, capable soul able to embrace any challenge that life chooses to grace me with. To me, that's what our HRLTT did. —CL

> I remember almost two years ago sitting in a HR training thinking please just stop the racing in my mind. . . . Drinking, drugging, anything—to try to make it stop. I don't have racing thoughts any more—not ever. My mind is clear on a day to day basis. . . . I have the power to create my own experience every moment of my life. I have hope. I see my past and myself in a new light. . . . I can experience hope, gratefulness, stress, anger . . . nothing exists unless I create it. I learned the importance in letting go. . . . When I am in a low mood I am a thought away from happiness. . . . Feeling good is contagious . . . —MB

A year ago I needed pills to sleep and an antidepressant to get up in the morning. I stopped taking them a while ago, just realizing one day that I didn't need them any more. I feel free, alive, and open to the infinite possibilities we all have to create our lives. . . . I am the one creating *my life!*. . . . I learned that I am a good, smart, nice, trustworthy being. —AW

I have been depressed maybe for the last five years. I had postpartum depression and it seems it never went away. I took Prozac . . . I would cry in the morning while the kids were asleep. . . . All I really wanted was to be dead. . . . My depression was getting more intense, . . . HR teaches me how to listen better, and I immediately recognize my habitual thought of my morning sickness been nothing but a habitual thought! . . . There is no better place than in . . . your inner health, that place inside yourself that follows different rules than the ego rules, or all the above illusions we live under. . . . Because of HR I have the ability to observe and better discern thoughts from reality, and live in the moment every single minute . . . —DB

Similar results after Health Realization Long-Term Professional Trainings were replicated in Bemidji, Minnesota (Pransky, 1999), Columbus, Ohio (Pransky, 2004a), Waterbury, Vermont (Pransky, 2004b), and Topeka, Kansas (Pransky, 2007).

The list goes on. Although many of these individual studies may not meet rigorous scientific standards, the accumulation of evidence warrants a closer look at this principle-based understanding of Health Realization/ The Three Principles as a very promising approach to individual and community change.

IMPLICATIONS FOR THE FIELD

As suggested above, despite equal attention being paid in the research to both external and internal factors in determining resiliency and strengths, and despite suggestions in the literature that both are equally important, an examination of current practice in the fields reveals that internal factors do not receive equal attention in program planning or practice. Even when internal factors are equally emphasized, it is standard practice to rely innocently on external strategies to produce the internal. For example, in its listing of suggested ideas for building internal assets in youth, the Search Institute suggests such practices as, "provide a comfortable place for your teen to study without distractions," "include college and career issues in services and programming," "teach students skills in conflict resolution," "give youth opportunities to express their beliefs," etc. (Benson et al., 1994)—all external changes.

Perhaps one reason for programmatic emphasis on approaches from the outside in is that external factors are easier to understand and manipulate and therefore easier to plan strategies around. It is more difficult to grasp how to work with the mysterious internal world. Perhaps another reason is that a new paradigm, by its very nature, runs counter to the prevailing view of a field, and is therefore nearly always resisted at first by the proponents of the current view (Klein, 1983, Pert, 1997; Wilson, 1998).

Given the aforementioned evidence from resiliency and Health Realization/ Three Principles, we would suggest that if the field is truly interested in maximizing efficacy, then equal attention and resources must be devoted to inside out study and practice. The evidence suggests that the fields of human services, social work, and prevention would be dramatically improved by focusing on what appear to be the two most crucial elements of what actually changes people and improves behavior:

1. People change *only* if they have a change of *thought.*
2. When people are guided by their *wisdom,* they do not commit the acts we are trying to prevent or treat, and this wisdom occurs naturally when people's minds clear or calm down. (Pransky, 2003)

If the fields of social work, human services, and prevention are truly interested in constructive change, emphasis needs to be placed on these two critical factors: thought and wisdom. We would assert that people's greatest strength is their ability to use the power of thought wisely. People need only to truly understand how thought and wisdom work within them to give them the experience of life they want for themselves.

Practical Applications

What would this look like in practical terms?

When working with someone from the inside out, we begin with the premise (or knowing) that everyone has innate health and wisdom inside. It can never disappear, even when it often appears to because it is the human spirit, the spiritual essence of human beings. People could not get away from it even if they wanted to. It can only be obscured when people use the power of thought unwisely against themselves, usually inadvertently, always innocently. (Innocently in the sense that they don't know they are letting their thinking rule them and that they don't have to.) Yet their inner health and wisdom is available to reveal itself at any time, even for a moment, as soon as their typical thinking lets go of its grip.

All one has to do to see if this is true is to look inside oneself and see if it works this way. See if when your mind calms down is when you get your best ideas and when you are less likely to act in unwise ways.

Another way of putting this is that all people are pure resilience, pure strength at their very core, and when we realize this fact and what keeps us from experiencing it (our own thinking that we have created and that will change eventually), we feel it. When we truly realize that thought is the power allowing us to experience this resilience or not at any moment, our level of consciousness automatically rises and we experience resilience and internal strength. Wisdom tends to speak with a soft voice; it is less readily heard and recognized because our typical thinking often speaks to us as if a heavy metal band is playing in our heads.

We have stated before that most people tend to think/believe that the outside world is what causes them to feel badly; in other words, that their circumstances or the situations in which they find themselves or that other people cause their emotions. Sometimes this is more easily seen in others than in ourselves. A case in point is the amount of stress we often feel when we have a lot of homework and too little time in which to do it. But if we look closely we will see that not everyone feels the same amount of stress given the same amount of homework. Why is that? People think differently about it. Some don't care. Others just know they can pull it off. Besides, sometimes given the same amount of homework we feel more stressed than we do at other times. Why? In those moments we are simply thinking differently about it. Therefore, it is not the homework causing our stress; it is our own thinking about it. Realizing this can be humbling, but also empowering.

At a more extreme level people who cause difficulties for themselves and/or others tend to believe the outside world makes them behave as they do. As examples, some people believe it is the presence of a drug such as crack, alcohol, or marijuana that makes them need it. It is the child acting out that makes the mother have to beat him. It is a woman acting in a provocative way that makes the man feel like he has to rape her, or beat her if she happens to be his wife or girlfriend. Examples abound. Imagine if all these people realized it was only their own thinking making them feel that way in the moment, and because it was their own creation they didn't have to take it that seriously or follow it. Imagine if they realized that even if they might not be able to stop such thinking in the moment, it will change at some point and therefore look less compelling. So all they have to do is ride it out for a while, and they will eventually get back more in touch with their health and wisdom. Imagine how many fewer problems would be acted out and therefore prevented.

THE UNFURLING OF HEALTH
INTO THE COMMUNITY

How, then, do we help an entire community or organization to see from this perspective? How is the inside out approach actually applied?

Below are the essential components of successfully applying the inside out approach. These components are not so much "steps" as bases to be covered (Pransky, 2003). For this chapter what can be said about each only scratches the surface.

1. **The Health of the Helper:** First and foremost, practitioners working from the inside out must generally model the "health" and perspective they attempt to bring forth in others. This means the practitioner must radiate and maintain a good feeling, understand the source of this feeling, and know how this feeling gets lost. [See component 4 for more detail about how one can get there.]

2. **Creating a Good Feeling:** The idea here is for people's minds to relax, to calm or slow down so their typical thinking loosens its grip. This occurs when the practitioner creates a climate around people of warmth and lightheartedness, and when the practitioner sees people's health and innocence, offers hope, and establishes rapport. All this helps people's minds be open to the new.

3. **Deep Listening:** Unlike in "active listening," practitioners using this approach listen deeply to others with an empty, clear mind, "being with" the person, taking him or her in not unlike how one normally listens to music (not really listening to the words), seeing the person with genuine interest and gaining a feeling of closeness. This is listening intuitively. The listener becomes curious about what the other person's world looks like. Deep listening is the key to knowing in what direction to go with people.

4. **Teaching, Conveying, or Drawing Out the Inside Out Understanding:** When all three components above are realized and wisdom indicates the moment is right, the practitioner helps others gain an understanding of the following notions:

- That thought is what creates people's experience, and thoughts will change.
- That innate health (containing everything people are truly looking for in life, such as peace of mind, love, self-esteem, etc.) and wisdom are always present and accessible and can only be obscured by people's own thinking.
- That a clear or quiet mind is the pathway to wisdom.
- That people's feelings tell them whether they can trust (and therefore whether they want to follow) their thinking.

When people realize their own freedom either to live allowing their healthy thinking process to flow through them or to live controlled by their unhealthy thoughts, they begin to see problematic experience as something created in their own minds. Thus, their problem behaviors diminish because what has been driving those behaviors simply doesn't look as "real" any more.

Perhaps the most difficult thing to comprehend about the Three Principles is that they cannot be understood by the intellectual mind. They have to be *realized* from beyond the intellect. Hence the next "step" in the process.

5. **Insight—A Shift in Perspective:** All the component steps above are solely for the purpose of spawning an insight of enough magnitude so that when people see their lives change for the better, their thinking, feelings, and behaviors follow. No one can make an insight happen in anyone, yet it is *the critical point of change.* By insight we mean a moment of understanding, a vertical jump in one's "level of understanding" that lifts people into a new reality where they see a bigger picture and take external events and circumstances less personally. New insights and new possibilities appear more often when the mind clears or quiets down.

6. **The Ripple Effect:** When people see their lives improve, they tend to want to share what they have learned with others. Their own lives reflect more well-being, and therefore relationships change in one's family and among neighbors. Then, when a critical mass gains this new perspective, they naturally come together to change unhealthy community conditions. Hence, change from the inside out.

CRITIQUES AND CAUTIONS

To some this [entire approach] will sound suspiciously like "blaming the victim," or telling people to pull themselves up by their bootstraps. "Do you mean to tell me that getting beaten or getting raped is not a horrible experience that causes great harm?!" Of course it is horrible and harmful! Of course, it is not the fault of the victim or survivor. But if we look closely we will see that different people experience the beating or the rape in different ways, and its effects on people's lives vary. For some, it will ruin their lives; others will chalk it up to a very unfortunate experience in their past but not let it affect their lives; others will see it as a turning point in their lives; as well as a wide variety of views in between. The only difference is their thinking. I put no value judgment on whether any particular thinking is good or bad, right or wrong. I am only saying that whatever we think about it is what we experience of it. Again, I am *not* saying that our own thinking creates these situations. I am *not* saying that our thinking attracts such experiences to us. I *am* saying that whatever we make of these circumstances and situations—however we look upon them, think about them, feel about them, and see them—happens via our own creative power of thought. (Pransky, 2003, p.82)

A SKEPTIC GETS TURNED AROUND:
DR. McMILLEN'S ODYSSEY OF DISCOVERY

This story begins more than thirty years ago, in my earlier life as a protective service worker. From my first days as a social worker I longed for an approach that would actually *help* people have happier and healthier lives. Instead, I witnessed a very uneven playing field, people victimized by their circumstances, individuals blamed for their predicaments. I saw my clients mostly as people with good intentions who loved their children and cared about the future; they just needed a break, an opportunity to "do the right thing." At that time, and with the best intentions, I believed what they needed was something outside of them: a different circumstance or a different "event" to occur so they could have a different outcome. Because I was looking in that direction I decided *the* answer lay in social reform and systems change; meaning, if we wanted people who lived in poverty, people who are different, all who are oppressed to have a chance to be more than their circumstances allowed, then we needed to direct our attention to the unfairness and inequity of the system. I spent years teaching passionately about what we needed to do to "fix" the helping profession. I targeted both the ineffectiveness of our fragmented, humiliating, and stigmatizing service delivery system and how services were delivered (victim-blaming, pathology-based, deficit-driven, etc.). Then something unexpected happened.

The Discovery

For a number of years I had been teaching a class called, "Prevention in Human Services." I added the book, *Modello: A Story of Hope for the Inner-City and Beyond* (Pransky, 1998) to my class, and it had an unbelievable impact on my students. Although my students didn't fully understand the approach and why it worked so well, they resonated with the people in the book and were very intrigued by the changes that occurred in the community. Their enthusiastic response, plus the astounding outcomes of this intervention, ignited my interest to understand this approach for prevention and community change.

Despite my curiosity, I was still doubtful and skeptical. Something about this approach seemed too simple to be believable. I argued that unless the deplorable social conditions were changed it would be extremely difficult for people's lives to improve. Yet I was drawn to the possibility of this new paradigm and could not turn away. If people's lives were truly impacted in the way described, this was worth investigating. Might this be the approach I had been searching for that could really help people have better lives? I decided to undertake an in-depth study of Health Realization/ Three Principles. I wanted to visit sites where I could interview people who were "living in their health" and using this understanding in their work. I was awarded a sabbatical from my university and decided to embark on a cross-country tour to see the three principles being applied in a variety of settings. These included housing projects, elementary schools, prisons, a parenting program, a university school of medicine, drug treatment programs, private practice (individual and corporate consulting), residential programs for individuals, county social services division, jails, juvenile hall, work furlough programs, mental health programs, drop-in support groups, etc.

Looking back, I don't think I had *any* idea what I was going to be exposed to or encounter. I was despondent about my work and desperately needed a vacation, thus I entered my sabbatical almost as an adventure, with no understanding of the magnitude of the experience that lay ahead of me. I know I started out naïve and skeptical, but the people I met in those first few months did not react to my doubts; they were simply willing to share what they knew and were open to my questions and skepticism. I kept waiting for that bolt of lightning that would make this all eminently clear. It never arrived. Quite unbeknownst to me, however, over time, quietly and incrementally, I developed new eyes with which to see the world and the people in it. I never really felt it happening, but I know something changed.

If It Ain't Broke, Don't Fix It

As I traveled from coast to coast, I saw more and more deeply how powerful this understanding is and how it affects the providers and the programs that deliver services. One of the first things I noticed was how differently people entered the role of helping. Helpers working from this understanding operate from a firm belief that they do not need to "fix" people or solve their problems for them. Over and over I saw helping professionals who clearly understood that the power to change and rise above their circumstances is within people, and people know what they need to do for themselves much better than the helper ever will. This was evident in the housing developments where residents were actively engaged in their own community development projects.

One example is Visitacion Valley in San Francisco, California. The Community Resiliency Project employs women who were once among the "problems" in this low-income housing project. They are now the providers of the Health Realization classes and are inspirations in the community. These women are truly changing their world. Despite all of their own previous trials and tribulations, they were so comfortable and confident as they planned their next steps that it was hard to imagine they had ever lived in doubt and insecurity.

I saw a similar response in two prison settings (Boston and San Jose, California), where this approach to seeing health in individuals truly changes the dynamics of helping. Great rapport existed among the inmates attending the weekly Health Realization groups. Despite their environment and, for some, a level of pent-up anger and frustration, they treated each other with respect, were open and talkative, and shared a real connection. They described how this class was one of the most important hours of the week. One man summed up the sentiment with the comment, "This program is a *must*. It could save your or someone else's life."

I observed this mutuality of helping in a *Parenting from the Heart* (Pransky, 2001/1997) group on Martha's Vineyard that uses this understanding as the foundation of the class. This was a profound experience that restored my faith that people can regain health, and it is not as hard as I had thought. As I listened to people, many of whom revealed that they had been consumers of traditional mental health services, I could feel their calm confidence. Over and over, people expressed how this understanding has allowed them to face personal challenges with a very different sense of their ability. It didn't matter whether they were coping with a nasty divorce, grieving the loss of a child, dealing with a new job, or trying to enforce a cur-few, they knew they had inside them everything they would ever need to get through.

It's A "Friday Afternoon Feeling" All Week

The second thing I noticed is the "climate" of the environment (be it an agency, school, or program) where people are operating from this understanding. I visited Thatcher Brook Primary School in Waterbury, Vermont, where teachers and staff had participated in Health Realization training. Despite the fact that not everyone in the school had received the training, I could tell when I walked in that something was different about this school. The greetings were warm, the energy was good, and people did not seem frantic or stressed out. The people I interviewed said they simply did not have as many difficulties with anyone or anything. They expressed that nothing seemed to be as personal as before they had taken the class. Issues with the children and their parents, with their colleagues, or with their own families were less problematic. I couldn't help but think this environment would be every parent's dream for their child's school.

Another example of healthy environment is Pransky & Associates in LaConner, Washington, a counseling center where all the clinicians work from this understanding. I observed a four-day intensive session where the client changed right before my eyes—the person became very confident about handling a huge job that had previously seemed over-whelming. But, an equally impressive part of this visit was seeing the nature of the inter-actions and the quality of the climate in their office. I have never been in an office where there was so much laughter, high spirits, and good energy while so much work was being done. I have seen for myself that helping agencies do not have to be the pressure cookers they so often are. A happier healthier work environment is possible.

The Health of The Helper

Connected to the idea of climate is a third theme that emerged, the undeniable health of the helpers I encountered. It seems that for helping professions the stress of our work has increased; we no longer are only facing the possibility of burnout, many of us now suffer "compassion fatigue" and "secondary trauma." To see such wise and happy service providers work from this new, inside out understanding struck a deep chord.

I visited a multiservice alcohol and drug treatment center in Portland, Oregon, that pro-vides services for both adults and youth, people who are homeless, and many "chronic users" of the social service system. Everyone at this center receives training based on the three principles, thus the approach is always strengths-based. The director truly impressed me with how much she enjoys her work and how well she manages the pressure of the position she holds, while maintaining her health, humor, and her easy-going nature. I rarely see such characteristics in people who have spent thirty-plus years in social services. She is full of hope and believes when people discover they *can* change, they do.

I interviewed a psychiatrist at West Virginia University in Behavioral Medicine and Psychiatry. He teaches in the school of medicine and provides direct services, including working with patients who have been hospitalized for mental health issues. His way of "being" shook me to my foundations because almost all my previous experiences with psychiatrists had been negative. I have never heard a psychiatrist laugh so much, talk about how much he loved his work and his clients, and be so humble about knowing so much.

This was an intensely important piece of my research and travels. I was stunned with how amazingly happy and healthy the people I had been meeting on my sabbatical journey appeared to be. It is clear to me that the people who work from this understanding have a confidence and a joy in their work that is palpable. I am as reassured to see such healthy helpers as I am to know that the people being served are receiving services in a manner that is actually helpful. Likewise, I also saw that it doesn't take overall systems change to experience an improved climate; in most of the places I visited, only a few people in relation to the whole had been trained in and were living and using the principles in their work. Yet, I could feel something different in how people interacted with each other.

Fast Forward

For me this story was just a beginning. I am now teaching *Prevention from the Inside Out* (Pransky, 2003). With the coauthor of this chapter I trained a cadre of co-trainers in Topeka, Kansas. A Health Realization/Three Principles project has started with the Topeka Housing Authority. I have offered training to several social services agencies and schools. I have already seen more changes in students', professionals', and residents' lives than I have seen in all my other years. This is especially heartwarming from someone who was, initially, such a skeptic.

Yet, even equipped with my new understanding I know I will have moments of insecurity and thoughts that distress me. Now I know, however, that I am creating my own experience, and that I can move to a happier, healthier place in another moment as easily as I can have a new thought. There is a great deal of peace in realizing that I am responsible for creating my experiences.

I am struck by the implications of title of the book that first exposed me to Health Realization: *Modello: A Story of Hope for the Inner-City and Beyond.* Hope has been restored in my life. I have hope for my students and for all the people whose lives will be touched by their work. I have hope for the agencies, programs, and communities where people are pointed toward the understanding that Health Realization offers. It gives me hope for the field of prevention, which gives me hope for the future. It is not the naïve hope of a 22-year-old, fresh out of college with her bachelors degree in Social Work, believing she can change the world. It is the thoughtful and tempered hope of a person who has worked in the field for a very long time, who has seen a lot, and who had started to doubt. Hope is a wonderful feeling to have come back into my life!

CONCLUSION

What does all this mean, then, in terms of how we enter the act of helping with a desire to facilitate individual and community change? Does our thinking, especially our thinking about others, affect the way we approach our roles as helping professionals?

One of the most common laments of those who work in human service is how stressful the work is. To help people who live in deplorable conditions or in misery is very noble but difficult work. Helping professionals have a notoriously high rate of burnout. Some leave their social services positions for other lines of work. Others stay, but the quality of their work deteriorates, their relationship with co-workers often become strained, their home life suffers and ultimately their clients are not well served. Is this an inevitable outcome of our work in social services? No!

Would knowing that everyone has an ultimate place of strength and resilience inside of them change the nature of the helping relationship and the role of the helper? We believe this knowledge changes our entire approach. When we operate from a place of health and well-being ourselves, we know that everyone has within them everything they need to be healthy and happy and to live productive and meaningful lives. We have already explored the concept of resilience as relevant to our approach to helping. The explosion of research in this area demonstrates that despite the risks and challenges, most children and young adults manage to emerge successfully from even the most highly stressed and socially and economically deprived environments (Werner & Smith, 2001). When resilience is thought of fundamentally as the "self-righting mechanism" inherent in all people, if we heed this understanding, then the helping professional is not burdened with the expectation of responsibility for providing some missing ingredient.

When service workers enter the helping relationship firmly grounded in the understanding of this inherent or innate capacity of people to "bounce back" and overcome serious adverse family and living conditions, they enter equipped with hope. They see possibility and they trust the potential that exists within every individual. And if they are unable to see it in the moment we are with them, they might see it after we leave, or they may see it some other time, or they may not ever see it, but it's all okay because we can never do more than our best. When we know that all change happens via insight and that it is impossible for us to make insights happen, it takes the burden of responsibility off of us as helpers. Does this mean we do not care as much? No! Does this mean we are less effective? No! If anything, we are more effective. We simply have hope for all and do our very best to help them see with new eyes and know where the true responsibility for change really lies.

When the helping relationship is premised on an understanding that the social worker's role is to help uncover natural strengths and point people in the direction of their innate abilities and how their thinking creates their experiences, the relationship shifts. Social workers do not shoulder the burden of seeing themselves as the "answer" to the problems that a person is facing. They do not see people as broken or damaged, and they do not think they need to "fix" anyone. They trust the person's natural tendency to "self-right" to "bounce back" and see helping as an opportunity to teach the person about mental health and how humans so often use thought against themselves to cover up their natural wisdom, rather than to help themselves.

At best the helper is a catalyst for individuals to have insights about their innate power and inner wisdom. The helper functions like a mirror that reflects what they have not yet been able to see about themselves. Helping professionals who understand this are not so personally invested in their client's success. They do not see the failure (or success) of a client as a reflection of their skill or talent as a helper. They relax into their helping role with confidence that people have it in them to find their answers and take the right steps. The person receiving the help may not be able to take action at that particular moment—and may even reject it—but that does not change the helper's belief that the person can and will make a change when she or he "sees" that he or she can.

It is easy for a helper to become overwhelmed by the enormity of chaos in one individual's life. When workers enter entire communities with multitudes of needs, it can be paralyzing. It is empowering and freeing for social workers to recognize that they are not responsible for "fixing" the situation. It is not up to them to remedy the problems. With a foundation firmly grounded in understanding the three principles we can enter the most complex individual, family, or community environments trusting that we have what it takes to make a difference, and that the people we serve do too.

It is important to recognize that the three principles are not some new theory or a set of beliefs. They are simply *facts* about the way people function and what brings people their experience of life. What are these facts? That everyone has a power within them that allows them to think thoughts; that thoughts come into people's minds continuously and are continuously changing; that everyone alive has consciousness, meaning the power to experience what he or she perceives, of life; that whatever people experience of life is experienced through their consciousness. These are obvious facts that cannot be refuted. The next fact is not so obvious, so we have to rely on what physicists assert: that there is some formless energy behind all life and all things, and this formless energy is somehow created into various forms.

What people don't often realize is that from the interplay of these three facts, everything else within the human psychological experience comes. What comes and the way it comes are not as obvious, but if people look inside themselves to the way it really works for them, they will at least be able to see other "facts" for themselves that pertain to their own particular experience. For example, is it true that when their minds calm down, people seem to feel better and act more wisely? Is it true that different people can see the exact same situation or person differently and therefore have a different experience of whatever is happening? Is it true that one person can see the same situation or person differently at different times? What makes that happen? What are the implications? These are only a few possible questions that encourage people to explore what is behind acting, feeling, and thinking the way they (and therefore others) do, and to question whether even though their experience of life appears to come to them from the outside world, is it not really created from within? If true, what are the implications for our lives and for helping others? Together we are exploring what internal resilience really is and where it comes from. Then, armed with new understanding of these facts, people draw their own conclusions and do whatever they want and live however they want. Odds are many will choose more health and well-being for their lives, accordingly. In summary, then, what we are really talking about here is an exploration into the true nature of internal resilience.

The one last thought we would like to share with you are the words of the sixth-century philosopher Lao-Tse.

> *If there is radiance in the soul, it will abound in the family.*
> *If there is radiance in the family, it will be abundant in the community.*
> *If there is radiance in the community, it will grow in the nation.*
> *If there is radiance in the nation, the universe will flourish.*

All we would add to this powerful sentiment is that, from this understanding, the "if" is not in question.

DISCUSSION QUESTIONS/EXERCISES

1. This chapter suggests that we have a powerful force within us; a power that may change not just what we do and how we think, act, and feel, and might change others. What is your response to this, as a person and as a helper?

2. Sit down with a colleague and/or friend and discuss the possibility that change is not so removed from how we think and act, but is always possible. How would that change your approach to your own life and the life of those you help?

3. Do you personally feel that there are powers and forces within you that have not been fully tapped? If so, what would that mean for your personal and professional life? If not, why not?

4. How do you think we can transform this energy and power to communities that we might be working in? That is, for example, how would it change our ideas about community practice?

REFERENCES

Bandura, A. (1989). Human agency in social cognitive theory. *American Psychologist, 44,* 1175–1184.

Banerjee, K., Howard, M., Mansheim, K., & Beattie, M. (2007). Comparison of health realization and 12-step treatment in women's residential substance abuse treatment programs. *The American Journal of Drug and Alcohol Abuse, 33,* 207–215.

Banks, S. (1998). *The missing link.* Renton, WA: Lone Pine Publishing.

Benard, B. & Marshall, K. (1997). A framework for practice: Tapping innate resilience. Research practice. (Spring), 9:15. Minneapolis, MN: University of Minnesota, Center for Applied Research and Educational Improvement.

Benson, P. L., Galbraith, J., & Espeland, P. (1994). *What kids need to succeed.* Minneapolis: Search Institute/Free Spirit Publishing.

Bowman, M. (1997). *Individual differences in posttraumatic response: Problems with the adversity-distress connection.* Mahwah, NJ: Lawrence Erlbaum.

Henderson, N., Benard, B., Sharp-Light, N., & Richardson, G. (1996). The philosophy and mission of resiliency in action. *Resiliency in Action, 1*(3), 4.

Marshall, K. (2000). *Experiences implementing resilience/Health Realization in schools.* Minneapolis: University of Minnesota, National Resilience Resource Center.

Marshall, K. (2005). Resilience in our schools: Discovering mental health and hope from the inside out. In D. L. White, M. K. Faber, & B. C. Glenn (Eds.), *Proceedings of Persistently Safe Schools, 2005* (pp. 128–140). Washington, DC: Hamilton Fish Institute, George Washington University.

Klein, D. C. (1983). A transforming view of mental health. *Journal of Primary Prevention, 836,* 202–206.

Pert, C. B. (1997). *Molecules of emotion: Why you feel the way you feel.* New York: Scribner.

Pransky, G. S., Mills, R. C., Sedgeman, J. A., & Blevens, J. K. (1997). An emerging paradigm for brief treatment and prevention. In L. Vandecreek, S. Knapp, & T. J. Jackson (Eds.), *Innovations in clinical practice: A source book* (pp. 76–98). Sarasota, FL: Professional Resource Press.

Pransky, J. (1998). *Modello: A story of hope for the inner-city and beyond: An inside out model of prevention and resiliency in action through Health Realization.* Montpelier, VT: NEHRI Publications.

Pransky, J. (1999). *The experience of participants after Health Realization training: A one-year follow-up phenomenological study.* Doctoral dissertation/Project Demonstrating Excellence prepared for The Union Institute, Cincinnati, Ohio.

Pransky, J. (2001/1991). *Prevention: The critical need.* Bloomington, IN: AuthorHouse.

Pransky, J. (2001/1997). *Parenting from the heart.* Bloomington, IN: 1stBooks Library. Cabot, VT: NEHRI Publications.

Pransky, J. (2004a). *Preliminary findings of pre/post test after health realization training of trainers for Ohio Resource Network for Safe and Drug Free Schools and Communities.* Montpelier, VT: NEHRI Publications (unpublished manuscript).

Pransky, J. (2004b). *Preliminary findings of pre/post test after 45 hour, 7 month Health Realization course for the Thatcher Brook Primary School in Waterbury, Vermont.* Montpelier, VT: NEHRI Publications (unpublished manuscript).

Pransky, J. (2007). *Preliminary findings of pre/post test after Health Realization long-term professional training in Topeka, Kansas.* Montpelier, VT: NEHRI Publications (unpublished manuscript).

Pransky, J. & Geber, M (2005). *Preliminary findings of pre/post test after Vermont (Central Vermont) Health Realization long-term professional training.* Montpelier, VT: NEHRI Publications (unpublished manuscript).

Pransky, J. (2003). *Prevention from the Inside Out.* Bloomington, IN: AuthorHouse.

Roy, A. F. (2007). *An examination of the principle-based leadership trainings and business consultations of a group private practice.* Unpublished doctoral dissertation. Boston: Massachusetts School of Professional Psychology.

Sedgeman, J. (2005). Health realization/innate health: Can a quiet mind and a positive feeling state be accessible over the lifespan without stress-relief techniques? *Medical and Scientific Monitor, 11*(12), HY47–52.

Singh, N. (2003). *Summative evaluation report ATOD program.* Minneapolis, MN: University of Minnesota Center for Applied Research and Educational Improvement. www.education.umn.edu/CAREI/Reports/SIG/Eval-plans/printable-evals/2003Summative/StPaul-Police.rtf January 17, 2007.

Stewart, D. L. (1988). *State-dependent learning: The effect of feeling and emotions on reading achievement.* Bend, OR: Philosophy of Living Center.

Werner, E. E. (1996, Winter). How children become resilient: Observations and cautions. *Resiliency in action,* 18–28.

Werner, E. E. & Smith, R. (2001). *Journeys from childhood to midlife: Risk, resilience and recovery.* Ithaca, NY: Cornell University Press.

Wilson, E. O. (1998). *Consilience: The unity of knowledge.* New York: Knopf.

CHAPTER FOURTEEN

POVERTY THROUGH THE LENS OF ECONOMIC HUMAN RIGHTS

MARY BRICKER-JENKINS

ROSEMARY A. BARBERA

CARRIE YOUNG

How does our practice change when we see people, not as "impoverished," but as targets of human rights violations? For over a decade, a group of social workers representing many fields of practice and modalities has been developing an economic human rights approach to practice along with people in client status. This chapter illustrates their work, its potential for freeing social work from the theoretical shackles of "poverty practice," and the tools it provides for unlocking people's strengths. Examples are drawn from the United States and Chile.

A woman with three jobs and two children finds that her tiny apartment, for which she pays over $500 per month, is in a building that has been condemned. For over two years she has made ends meet working a few jobs, finding friends to watch her children so she did not have to pay childcare, relying on local soup kitchens and food banks, and walking four miles a day to save transportation costs. But now she is not sure what she will do.

Almost 6,000 miles away, in a shantytown on the outskirts of Santiago, Chile, a family faces a similar predicament. They have been living *allegado* (in an already overcrowded home) with family members. Both parents do "home work," sewing clothing in their home for a large importer/exporter. Their work day typically runs fourteen hours, but they are pleased that they can be close to their three children. The family members with whom they live with just found out they are expecting another child and have told them that they will have to move.

A social worker who works from a strengths perspective can easily see in both of these stories the resilience, determination, and resourcefulness of these families. A strengths-based social worker will immediately recognize that, despite the odds being stacked against them, these are ingenious people who do what it takes to make ends meet and that these internal resources will serve them well as they face yet another devastating life experience.

But is that enough? We think not. While it is necessary to recognize the strengths and resourcefulness that individuals have used to survive in exploitive conditions, that is not sufficient. It is certain that these families can build upon their past strengths in order to forge ahead into yet another precarious situation. But how long until the next emergency? How long until they once again fall prey to a system that feeds on their hardships? The conditions they face are the result of structural forces and arrangements; they require not only mobilization of their strengths to meet an immediate problem, but also concrete resources to meet their basic human needs and, *therefore*, a change in the structures that gave rise to the problem in the first place.

For the past decade in the United States, and for decades longer in other nations, social workers and people living in poverty have together been inventing a practice rooted in the concepts of human rights, and particularly economic human rights. This chapter provides an overview of that practice in two nations, Chile and the United States. In this practice, we work in many ways on the problems of daily living; however, our focus is not on the poverty of the people, but on the poverty of policies that deny people the basic necessities of life. This focus not only illuminates individual strengths, but reveals opportunities to engage those strengths to challenge injustice, promote health, and create community.

In fact, that is what happened in both of the situations described above. In the first instance, social workers who work with the Poor People's Economic Human Rights Campaign (PPEHRC) helped the family get its immediate housing needs met, but also involved the mother in a community organization where she could be a member of a group claiming the right to housing through public education, demonstrations, sit-ins, and takeovers of vacant federally owned houses. In the second example, a Chilean social worker referred the family to its local *Comité de los Sin Casa* (Committee of Those Without Homes) that was working with over 100 families to solve the housing crisis in the neighborhood.

WHAT ARE ECONOMIC HUMAN RIGHTS?

The concept of "human rights" is common currency in mainstream USian[1] political discourse, but that discourse is somewhat misleading. In general, it refers only to civil and political rights, and excludes economic, social, and cultural rights (Howard-Hassmann & Welch, 2006). The keystone instrument of human rights is the Universal Declaration of Human Rights (UDHR), adopted unanimously by the United Nations' General Assembly in 1948. Eleanor Roosevelt chaired the committee that drafted the document. Two subsequent treaties were derived from it: the International Covenant on Civil and Political Rights (ICCPR) and the International Covenant on Economic, Social, and Cultural Rights (ICE-SCR). The United States signed and ratified the former; President Carter signed the latter, but it has never been ratified by the U.S. Senate. Therefore, the range and force of obligations of the U.S. government is a matter of legal debate. There is consensus among international legal scholars, however, that most of its rights are specifically guaranteed in the ICCPR and other instruments already ratified by the Senate (Melish, 2006, 2007; Soohoo,

---

[1]We use the term USian to denote the fact that "America" has many nations and cultural groups, of which the United States is only one. Indeed, "North America" has several.

Albisa, & Davis, 2007). Further, its moral force is unquestioned—except, perhaps, by those whose political and economic interests would be compromised by its elevation.

Such was the case with an earlier iteration of economic rights in the United States, Franklin D. Roosevelt's "Second Bill of Rights." In the spirit of and implementing his famous 1941 "Four Freedoms" speech, he proposed to Congress in January 1944 that

Every American is entitled to

- The right to a useful and remunerative job in the industries or shops or farms or mines of the Nation;
- The right to earn enough to provide adequate food and clothing and recreation;
- The right of every farmer to raise and sell his products at a return which will give him and his family a decent living;
- The right of every businessman, large and small, to trade in an atmosphere of freedom from unfair competition and domination by monopolies at home or abroad;
- The right of every family to a decent home;
- The right to adequate medical care and the opportunity to achieve and enjoy good health;
- The right to adequate protection from the economic fears of old age, sickness, accident, and unemployment;
- The right to a good education.[2]

Contrary to popular belief—which was heavily shaped by the anti-communist rhetoric of the McCarthy and Cold War eras and promoted by the wealthy and their political allies—the majority of USians supported these rights (Kaplan & Kaplan, 1993; Sunstein, 2004). In today's period of U.S. economic decline and the vulnerability of people who have thought of themselves as middle class, it is likely that this is true today.

For this reason, among others, we have recently seen a resurgence of interest in economic human rights in the United States. For the most part, the focus has been on using the various human rights instruments in legal strategies, but there is one organization—the Poor People's Economic Human Rights Campaign—that has focused specifically on economic human rights in an effort to build a movement to abolish poverty in the United States and, in fact, around the globe. PPEHRC is a national organization that grew out of the experience of Philadelphia's Kensington Welfare Rights Organization (KWRU). It consists of approximately 100 grassroots organizations, most of them led by people living in poverty, each with its own focus and program, but united by a commitment to this mission:

The Poor People's Economic Human Rights Campaign is committed to unite the poor across color lines as the leadership base for a broad movement to abolish poverty. We work to accomplish this through advancing economic human rights as named in the Universal Declaration

---

[2]The complete text of this address is available at http://en.wikisource.org/wiki/Franklin_Delano_Roosevelt%27s_Eleventh_State_of_the_Union_Address

of Human Rights, such as the rights to food, housing, health, education, communication, and a living wage job.

Not all of the members of PPEHRC organizations live in poverty, but their commitment is to the program of the organized poor—that is, to abolish poverty. This means that services, while necessary, are no substitute for resources; that "reducing" or "ameliorating" poverty is insufficient, that programs directed only at "extreme" poverty are divisive and deficient, as are programs that are directed at the poverty of one identity group to the exclusion of others. PPEHRC builds its movement on the foundation of the economic rights most directly expressed in Articles 23, 25, and 26 of the UDHR; Article 19 is included as it affirms the right to communication, deemed essential for securing all others[3]:

ARTICLE 19.
Everyone has the right to freedom of opinion and expression; this right includes freedom to hold opinions without interference and to seek, receive and impart information and ideas through any media and regardless of frontiers.

ARTICLE 23.
(1) Everyone has the right to work, to free choice of employment, to just and favourable conditions of work and to protection against unemployment.

(2) Everyone, without any discrimination, has the right to equal pay for equal work.

(3) Everyone who works has the right to just and favourable remuneration ensuring for himself and his family an existence worthy of human dignity, and supplemented, if necessary, by other means of social protection.

(4) Everyone has the right to form and to join trade unions for the protection of his interests.

ARTICLE 25.
(1) Everyone has the right to a standard of living adequate for the health and well-being of himself and of his family, including food, clothing, housing and medical care and necessary social services, and the right to security in the event of unemployment, sickness, disability, widowhood, old age or other lack of livelihood in circumstances beyond his control.

(2) Motherhood and childhood are entitled to special care and assistance. All children, whether born in or out of wedlock, shall enjoy the same social protection.

ARTICLE 26.
(1) Everyone has the right to education. Education shall be free, at least in the elementary and fundamental stages. Elementary education shall be compulsory. Technical and professional education shall be made generally available and higher education shall be equally accessible to all on the basis of merit.

(2) Education shall be directed to the full development of the human personality and to the strengthening of respect for human rights and fundamental freedoms. It shall promote understanding, tolerance and friendship among all nations, racial or religious groups, and shall further the activities of the United Nations for the maintenance of peace.

---

[3]See PPEHRC's website, www.economichumanrights.org, for ways these are used "on the ground." For useful explanation of the rights, see the essays at the website of The National Economic and Social Rights Initiative (NESRI), www.nesri.org/economic_social_rights/index.html

(3) Parents have a prior right to choose the kind of education that shall be given to their children.[4]

In other parts of the globe, economic human rights are not only familiar to citizens, but incorporated in varying degrees into the national and supranational legal frameworks (Gough, 2000). In Central and South America, for example, most nations have agreed to be bound by the adjudications of the Inter-American Court of Human Rights (IACHR), a body charged with enforcing and interpreting the provisions of the American Convention on Human Rights. This instrument is very similar in its provisions to the UDHR. To become a member of the Organization of American States (OAS), the United States was required to agree to its principles, but it has not acceded to the authority of the IACHR (see, for example, Human Rights Education Associates, www.hrea.org). Thus, when in 1999 PPEHRC filed a petition with the IACHR claiming that the United States had violated economic human rights by eliminating rights and entitlements under "welfare reform" provisions, they were aware that the petition would have greater moral force in Central and South America than in the United States, and would serve to build the movement in the United States and alliances among people living in poverty across national boundaries (Weiss, 2000).

Chile has organizations based in poor communities, but given the "culture of rights" among the people, they are more woven into social and political fabric of the people than is PPEHRC in the United States. Approaches to feeding the hungry illustrate this point well. In Chile, this is typically accomplished through *Ollas Comunes*. These are similar to, but critically different from, a soup kitchen. In soup kitchens in the United States, people from outside the community find the ingredients, prepare and serve the meal for people who are, according to neoliberal discourse, "food insecure." In Chile that would be seen as inappropriate. An *Olla Comun* is an organization run by the very people who are hungry. The organizational form dates back to the early years of the Republic and the first miners' strikes in the North of the country. The workers and their families would pool their food resources and cook together in order to be sure that all had something to eat. This practice became a tradition in Chile as exploited Chileans organized for their human rights throughout the history of the country.

SOCIAL WORK AND HUMAN RIGHTS

It is not surprising, given this cultural difference, that human rights—and particularly economic rights—have been more fully integrated into social work in Chile, among other nations, than in the United States. Social workers have played key roles in grassroots organizations in Chile, not as managers, or leaders, but as partners in the struggle for human rights. Historically, social workers in Chile have seen their role as partners in solidarity with exploited Chileans (Sánchez, 1989). This is one of the reasons that the Pinochet military

[4]Adopted and proclaimed by General Assembly resolution 217 A (III) of 10 December 1948.

regime closed the School of Social Work at the *Universidad de Chile;* they saw it as a breeding ground for subversion and terrorism against the state. During the military regime, most schools of social work became much more conservative and began teaching the case management approach to social work without content in human rights. Prior to the military regime, social workers fought side by side with union members, shantytown residents, peasants, students, and other exploited groups demanding that economic human rights be respected. After the military coup, they also found the need to fight against the rampant abuse of political and civil human rights. Today, with the gradual restoration of democracy in the country, social workers are reclaiming their social transformation mission and rights framework, and they continue to fight for the human rights of all, including the rights of the original people of Chile, the Mapuches (Eroles, 1997; Sánchez, 1989).

In the United States, despite a few notable exceptions (Baptist, Bricker-Jenkins, & Dillon, 1999; Gil, 1998; UN, 1992; Witkin, 1999; Wronka, 1992) and chapters in previous editions of this text, little has been available on human rights in the U.S. social work literature until recently. Since the turn of the decade, the integration of a human rights perspective into social work practice and education has been aided by recent publications from English-speaking nations more familiar with the concepts (see, for example, Dominelli, 2005; Ferguson, Lavelette, & Whitmore, 2004; Ife, 2001; Mullaly, 2001, 2002; Thompson, 2002). Only in the last few years have a few social work texts appeared that have presented or attempted specifically to integrate a human rights perspective (Lee, 2001; Reichert, 2003, 2007; van Wormer, 2004; Wronka, 2008). There are few resources specific to economic human rights practice (for example, Bricker-Jenkins, Young, & Honkala, 2007; Bricker-Jenkins, 2004).

So we have to continue to reflect and act upon what human rights mean to us as social workers. How do we move beyond the discourse of human rights, beyond a theoretical belief in human rights, to a social work practice permeated by human rights in the United States as it is in, for example, Chile? Most urgently, given the rising tide of poverty and pervasive economic vulnerability accompanied by a crumbling seawall of civil and political rights in the United States, and given the fact that we and nearly all with whom we work are together experiencing economic stress, how can an economic human rights framework mobilize our strengths to accomplish our transformative agenda?

That has been a central question for the scores of social workers who have worked with PPEHRC member organizations since the mid-1990s as allies and, in some cases, as members. They have built a practice from dialog and shared experiences with people living in poverty (Baptist, Bricker-Jenkins, Gentry, Johnson, & Novak, 2006; Jones, 2000; Jones & Bricker-Jenkins, 2002). How and where this practice is conducted has depended largely on two factors: relationships and auspices.

For those who have had opportunities to work in collaboration with people living in poverty, especially those who are members of organizations led by the poor, the practice is much like the practice of social workers in Chile. They have counseled and comforted, participated in direct actions, organized events, accessed resources, advocated and intervened with social service and healthcare organizations, researched and promoted change in social policy arenas. They have organized "underground railroad depots"—groups of allies who mobilize resources and support PPEHRC groups. They have co-authored publications with leaders of the organizations, co-created field placements and other experiential learning activities. For the larger social work community they have developed a substantial training and educational curriculum and materials and made these available through PPEHRC's educational arm, the University of the Poor. Several whose social work practice was incubated in PPEHRC organizations, or later influenced by their collaborative work, now teach in schools of social work and infuse economic human rights perspectives into their courses.

Most U.S. social workers, however, do not have the benefit of working with PPEHRC and similar organizations, neither as allies or members. They work in traditional settings—auspices that govern and define the range of "appropriate" relationships they have with people who are in client status. Some can work after hours—that is, under different auspices—with people living in poverty in true partnership relationships, but there remains the need for integration of an economic human rights perspective into practice in conventional settings. In the remainder of this chapter, we turn to that need and opportunity.

PRINCIPLES OF ECONOMIC HUMAN RIGHTS PRACTICE[5]

At this stage of development, we are constructing an economic human rights (EHR) practice using the scaffolding of a set of practice principles. These have been based on Jones's 2000 study of perceptions of needed and desired social work approaches by PPEHRC leaders living in poverty (Jones, 2000; Jones & Bricker-Jenkins, 2002), organized conversations among social workers working in or with PPEHRC organizations, and the Chilean experience. Some of these principles are identical with those of other politically oriented and strengths-based approaches, but have a particular meaning and application in an EHR framework. In the next section, we will discuss and illustrate each of the following six elements of the scaffolding:

1. Human rights are indivisible and universal; everyone has economic human rights.
2. We must examine and challenge false assumptions about the poor behind our work and behind the policies of our agencies and government.
3. There are narratives of people's lives that are not being told in the media; they must be told and legitimized.
4. There is power in collectivity
   - to break isolation.
   - to provide support.
   - to create change.
5. Individual problems are social and political problems:
   - the personal *is* political.
   - there is no divide between clinical social work and political social work.
6. Ending poverty is possible and essential for our survival.

---

[5]Created by members of the KWRU Social Work Strategy Committee and the School of Social Work and Social Transformation of the University of the Poor, Poor People's Economic Human Rights Campaign.

THE PRINCIPLES IN ACTION: CASE EXAMPLES

Indivisibility and Universality of Human Rights

First and foremost, human rights in all their manifestations are indivisible. This means that civil and political rights cannot be ensured without social, economic, and cultural rights, and vice versa. This is a fundamental principle in human rights theory and law; the fact that the United States ignores this principle does not obviate it. In the following case example, a social worker is working in a prison setting with women who do not have the economic power to protect their legal and civil rights from *de facto* suspension by the public child welfare agency. The consequences for their children—and, ultimately, for the social fabric—are devastating.

> I have been working with mothers who are incarcerated in the county jail. The vast majority of these women are serving relatively short sentences (less than 3 years), mostly involving drug charges. In the jail, I run a parenting support and education group and also work one on one, as needed by individual members of the group, on "problem solving" related to their children and their DHS cases. Most of the women do not receive visits with their children (DHS social workers tell them they can't do visits in jail, even though the only person who can suspend visits for any reason is a judge, and a mother being in jail is not automatic grounds for suspending visits.) Furthermore, many of the women have no information about their children; they do not know where they are, with whom they are living, how they are doing in school. They do not receive medical reports on their children, school reports, psychologist/psychiatrist reports, service plan documents from DHS, or even court reports. All of this, of course, not only violates their economic human rights, but also their civil rights and even DHS policy and procedure. Everything about jail is just awful. I'm glad to be there (and glad I'm not there more than two afternoons a week), but it's so clear to me how completely ineffective it all is.

In this climate that dismisses and debases the women's most basic rights and human needs, it is not surprising that the women internalize the shame and blame heaped upon them and "act out" in the group—especially when the agency that is keeping their children away from them tell them what they must learn in the group. The worker deals with the behaviors and the false assumptions about the women by reframing their situations in economic human rights terms. She shows a film that portrays the political context of the drug scene, and she validates the violation of their rights by having them document their stories.

> I have really been struggling with process in my group, but I figured out to just ditch the suggested curriculum and activities and facilitate a more general discussion, integrating the content as appropriate. It's working much better. Women in the jail get yelled at all day long, and I am not going to yell. I couldn't pull it off even if I wanted to, which I don't. So figuring out what else to do to balance the tendency toward chaos has been an interesting challenge. Most of the women are ultimately in the group to satisfy a DHS requirement, but I've tried hard to convey—without jeopardizing my job, I hope—that I don't think DHS is effective as a system and that I am willing, if they should want, to assist them in navigating/dealing with DHS. Over half the women in the group have approached me asking specific questions about their own experiences with DHS, and I take that as a good sign. I regularly

include content on economic human rights in my groups, and I have shown PPEHRC films (especially the Drug War Reality Tour film) in my groups to stimulate discussions of economic human rights violations. The women fill out economic human rights violations forms as part of the group, as well.

Universality is another fundamental principle of human rights that has a particular import for social workers. With our penchant for categorical thinking and policymaking in the name of efficiency and effectiveness, now aggravated by privatization of services, we have lost track of the fact that everyone has economic rights. In the following illustration, an agency works within an intractable system toward the goal of ensuring that everyone can claim the right to health. It should be noted that the right is the right to health, not merely to healthcare, and most certainly not just health insurance. But the agency seizes every opportunity to get closer to that goal.

> The mission of my agency is to improve the systems and supports that affect people with low incomes so that they can live with dignity and economic security. We advocate with and on behalf of them in the areas of healthcare, food assistance, income supports, employment, and education and training by providing representation in the courts, the Legislature, and administrative agencies; legal policy research and analysis; and education and training about legal rights and opportunities to participate in public policy reform. In other words, we work to help ensure the economic human rights of people in our state.
>
> Reading the inspiring language of the Universal Declaration of Human Rights leads many people to wonder how to operationalize its ideals. My agency's work to protect Medicaid coverage for the so-called "non-categoricals," a group of individuals with low income who are not entitled to federally protected Medicaid coverage like the "categoricals" are, provides one example of translating Article 25 and its aspiration to ensure "the right to a standard of living adequate for the health and well-being of themselves and their family, including. . . medical care. . ." into policy.
>
> Federal Medicaid entitlement is based on low-income status within a coverable group, or category: children through age 20, parents of children, pregnant women, disabled adults, and seniors. What, then, of the many adults age 21 to 64 who are not living with dependent children and do not meet the strict standards for "qualifying" as disabled (or who are unable to provide the necessary paperwork to document a disability)? Much of our homeless population falls into this "non-cat" category. From working to obtain the waiver necessary to offer Medicaid coverage to this special group back in 2002 to ongoing efforts to protect further cuts to the enrollment cap and restrictions on healthcare services provided to this group, Maine Equal Justice has helped ours to be one of a small handful of states that offers Medicaid to the non-cats. In this way, we can be proud to have a policy that represents one path toward the commonly held value to ensure healthcare for all people.

It is unlikely that we will soon be thinking and acting in "universal" terms. The pervasiveness of racism, sexism, heterosexism, and myriad other forms of institutionalized prejudice and domination have served well the interests of those who cleave our unity to cling to their power. As long as some groups of people are, by these forces, rendered more vulnerable than others, it is likely that we will need "identity-based" programs and practices. But if we are to claim our universal rights, it is essential to understand even as we work in and for these programs that we are also serving the interests of those who would be threatened by unity.

That is why PPEHRC organizes across color lines. Most people living in poverty in the United States are white, but most images of poverty are colored in black and brown. This is not an accident (Neubeck, 2006). We are hindered as well in the United States by false notions of "class." We tend to think of class as culture, we conflate income with class, and we are encouraged to think of multiple rungs on a ladder of class—each of which separates the huge majority from the tiny minority that owns the majority of the wealth. This too is not an accident. Thus, USians consistently vote for programs and policies that run counter to their economic interests. Acting from an economic human rights framework, with its principles of indivisibility and universality, is a corrective to that (Bricker-Jenkins & Baptist, 2006).

Assumptions About "Poor People" and Poverty

False assumptions about poverty and people living in poverty pervade our policy and practice; we must examine and challenge these assumptions. Do we really understand, for example, how economic policies and decisions actually work to violate human rights? Do we understand how these same economic decisions tie our hands as social workers and keep from us the valuable resources we need to effectively and ethically engage in our practice? More insidiously, people living in poverty share these assumptions. We have found that, when we listen deeply to people, they apologize for being poor and reveal their fear and the shame of poverty. In the following illustration we see how the use of an economic human rights lens helps a therapist see the dynamics of poverty-based blame and shame, surface them, and move toward resolution.

> Kate, a white woman in her twenties, was coping with her very ill mother moving in with her. Kate had a very conflictual relationship with her mother, whose depression and many physical health problems often got in the way of meeting Kate's emotional needs growing up. As Kate was trying to come to terms with and express the anger she had toward her mother, I realized that Kate may have lacked understanding and empathy for the social and economic struggles that her mother had had and that Kate herself was currently having.
>
> Kate grew up in a rural part of the state, where her single mother struggled to provide for her two children. Kate, who attended college, realized in our explorations that she often felt "out of place" because her friends and colleagues did not know the economic hardships that she and her family experienced. Kate felt ashamed that her mother's home was foreclosed and that she was now having to support herself and her mother. Kate faulted her mother for shopping compulsively on TV shopping networks, but not having money to pay the taxes on the family home. After allowing Kate to express her anger, I suggested that maybe her mother did the best she could considering the economy, the lack of financial support, the lack of quality physical and mental health care available in poor rural areas, and the possible shame her mother felt for being poor and especially white and poor.
>
> Kate expressed an immense amount of relief at the thought that, yes, she didn't get what she needed from her mother, but her mother loved her and did the best she could under the economic conditions of a country that, despite all its wealth, does not make sure people have adequate housing, healthcare, and education. Kate was able to let go of some of the shame she felt about growing up poor and continuing to struggle financially. Kate was able to take some of the anger she felt toward herself and her mother for being poor and express it outward toward a society and government that allow the needs of corporations to come

before the needs of Kate's mother and Kate. Kate now works for an agency advocating for the rights and needs of people without healthcare, and her sense of self is stronger.

The next illustration is from an agency that had a "critical mass" of workers who consciously used an economic human rights framework. That fact helped them create a service and practice that stood in marked contrast to the prevailing drug and alcohol approach, to which youth seldom respond well.

> The setting is a harm-reduction-based youth organization with a drop-in center and supportive services for those who access this center. As a social worker working one-on-one with our participants on their journey toward risk reduction and increased health, I used a cognitive-behavioral model, but my commitment to the EHR framework eliminated the "blame the victim" mentality that runs rampant in the drug and alcohol field. Almost all of our participants are victims of trauma in one capacity or another, making quitting their self-medication practices increasingly difficult, especially in a world where mental health services are near-impossible to access. The cycle of decreased use leading to increased PTSD-induced flashbacks, leading to a return to the one coping mechanism they have—relapse—was a continual battle we faced together. Without a true understanding of the systemic causes of poverty and the gross lack of access to economic human rights, it would have been too easy to blame my participants for this cycle and inevitable relapse. Once out of rehab, why do they continually return to their drug of choice? The lack of housing, living wage jobs, adequate mental healthcare, especially D&A treatment, in a world where "personal responsibility" removes any responsibly from the system to make such things available—that results in a reality where many are doomed to fail.
>   My commitment in the fight to change this system, work to get economic human rights for all, and basing all I do in my social work practice upon the EHR framework has resulted in my being able to practice in a manner based on human dignity and respect, and to work in solidarity with my participants toward a world where we are not forced to self-medicate due to lack of adequate healthcare and D&A services, to do sex work to survive due to lack of housing and living-wage jobs, to break the law to feed ourselves due to a lack of accessible food and nutrition.

An EHR practice also challenges some of the conventional wisdoms of social work. We have been taught, for example, to "help those who cannot help themselves" and to "empower others." While based on good intentions, and appropriate in some cases, these concepts are often misunderstood and misapplied because of the assumptions we make. As in the case of the Chilean *Olla Comunes,* EHR practice is really strengths and empowerment in action. It so eloquently demonstrates that no one can empower others, but that given the proper conditions people can and will empower themselves. The following comes from a social worker in the United States; in this case the practice helped to create the requisite conditions.

> I absolutely love my job [in childcare]. We successfully engaged in a state budget campaign to lift the five-year-old freeze on income eligibility for subsidized childcare, which put in 67 million new dollars into the childcare system. Low-income parents led the campaign, testified at budget hearings, and held a rally outside the state capitol (600 parents!) to inform legislators about the need for quality affordable childcare. The experience I shared with all of you [in my field placement at a PPEHRC organization] really taught me about the

social worker I want to be. The stories of these parents inform my work; they have the expertise and knowledge about their children and their families, and it's so vital that they are at the forefront making their voices heard in order to effect change. All I have to do is put a mirror in their face to let them know and realize they have power, they can lead, and they can destroy the myths about poor people.

Untold Narratives of "The Disappeared"

In Chile, the military regime "disappeared" thousands who were fighting for their rights, including many social workers. In the United States, "disappearing" people takes a different form. People living in poverty are stripped of the truths of their lives. Their truths are replaced with myths and legends that justify punitive policies and controlling practices. So there are narratives of many people's lives that are not being told in the media and even professional literature; they must be told and legitimized. Further, we must work not to "give voice to the voiceless"; all people have a voice. Rather, we must work to make sure all voices are heard.

One of the ways we do that is to organize "truth commissions" and help people participate in them. Truth commissions are used in the global South as part of a formal reconciliation process. Through them, people publicly tell their stories and reclaim their lives and their rights. In the United States, there is no formal sanction for them, but PPEHRC organizes local and national truth commissions to document and analyze violations of economic human rights, fix responsibility, and mobilize participants to claim their rights.[6] Social workers—and social work students—have not only helped to organize these, but have collected documentation for them and even testified about the violations they and their own families have experienced. Truth commissions help us understand that the individual problems we experience are really social and political problems that we share with millions of others. The following illustrates one EHR social worker's political and therapeutic approach to case management in a mental health setting. In this case, given the circumstances, the testimony might be read by someone else, but the story will be told and validated.

> [Laura] receives case management services. She is in hiding from an extremely violent spouse and has three children. They all have a rare genetic medical condition. She has had to fight to stay in hiding and change her identity with welfare and social security. She is also fighting everyday to get to the appropriate specialists for the family's medical condition. She has been introduced to [our local PPEHRC organization] and the concept of economic human rights. We are now working on her testimony for a truth commission we are planning for April.

Collectivity and the Unity of the Poor

EHR practice is fueled by the power of collectivity. We live in a U.S. society that wants to keep us apart. Our neoliberal economic model is designed so that we work in isolation. Working together in a collective permits us to break out of this isolation, provide support to

---

[6]See the brief report at www.economichumanrights.org/ntc_report1.shtml A full report, which includes a "how to" section for collecting documentation and organizing local truth commissions, is in production and will be available from PPEHRC in mid 2008.

one another, and create change. In the United States, we must be countercultural and work together, learning from those in places like Chile where collectivity is more culturally consonant. Here a social worker speaks to the cultural differences and to an appropriate social work role in a collective of people living in poverty.

> When I explain to people in the global North, especially the United States, the work I have been doing in Chile for the past twenty years, I have to spell out the differences as folks do not always get it. For example, for a number of years I worked with Ollas Comunes in the shantytown La Pincoya, where I lived. In the Olla Comun, the members continue to pool their resources and search for more resources so that they can cook together and so that no one goes hungry. Sometimes that means that the organization has to carry the weight of the poorest members since they often have nothing to share, but the practice of solidarity is one that is very important in Chile and in all grassroots organizations. So, one might ask, if the Olla Comun is self-sufficient, why would a "gringa" be needed? I worked with the Ollas providing assessment, support, and training along with the social workers at the Vicariate of Solidarity of the Roman Catholic Church.

Collectivity can be an antidote even to the most extreme suffering:

> During the dark days of the military regime, poor Chileans continued to organize for their human rights, at great personal risk and cost. Luzmenia Toro Sepúlveda, one of the founders of La Pincoya, was arrested on 11 September 1973 and tortured at a local police station. When she was released, one of the first things she did was to begin an Olla Comun with those families who were suffering at the hands of the U.S.-sponsored and supported military regime. She and her family would pay dearly, but that did not stop them.

The right to housing—not homeless shelters, but housing—is one that has spurred collective action in the United States. With many social workers directly and indirectly involved, some PPEHRC have occupied federally owned vacant properties, declaring them "human rights houses," when all attempts to house people through the social service systems have failed. Since the lack of available and affordable housing—and not family pathology—appears to be the largest factor preventing reunification in child welfare cases, EHR social workers have been particularly supportive of these actions. The right to housing applies to all individuals, but can best be claimed collectively in environments that elevate the right to profit over the right to housing. Again, we learn from Chilean experience:

> The Comités de los Sin Casa are another example of people organizing themselves to get their needs met. Housing has been a perpetual problem in the poor areas of Chile's cities. And, since the Chilean winter can be harsh, adequate housing is important. In order to deal with the lack of housing, shantytown dwellers in Santiago in the 1950s organized the first Comité de los Sin Casa. These leaders worked with members to raise and save money for downpayments on public housing, but when their attempts to work with the government failed, they decided it was time to be the protagonists. They organized the first land occupation in Latin America and named it La Población La Victoria (The Victory) because they had attained a "victoria contra la miseria"—a victory over misery (Lagos et al., 2002, p. 3). Other land occupations followed.

In EHR practice, collectivity is also cultivated among organizations and between practitioners and organizations who meet people's needs based not on conventional social service philosophies and program categories, but on an EHR framework:

> One of the women in my group, Gina, has been struggling with an addiction to crack cocaine for the last twenty-six years. She has two living children, ages 9 and 5, both living with Gina's mother. She has seen her children once in the past five months, although she speaks to them on the phone nearly every day. Gina has been in and out of jail for years, always for relatively short sentences. She will be leaving jail again soon and is terrified of leaving and relapsing. (She has not been using while incarcerated, although drugs are widely available in jail.) Gina has been requesting that she be "court-ordered" into a recovery program upon release, but has been told that she is not eligible for such a program and has been repeatedly denied. Her probation officer says that she may be able to get into an outpatient program, but Gina is convinced that she will use again if she is back on the street right now.
>
> When she raised this with me, she was both devastated and scared. She and I talked for a while about the "right to recovery" and how that right doesn't change just because someone has been an addict for a long time or relapsed many times. We talked about how common relapse is and we talked about how and why drugs impact our community, referring specifically to the Drug War Reality Tour film I had shown in group. I contacted New Jerusalem, a long-term inpatient drug treatment program with significant connections to the PPEHRC. New Jerusalem was willing to accept her right from jail, no questions asked. Gina took the information and was very relieved and happy. We talked about the difference between this program and others with regard to their policies on eligibility, insurance, intake, etc.

The Personal Is Political

This adage is truer today than it ever was: The personal *is* political. In the throes of our daily practice, it is easy to lose sight of the fact that the conditions we face are the result of conscious decisions made by people we've entrusted with formal power, whether they be government officials, professional leaders, or academics. We must take back the political—"by the people"—so that we can effectively govern ourselves to ensure our human rights. This can begin by identifying the ways that decisions that we think of as necessary and inevitable were the result of choices.

> I got a call after work from a deputy sheriff. He knew I had an extra refrigerator and asked if he could have it. He explained that he was called on a child abuse case that day because DHS was going to remove the children. The mom had no food and no way of getting any. He asked the DHS worker about the emergency funds the department had to prevent placement, but she said they were all gone for the year, all spent in six months. He and the social worker agreed "there was nothing wrong with this family but they was poor," he said, but the worker's hands were tied, she said. He went to his church and got a week's food, but the worker said the family had to have a fridge, so he called me. He had to get it right away because the social worker, who "was a good person that really wanted to help," was required to meet a deadline for action on the case, and she had other families she had to see that day. Of course, I gave him the refrigerator, but I have to ask what's wrong with this picture— the cop is doing the social work because the social worker is required to be the cop. Who decided that's the way it should be, and who is letting it continue? I keep hearing the words, "There was nothing wrong with this family but they was poor."

In Kentucky a group of BSW students—all from the ranks of the poor themselves—founded a "self-help" group called Women in Transition (WIT). They stayed together after they graduated and affiliated with PPEHRC. Over time they realized that the greatest problem facing women in their community was the threat of losing their children for economic reasons. Their civil rights were also being violated, and their shame and isolation were rendering them even more vulnerable. The WIT women began a project called CORROC—Claiming Our Rights/Reclaiming Our Children. They put out the word that people contacted by DHS could contact them. Their "posse" would be there to walk through the investigation process with them. WIT has had demonstrations and truth commissions to reveal the link between economic human rights violations and child removal, the enormous cost of child removal compared to meeting families' needs, and the ways that families' legal rights are violated. Their work has resulted in many changes in child welfare policies and practice in the state, but they are not finished. Political decisions are being made that are hitting close to—and may be destroying—people's lives.

The same is true, of course, in Chile, but EHR practice grown more easily in that climate, and this illustration demonstrates:

> Chela is a social worker who has been working in human rights for decades. A Mapuche from Santiago, she began her work during the military regime protesting the violent violations of human rights. She has worked in many areas of human rights, with women, with youth and with the struggle of her Mapuche people. One of the most important sites of her work, however, was with young girls who were forced into prostitution to help their families make ends meet in La Pincoya. Instead of condemning these girls, or approaching them from a conventional social service or case management perspective that was the predominant approach at the time, Chela worked with them from a human rights perspective. She spent vast amounts of time listening to the girls and their stories, getting to know them and their realities. She engaged them in deep discussions and asked them about their dreams for themselves. She then talked to them about their rights as human beings, introducing them to the United Nations Convention on the rights of the child. She helped facilitate a process where the girls could understand the economic conditions, specifically the rise of neoliberalism in Chile, that forced them into prostitution. Finally, she worked with them to form cooperatives where they could learn trades, organize for their rights, and build a future not based on prostitution.

If the personal is political, our practice must reflect that reality. The false divide within social work itself between clinical social work practice, political social work practice, and activist social work practice does not serve social work and certainly does not serve the advancement of human rights. The following illustrates one way that EHR practice integrates the personal and political, bringing practice into line with lived experience and unleashing personal political power for a collective struggle.

> I saw this particular man for grief counseling services. He was 74 years old and his wife had died after a long illness. There were outstanding medical bills after his wife's death, and he was trying to pay them in full. This was a terrible problem because he certainly could not afford this and got behind in his other bills. In working together we discovered that he felt it would dishonor his wife not to pay the medical bills, and he was also someone who always paid any bill sent to him. I introduced him to Economic Human Rights. We established that healthcare is a human right guaranteed to all. We used this as a framework for him to see that

some of the bills were unjust, and we explored the idea that his wife would not want him to have financial stress and worry in order to pay these bills. We discussed the profits made by the healthcare industry and used this disconnect with his experience of trying to pay his bills of daily necessity to free him of this obligation and to reframe the duty he was feeling to his wife and a corporation he owed money to. He will pay the bills as he can, but he is in charge of the process now. He will be testifying at our Truth Commission.

Ending Poverty Is Possible and Necessary

Finally, we must believe that ending poverty is possible and essential for the survival of all—ourselves as much as those persons currently in client status. Fulfilling the vision of the UDHR will end poverty. Poverty is not a natural state, but the result of collective decisions. Changing those big decisions will require a big movement, and that's what PPEHRC and other groups around the globe are building together. Social workers can be a part of that, and not only after hours. Just as Chilean social workers have done in large measure, practice can be transformed to integrate the work of claiming economic human rights. The following illustration is summative, reflecting all the principles of EHR practice, including an approach to fostering hope that poverty can end and supporting action to end it.

> As a social worker in a legal clinic, I was asked to work with a man, David, who had lost his house due to a mortgage foreclosure. The attorney suggested that I could help him find new housing, without having much sense of what exactly that might involve.
>
> David was a 47-year-old African American man who had lived in his home for fifteen years. He was divorced and a stepparent, but did not have regular contact with his step-children. His only other family was a younger sister and her husband, both of whom lived nearby. David was permanently disabled and received Social Security Disability payments monthly. This was before there was any prescription drug benefit for people receiving Medicare, so over half of David's monthly $750 Social Security payment went to pay for his needed prescription medications. Because David was considered permanently disabled, there were subsidized housing options that didn't involve a 10+ year waiting list, but not many options, and we had less than four months.
>
> David had a long history of community involvement and felt very connected to his community. He had been his block captain for years before he became too ill to continue. He had received a special recognition from City Council for his service to the city. David and I talked extensively about economic human rights, with specific focus on the right to healthcare and housing. Together, we filled out an economic human rights violation form.
>
> In the course of filling out applications for subsidized buildings for disabled adults, David and I decided to rely on his City Council connections. "I helped people for a lot of years, and now it's their turn to help me, too." He was fortunate to get an apartment with a move-in date only three weeks after his scheduled eviction date. He himself wrote a letter to the foreclosing bank, demanding that they respect his human rights to housing and not forcibly evict him. He also threatened to go to the news media, should they not grant him an exten-sion. (They did grant it.) I applied for a small grant that covered his moving expenses, as he was not able to pack and move his belongings and needed significant help to do so. Once he was all moved in to his new building, he and I met one last time (he cooked dinner for me, even), during which he told me his intention to educate others about the rights to housing and healthcare. He had written a number of letters to elected officials at statewide, local, and federal levels, demanding universal healthcare and housing for all.

David's story also reminds us that the movement we must build, while led by the poor, is not a "poor people's movement." It is a movement to end poverty by guaranteeing everyone's human rights. It is sometimes difficult for social workers, steeped in a social services model, to grasp their solidarity with people living in poverty. But it can happen. In Pennsylvania, members of the founding PPEHRC organization, the Kensington Welfare Rights Union, worked with members of the state legislature and with the state chapter of the National Association of Social Workers in a multiyear economic human rights campaign (Bricker-Jenkins, 2004). At the beginning of the project, many social workers from across the state "helped out." At the final legislative hearing, however, many of those social workers sat side by side with people in client status and testified about the economic human rights violations they had experienced. This work eventually came together as the PA-PPEHRC, which is an affiliate of the national PPEHRC and whose membership includes people living in poverty, community organizations, and social workers from across the state. This represents a fundamental change in thinking about "class," and transforms the social work relationship from service to solidarity—a pragmatic solidarity (Farmer, 2005) grounded in our commonalities and not in a particular "techniques de jour."

CONCLUSION

In order to engage in practice from an economic human rights framework, social workers need a sense of history to begin the long journey to justice. We must move beyond the false dichotomies of shame and blame, deserving and undeserving poor, that have been in place over 500 years and advocate for laws and policies that will actually permit us to engage in social work practice rather than case management or, worse, poverty management. As our "harm reduction" worker said,

> This framework removes the foundation upon which the culture of poverty and the blame the victim philosophy have been built. This framework showed me a sure way to be the social worker I am proud to be and work in partnership with those who come before me with so much self-blame and hatred for believing they have failed—instead of knowing it was in fact a system that had failed them.

Finally, EHR practice enables us to engage in thoughtful, reflexive study that leads to concrete action—that is, the process of praxis as described by Brasilian educator Paulo Freire—reflection, study, action that is necessary to bring about social change (Freire, 1970). It helps us do the work that we chose to do when we chose social work.

DISCUSSION QUESTIONS/EXERCISES

1. If you can, in a group that you are familiar with or in a class or in an in-service training and where it would be appropriate, initiate a discussion about our failure to recognize economic human rights and how we can begin, in our small way, to advocate for economic human rights.

2. What does it mean to say the personal is political? And how does that affect your social work practice? How should it affect your practice?

3. Go to a local food pantry or soup kitchen and observe how things are run. Keeping in mind what the authors say about the importance of critically involving those who make use of the service in delivering, how does this operation stack up?

4. What does use of the term *USian* mean to you?

REFERENCES

Baptist, W., Bricker-Jenkins, M., & Dillon, M. (1999). Taking the struggle on the road: The new freedom bus—freedom from unemployment, hunger, and homelessness. *Journal of Progressive Human Services, 10*(2), pp. 7–29.

Baptist, W. & Bricker-Jenkins, M. (2001). A view from the bottom: Poor people and their allies respond to welfare reform. *The Annals of the American Academy of Political Science, 577,* 144–156.

Baptist, W., Bricker-Jenkins, M., DGentry, S., Johnson, M., & Novak. (2006). "That history becomes you": Slave narratives and today's movement to end poverty. In D Saleebey (Ed.). *The strengths perspective in social work practice.* Boston: Allyn & Bacon/Longman.

Bricker-Jenkins, M. (2004). Legislative tactics in a movement strategy: The Economic Human Rights-Pennsylvania Campaign. *Meridians, 4* (1), 108-113.

Bricker-Jenkins, M. & Baptist, W. (2006). The movement to end poverty in the United States. In R. E. Howard-Hassman & C. E. Welch, Jr. (Eds.), *Economic Rights in Canada and the United States* (pp. 103–117). Philadelphia: University of Pennsylvania Press.

Bricker-Jenkins, M., Young, C., & Honkala, C. (2008). Using economic human rights in the movement to end poverty: The Kensington Welfare Rights Union and The Poor People's Economic Human Rights Campaign. In E. Reichert (Ed.), *The Other Human Rights: Perspectives on Economic, Social, and Cultural Rights* (pp. 180–201). New York: Columbia University Press.

Dominelli, L. (2005). *Social work futures: Crossing boundaries, transforming practice.* New York: Palgrave Macmillan.

Eroles, C. (1997). *Los derechos humanos: Compromiso ético del trabajo social* [Human rights: An ethical imperative for social work]. Buenos Aires: Espacio Editorial.

Farmer, P. (2005). *Pathologies of power: Health, human rights, and the new war on the poor.* Berkeley: University of California Press.

Ferguson, I., Lavalette, M., & Whitmore, B. (Eds.). (2004). *Globalisation, global justice and social work.* London: Taylor and Francis.

Freire, P. (1970). *Pedagogy of the oppressed.* New York: The Continuum Publishing Company.

Gil, D. G. (1998). *Confronting injustice and oppression: Concepts and strategies for social workers.* New York: Columbia University Press.

Gough, I. (2000). Why do levels of human welfare vary across nations? In I. Gough (Ed.), *Global capital, human needs, and social policies: Selected essays, 1994–99,* (pp. 105–130). New York: Palgrave.

Gough, I. (2004). Human well-being and social structures: Relating the universal and the local. *Global Social Policy, 4*(3), 289–311.

Howard-Hassmann, R. E. & Welch, Jr., C. E. (Eds.). *Economic rights in Canada and the United States.* Philadelphia: University of Pennsylvania Press.

Human Rights Education Associates Retrieved February 12, 2008, from www.hrea.org/index.php?base_id=150

Ife, J. (2001). *Human rights and social work: Towards a rights-based practice.* Cambridge, UK: Cambridge University Press.

Jones, J. (2000). *Doing the work: A collaborative study conducted with members of the Kensington Welfare Rights Union, Philadelphia, PA.* Northampton, MA: Smith College School for Social Work.

Jones, J. & Bricker-Jenkins, M., with members of the Kensington Welfare Rights Union. (2002). Creating strengths-based alliances to end poverty. In D. Saleebey (Ed.), *The strengths perspective in social work* (3rd ed., pp. 186–212). New York: Longman.

Kaplan, C. P. & Kaplan, L. (1993). Public opinion and the "Economic Bill of Rights." *Journal of Progressive Human Service, 4*(1), 43–59.

Lagos, J., González, J.M, Núnez, N., Rodríguez, G., & Finn, J. (2002). *La Victoria: Rescatando la historia* [La Victoria: Recuperating history]. Santiago, Chile: Junta de Vecinos de La Victoria.

Lee, J. A. B. (2001). *The empowerment approach to social work practice: Building the beloved community,* (2nd ed.). New York: Columbia University Press.

Melish, T. J. (2006). Rethinking the "less as more" thesis: Supranational litigation of economic, social and cultural rights in the Americas. *New York University Journal of International Law and Politics (JILP), 39,* 1. Available at SSRN: http://ssrn.com/abstract=955920

Melish, T. J. (2007). The Inter-American Commission on Human Rights: Defending social rights through case-based petitions. In M. Langford (Ed.), *Social rights jurisprudence: Emerging trends in comparative and international Law.* New York: Cambridge University Press. Available at SSRN: http://ssrn.com/abstract=1000275

Mullaly, B. (2001). Confronting the politics of despair: Toward the reconstruction of progressive social work in a global economy and postmodern age. *Social Work Education, 20*(3), 303–320.

Mullaly, B. (2002). *Challenging oppression: A critical social work approach.* Don Mills, OT: Oxford.

Neubeck, K. J. (2006). *When welfare disappears: The case for economic human rights.* New York: Routledge.

Reichert, E. (2003). *Social work and human rights: A foundation for policy and practice.* New York: Columbia University Press.

Reichert, E. (2007). *Challenges in human rights: A social work perspective.* New York: Columbia University Press.

Sánchez, M. D. (1989). Trabajo social en derechos humanos: Reencuentro con la profesión [Social work in human rights. A reunion with the profession]. In Colectivo de Trabajo Social (Colectivo), *Trabajo social y derechos humanos: Compromiso con la dignidad. La experiencia chilena* [Social work and human rights: A commitment with dignity. The Chilean experience] (pp. 17—30). Buenos Aires: Editorial Humanitas.

Soohoo, C., Albisa, C., & Davis, M. F. (2007). *Bringing human rights home* (three volumes). New York: Praeger.

Sunstein, C. R. (2004). *The Second Bill of Rights: FDR'S unfinished revolution and why we need it more than ever.* New York: Basic Books.

Thompson, N. (2002). Social movements, social justice and social work. *British Journal of Social Work, 32,* 711–722.

United Nations Centre for Human Rights. (1992). *Teaching & learning about human rights: A manual for schools of social work and the social work profession.* New York: United Nations.

Van Wormer, K. (2004). *Confronting oppression, restoring justice: From policy analysis to social action.* Alexandria, VA: CSWE.

Weiss, P. (2000). Economic and social rights come of age: United States held to account in IACHR, in *Human Rights Brief,* 7(2), accessed February 12, 2008 at www.wcl.american.edu/hrbrief/v7i2/economic.htm

Witkin, S. (1999). Constructing our future. *Social Work, 44,* 5–8.

Wronka, J. (1992). *Human rights and social policy in the 21st century.* New York: University Press of America.

Wronka, J. (2008). *Human rights and social justice: Action and service for the helping and health professions.* Lanham, MD: Sage Publications.

ACKNOWLEDGMENTS

The authors wish to thank the following for their contributions of case material: Janine Corbett, Mary Ignatius, Jennifer C. Jones, Kristin Smith Nicely, Laura Rodgers. All are members of the Poor People's Economic Human Rights Campaign (PPEHRC) and its educational arm, the University of the Poor, School of Social Work and Social Transformation.

..... ▬▬▬▬▬▬▬▬▬▬▬▬▬▬▬▬▬▬

CHAPTER FIFTEEN

THE STRENGTHS PERSPECTIVE
Possibilities and Problems

DENNIS SALEEBEY

Focusing and building on client strengths is not simply a counterweight to the prevalence of the deficit model. It is an imperative of the several values that govern our work and the operations of a democratic, just, and pluralistic society. Such values include distributive justice, equality, respect for the dignity of the individual, inclusiveness and diversity, and the search for maximum autonomy within maximum community. Some critics score practitioners of the strengths perspective for turning their backs on the realities of poverty, injustice, racial and class discrimination, and institutional and interpersonal oppression.

John Longres (1997) makes the case that devotion to the strengths perspective may lead to the scrapping of those sociological and political ideas (e.g., Marxism, symbolic interactionism, and functionalism) that give an invaluable slant on the withering realities of oppression, alienation, and anomie. This is a serious criticism, if true. A review of writing and thinking in the fields of resilience practice as well as strengths-based approaches leads me to believe that there is little in either system that makes shrinking from other theories and frameworks a requisite—either implicit or explicit. Whether social work practitioners or theorists operate from, say, a cognitive behaviorist scheme or a neo-Marxist structuralist one, they still can infuse their professional thinking and acting with appreciations that reflect and employ the basic resources and assets of individuals, families, communities—even if it is not inherent in their tradition. Most, but certainly not all, orientations are conflicted about basic human nature and the human condition—the good, the bad, and the ugly. The strengths perspective, not as grand as a theory, nor as evolved, by any means, recognizes the fallibilities of people and the grinding problems that they face, but it is an attempt to restore, beyond rhetoric, some balance to the understanding of the human condition such that we recognize and honor the strengths and capacities of people as well as their afflictions and agonies.

In a sense, everything depends on the vitality and fairness of the developmental and social infrastructures of the community and state. In Walzer's (1983) view, justice and equality do not call for the elimination of differences, but the elimination of certain kinds of differences—those defined or created by people in power that are the bedrock of their domination of fellow citizens, whether the differences are couched in the language of race, class, gender, sexual orientation, or religious belief. In his words:

> It's not the fact that there are rich and poor that generates egalitarian struggle but the fact that the rich grind the faces of the poor. It's always what one group with power does to another group—whether in the name of health, safety or security—it makes no difference. The aim, ultimately, of the fight for equality is always the elimination of subordination . . . no more toadying, scraping and bowing, fearful trembling. (p. xiii)

For us, the message is that some models and institutions of helping throughout the years have become pillars of this kind of inequality. Sometimes, in the name of the good, welfare, or assisting, we inadvertently or, on occasion, deliberately, subdue or suppress the natural energies and motivations for becoming and for becoming better. We become operatives in systems that are sometimes not well designed or intended to promote the inner and outer assets and capacities of individuals, families, and communities. The doing of this, when it happens, is sometimes based on mistaking what is, in truth, a social phenomenon for an individual one. As William Ryan (1976), in his classic, *Blaming the Victim*, observed: ". . . the basic ideological maneuver in *Blaming the Victim* is to apply exceptionalistic analysis to universal problems" (p. 256). The exceptionalistic position argues that all observable social problems and defects are the result of unusual and probably unexpected circumstances that affect individuals and families in particular ways. These produce problems that cannot be predicted and cannot be solved except in each individual case and, even then, not completely. The universalist position sees social problems as rooted in social causation and, as such, they may be predictable and managed at the level of social program and policy. To mistakenly define structural problems as individual defects is to, therefore, blame the victim. In terms of a strengths point of view, this means that we have to fight what may be a heavy institutional or organizational inclination to see the problem in the individual. This effectively thwarts the knack for seeing the assets that lie within and around that individual or family or community.

Froma Walsh (1998), an experienced family practitioner, researcher, and educator, writes this about the mental health and, by implication, family fields of practice:

> In the field of mental health, most clinical theory, training, practice, and research have been overwhelmingly deficit-focused, implicating the family in the cause or maintenance of nearly all problems in individual functioning. Under early psychoanalytic assumptions of destructive maternal bonds, the family came to be seen as a noxious influence. Even the early family systems formulations focused on dysfunctional family processes well into the mid-1980s. More recently, popular movements for so-called "survivors" or "adult children of dysfunctional families" have spared almost no family from accusations of failure and blame. . . . With the clinical field so steeped in pathology, the intense scrutiny of family deficits and blindness to family strengths led me to suggest, only half-jokingly, that a "normal" family could be defined as one that has not yet been clinically assessed. (p. 15)

All of our knowledge (theories, principles) and all of our technical orientations must be examined, "critiqued, challenged, or corroborated in the light of their relationships to power and interest" (Kondrat, 1995, p. 417). Whether we discover that we are serving corporate interests, malignant political claims, or benighted professional frameworks, if they, in any way, obfuscate or distort local knowledge, ignore and suppress personal and communal strengths and powers (cognitive, moral, behavioral, political), then we, too, have committed a root act of oppression.

Whatever else it is, social justice is understood only in terms of domination—domination of the distribution of social goods, those resources essential for survival, growth and development, transformation, simple security and safety. Welfare, communal support and connection, commodities, goods, health, education, recreation, and shelter all underwrite identity as well as personal resourcefulness and strength—the tools for becoming as human and competent as possible. A more just and equitable distribution system is at the heart of the development and expression of individual and collective powers and capacities. As social workers, we confront and promote the idea of strengths at two very different levels—policy (philosophy) and practice (principles)—but they always meet in the lives of our clients.

In the 1960s, we talked of "power to the people." That apothegm had many different meanings. Not the least of these was that a government or social movement must dedicate itself to returning social, economic, material, and political goods to the people who had been systematically denied them. The idea of returning power to ordinary and oppressed citizens alike raised nettlesome questions. What, in fact, do people need? What are citizens entitled to? Whose claims to scarce social goods shall prevail? How shall these goods be distributed? When the ardor of the 1960s was stanched in the mid-1970s, these questions had not been answered. Today, collectively, we seem no closer to answers.

In the 1980s, the New Federalism—Reaganomics, for some—made the idea that these social resources could be disbursed through the devices of the marketplace exceedingly attractive. But the marketplace, at best, can provide only limited resources, often on quite a selective and preemptive basis. And, it should be obvious to anyone who shops, trades, sells, or invests, that the marketplace is no venue for the pursuit of justice, equity, or recompense. Unless it might sell beans, philosophic assertions about fertilizing the roots of democracy seem frightfully out of place in the private, for-profit sector of the economy. One would think, however, judging by all the books, talk shows, workshops, and infomercials available that the marketplace distribution of social and psychological capital has been a tremendous success. I think, rather, that this procession of pop-psych, pop-soc nostrums indicates that we have failed through conventional socializing institutions to help many individuals develop a sense of autonomy, personal mastery, or communal connection and failed to assist neighborhoods, communities, and cultures to retain their sense of value and distinctiveness.

As we lurched toward the millennium in the 1990s, the impetus for slicing the traditional ties between government and vulnerable people, between workers and corporations gained momentum. The welfare reforms of 1996 (the Personal Responsibility and Work Opportunity Act), all gussied up in the language of familial responsibility and participation in the workplace, still leave almost 14 million children poor. And while officials chortle at the success of getting people on welfare back to work, they ignore some obvious facts. First, most people (usually women and their children) used welfare as it was intended: as a temporary socioeconomic respite when work was not available. Roughly 70 percent of all AFDC recipients fell into this category. The other 30 percent had much more tenuous ties to the workplace because of lack of skills, personal difficulties, searing intergenerational poverty, mental and physical illness. Even given that, the total time spent on AFDC by all who ever received it is six years. Second, it is unlikely at this point that welfare reform will touch the dire circumstances, the problematic motivation, the dearth of ways into the opportunity structure of the latter group. The other 70 percent will do as they have done in the past (Albelda & Folbre, 1996; Edelman, 1997). This is not to say that AFDC was a smashing success. But it is to say that the values that originally inspired it were closer relatives of the considerations and necessities of social justice. Finally, the debate that led to these changes turned on old stereotypes of the poor; ignored many of the structural foundations of enduring poverty; smelled more than a little bit of racism; and ignored the fact that a dead-end job with few or no benefits, or a transient one, is worse in some ways than welfare, in that it does not assure, to as great a degree, the health and security of the children and other dependents involved.

In 2004, 12.7 percent of all persons lived in poverty. Between 1993 and 2000 the poverty rate fell, bottoming out at 11.3 percent in 2000. So there has been a significant increase in poverty in the last eight years. Poverty rates are highest in single-parent families headed by women. The rate is even higher for Hispanic and African American women, yet higher for foreign-born residents, and even higher for foreign born non-citizens (National Poverty Center, 2007).

So, social justice turns on the ethics of *empowerment, inclusion*, and *equality*. From this vantage point, a just society (or organization, for that matter) is one in which every individual, family, and community has access to those social resources (shelter, education, safety, nutrition, medical care, and employment, for example) that are presumed to underlie the development of personal resources—capacities and strengths, interests, agency, a sense of worth and value, talents, as well as systems of meaning: spiritual, philosophical, political, and social.

We have argued in this book for a subtle change in the basic equation between equality, justice, community, and autonomy and asserted that there is power in the people and their environments. No matter how subordinated, marginalized, and oppressed individuals and communities may appear, people, individually and collectively, can find nourishment for their hopes and dreams, tools for their realization somewhere. These tools may be damaged, hidden, or out of circulation, but, whatever their condition, they are there awaiting discovery and/or expression. When we talk of building on client strengths, of respecting people's accounts of their lives, of regard and respect for a people's culture, we are, in a sense, giving testimony that, in spite of injustice and inequity, people do have prospects. People do show a kind of resilience and vitality that, even though it may lie dormant or assume other guises, is inward. In some ways, the work of the strengths perspective is a modest form of locality justice: aligning people with their own resources and the assets of the neighborhood or community. In the end, this work is about citizenship: helping individuals, families, and communities develop a portfolio of competencies and resources that more fully allows them to enact the duties and receive the rights of full citizenship. The quest for social resources and justice should never end, but we do not have to wait for the Godot of ultimate justice to do this work well.

UNCERTAINTIES AND CAUTIONS ABOUT THE STRENGTHS PERSPECTIVE

Those of us who have been involved in practice, education, research, and training using the strengths perspective have encountered a number of concerns and countervailing ideas expressed by practitioners and students.

The strengths perspective is just positive thinking in another guise. The United States has a long and honored tradition of positive thinking that even today is alive and well. From Mary Baker Eddy to Norman Vincent Peale to Anthony Robbins to Suze Orman, our society has enjoyed an array of positive thinkers purveying their own nostrums and panaceas on television, in books, in workshops, from the pulpit, and through other media. My view is that the strengths perspective is not the mindless recitation of uplifting mantras or the idea that relief and surcease from pain and trauma is just a meditation or glib reframing away. Rather, it is the hard work of helping clients and communities build something of lasting value from the social wealth and human capital within and around them. There is little else from which to create possibility and prospects where none may have existed before.

Your expertise as a professional social worker is obviously one of the resources to be used, but by itself professional cunning and craft is not enough; social services are not enough. We must help find, summon, and employ the resources of the client or community. But many people, especially those living against the persistent rush of dire circumstance, are not prone to think of themselves and their world in terms of strengths or as having emerged from scarring events with something useful or redeeming. In addition, if they also happen to be or have been clients of the health, mental health, or welfare systems, they may have been indoctrinated in the ideology of weakness, problems, and deficiencies. They are not easily dissuaded from using these ritual symbols to understand themselves and their situation. The strengths perspective requires us, as well, to fashion collaborative, appreciative client relationships that we have been taught are the basis for effective, principled work with clients. Establishing such relationships obliges us to a strict and accurate accounting of client assets. Finding these and utilizing them compels arduous and careful work.

The strengths perspective takes a kind of heroic view of itself, doesn't it?—Gathering up those who suffer under its wing and basically ignoring the real problems these individuals have. In a recent sly polemic about the strengths perspective, an approach suspect because it pays no attention to problems and is ignorant of the capacity-building history of social work, McMillen, Morris, and Sherraden (2004) write:

> In one corner, in black spandex, we can find the social worker therapist with a keen focus on his client's psychopathology, waving above him a copy of the American Psychiatric Association's *Diagnostic and Statistical Manual of Mental Disorders.* In the other corner, with her white flowing robes, open arms, and olive branch in her teeth, stands the social work partner ready to work as an equal with her disempowered neighbors to create sustainable change. (p. 317)

Pretty funny stuff, the insinuation of sexism aside. What we seek is a balance, a balance that is hard to come by, given the realities of contemporary practice heavily influenced as it is by diagnostic injunctions of medicine and psychiatry (the National Institute of Mental Health has virtually assured that it will only fund research and projects that use the DSM as the standard for defining disorders to be treated and investigated [outcome research]) (Duncan & Miller, 2000), the reimbursement styles of insurance companies and the sway of the pharmaceutical industry (see Chapter 1 for some of the problems of medication as treatment). We want to assure that the often overlooked capacities and resources, and resourcefulness of individuals, families, and communities are not disregarded but are part of a serious assessment and a vital framework for understanding and helping. In the recovery (from serious and debilitating mental illness) movement, you will hear narratives from all kinds of people from all walks of life that tell the story of having one's identity consumed by the label schizophrenic, for example (Ridgeway, 1999). How, for many, maybe most, people who suffer from this most serious mental disorder the possibility of recovery rides on the wings of hope for a better day—even if only better because one now has her own apartment, or has a real job.

Case management with people who have serious and persistent mental illness begins with these assertions: that these individuals have had and do suffer from a serious human condition that has biopsychosocial and spiritual components; that they have had or do have hallucinations or delusions; that they have probably experienced serious ruptures in the tempo and pace of their lives; that they may need medication and support for a lengthy period of time. But the strengths perspective is driven by the idea that each of these individuals has prospects and possibilities. The essential presumption is that they will recover and that there are a variety of internal and external resources still available to them. In a pilot study of the recovery of people with serious mental disorders, the seventy-one consumers who were interviewed identified several factors critical to recovery. The most important elements, in order, were the ability to have hope; developing trust in one's own thoughts and judgments; and enjoying the environment—basking in the warmth of the sun, listening to the sounds of the ocean, sitting in the shade of a tree. Simple pleasures and ready possibilities (Ralph, Lambric, & Steele, 1996). Charles Rapp, as mentioned before, a real leader in the strengths model of case management with people with serious and debilitating psychiatric disorders, and Rick Goscha (2006) talk of those professional behaviors that are either spirit-breaking or hope-inducing. "We refer to spirit-breaking behaviors as those behaviors that diminish or even possibly extinguish the hope held by the person that he or she can move forward in the journey of recovery. Hope-inducing behaviors are those that enhance and strengthen the hope that individuals hold" (p. 77).

If practitioners using a strengths framework do disregard the real problems that afflict clients and those around them and, thus, end up contributing to the damage done to people's lives, that is capricious, perhaps even reckless. There is nothing, however, in the strengths approach that mandates the discounting of the problems of life that people bring to us. In each of the chapters of this book, authors call for a responsible, balanced assessment and treatment plan, seeking to undo the too-often imbalanced deficit or problem assessments. All helpers should evaluate and come to a reckoning of the sources and remnants of individual and family troubles, pains, difficulties, and disruptions. Often, this is where people begin, this is what they are compelled to relate, these are matters of the greatest urgency. There may well be the need for catharsis, for grieving and mourning, for the expression of rage or anxiety. We may also need to understand the barriers, both presumed and real, to the realization of hopes, dreams, and expectations. As Norman Cousins (1989) suggested, we shouldn't "deny the verdict" (diagnosis/assessment) but "defy the sentence" (prognosis/outcome).

Once having assessed the damage and the disappointment, we must ensure that the diagnosis—the assessment—does not become the cornerstone of an emergent identity. To avoid that possibility, we want to calculate how people have managed to survive in spite of their troubles, what they have drawn on in the face of misfortune or their own mistakes. We want to understand what part of their struggle has been useful to them. We want to know what they know, what they can do, and where they now want to go. Whatever else the symptoms that so bemuse us are, they are also a sign of the soul, of the struggle to be more fully alive, responsible, and involved (Moore, 1992). For social workers, the goal may not be the heroic cure, but the constancy of caring and connection and working collaboratively toward the improvement of day-to-day living, in spite of, or because of, symptoms. So what is of interest to us is how people have taken steps, summoned up resources, and coped. People are always working on their situations, even if just deciding for the moment to be resigned. As helpers, we must tap into that work, elucidate it, find and build on its promise. In some contexts, even resignation about or acceptance of one's condition may be a sign of strength. Susana Mariscal (2007), a Ph.D. student at the University of Kansas, School of Social Welfare, an experienced practitioner, and a devotee of strengths-based thinking, recounts this story, based on her work with Latina immigrants in the local school system:

> All participants refer to the inner drive to push forward in spite of all the challenges they encounter, such as learning a new language and the loss of friends. For them, this drive usually starts shyly in dialogue with a person they trust, someone who believes in them. It grows and feeds from their own hope, as they start achieving their goals. For instance, referring to learning English, making friends, and understanding class materials, Esmeralda, a 15-year-old Latina immigrant says, "Once you do it you keep doing it. . . . you have the power to keep going."

It is well, too, to keep in mind that labels always bespeak the reality of an outsider, they collectivize and abstract real experience, and make the client's own experience and stories seem alien and contrived. We must use labels judiciously if at all, and with a profound respect for their distortions and limitations, and also with an equally profound respect for their potential to "mortify" individuals (Goffman, 1961), stripping them of their distinctive identity, and overwhelming them, through a variety of rituals and social processes, with their new and exotic identity. It may be useful, however, to think of a label as a designation given too quickly, without sufficient biopsychosocial assessment, and delivered through the efficacies and efficiencies of the power inequality between professional (and institution) and client.

I have been a practitioner for many years and have worked in many fields. In my experience people who seek help don't really seem like an advertisement for strengths and resilience. Mostly, they seem beaten, angry, depressed, and at a loss. Dominated people are often alienated people; they are separated from their inner resources, external supports, their own history and traditions. People struggling with cruel circumstance, the betrayal of their bodies in disease, or foundering in the larger social and economic world also find themselves isolated, alienated from their own resources and sense of self and place. One of the key effects of alienation is identification with the oppressor. Such identification may assume many forms but it is, regrettably, common. One of its forms is the assumption of the self-identifying terms of a diagnostic label: Or, in other words, to be what the oppressor says I am (Freire, 1973). Herb Kutchins and Stuart Kirk (1997) remind us that the mental health enterprise turns on the administration of people's minds and the bureaucratization of their health. Both depend on the power to define. The more specific the definition, as in DSM IV, now the DSM IV TR (Text Revision) (American Psychiatric Association, 2000), the more the authenticity of inner experience and perception, the more the availability of capacities becomes lost. In writing of "impossible cases," working with clients who are old hands in psychotherapy, Duncan, Hubble, and Miller (1997) write: "Looking beyond labels and giving clients the benefit of a doubt is critical with psychotherapy veterans. Behind every label used as explanation lies an invalidation. Chronic invalidations characterize impossibility. Replace that history with a competing experience of acceptance and validation and watch what clients can really do" (p. 71).

My observation, as someone who practices from a more psychodynamic perspective, is that practitioners using a strengths approach reframe, for example, something devastating like schizophrenia so that it becomes nothing more than an exquisite sensitivity to external and internal stimuli. I have heard social workers who practice from a strengths approach accused of simplifying the complexity of people's lives and cleansing the inevitable messiness of the human condition with soothing words and applying potions that slather naïve optimism on the wounds of dire circumstance. Thus, clients and workers do not do the hard work of transformation, normalization, and amelioration, risking action and building bridges to a larger world. But, for example, the strengths approach does honor the pains of what has been called schizophrenia. The approach's tenets, principles, and methods were forged in intense work with people thought to have severe and persistent mental illness. In every case, to the extent that they apply, the authenticity of symptoms, delusions and hallucinations, the neurochemical and structural abnormalities, and the necessity of medication are acknowledged and become part of the work of constructing a world of possibility and opportunity for the individual and family. We are not in the business of talking people out of painful realities. Remember, *it is as wrong to deny the problem as it is to deny the possible!* But there is a kind of reframing to be done—to fashion an attitude, a vocabulary, a story about prospects and expectation, and a four-color glossy picture of the genuine individual lurking beneath the diagnostic label. This is work—creating access to communal resources so that they become the ticket to expanded choices and routes to change.

As a social worker, this is pretty much the way I practice, although I don't necessarily refer to it as strengths-based work. So what's the big deal? If we are to believe advertisements for ourselves, maybe not such a big deal. But both loudly and implicitly, the chapters herein have decried the hegemony of the medical model, the caricature of the helper as sly and artful expert, as applied technologist, the idea that the world of the professional social worker travels a different orbit than the clients'. So, must we surrender our status as experts, our esoteric and practical knowledge and lore? While we might want to reexamine the notion of expert, especially the implicit paternalism nestled within it, we do have special knowledge and would be foolish to deny that. But, it might be very important to critically analyze and rethink the assumptions and the consequences of the use of our knowledge, as well as their cultural, racial, class, and gender distortions and biases. Many have commented on the attractive alternative to the usual construction of professional intervention developed by Donald Schön and Chris Argyris (Schön, 1983)—reflective practice (see discussion in Chapter 1). Opting for relevance rather than rigor, Schön's description of the reflective practitioner not only highlights the considerable artistry, intuition, and extemporaneousness of practice, but also a radically different contract between client and professional, very much in keeping with the strengths perspective.

A reflective contract finds the practitioner with obvious knowledge and skills to offer for service but also recognizes that the professional is not the only one in the contractual relationship with the capacity for enlightenment. The professional defines the work as a mutual quest in which the client is joined in a search for solutions, surcease, and success. Both parties to the contract have control: In a sense, they are independent but bound together. The professional asks the client to continually judge the work that is done and to revise its content and course as necessary. In any case, the core of the contract is in the establishment of an authentic connection to the client.

Like Schön, Duncan and Miller (2000) regard the therapeutic, helping relationship as a mutual, collaborative one, one in which all of the parties have knowledge, theories, experience, and wisdom that may be called upon to bring about desired changes, changes that are under the direction of the client.

> The client's judgment regarding experiences relevant for discussion and revision is respected. The therapist, an active participant, draws upon possibly relevant ideas to interject into the conversation. This input grows into meaningful dialogue or fades away depending on the client's response. (p. 151)

The nature of the helping relationship changes in the direction of power equalization, mutual assessment, and evolving agreements. In a sense, the worker is the agent of the individual, family, or community. This may put the social worker in direct conflict with the agency, as discussed further in this section.

Perhaps the biggest change in practice will be a change in vision, the way in which we see and experience clients, even the most disreputable and frightening clients. Suspending skepticism, disbelief, and even our cynicism about clients and client groups will probably not be difficult for many social workers. We are of good heart, after all. But beyond that, to see in the internal and external environments of misery, pain, self-delusion, even self-destruction, the glimmer of potential, the glint of capacity, virtue, and hope asks of us a significant deepening of our consciousness of, and openness to, clients' worlds.

Working from a strengths perspective is a great idea, but, unfortunately, I work in an agency that is absolutely brimming with deficit and disorder talk and conversation. I must say, I bow to the culture of the agency and find myself talking their talk and walking their walk. I wish I didn't, but . . . We can hardly be about the business of empowering clients if we feel weak, powerless, defenseless, and alienated from our own work because of agency policies, philosophies, and attitudes toward clients. There is little doubt that in agencies where social control trumps the socialization of clients, deep pessimism about client motives exists. Negative expectations of clients hold thrall, work is defined in terms of controlling damage, clients are defined in terms of degrees of manipulation and resistance, and the health of workers is compromised (Benard, 1994; Duncan et al., 1997). Burnout, turnover, dissatisfaction, and fatigue are too often the fruits of work conducted under these conditions. In my own experience, these conditions exist far more commonly than we think. They create an atmosphere polluted with negative or shrunken expectations of clients, and shrouded in a fog of anger, disappointment, and cynicism on the part of professionals.

If you work in such an agency, must you succumb to the blandishments and protective seductions of such a view of clients? I don't think so. There is always choice. For example, you can choose how you will regard your clients. You can take the time and make the effort to discover the resources within the client and in the environment. You can choose how you will interpret and use information about the client as well as deciding what information you will seek. Over the years, in a class on the biopsychosocial understanding of mental health and mental disorder, two suggestions from students stand out. In our state, as in many others, to be licensed as a social worker at the highest level, you must have had a course in psychopathology (understanding and making diagnoses using the DSM IV). The document itself is unremittingly negative and, as was observed before, turns each individual into a case. A student suggested that the five axes of assessment should be expanded to six. Axis VI would be a detailed accounting of the resources and strengths of the individual. She added that in every staffing you would be obligated to declare and demonstrate the positive attributes and environmental resources of the client—no matter how modest.

A second student once asked why there wasn't a diagnostic strengths manual—an attention-grabbing suggestion to say the least. With the suggestions of students, I embarked—somewhat tongue in cheek—on such an endeavor. This comes from the observation that it is difficult to employ a strengths perspective if you do not have a language or lexicon for doing so. One example: Under the section, 300.00 Estimable Personal Traits, we find 301.4 *Integrity*.

> **Criterion A.** For at least six months, nearly every day, the individual has exhibited at least three of the following:
>
> 1. Did what he or she promised.
> 2. Told the truth no matter the personal cost to self.
> 3. Refused to participate in ethically dubious practices in the workplace.
> 4. Lived by the values that he or she claims in a situation where it would have paid handsomely not to.
> 5. Stood up for an individual(s) who was reproached for doing what he or she thought was in the interest of the larger group.
>
> **B.**   This is not better explained by a "holier-than-thou" attitude or a sense of moral superiority.
>
> **C.**   Such behavior benefited others more than the person.
>
> **D.**   Rule out the possibility that the person acts in this way to secure a long-term advantage over the others involved.

I don't think it is prudent to give up the deficit model of the human condition or the problem-based approach to helping. This is the language of our culture and our profession. I really don't want to be an outlier. Even though the devolution of health and mental health-care toward managed care, the rise of third-party payments and vendorship, licensing, and the spread of private practice all play a part in the amplification of the disease model, it is, ultimately, an act of your individual intention and purpose to put it in proper perspective. To do so you must examine it critically, examine the consequences of its exclusive employment in your work, and consider the advantages that the addition of a strengths-based approach would confer on your professional work and on the welfare of your clients. The disease model has reigned in many fields, in some since the nineteenth century (psychiatry, for example), but it has produced very little in the way of positive results. By almost any measure, the problems we oppose with the tools and dispositions of the disease/medical model remain rampant and poorly understood, except at the most general level (Kutchins & Kirk, 1997). As Hillman and Ventura (1992) claim, in a different arena, "We've had one hundred years of psychotherapy and the world is getting worse!"

The disease framework has reproduced itself over and over again in many different contexts. In spite of notable failures in treating common human frailties and conditions, more and more behavior patterns, habits, life transitions, life dilemmas, and personal traits—from excessive shopping to extremist thought, from persistent sexual activity to adolescent turmoil—are regarded as illnesses. This is not to ignore some successes. The neurobiological understanding (and psychopharmacological treatment) of some major mental disorders; the gradual unraveling of the mystery of the genetic components (and their interactions with the environment) of temperament; and the neuropsychological bases of emotions, memory, cognitive states of all kinds, as well as those of mental disorders, all have been remarkable (Le Doux, 2002). It is also instructive to note that many interpersonal psychotherapies work. (Asay & Lambert, 1999; Strupp, 1999). Many of them are successful to the extent that they capitalize on the assets and resources of clients and their environments and have the prospect of hope embedded in their philosophies and practices. It was Jerome Frank (1973) who first pointed out that people usually come to psychotherapists because they are demoralized. Often they are demoralized because they cannot get what they want or get to where they want to go. Restoring hope by dismantling the blockage to hope is a central part of effective psychotherapy and healing. But the impudence and truculence of the human condition, in all its astonishing variety, still remains.

The disease framework, whatever else it is, is a kind of cultural discourse or conversation. It is a vocabulary that has consequences for those who are designated or defined under its lexicon or those who employ it. Kenneth Gergen (1994), taking a social constructionist[1] view of the situation, comments on the power of the deficit discourse promoted in the mental health field: to encourage social hierarchies (doctor/expert knows best and has the power to act on that knowledge) heightens the erosion of community (we focus almost always on individuals and ignore the context of their suffering or struggles) and fosters what he calls "self-enfeeblement."

> Mental deficit terms . . . inform the recipient that the "problem" is not circumscribed or limited in time and space or to a particular domain of his or her life; it is fully general. He or she carries the deficit from one situation to another, and like a birthmark or a fingerprint, as the textbooks say, the deficit will inevitably manifest itself. In effect, once people understand their actions in terms of mental deficits, they are sensitized to the problematic potential of all their activities, and how they are infected or diminished. The weight of the "problem" now expands manyfold; it is as inescapable as their own shadow. (pp. 150–151)

Yes, but . . . many social workers and agencies claim that they already abide by a strengths regimen. A review of what their practices actually involve often reveals applications that stray from an orientation to client strengths. The question is, "How would you know if you or your agency was practicing from a strengths perspective?" To be able to answer

---

[1]Roughly, social constructionism is an emerging point of view that emphasizes the role of interpretation, discourse, relationships, and language in understanding and making sense of human experience.

this, as Charlie Rapp has commented, would move everyone along in the articulation and use of this perspective. Let us give it a try. First, the emotional atmosphere in the agency and your own emotional state would be more passionate and buoyant. The expectations of both clients and staff would be more heartening and hopeful, creating a more uplifting ambience in the agency. Second, clients and their families would be more actively involved in their own journey to a better life, but also in the agency, participating as real partners and collaborators in program, policy, and helping (e.g., mentorship) to the extent that they wished. Third, the language and ethos of the agency (and the records and archives) and everyone in it—clients included—would be abundant with terms, phrases, metaphors, and categories that directly refer to the resources and capacities of clients and communities, the range of possibilities in people's lives, individually and collectively, and the shades and facets of enriched and collaborative helping relationships. It would also reflect clients' native languages and discourse metiers. Fourth, the realization and expression of health and hopefulness would be intense and embracing. Finally, the level of expertise of social workers would be expansive and balanced as they work to understand the continuing interplay of problems and possibilities in people's lives. This is a minimal list but perhaps a beginning. So, look around the agency or organization where you work or have a field placement. What do you see? Feel?

It seems to me that you are blithely ignoring the mess that the world is in. Some people, individually and collectively, are dominating and brutalizing other people. Violent crimes are committed. Wars are started for no good reason. People are denied the basics of life. What about that? It would be naive and disingenuous to deny the reality of evil. Apart from any philosophical efforts to define what it is, there is little doubt that there are individuals (and groups) who commit acts that are beyond our capacity to understand, let alone accept (see Chapter 1). But writing off such individuals and to circumscribe certain behaviors as irredeemable is an individual moral decision that you must make. Such a decision is not always rendered with clarity or certainty. For example, would you agree with George Bernard Shaw that "[t]he greatest of our evils and the worst of our crimes is poverty"? Or would Sophocles' cry, "Anarchy, anarchy! Show me a greater evil!" be more compelling? Certainly the world has endured, on both small and large scales, horrendous destruction of both spirit and life itself. Every day brings with it another disclosure of tyranny of the soul and body—the capture of the minds and bodies of others. But in terms of our work, there are at least three things to consider in answering this difficult question:

1. There may be genuinely evil people, beyond grace or redemption, but it is best not to make that assumption about any individual first, even if the person has beaten his spouse or if he has sold crack to school-age kids.

2. Even if we are to work with people whose actions are beyond our capacity to understand or accept, we must ask ourselves if they have useful skills and behaviors, even motivations and aspirations that can be tapped in the service of change to a less destructive way of life.

3. We also must ask if there are other more salutary and humane ways for these individuals to meet their needs or resolve their conflicts. We cannot automatically discount people without making a serious professional and moral accounting of the possibility for change and redemption.

Finally, in my experience when the judgment of clients as being beyond hope is made, it often relates more to the rendering of them as manipulative, threatening, or resistant within the treatment process.

In Erich Fromm's view, there is an uncanny commonality underneath those behaviors that destroy and demolish human spirit and those that uplift and affirm it. Each individual or group bent on either the destruction or the affirmation of humankind does so from the requisite meeting of basic existential needs—for something to be devoted to, for roots, a place, and affective ties to others, and for a sense of coherence and integration, among others. These essential and compelling needs can be met through the blandishing of weapons, or the extension of the hand of friendship and care (1973).

Does the strengths model work? We can argue about what constitutes evidence, but given our usual methodological appetites, both quantitative and qualitative research shows that the strengths perspective has a degree of power that would suggest its use with a variety of clients. The most current research summary compiled by Rapp and Goscha (2006) does imply that the strengths model, when evaluated on its own or compared to other approaches, is efficacious in working with people with severe and persistent mental illness. If we examine various outcome measures—hospitalization rates, independence, health, symptoms, family burdens, achievement of goals, degree of social support among others—between and within studies, the strengths model consistently shows that it delivers results with populations that typically, over time, helped with more conventional methods, do not do as well on these measures.

It must be stated that modesty is appropriate here. But the fact is that research continues on the strengths model of case management and, at best, is suggestive. Rapp and Goscha (2006) report that there have been two experimental, two quasi-experimental, and five nonexperimental studies. Sample sizes were relatively small. The measures used across the studies were diverse, and one may legitimately question if they were stringently relevant to all of the activities and processes of case management. Nonetheless, in none of the studies did clients involved with strengths-based case management do worse than clients experiencing standard case management practice. In fact, in one experimental study the ratio of positive outcomes to no differences was 13:5. Rapp and Goscha (2006) report that the two spheres where results have been solidly and consistently positive are reduction of symptoms and improved social functioning. These are important and vital areas in the lives of people struggling with serious mental disorder, social dislocation, and intolerance. Rapp and Goscha (2004) compared the structural principles or active ingredients that make SBCM and ACT more effective than standard services. Twenty-two quasi- or experimental studies were reviewed and some of the ten structural principles that make ACT and SBCM more effective than standard services include case managers delivering as much of the services as possible, natural community resources being the primary partners, and the combining of both individual and team case management as helpful. These results, however, do not include any of the studies reported in this volume. Likewise, it does not include the substantial research done from other but related vantage points, such as the health realization work reported in Chapter 13. Nor does it include the research done on the factors that make helping, regardless of school, theory, or perspective, efficacious. (See Chapter 5.) It does not include the newly emergent studies of the recovery process for people with serious mental illness. Much remains to be done. But if we add to these studies the reports of practitioners around the country, the testimony of clients, and the witness of our own experience (these are data, too), there is no compelling reason to shrink from the strengths approach to practice.

Whatever else it might be, however else it might be construed, the strengths perspective, like other perspectives, is a manner of thinking about the work you do. The test of it is between you and those with whom you work. Do they think the work has been relevant to their lives? Do they feel more adept and capable? Have they moved closer to the hopes, goals, and objectives that they set before you? Do they have more connections with people and organizations, formal and informal, where they find succor, a place, occupation, project, time well spent, or fun? Do they have more awareness and respect of the energy and aptitude that they have forged in the fires of anguish and trauma? Do they have the sense that you will be with them and for them as they try to construct a better life for themselves? Do they know that you trust them eventually to continue on a path without your help, guidance, and good will?

When we apply diagnoses, do assessments, develop and employ theories and conceptual schemes, we are, in essence, making meaning. Jerome Bruner (1990), the legendary and esteemed social psychologist, says, "Our culturally adapted way of life depends upon shared meanings and shared concepts and depends as well upon shared modes of discourse for negotiating differences in meaning and interpretation" (p. 13). What is true of our culture is true of our profession. The language, frameworks, metaphors, and linguistic devices that we use and share, and that we, whether we are aware of it or not, inculcate in our clients, are systems of meaning designed to make sense and order out of an untidy world. It may be that the extent to which we think clients are getting better may be that degree to which they enter into our world of meaning, and abandon their own "folk psychology." I hope this is not the case, and many newer approaches to helping seem to foster clients' theories of problem, change, and their hopes for the future.

In the end, the superordinance of the disease model should be foresworn because it discourages two facets of good social work practice:

- Searching the environment for forces that enhance or suppress human possibilities and life chances.
- Emphasizing client self-determination, responsibility, and possibility so cherished in the rhetoric of social work practice.

An unthinking and monolithic devotion to the disease model undercuts, in the broadest and deepest way, the possibility of personal autonomy and community responsibility by sparing no human behavior from the intimation of disease. Even when we acknowledge the reality of an illness, we are not absolved from finding resources within that person, her environment, and her relationships, and assisting her in capitalizing on those in living beyond or even with the disease and improving the quality of her life.

OF PARADIGMS AND PROSPECTS: CONVERGING LINES OF THOUGHT

In many different places and through many different means, it is claimed that Western culture, perhaps the world, is undergoing a fundamental paradigm shift. If we define a paradigm as a framework crafted of symbols, concepts, beliefs, cognitive structures, and cultural ethos so deeply embedded in our psyches that we hardly know of its presence, the crumbling of an existing paradigm and the rise of another can be a deeply disturbing phenomenon. While there is profound disagreement and even conflict about what the old paradigm is, and what it is being replaced with, some have seen the hegemony of the rational, linear, scientific worldview challenged by the rise of a perspective that is more interpretive—a paradigm that claims that, when it comes to the human condition and human nature, there are no singular, objectively wrought truths to be had. No perspective is final, and maybe even no perspective is superior to another. All are deeply rooted in a particular social context, linguistic and discourse traditions (psychiatrists talk differently than car salespeople or nuclear physicists who talk differently and see a different world than school teachers, and so forth) and, thus, make sense in that context, but might appear as sheer lunacy in another time and place.

There is comfort here for voices that have struggled too long to be heard, for cultures and peoples whose understanding of the world has been thrust aside or debased, for all those who have something to bring to the intellectual, moral, and spiritual marketplace. There is also encouragement here for other paths of knowing and being in the world. Others disagree with this perspectivalism. But, it does seem to many that "for better or worse, the world is in the midst of the torturous birth throes of a collective emergence of an entirely new structure of consciousness" (Wilber, 1995, p. 188). It may be that we are moving in the direction of some sort of integration of the spheres of life, seeing and expressing the intricate and still-evolving connections between the body, mind, and environment; the earth, cosmos, and spirit. None of this will occur without tremendous upheaval and resistance, and no one can be certain, if the older paradigm is shattering, what will appear in its place.

As I write this (January 29, 2008), the nominating process for the Democratic and Republican candidates is in full swing even though we have months to go before the conventions and then the general election. As I hear the candidates debate each other, give campaign speeches, and do interviews, it occurs to me that there is a tension between the candidates who represent a more modernist view of the world and those who, however fuzzily, represent a view of the world that lurches toward the postmodern and constructionist—that we can fashion our future world out of sincere and deep dialogue with each other, with all voices heard.

What has all this to do with the strengths perspective? In a modest way, the strengths perspective moves away from the disease paradigm that has dominated much of the professional world, the scientific and technological realms. That model, described in various ways throughout these chapters, assumes a different viewpoint on clients and our work with them than the strengths model does. So to begin to surrender it can be a wrenching experience—in a moderate fashion, as disruptive as larger, more cosmic shifts in consciousness. But it is nonetheless a shift in consciousness, a change in the way that we see our clients and regard our work. Fortunately, we are not alone in this transformation of our professional consciousness. In other disciplines and professions, fault lines have appeared, and new conceptual and practical structures are becoming visible. Some of these have been alluded to in the previous chapters. There are five that I want to briefly emphasize in this concluding chapter.

Resilience

In the fields of developmental psychology and developmental psychopathology in particular, it has become clear that children exposed to risk in their early years do not inevitably consummate their adult lives with psychopathology or sink into a morass of failure and disappointment. The field is not of one mind here, but after arising out of the presumption that there are specific and well-defined risks that children will face, and these will always end in some sort of developmental disaster, it now seems clear that most do not; most children surmount adversity and, while bearing scars, do better as adults than we might have predicted. Yes, some children do face trauma, institutional and interpersonal, so toxic that to emerge unscathed or relatively functional would be miraculous. But even here, there are miracles. We need to understand better what makes them happen. Consider alcoholism and children growing up in homes where alcohol abuse and its attendant profligacy on the part of one or both parents is a frequent phenomenon. The literature has it that these children are at serious and elevated risk for alcohol abuse as adults as well as other assorted personal struggles and failings. But most children of parents who have serious alcohol problems do not become alcoholic drinkers; many deliberately structure and restructure their lives to avoid such an eventuality.

It is a mixed and sometimes bewildering picture that we have. There are reports of people who have recovered from alcoholism on their own. Not really on their own, as George Vaillant (1993) points out, but with some mix of the following: social supports, hope (again) and faith, luck, timing, social context, temperament, the incidence of protective factors in the environment (often the most important, as others have pointed out, is the presence of one person—a friend, spouse, peer, coach, etc., who cares and is steadfast in that attention). Scott Miller and Insoo Kim Berg (1995) remark:

> However, [one] surprising finding from our own work is that the solution to a person's alcohol problem need not look like or even be related to the problem. Indeed we have personally worked with and met hundreds of clients who solved their alcohol problems by doing things that are not related to in any direct fashion. These have included spending more time with the family, developing an exercise regimen, finding a satisfying hobby, joining a social or religious group, changing friends, eating three good meals a day, and getting a job. (p. 19)

Vaillant (1993) reports a similar scenario for one of the subjects of the decades-long Harvard Study of Adult Development, Robert Hope (a pseudonym). Unemployed and in the grip of alcoholism in his twenties, by the time he was in his thirties, he had stopped drinking. He attributed that to marriage to a strong and sympathetic spouse. But after their divorce some ten years later, he continued, with difficulty, on his path to recovery. Those things that seemed to make a difference? Learning to more productively express his anger, developing the ability to elicit social supports, and becoming more honest and open about himself.

But one thing is clear from the research, not just on children growing up under these circumstances but other stressful and challenging ones as well: These children, when they become adults, most of the time (one-half to two-thirds) do not succumb to the particular risks and vulnerabilities that supposedly inhered in their childhood experience. That they suffered is clear, but it is not the issue here (Wolin & Wolin, 1993).

Any environment is a welter of demands, stresses, challenges, and opportunities, and these become fateful, given a complex array of other factors—genetic, constitutional, neurobiological, familial, spiritual, communal—for the development of strength, resilience, hardiness, or diminution of capacity. We are only now learning what factors lead to more hopeful outcomes. Clearly, in almost every environment, no matter how trying, there lurk not only elements of risk, but protective and generative factors as well. These are people, resources, institutions, and contingencies that enhance the likelihood of rebound and recovery, or may even exponentially accelerate learning, development, and capacity. To learn what these elements of the body/mind/environment equation are, we have to go to the community, the family, and the individual and learn from them how transformation or resilience developed.

After reviewing most of the literature on genes and personality, twin studies, socialization, relationship networks, and status systems for clues about what makes us uniquely who we are, and how being members of a biopsychosocial group affects us, Judith Rich Harris (2006) argues that while our genetic inheritance accounts for the lion's share of what makes us different, and our parents,' step-parents,' and/or other caretakers' behavior and relationships with us may account for a small bit of the difference; for the rest, however, it is the environment—especially our relationships with our peers. Children (and adults) want to be like their peers and liked by their peers. More than that, they want to succeed with their peers. Children get ideas about appropriate behavior by observing and copying their friends and other peers. There is a status element here as well. Children want to be better than their peers, to succeed among them. Being like their parents, or copying parents' behaviors, is not a good strategy for children in developing relationships with peers and succeeding in their various social worlds. For parents, this means the baffling disconnect that often exists between behavior at home and behavior at school and in the neighborhood.

One of the more celebrated studies of the development of resilience in children as they grow into adulthood was the longitudinal research begun in Kaua'i, Hawaii, in 1955 by Emmy Werner and Ruth Smith (1992). In their earlier report (1982), they reported that one out of every three children who were evaluated by several measures to be at risk for adolescent and adult problems developed, as it turned out, into competent and confident youths at age 18. In their follow-up, Werner and Smith (1992) found that a surprising number of the remaining two-thirds had become caring and efficacious adults at ages 32 and 40. A more specific and telling example: Only one third of the children who had developed serious emotional and behavioral problems in adolescence had some continuing midlife problems. More surprising yet, by age 40 only 4 percent of the delinquent youths in the study had committed additional crimes (Werner, 1998). One of their central conclusions is that most human beings have self-righting tendencies and are able to effect a change in life trajectory over time, but this tendency must be supported by internal and external factors. One of the many factors that contributes to that is the presence of a steadfast, caring adult (or peer in a few cases). It need not be a parent nor need the relationship be an everyday affair. Other factors included a sense of faith and coherence of meaning, even during times of turmoil and trouble; schools that fostered and encouraged learning and the development of capacities and that had a buoyant, optimistic spirit in the classroom; teachers and mentors who instructed, guided, supported, and acted as protective buffers to the incredible stresses that some of these children faced. The children themselves often showed problem-solving abilities and a persistent curiosity. But if we take the research of Harris (2006) described above seriously, peers undoubtedly played an important role as well.

But as discovered in Werner and Smith's study, over the past few years, elements of communities and neighborhoods are now seen as important in maintaining the balance among risk, protective, and generative factors. In those communities that seem to amplify individual and familial resilience, there is awareness, recognition, and use of the assets of most of the members of the community, through informal networks of individuals, families, and groups. Social networks of peers and intergenerational mentoring relationships provide succor, instruction, support, and engagement.

In our (the School of Social Welfare, University of Kansas) work over ten years in two public housing communities, we met with varying degrees of success in helping the residents who were interested in building the kind of community that they would like and be proud of. But where there was accomplishment and success, three factors seemed to be involved. First, some residents took charge after we helped them lay some of the groundwork. These individuals were usually regarded as leaders by many other residents. Second, we had to have some ideas about tangible programs and structures that the residents could modify and mold to fit their needs and achieve their goals. And it had to be made clear, to the extent that public housing policy allowed it, that nothing was off the table in terms of possibilities. Third, we needed to celebrate, acknowledge, and elaborate the accomplishments of residents—individually and together. One of the more successful programs was a mini-grant program. In it, thanks to a generous contribution from a private donor, residents, individually or together, were given grants of up to $200 to develop a program that would benefit some part of the community. They had to fill out an application, and the application had to be approved by a panel of residents and students (in the field program of the School of Social Welfare). Some of the efforts were ingenious and would never have occurred to an outside agent coming in with a prepackaged program. One small grant was given to have a block party with games, prizes, entertainment provided by young and old residents, food prepared by the residents, and items the residents had made put up for sale. While this only lasted for a day, it did have reverberating effects. One of the most obvious was that people had the opportunity to meet each other. For a variety of reasons—fear, uncertainty, who knows?—many residents only ventured out if they had to (to go shopping, to work, etc.). Thus, they had not yet formed the critical mass of relationships that are the foundation of many communities. But a new dynamic (aided by other events and happenings) was put into place on that day and slowly grew. We did what little we could to nurture it, but it was the residents who did the work.

But if we do have programs designed to enhance capacities and the rebound from adversity, Lisbeth Schorr (1997) in her review of programs that work to prevent poor or "rotten" developmental outcomes for children found they typically had seven qualities: (1) They were comprehensive, flexible, and responsive to local needs and interests; (2) they crossed traditional professional and bureaucratic boundaries; (3) they saw the child in the context of the family; (4) they saw the family in the context of the community; (5) they had a long-term commitment to prevention; (6) they were managed by competent and caring individuals; and (7) their services were coherent and easy to use.

There is also a relationship between health, adversity, and resilience. In a comprehensive review of studies that have documented how people may benefit from adversity, McMillen (1999) culled out and fashioned from the data the following factors. First, a difficult, even traumatic event, once faced, may lead to greater confidence that another challenge can be met, bringing with it an increase in the perceived efficacy of one's ability to handle adversity, making future stressful events seem less toxic. Second, as many people have discovered, a seriously adverse event may encourage a deep review of one's values, beliefs, priorities, commitments, relationships, and pastimes. Such changes may really enhance one's health and lifestyle. Third, when trouble surfaces, a person may discover unrealized sources of support from other people, as well as realizing their own vulnerability. Both of these may, in turn, lead to a revised and more positive, balanced view of other people. Finally, in the struggle to cope with an aversive and forbidding event, a person may find the seeds of a new or revised meaning. The questions, "Why me? Why now?" may lead to an authentic existential shift of gears.

So resilience is dependent on the interaction of factors at all levels, from biological to personal, to interpersonal, to environmental, and to spiritual. Not only do children and adults learn about themselves and develop strengths as they confront challenge and adversity, if they are lucky they find and make connection with compatriots in the making of a better life, and they find themselves in a community where natural resources are available, no matter how sparse they might seem.

According to many resilience researchers, it turns out that resilience is a common facet of the human condition. Ann Masten (2001) argues that:

> What began as a quest to understand the extraordinary has revealed the power of the ordinary. Resilience does not come from rare and special qualities, but from the everyday magic of ordinary, normative human resources in the minds, brains, and bodies of children, in their families and relationships, and in their communities. (p. 9)

Health and Wellness

In the last decade or so, there has been something of a revolution in the way that we think about our health and wellness, individually and collectively. More and more, ordinary people and many professionals in the health field are looking at natural and native treatments and cures for illnesses—whether in the form of diet and exercise, supplements and herbs, lifestyle changes, meditative and spiritual practices, holistic health treatment and naturopathic remedies, and environmental modifications. For many, treatment and the responsibility for wellness is no longer a narrow and exclusive medical matter. Many qualified and well-known physicians have been a part of this change as well. See, for example, Andrew Weil, MD (1995), Stephen Sinatra, MD (2008), Julian Whitaker, MD (2008), David G. Williams, MD (2008), and Al Sears, MD (2006); each of them has newsletters, reports, pamphlets, and, in some cases, books in which they outline their findings from the research, from clinical experience, and from nontraditional sources. The net effect of their efforts, I would guess, is to give people a sense of their own power and responsibility in promoting wellness, and handling disease.

It would be foolish to even begin to summarize their approaches here, but I think it is fair to suggest the following.

1. There are effective, often natural, treatments known in various parts of the world and, often, passed through many generations. Usually, they are inexpensive and readily available and, in some cases, have been studied by medical anthropologists, anthropologists, nurse practitioners, medical researchers, interested physicians, and, of course, native healers.

2. These treatments are usually cheap and, more often than not, do not carry the sometimes inimical side effects of more conventional treatments and medicines.

3. Part of the ethos of this shift in medicine is to return power to persons seeking help based on the idea, although variously expressed, and as has been said before in this book, that people do have an innate capacity for health and wholeness.

4. I suspect another urge that drives these developments is to make it possible financially for large numbers of people to have access to effective treatments.

I would be remiss if I didn't say that conventional medicine still has the tools and ideas to treat a vast array of illnesses and conditions. There are undoubtedly physical states that require what allopathic (conventional) medicine has to offer, but naturopathic and alternative medicine, for example, have their advocates and practitioners and some research to support their claims (Dossey, 2003).

The resilience and health and wellness literature run parallel in many regards. Both assert that individuals and communities have native capacities for restoration, rebound, and the maintenance of a high level of functioning. Both suggest that individuals are best served, from a health and competence standpoint, by creating belief and thinking around possibility and values, around accomplishment and renewal, rather than focusing on risk and disease processes. Both indicate that health and resilience are, in the end, communal projects—an effect of social connection, the pooling of collective vision, the provision of guidance, and the joy of belonging to an organic whole, no matter how small.

Story and Narrative/The Therapies of Meaning Creation

The constructionist view, in its many guises, urges us to respect the importance of making meaning in all human affairs. Human beings build themselves into the world, not with their meager supply of instinct, but with the capacity to construct and construe a world from symbols, images, icons, language, and ultimately stories and narratives. While culture provides these building blocks, we impart, receive, and revise meanings largely through the telling of stories, the fashioning of narratives, and the creation of myths. Many are given by culture, some are authored by families, individuals, and subcultures. And there is always some tension between the culture and the self in this regard. But individuals and groups do tell their own stories. Stories serve many purposes. They are about dreams, discovery, redemption, trouble, courage, love, loss—every element of the human experience and condition. They instruct, chasten, guide, comfort, and surprise. They provide a sinew of connection between those who share them. They survive because they have human value and humane consequences. We are prepared by our own history as a species and as individuals to respond to the medium of stories. Good stories grounded in our experience can elevate us or put us firmly in the bed of familial, intimate, and cultural relationships in ways of our own making, not somebody else's. Children are socialized in large part by stories and narratives.

Ann Lamott in *Bird by Bird*, the autobiographical account of how she turned to writing in her life, says this about what she did with the stories her friends told her.

> I started writing a lot in high school: journals, impassioned antiwar pieces, parodies of writers I loved. And I began to notice something important. The other kids always wanted me to tell them stories of what had happened, even—or especially—when they had been there. Parties that got away from us, blowups in the classroom or on the schoolyard, scenes with their

parents that we had witnessed—I could make the story happen. I could make it vivid and funny, and even exaggerate some of it so the event became almost mythical, and the people involved seemed larger, and there was a sense of larger significance, of meaning. (p. xix)

Some single mothers in a public housing community were encouraged to relate their stories of survival under what were often siege conditions (O'Brien, 1995). Reluctant at first, they often reiterated the public's and media stories about people like themselves, and their initial attempts were not very flattering. But once they got into it, they all had distinctive, sometimes buried, stories to tell about survival. These stories were often about courage, wiles, faith, relationship, struggle, and uniqueness. These women were not saints; they were simply human beings who, facing the enormous difficulties of being poor, isolated, often unemployed, and raising children alone, had somehow managed to make it. If there was a persistent theme in these stories, it was resilience. And it was important for these women to share their stories. Most times, no one cared how they happened to see their worlds. Without encouragement to tell, some of their world was unconstructed, or not of their making. It was, they said, important for their children to hear these stories. These were in some ways cautionary tales admonishing the listener—children, too—on the dangers out there and how to avoid them. They were ennobling as well. Listeners were instructed on the managing of hardship and ordeals, and the mounting of internal and external resources in its face.

Groups who suffer under the domination of the larger culture and social institutions frequently do not have their stories told or heard in the wider world nor, regrettably, sometimes in their own world (Rosaldo, 1989). One of the human costs of being oppressed is having one's stories buried beneath the landslide of stereotype and ignorance. This means, then, that one of the genuine strengths of people(s) lies in the fabric of narrative and story in the culture and in the family. These are generative themes (Freire, 1996), and they capture the hopes and visions, the trials and tribulations, the strengths and virtues of a people, of a family. It is part of the work of liberation, renewal, and rebuilding to collaborate in the discovery, projection, and elaboration of these stories and accounts. A story told and appreciated is a person, family, or culture affirmed. While we understand that there is an innate capacity or urge toward health in the human body, we may not understand as well that in a story or narrative may be the health of a culture.

Solution-Focused Approaches

Coming from the work and philosophy of Steve de Shazer, the clinical work and writing of the late Insoo Kim Berg and Peter De Jong, and the recent work of Scott Miller, Mark Hubble, and Barry Duncan, the solution-focused approach (see Chapter 6 by Weick, Krieder, and Chamberlain) to helping has gained ground, both in terms of its clinical use, but also in terms of increasing empirical support. Although it does not attend pointedly to strengths, it does have an implicit and abiding interest in the strengths of individuals and families (Miller, 2006). And, as yet it has not, in my view, really concentrated on the resources and solutions in the environment. John Walter and Jane Peller (1992) say the basic question asked by this approach is "How do we construct solutions?" And such a question, they argue, harbors certain assumptions: There are solutions; there is more than one solution; solutions can be constructed; therapists and clients do the constructing; constructing means the solutions are invented or made up, not discovered; and how this is done can be said and shown (Walter & Peller, 1992). From the outset, in solution-focused work, the eye is always on the goal, the end, and the solution and the thinking, imagining, motivating, and relating that takes place around solution development is independent of the processes that sustain problems. Furthermore, the emergence of solutions obscures and trumps the further development of problems.

Of great importance to the practitioners of this approach is this question: How do theories, methods, and practitioners actually contribute to the elaboration and intensification of the problems presented to them by clients? Duncan and others (1997) suggest the following:

1. Certain conditions invite the expectancy of difficulty or impossibility (think of borderline personality disorder or urban ghetto youth) and "attribution creep"—the expansion of negative impressions based on the expectancy that things will not get better, probably worse. These impressions are hardy blooms and difficult to prune.

2. Theories often have within them negative countertransference. That means that they create word pictures of groups of clients that are often pessimistic or invalidating (the psychodynamic view of schizophrenia, for example, or the at-risk view of certain groups of children and their neighborhoods). Likewise, they mute the theories and language of the individual and culture.

3. Often, when solutions of one kind or another do not work or the problem turns out to be refractory, practitioners (parents, teachers, all of us sometimes) do more of the same. And as more of the same produces a hardening of the problem, we do even more of the same. Think of parents and their adolescent children. A midnight curfew on the weekend doesn't do it? How about an 11:00 P.M. curfew? Not effective? How about a 10:00 P.M curfew for the whole week? Or consider a psychiatrist with little time to see each patient. One antidepressant doesn't do it? How about another? And another?

4. It is common to think of many individuals or families as unmotivated or treatment resistant if they do not respond to our blandishments. Sometimes we make things worse by overlooking or misunderstanding the client's motivation. The fact is that every client has some range of motivations. They just may be out of the purview of our approach and intent. It is also true that clients have their own theories about what is wrong.

Duncan, Hubble, and Miller (1997) recount the work they did with 10-year-old Molly. Suffering from debilitating nightmares, sleeplessness, night terrors of various kinds, she was unable to sleep in her own room. Part of the work of solution-focused therapists is to find out what the individual thinks is the problem and how she or he would propose to fix it. What Molly offered was a way to rearrange her room so it was more defensible and comfortable. She barricaded her bed with pillows and stuffed animals against unwanted nightly visitors. This was a young girl who had been seen by four different professionals, was on imipramine for depression and anxiety, and was thought to be in the midst of a dysfunctional family. But the effecting of her solution brought immediate relief. This is also what Malcolm Gladwell (2000) calls a band-aid solution. These are ways out of predicaments and they are "inexpensive, convenient, and remarkably versatile solution[s] to an astonishing array of problems" (p. 256).

Positive Psychology

In recent years, some psychologists have been looking at the detrimental effects of always emphasizing what is wrong, what is missing, what is pathological, and the like and have begun to turn their gaze to the strengths and virtues of people. I must say here that psychology seems oblivious to the strengths approach in social work practice, which has predated many of the "new" ideas of positive psychology. Martin E. P. Seligman (2002), the putative founder of positive psychology, has this to say, "I believe it is a common strategy among all competent psychologists to first identify and then help their patients build a large variety of strengths, rather than just deliver specific damage-healing substances" (pp. 6–7). Among the strengths he speaks of are courage, rationality, optimism, honesty, perseverance, realism, capacity for pleasure, and others. Three of the major differences between this budding approach to psychological understanding and practice and the strengths approach in social work is that our profession recognizes that: (1) Almost anything, given circumstances and context can be a strength or asset; (2) many strengths and resources are to be found in relationships, and in environments—social, physical and built, large, and intimate; and (3) that strengths practice often involves helping people put together their personal assets and their environmental resources toward the building of a better life. One without the other makes for very difficult practice.

Clearly, there is a convergence in these approaches of appreciations, perspectives, and points of view. While differences remain, the union of certain assumptions and standpoints is heartening to say the least.

CONCLUSION

The contributors to this volume—most of whom are practitioners as well as scholars and educators—hope that you find something of real value here that can be translated for use with the individuals, families, and communities that you serve. We all believe that the initiatory act in employing a strengths perspective is a commitment to its principles and underlying philosophy—a credo that, in many regards, is at serious odds with the approach we have variously labeled the deficit, problem, or pathology orientation. We firmly believe that once committed you will be surprised, even amazed, at the array of talents, skills, knowledge, and resources that you discover in your clients—even those whose prospects seem bleak. In a nutshell, that is, for us, the most convincing rationale for embracing a point of view that appreciates and fosters the powers within and around the individual. The authors also hope that you have found some tools to assist you in the promotion of the health, resilience, and narrative integrity of your clients. But, in the end, what will convince you to stay with this perspective is the spark that you see in people when they begin to discover, rediscover, and embellish their native endowments. That spark fuels the flame of hopeful and energetic, committed and competent social work.

DISCUSSION QUESTIONS/EXERCISES

1. You have finished the book. Where do you stand now on the utility and relevance of the strengths perspective? How will you understand problems that people bring to you now?

2.   Do you think that you can practice from a strengths perspective no matter what sort of organization or agency you work at?

3.   You and your colleagues are working in La Paz, Bolivia, as a part of an international outreach program to street kids all over the world. About 60 percent of these children left home because of physical abuse, 20 percent due to extreme poverty, and another 20 percent were abandoned by their parents. On the street, these kids form peer cliques that act like families, and they strive to take care of each other and provide a sense of belonging. However, many of the children sniff glue ("clefa"), and they are sometimes terrorized by older gangs, some community members, and even the police. Taking a strengths approach, what would be the first step(s) you would take to begin to confront this situation?

REFERENCES

Albelda, R. & Folbre, N. (1996). *The war on the poor: A defense manual.* New York: New Press.

American Psychiatric Association. (2000). *Diagnostic and statistical manual of mental disorders* (4th ed., Text Revision.) Washington, DC: Author.

Asay, T. P. & Lambert, M. J. (1999). The empirical case for the common factors in therapy: Quantitative findings. In M. A. Hubble, B. L. Duncan, & S. D. Miller (Eds.), *The heart and soul of change: What works in therapy.* Washington, DC: APA Press.

Benard, B. (1994, December). *Applications of resilience.* Paper presented at a National Institute on Drug Abuse conference on the role of resilience in drug abuse, alcohol abuse, and mental illness, Washington, DC.

Bruner, J. (1990). *Acts of meaning.* Cambridge, MA: Harvard University Press.

Cousins, N. (1989). *Head first: The biology of hope.* New York: Dutton.

Dossey, L. (2003). *Healing beyond the body: Medicine and the infinite reach of mind.* Boston: Shambhala Press.

Duncan, B. L., Hubble, M. A., & Miller, S. D. (1997). *Psychotherapy with 'impossible' cases: The efficient treatment of psychotherapy veterans.* New York: Norton.

Duncan, B. L. & Miller, S. D. (2000). *The heroic client: Doing client-directed, outcome-informed therapy.* San Francisco: Jossey-Bass.

Edelman, P. (1997, January). The worst thing President Clinton has done. *Atlantic Monthly, 282,* 43–58.

Frank, J. D. (1973). *Persuasion and healing.* Baltimore: Johns Hopkins University Press.

Freire, P. (1973). *Pedagogy of the oppressed.* New York: Seabury.

Freire, P. (1996). *Pedagogy of hope.* New York: Seabury.

Fromm, E. (1973). *The anatomy of human destructiveness.* New York: Holt, Rinehart, & Winston.

Gergen, K. J. (1994). *Realities and relationships: Soundings in social construction.* Cambridge, MA: Harvard University Press.

Gladwell, M. (2000). *The tipping point: How little things can make a big difference.* Boston: Little, Brown & Company.

Goffman, E. (1961). *Asylums.* New York: Doubleday/Anchor.

Greenwald, G. (2007). *A tragic legacy: How a good vs. evil mentality destroyed the Bush presidency.* New York: Crown Publishers.

Harris, J. R. (2006). *No two alike: Human nature and human individuality.* New York: W. W. Norton & Co.

Hillman, J. & Ventura, M. (1992). *We've had one hundred years of psychotherapy and the world is getting worse.* San Francisco: HarperSanFrancisco.

Kondrat, M. E. (1995). Concept, act, and interest in professional practice: Implications of an empowerment perspective. *Social Service Review, 69,* 405–428.

Kutchins, H. & Kirk, S. A. (1997). *Making us crazy: DSM: The psychiatric bible and the creation of mental disorders.* New York: Free Press.

Lamott, A. (1995). *Bird by bird: Some instructions on writing and life.* New York: Anchor Books.

LeDoux, J. (2002). *Synaptic self: How our brains become who we are.* New York: Viking.

Longres, J. (1997). Is it feasible to teach HBSE from a strengths perspective? No! In M. Bloom & W. C. Klein (Eds.), *Controversial issues in human behavior and the social environment.* Boston: Allyn and Bacon.

Mariscal, S. (Dec. 11, 2007). Personal communication: Case studies.

Masten A. (2001). Ordinary magic: Resilience processes in development. *American Psychologist, 56,* 227–238.

McMillen, J. C. (1999). Better for it: How people benefit from adversity. *Social Work, 44,* 455–468.

McMillen, J. C., Morris, L., & Sherraden, M. (2004). Ending social work's grudge match: Problems versus strengths. *Families in Society, 85,* 317–325.

Miller, J. (2006). Critical incident debriefings and community-based clinical care. In A. Lightburn & P. Sessions (Eds.), *Handbook of community-based clinical practice* (pp. 529–541). New York: Oxford University Press.

Miller, S. D. & Berg, I. K. (1995). *The miracle method: A radically new approach to problem drinking.* New York: W. W. Norton & Co.

Mills, R. (1995). *Realizing mental health.* New York: Sulzburger & Graham.

Modricin, M., Rapp, C. A., & Poertner, J. (1988). The evaluation of case management services with the chronically mentally ill. *Evaluation and Program Planning,* 307–314.

Moore, T. (1992). *Care of the soul.* New York: HarperCollins.

National Poverty Center, University of Michigan, Gerald R. Ford School of Public Policy. (2007). *Poverty in the United States.* Retrieved Feb 15 2008 from www.npc.umich.edu/poverty.

Ornstein, R. & Sobel, D. (1989). *Healthy pleasures.* Reading, MA: Addison-Wesley.

O'Toole, J. (1995). Goods in common: Efficiency and community. In M. Adler (Ed.), *The great ideas today: 1995.* Chicago: Encyclopedia Britannica.

Pelletier, K. R. (2000). *The best alternative medicine: What works? What does not?* New York: Simon & Schuster.

Ralph, R. O., Lambric, T. M., & Steele, R. B. (1996, February). *Recovery issues in a consumer developed evaluation of the mental health system* (pp. 1–13). Paper presented at the 6th annual conference of *Mental Health Services Research and Evaluation Conference.* Arlington, VA.

Rapp, C. A. (1998). *The strengths model: Case management with people suffering from severe and persistent mental illness.* New York: Oxford University Press.

Rapp, C. A. & Goscha, R. (2004). The principles of effective case management of mental health services. *Psychiatric Rehabilitation Journal, 27,* 319–333.

Rapp, C. A. & Goscha, R. J., (2006). The strengths model: Case Management with people with psychiatric disabilities (2nd ed.) New York: Oxford University Press

Ridgeway, P. (1999). *Recovery.* Lawrence, KS: School of Social Welfare, University of Kansas.

Rosaldo, R. (1989). *Culture and truth: The remaking of social analysis.* Boston: Beacon Press.

Ryan, W. (1976-revised edition). *Blaming the Victim.* New York: Vintage Books.

Schön, D. A. (1983). *The reflective practitioner.* New York: Basic Books.

Schorr, L. B. (1997). *Common purpose: Strengthening families and neighborhoods to rebuild America.* New York: Anchor/Doubleday.

Sears, A. (2006). *Rediscover your native fitness.* Wellington, FL: Author.

Seligman, M. E. P. (2002). Positive psychology, positive prevention, and positive therapy. In C. R. Snyder & S. J. Lopez (Eds.), *Handbook of positive psychology.* New York: Oxford University Press.

Sinatra, S. (2008). *Heart, health and nutrition.* Monthly newsletter. Potomac, MD: Healthy Directions, LLC.

Snyder, C. R. (2000). Hypothesis: There is hope. In C. R. Snyder (Ed.), *Handbook of hope: Theory, measures, and applications.* San Diego: Academic Press.

Snyder, C. R. & Feldman, D. B. (2000). Hope for the many: An empowering social agenda. In C. R. Snyder (Ed.), *Handbook of hope: Theory, measures, and applications.* San Diego: Academic Press.

Stanard, R. P. (1999). The effect of training in a strengths model of case management on outcomes in a community mental health center. *Community Mental Health Journal, 35,* 169–179.

Strupp, H. H. (1999). Essential characteristics of helpful therapists. *Psychotherapy, 36,* 141–142.

Vaillant, G. E. (1993). *The wisdom of the ego.* Cambridge, MA: Harvard University Press.

Walter, J. L. & Peller, J. E. (1992). *Becoming solution-focused in brief therapy.* New York: Brunner/Mazel.

Walzer, M. (1983). *Spheres of justice.* New York: Basic Books.

Walsh, F. (1998). *Strengthening family resilience.* New York: Guilford.

Weil, A. (1995). *Spontaneous healing.* New York: Knopf.

Werner, E. E. (1998). Resilience and the life-span perspective: What we have learned—so far. *Resiliency in Action, 3,* 1–8.

Werner, E. E. & Smith, R. S. (1982). *Vulnerable but invincible.* New York: McGraw-Hill.

Werner, E. E. & Smith, R. S. (1992). *Overcoming the odds.* Ithaca, NY: Cornell University Press.

Whitaker, J. (2008). *Health and healing: Your definitive guide to wellness medicine.* Monthly newsletter. Potomac, MD: Healthy Directions, LLC.

Wilber, K. (1995). *Sex, ecology, and spirituality: The spirit of evolution.* Boston: Shambhala.

Williams, D. G. (2008). *Alternatives for the health conscious.* Monthly newsletter. Potomac, MD: Mountain Home Publishing.

Wolin, S. J. & Wolin, S. (1993). The resilient self: How survivors of troubled families rise above adversity. New York: Villard.

Wright, B. & Fletcher, B. (1982). Uncovering hidden resources: A challenge in assessment. *Professional Psychology, 13,* 229–235.